CW00942267

BRITISH
SECRET PROJECTS
HYPERSONICS, RAMJETS
& MISSILES

To my dear wife Kirsten

British Secret Projects –
Hypersonics, Ramjets & Missiles
© Chris Gibson and Tony Buttler, 2007

ISBN (10) 1 85780 258 6
ISBN (13) 978 1 85780 258 0

First published in 2007 by
Midland Publishing
4 Watling Drive, Hinckley, LE10 3EY, England
Tel: 01455 254 490   Fax: 01455 254 495

Midland Publishing is an imprint of
Ian Allan Publishing Ltd.

Worldwide distribution (except North America):
Midland Counties Publications
4 Watling Drive, Hinckley, LE10 3EY, England
Tel: 01455 233 747   Fax: 01455 233 737
E-mail: midlandbooks@compuserve.com
www.midlandcountiessuperstore.com

North America trade distribution by:
Specialty Press Publishers & Wholesalers Inc.
39966 Grand Avenue
North Branch, MN 55056, USA
Tel: 651 277 1400   Fax: 651 277 1203
Toll free telephone: 800 895 4585
www.specialtypress.com

All rights reserved. No part of this publication
may be reproduced, stored in a retrieval system,
transmitted in any form or by any means,
electronic, mechanical or photo-copied, recorded
or otherwise, without the written permission of
the copyright owners.

Design and concept
© 2007 Midland Publishing and
Stephen Thompson Associates
Layout by Russell Strong.

Printed by Ian Allan Printing Limited
Riverdene Business Park, Molesey Road
Hersham, Surrey, KT12 4RG, England.

Visit the Ian Allan Publishing website at:
www.ianallanpublishing.com

Photograph on half-title page:
**Launch of a Bristol XTV.4 ramjet-powered
test vehicle for the Red Duster programme
that ultimately led to the Bloodhound surface-
to-air missile.**

Photograph on title page:
**Avro Vulcan carrying a pair of Douglas Skybolt
air-launched ballistic missiles. Not a British
weapon, but Skybolt and particularly its
cancellation, had a profound effect on British
weapons development and defence policy in
the early 1960s.** Author's collection

BRITISH
SECRET PROJECTS
HYPERSONICS, RAMJETS & MISSILES

CHRIS GIBSON & TONY BUTTLER

MIDLAND
An imprint of
Ian Allan Publishing

Contents

Introduction

Since the end of the Cold War in 1989 the interests of air enthusiasts have moved quite significantly away from current and future developments towards aviation history. There are two factors in this: with fewer new aircraft on the stocks and the trend towards multi-role types, the modern air forces, aircraft and uninhabited air vehicles are to be frank, less interesting. Many, including this author, have turned to the past, a time when test pilots and aircraft designers were household names and each year's Farnborough Air Show included a New Types enclosure, surrounded by the curious, both amateur and professional. Tony Buttler acknowledges the 1976 'Project Cancelled' by Derek Wood as having sown the seeds of this change, with Wood's analysis of the death of an industry sparking off the interest in less well-known British aircraft projects. The past is another country, with a diverse assortment of aircraft to maintain our interest, and an undiscovered country to boot, where surprising 'new' projects are found. The other change is the opening up of company and Government archives, allowing researchers to examine the background of aerospace projects, particularly from the policy and funding viewpoint.

The reader might wonder why this book, the fourth in the British Secret Projects series, covers 'Hypersonics, Ramjets and Missiles'. The truth is these fields represent the most advanced technological development work ever carried out in the United Kingdom. The three subjects are so closely related that telling the story of one cannot be done without the story of the others. Another reason is that the aircraft described in Volumes 1 to 3 were intended to carry weapons and, in an era when the weapon system came to the fore, the story of the guided weapon therefore completes the picture.

Hypersonics are of great interest, a field that has promised much for over 50 years, and is a field that Britain pretty much made its own in the decade from 1957. Hypersonic aircraft research in Britain hinged on the availability of powerplants, that is ramjets. Ramjets in turn grew from the need for a long-range guided weapon, so the three fields are inextricably linked.

This book is intended to show how British industry rose to the challenge of two very advanced fields: guided weapons and hypersonic flight. The research for this book has exploited the new open attitude of the Government Ministries, which allows analysis of some of the controversial projects and the decisions that affected them.

All the source material in this book comes from open sources, with much of it from the UK National Archives and other repositories. While the Government for the most part is willing to open up its documentation, the manufacturers are still reticent to release information on many of their wares. The phrase 'that project formed the basis of a current operational system' became a standard response to requests for information: understandable, given the nature of the business and world situations past and present. Nor is the information published previously always strictly accurate, performance figures are massaged to boost or degrade perceived performance and what appears initially to be inaccurate reporting may turn out to have been a deliberate Government policy of deception. In some cases such as the deterrent gap in the 1960s, deception was the only real weapon available. Despite the official reassurances, RAF aircrews were left with no option but to carry out missions with a weapon the Americans had considered obsolete in 1957.

This raises the controversial matter that no discussion on British weaponry can ignore: the Sandys question. Normally associated with the phrase 'The man who killed the British aircraft industry', Minister of Defence Duncan Sandys was given the brief of providing Britain with armed forces suitable for late 20th century operational and economic climates. Sandys was appointed just after the Suez Crisis of 1956 and just before the aviation industry became the aerospace industry. Scrapping National Service saved considerable expense, but pound-for-pound, deterrence was the future. By 1956 it was obvious that the large manned bomber in RAF service had little potential other than as stand-off missile carriers and fighters impotent against ballistic missiles. The ballistic missile and its

invulnerability was the way ahead, with fast low-flying strike aircraft for tactical work. From these views arose OR.1139 and OR.339 and Sandys based his defence plan on what became Blue Streak and TSR.2. Remember, it wasn't Sandys who scrapped these projects. Where Sandys did fall down was his assumption that the next war would be one of mutual destruction. Perhaps the rose-tinted spectacles, that have been used to view the British aviation industry for long and weary, should be discarded and archive material looked at in the clear light of day.

Historical research of any subject is dependent on the availability of material from which to construct the story. At first sight the recent arrival of the Freedom of Information Act should have seen the release of masses of material; but items concerned with military technology remain sensitive. There is no conspiracy to conceal such information, merely the fact that its declassification would require personnel with the relevant security clearances and knowledge. Such people do not work for minimum wage, which makes this a costly and time-consuming business. As a result there are large gaps in the documentation available to researchers, particularly the UK's hypersonic research work, much of which could be applied to ballistic missiles and re-entry systems.

When material is available it can also be somewhat contradictory, no doubt because designers were only given the minimum required to draw up their project; for example, aircraft designers were given an installation weight, thrust rating and fuel consumption information for engines, while the powerplant people were given estimates of all-up weights and flight regime. Fifty years later, with the engine company's data in one hand and the aircraft builder's data in the other, a historian has to decide whose information is 'more correct'. This may sound odd, but this author was initially surprised when, on being shown the aircraft design studies, a propulsion research engineer exclaimed 'Well, I always wondered what that looked like.' The result can be a seemingly confused story that will only be clarified as more information becomes available.

To this author the technology that produced the Red Top air-to-air missile or the Thor ramjet paved the way for items that make life easy in the modern world. Press a button on your TV remote control and the Infra-Red 'seeker' in your TV brings it back to life. Fifty years ago that detector's forebear was in a test vehicle streaking across Larkhill Range towards a propane gas fire. Next time you fly on a charter jet, ponder the technology that allows its Rolls-Royce turbofan to run for hours on end with little maintenance between flights other than a few visual inspections and a report from a diagnostic system. All of this came from the development of ramjet combustors for guided weapons and their associated telemetry systems. Again, step back fifty years and that print-out was a series of scratches on a strip of sooty foil showing the oscillating temperature of a stuttering ramjet burner in another test vehicle.

The first part of Volume Four covers the early history of the British guided weapon and the various test vehicles whose soggy demise in Cardigan Bay contributed to the process of development. The main guided weapon roles are examined as they evolved into usable weapon systems in use in the early 21st century. The second half looks at the development of ramjets and the related work carried out on hypersonic aircraft. While British work on hypersonics was mainly concerned with re-entry trials for ballistic missiles, the volume of work carried out on satellite launchers alone could fill a book. Therefore this volume concentrates on air-breathing, endo-atmospheric projects that could have, given a great deal of time and money, come closest to being built. While no attempt has been made to explain the true complexity of the engineering and technical challenges, the text hopefully gives the reader a better understanding of why these projects came to nought. The current aim of hypersonic research is a re-useable space launcher; this was a secondary role in the early 1960s, where a transport to reinforce the Empire was the goal. Since starting the research for this book, the author has been constantly amused by the ongoing assurances that London to Sydney in two hours is just around the corner. It was on the cards in 1959 as well, and yet probably won't happen in the author's lifetime.

This author has nothing but admiration for the people who invested their time, effort and ingenuity in developing these systems, only to see them cancelled as the threat or policy changed, in some cases, overnight. On asking the question 'How did that feel?' most reply with a pragmatic 'We just got on with the next one.' In time the 'next one' became a rarity and these talented people moved into other areas, taking their expertise and applying it in 'Civvie Street'. These are the people who built our modern world and they should be recognised for it.

Chris Gibson
Washington, Tyne and Wear, April 2007.

Acknowledgements

This book could not have been written without the help of a number of people. The generosity of fellow researchers and willingness to help someone embarking on a project such as this cannot be described. Most provided invaluable help with information and in keeping the author on the right track, not to mention much needed advice. For anyone researching guided weapons, the first port of call is Bill Gunston's 'Encyclopaedia of Rockets and Missiles' which has provided the most authoritative source, if not *the* source, on guided weapons since its publication in 1979. Steven R Twigge's 'Early Development of Guided Weapons in the UK 1940-1960' presents an in-depth analysis of the policies and finance behind Britain's effort in the field. Much has changed since their publication and the author respects Bill and Steven's courage in publishing, on a subject that had been largely ignored, at times when information availability was restricted.

Thanks are due to the patient and helpful staff of the National Archives, who provided a valuable and very efficient service for all the research for this book.

Early in the search for a British hypersonic project, the author was put in touch with Roy Hawkins of the Rolls-Royce Heritage Trust (Bristol Branch). Roy rapidly dispelled any illusions the author might harbour of ramjet-powered aircraft as hardware. He was completely unselfish in his willingness to help and this book could not have been written without him.

When it comes to knowledge of the Bloodhound SAM, few compare with Richard Vernon and David Mackenzie who provided invaluable help in the air defence and test vehicle chapters. Although many of the photographs in these chapters are credited to the Bristol Collection, Richard deserves a specific mention for their discovery and identification. His efforts are much appreciated.

Chris Farara of the Brooklands Museum, whose uncanny ability to turn up gems continues to amaze, deserves a special mention for his patience and meticulous archiving. Thanks are also due to another Brooklands volunteer, John Forbat, whose sterling work on raising the profile of Vickers' guided weapons turned up not just documents but long-lost hardware. However, neither Chris nor John could do this work without Brooklands' Curator of Aviation, Julian Temple. Harry Fraser-Mitchell provided much of the information on Handley Page's little-known guided weapons activities and allowed use of drawings and information.

The North West Heritage Group at BAE Systems, Warton whose P.42 study forms a major part of the story very kindly allowed use of drawings and documents and the author thanks Ian Lawrenson and Bob Fairclough for their help in making this material available.

When it came to tracking down some of the originators of guided weapons in the UK, Clive Richards of the Royal Air Force Historical Branch and Peter Elliot at the Royal Air Force Museum at Hendon were invaluable. The staff of the Royal Electrical and Mechanical Engineers Museum at Arborfield also contributed to the story of the early missiles and provided access to many original documents and drawings. A special thanks is due to John Hall for his superb models.

Others, without whose contribution this book could never have been produced, include: Bobbie Alexander; Brian Burnell; Phil Butler; Joe Cherrie; Steve Clifton; Clive Elliott; Nigel Evans; Dave Forster; Dr Paul Henney; David Mackenzie; Dr Richard Moore; John Pitfield; Dennis Poole; Mike Pryce; Bill Rose; Dr Jeremy Stocker; Ray Sturtivant; Robert Thornton, Richard Vernon.

Thanks are also due to Thales Air Defence PLC, BAE Systems and the crew of the Ensco 80.

Chapter One

The Origins of the
Guided Weapon in the UK

Guided weapons in UK service date back to the wire-steered torpedoes developed by Australian watchmaker Louis Brennan in the late 1890s and used by the Royal Engineers for coastal defence from 1900 to 1920. Aerial guided weapons in the UK really date back to the Great War, to Prof A M Low, who was credited with the invention of the electrically controlled rocket and radio torpedo gear. He was a brilliant scientist, with a talent for original research, who could turn his hand to any scientific field, but was particularly interested in radio. He had in fact drawn up a theoretical television system in 1914. In this author's opinion Low was the father of the British guided weapon.

Early air-to-air weapons involved dropping explosive loaded grappling hooks, called the 'Farnborough Fiery Grapnel' from aircraft such as the Royal Aircraft Factory BE.2 and BE.12. This met with little success, mainly due to the poor climb performance of the aircraft allowing the German Zeppelin airships that were their targets to escape before the defenders had climbed above them.

Low was asked to adapt an explosive-packed biplane fighter so that it could be controlled from the ground and flown up a searchlight beam into the Zeppelins that were bombing London. This evolved into the radio-controlled Ruston Proctor A.T. monoplane (Aerial Target, a cover name to conceal its true purpose), designed by H P Folland, who later founded the Folland Aircraft Co. Unsuccessful, the A.T. was dropped and forgotten about after a lacklustre demonstration. However, Low's equipment was not discarded. After a brief collaboration with Cdr Brock of

Mid-1946 – A Vickers Type 432 attacks a Messerschmitt Me264 with an Artemis semi-active air-to-air missile. Adrian Mann

the Royal Navy on a radio-controlled rocket, the Navy saw potential in Low's equipment in the role of long-range bombardment.

The UK's next foray was the 'Long-Range Gun with Lynx engine', known as the Larynx, designed by the RAE in the late 1920s. Larynx, intended as an anti-ship weapon, used Low's control techniques and was catapult launched from Royal Navy warships such as HMS *Stronghold*. This was not strictly a guided weapon, because it used an autopilot to fly to its target. The Admiralty had high hopes for it, probably because it had a top speed higher than contemporary fighters and was thought to be immune from interception.

British Secret Projects: Hypersonics, Ramjets & Missiles

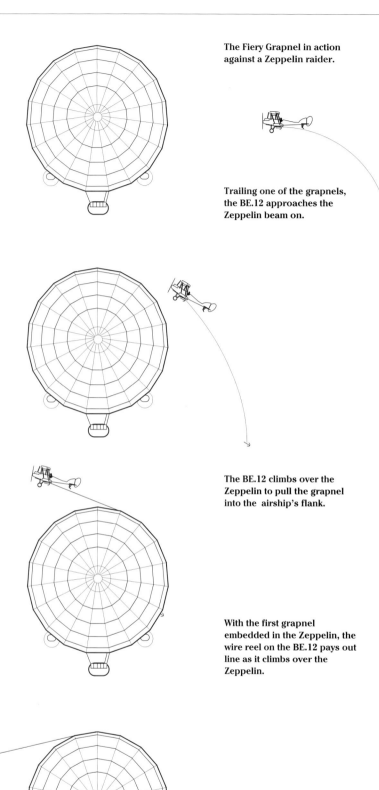

The Fiery Grapnel in action against a Zeppelin raider.

Trailing one of the grapnels, the BE.12 approaches the Zeppelin beam on.

The BE.12 climbs over the Zeppelin to pull the grapnel into the airship's flank.

With the first grapnel embedded in the Zeppelin, the wire reel on the BE.12 pays out line as it climbs over the Zeppelin.

When all the wire is paid out, a weak link on the BE.12 holding the second grapnel parts and this grapnel falls away to embed itself in opposite flank of the Zeppelin before both grapnels explode.

Ram

As well as surface-to-surface weapons such as Larynx, anti-aircraft guided weapons were also under consideration by Britain in the 1930s. In November 1935 the Royal Aircraft Establishment discussed the development of a guided anti-aircraft weapon for use against the air armadas that the Air Ministry expected to rain devastation on Britain. Called Ram, this weapon was more or less a longer-ranged Ruston Proctor Aerial Target. Unlike the AT, the Ram was to be guided from the air by a pair of aircraft that worked in unison. Referred to as the Shepherd, the first aircraft flew astern of the Ram and controlled its line and elevation. The second, called the Flanker, flew abeam of the enemy formation, out of the range of the bomber's guns and corrected the Ram's position before the 500 lb (227kg) warhead was detonated as the Ram closed up on the formation.

Four manned aircraft, complete with undercarriage and larger wings, were proposed for trials to prove the aerodynamics of the Rolls-Royce Kestrel-engined Ram. The radio control system from de Havilland Queen Bee target drones was suggested for Ram. However this was dismissed because that control system was incapable of rapid manoeuvres at speeds up to the 400mph (644km/h) the RAE believed would be needed to catch the bombers of 1940. Problems foreseen included: difficulties with night operation, the possibility that enemy formations would spread out to reduce attrition and the cost due to the use of expensive, high-performance engines such as the Kestrel. In the end the multi-gun fighter was deemed a more practical solution.

In the guided weapon context, one further application of the Ram is of interest. By 1935 the importance of radio frequency technology was becoming apparent, particularly in Britain which was then developing Radio Direction Finding, later known as radar. It was proposed that a Ram be fitted with equipment to home in on such equipment if it was used by an enemy. Ram was to be the first 'radar buster' or anti-radiation missile.

By the late 1930s the emphasis was still on an anti-ship weapon and this produced the Toraplane. First considered in 1918 by the RAE for a large glide bomb, the basic idea was dusted off just before World War Two by Sir Dennis Burney. Burney also invented the mine-sweeping device called the Paravane, the High Explosive Squash Head (HESH) anti-tank round, and later designed a propeller-driven railway system that was built and tested at Milngavie, near Glasgow. The Toraplane was essentially a winged torpedo to be

The Farnborough Fiery Grapnel fitted to a BE.12.
TNA AIR 1/863

delivered by Bristol Beauforts and its development continued with many delays until 1942, at which time an exasperated Coastal Command had it cancelled.

Elsewhere in 1942, Britain's Anti-Aircraft Command and the German Luftwaffe had reached similar conclusions on defence against bombing raids. Despite radar, ever more complicated predictors (early fire control computer) and high-speed gun laying systems to direct their fire, anti-aircraft guns were of limited effectiveness. While the proximity fuze provided better results against targets such as the V-1, it was against the high-flying heavy bomber that AA was least effective. Studies had shown that a direct hit, rather than proximity or time-fused bursts, was the only way to destroy bombers. Increased rate of fire and muzzle velocity were seen as ways to improve effectiveness but even so the 'Cost per Bird' for rapid-firing 3.7in (9.4cm) guns was £9,000 (at 1944 prices).

However, it was becoming apparent that despite all these improvements, it would still take massive and costly firepower to defend against bombers. A further spanner in the works was the advent of the jet aircraft, making predictors more or less obsolete overnight. This situation had been demonstrated clearly by the Luftwaffe's Arado Ar 234 undertaking reconnaissance flights over eastern England with impunity from September 1944. So, from an economic and operational point of view, a more efficient method of shooting down aircraft was required.

The Pilotless Interceptor

As it required two Shepherd aircraft for control and detonation, the Ram was a costly and manpower intensive weapon. By June 1941 the Air Defence Research and Development Establishment (ADRDE) considered that radar's evolution had reached the point where it could be used to track a target and interceptor with sufficient precision to allow an interception. L H Bedford of Cossors Ltd and J D Cockcroft of the ADRDE proposed using a small pilotless aircraft carrying a warhead to intercept a bomber. The Pilotless Interceptor would be under control from the ground, but tracked by radar rather than visually.

Two 10cm (3in) GL Mk.III gun-laying radar sets were required: The first used to track the incoming bomber, while the second tracked the Pilotless Interceptor Aircraft. This was a small high-wing monoplane with a span of

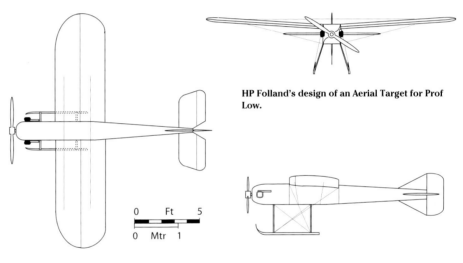

HP Folland's design of an Aerial Target for Prof Low.

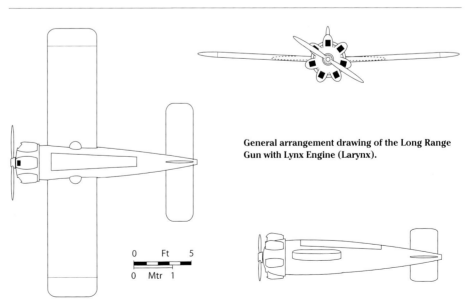

General arrangement drawing of the Long Range Gun with Lynx Engine (Larynx).

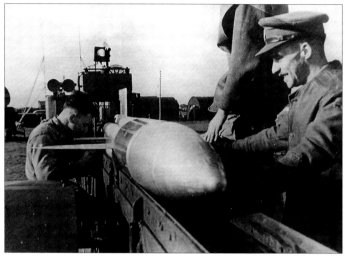

Above left: **Cossor / AA Command 'Brakemine' anti-aircraft weapon ready for launch on a modified 3.7in AA gun mount.** REME Museum

Above right: **Brakemine being readied for a trial flight.** REME Museum

Below: **Sole surviving Brakemine on display in the Royal Electrical and Mechanical Engineer Museum of Technology at Arborfield. Note drive shafts for tail controls.**

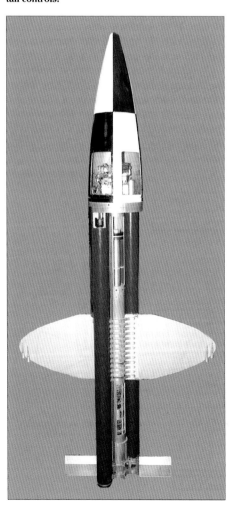

By April 1943 Watson-Watt had lost patience: 'I consider there has been a great and unjustifiable waste of official time in these discussions with Wg Cdr Lester, whose technical competence falls far below his own estimate of it.'

The conclusion was that the effort required could be better focused elsewhere, there being no pressing need for such equipment. Indeed, in March 1943 Ben Lockspeiser (Director General of Scientific Research at the Ministry of Aircraft Production) opined that: '...such devices should be best left to the better resourced Americans'.

By April 1943 Wg Cdr Lester was informed that his idea would not be taken up by any of the research establishments. His treatment by the Establishment may have been the final straw for Lester as he retired from the RAF in 1943.

Brakemine

While all this had been going on, two other independent teams came up with similar weapon guidance methods. In late 1942 Lt Col H B Sedgefield and Major W E Scott of the Royal Electrical and Mechanical Engineers (REME) had conceived a beam-riding method for guiding a rocket. Not long after, L H Bedford and S Joffeh, electrical engineers with the radio builder A C Cossors, spent an overnight train journey discussing how a weapon could fly along a radio beam. In mid-1943 the two teams got together and began working on a project called Brakemine.

This has been described as the pet project of the OC of Anti-Aircraft Command, Gen Frederick Pile, and was a small monoplane missile (or in the parlance of the time, guided anti-aircraft projectile or GAP), powered by six 3in (7.62cm) UP rocket motors and launched from a modified 3in (7.62cm) anti-aircraft gun mounting. Much bigger than

Spaniel, Brakemine offered more scope for development than the earlier studies.

First launched in unguided form in September 1944, subsequent guided Brakemines were 'gathered' (that is, guided into the beam), and would fly along the radar beam to the target. Control was by 'Twist and Steer', using the tailplanes differentially as ailerons to roll the missile, then as elevators to change the pitch. This control method is more correctly named polar control and the Brakemine trials also saw the first use of telemetry to assess vehicle performance.

And where, you might ask, was the RAF? The Air Ministry and the RAE had in fact been working on a guided anti-aircraft projectile that had been derived from the ideas of Flt Lt B S Benson of the RAE. Benson, a RAFVR pilot Officer in 1940, had been promoted to Acting Flight Lieutenant by the time he was seconded to the RAE. As one might expect, this GAP was named Ben and it possibly came the closest of any of the wartime projectiles to being considered for service since it could have been undergoing service trials by early 1946. Ben comprised a pair of 3in (7.62cm) Rocket Projectile (RP) motors mounted side-by-side with a nose fairing housing the warhead and control system. Manoeuvres were performed by selective thrust from four jets mounted around the fairing and four rectangular wings were fitted midway down the body to maintain stability.

Described as a searchlight-controlled GAP, guidance for Ben involved Radar, Searchlight Controller 9X, the searchlight itself and an aft-facing photoelectric sensor fitted to each wingtip. Why adopt photoelectric guidance? Firstly, as previously mentioned, the radars in use at the time could not generate a narrow enough beam for a beam-riding guidance system and secondly, homing systems on the missile were susceptible to jitter caused by radar reflections from the target's propellers.

The target was tracked by a radar-directed searchlight and Ben was fired from a launcher mounted on the searchlight. Shortly after launch, at a height of around 50ft (15.2m), Ben was steered into the searchlight beam and, using the photoelectric sensors, the control system kept Ben within the beam by directing thrust through a set of four nozzles arranged around the nose, the aim being to place Ben within 200ft (61m) of the target. When the radar return showed that the ranges of the target and Ben were coincident, the searchlight was switched off, triggering the warhead. The searchlight-guided Ben was seen as the best option for producing a practicable weapon against bombers in the shortest time. However, developments in radar and a change in threat overtook photo-electric Ben and a radar beam-riding version was under development from mid 1944, but with reduced priority.

With the tide of war turning in the Allies' favour, there was little need for an operational GAP for the air defence of the UK, so GAP development was put on the back burner. However, the war in the Pacific was not so clear-cut and this enhanced the priority of GAP development.

Defending the Fleet

The Royal Navy first considered guided weapons for air defence in late 1943 having seen HMS *Warspite* and HMS *Uganda* badly damaged in September 1943 by German guided weapons off the Salerno beachhead. In November 1943 Dr Charles Goodeve, he of the 'Wheezers and Dodgers' at the Department of Miscellaneous Warfare and by then Controller of Research and Development, had become involved and discussed US work on a small subsonic anti-aircraft weapon. While the official policy was that such things should be left to the USA, H R King, Director of Gunnery and Anti-Aircraft Warfare wrote the following prophetic sentence: 'No projectile of which control is lost when it leaves the ship can be of any use in this matter.' Thus was born the Naval GAP.

Meantime, US forces in the Pacific Theatre were conducting an island-hopping campaign that was intended to lead to an invasion of Japan. Japanese Naval and Army air forces formed special attack squadrons to take the fight to the Allies and on 15th October 1944 the USS *Franklin* was hit by an aircraft that appeared to have been aimed directly at the ship. The Kamikaze had arrived. The first massed Kamikaze attack on the US Fleet occurred on 25th October during the Battle of

the Leyte Gulf, resulting in the sinking of USS *St. Lo*.

The Royal Navy had learned to its cost in the Mediterranean, when under attack by German dive-bombers, that a diving aircraft was a very hard target to hit from a warship. Despite heavy anti-aircraft defences and the use of fighter screens, the Kamikaze continued to exact a heavy toll on Allied naval forces from late 1944. Damaging the aircraft with shrapnel was not sufficient, the incoming warhead had to be destroyed and only a direct hit could do this. The Kamikaze gave new incentive to development of guided aircraft projectiles, particularly in the US, but also prompted renewed interest in the UK.

In 1944 a four-panel committee on Guided Anti-aircraft Projectiles was being set up: Panel A covering propulsion; B aerodynamics; C radar and radio and D stabilisation.

The original need for a means to defeat German guided weapons had in April 1944 generated a requirement for a defensive GAP. The requirement stated that the GAP was: 'To counter directly approaching aircraft up to 40,000ft (12,192m) and 500mph (805km/h), at a point before they could release freefall bombs. To be fitted to destroyers and bigger vessels and weighing not more than 500 lb (a

depth charge is 500 lb (226.7kg) and destroyers can handle them). Also able to be guided close enough to a target to allow a proximity fuse to work.'

However, that weapon could also be used against the Kamikaze. Fairey Aviation, with G W Hall at the helm of the Research and Armament Development Division, was first on the scene producing a weapon that was more or less a small aircraft with a warhead. This weapon, called Stooge, was launched from a trestle using four 3in (7.62cm) boost rocket motors, with four Swallow rocket motors as sustainers and guided visually via a radio link. Stooge was subsonic, easier to control, but practically was not of much use. In fact the Director of Gunnery had dictated that any GAP should have a speed 50% faster than its quarry, a governing factor that would influence SAM design for more than a decade. Development of Stooge continued until 1947, marking Fairey's first foray into guided weapons.

Stooge was too slow for the Navy's liking, nor did they rate the radio command guidance particularly highly, preferring a 'self-guiding' weapon. Discussed as a weapon for destroyers, Ben in its beam-riding guise met the size and weight requirements, but its 3in (7.62cm) rockets couldn't provide the Navy

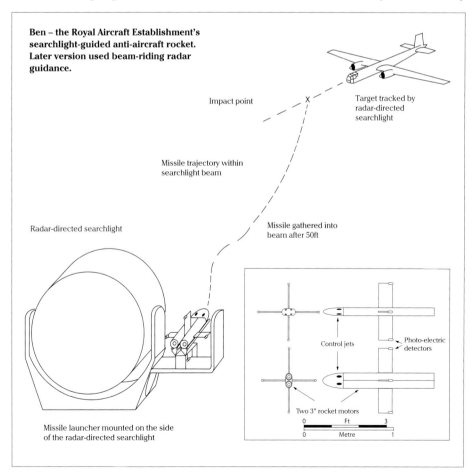

Ben – the Royal Aircraft Establishment's searchlight-guided anti-aircraft rocket. Later version used beam-riding radar guidance.

Impact point

X

Target tracked by radar-directed searchlight

Missile trajectory within searchlight beam

Radar-directed searchlight

Missile gathered into beam after 50ft

Control jets

Photo-electric detectors

Two 3" rocket motors

Missile launcher mounted on the side of the radar-directed searchlight

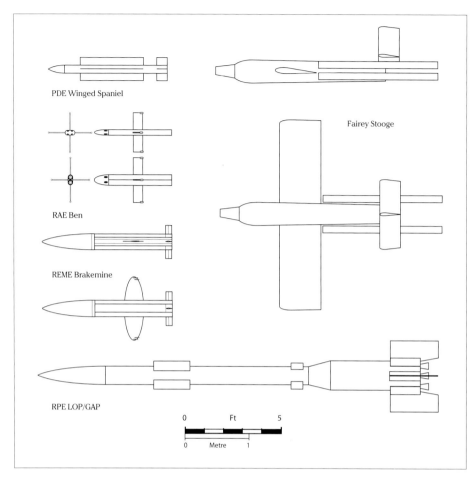

PDE Winged Spaniel

Fairey Stooge

RAE Ben

REME Brakemine

RPE LOP/GAP

0   Ft   5

0   Metre   1

Comparison of early British guided anti-aircraft projectiles. Note the transition from aircraft-type, low-speed configuration to the classic missile layout.

Guided weapons were viewed with some suspicion by airmen from the start.

GUIDED MISSILES DEPARTMENT
PRIVATE

Well, I'm working on a rocket now which goes up to 30,000ft, shoots down the enemy, returns back to base, reports to the debriefing room, and then shoots a line about itself in the mess.

with the required range capability. So the Navy turned to the more powerful liquid rocket engine with solid rocket boost.

Since 1941 Isaac Lubbock of the Asiatic Petroleum Co had been experimenting with a rocket engine called 'Lizzie' at the Rocket Propulsion Establishment (RPE) near Westcott. The intention was to develop an assisted take-off unit for the Wellington bomber, but the engine was soon adopted for projectile propulsion. Lizzie was fuelled with petrol and used liquid oxygen as its oxidiser. In 1944 the Ministry of Supply issued another requirement for a supersonic GAP with a ceiling of 40,000ft (12,192m). This led to the merging of the Brakemine and Ben GAP projects with the Lizzie engine, resulting in LOP/GAP (Liquid Oxygen and Petrol / Guided Anti-aircraft Projectile). Boosted by seven 3in (7.62cm) rocket motors, LOP/GAP formed the basis of the RTV.1 test vehicle that, as will be described in the next chapter, laid the foundations of post-war guided weapon development in the UK. In 1946 the name 'Seaslug' first appeared in Admiralty documents and it was still appearing 40 years later as Seaslug came to the end of its Royal Navy career. Those four decades would see phenomenal changes in guided weapons.

A Development Strategy

In late 1945 the Government felt that a single body should oversee the development of guided weapons and it proposed a Guided Weapons Committee to have overall control of research and development. The main problems were seen to be technological, however the committee's aims were to prevent duplication of effort and to co-ordinate that effort. Sir Henry Tizard had headed the Aeronautical Research Committee in the run up to World War Two and had overseen the development of radar. As an obvious choice to champion GW research, Tizard was asked to be chairman of the Guided Weapons Committee, but replied that he was too old. Sir Stafford Cripps, Minister of Aircraft Production, later President of the Board Of Trade in 1945, was asked to write to Tizard again, more or less begging him to take charge – 'Please say yes.' To which Tizard replied 'Don't press me.' Helpfully, Tizard suggested some alternatives: Sir Harry Ricardo, the engine developer, declined and eventually Sir Alfred Egerton, Professor of Chemical Technology at Imperial College, London agreed to become Chairman.

At the end of the war the Committee outlined the future needs of the UK armed forces:
1) Admiralty – long-range GAP 50,000ft (15,240m) ceiling, 700mph (1,126km/h) target, weight less than 0½ ton (452.6kg).
2) Admiralty – close-range GAP, 3,000-5,000yd (2,743-4,572m) range, 750mph (1,207km/h) target, very small size.
3) Weapon X – ship-ship, 30,000yd (27,432m) range, with three times the chance of hitting a target than a 16in gun with only a few hits to sink a battleship.
4) Weapon Y – ship-ship, guided projectile with a steep attack and hit equivalent to a 16in shell.
5) General Staff – long-range GAP similar to [item] 1) but without the weight restriction.
6) General Staff – long-range rocket.
7) General Staff – strategical (sic) rocket.

NB – Steep attack meant that the projectile plunged onto the target at a high angle.

Ambitious stuff, but in three decades British guided weapons had evolved from the primitive origins of aircraft flown at Zeppelins to the rocket-propelled, telemetered, radar beam-riding Brakemine. This had been achieved by hard work and perseverance by some of the most accomplished scientists and engineers in Britain. By 1946 the stage was set for the huge leaps in technology and expertise on guided weapons seen in the next decade. To do this a lot of testing would be required and that required Test Vehicles.

The Origins of the Guided Weapon in the UK

Chapter Two

Test Vehicles –
The Unsung Heroes

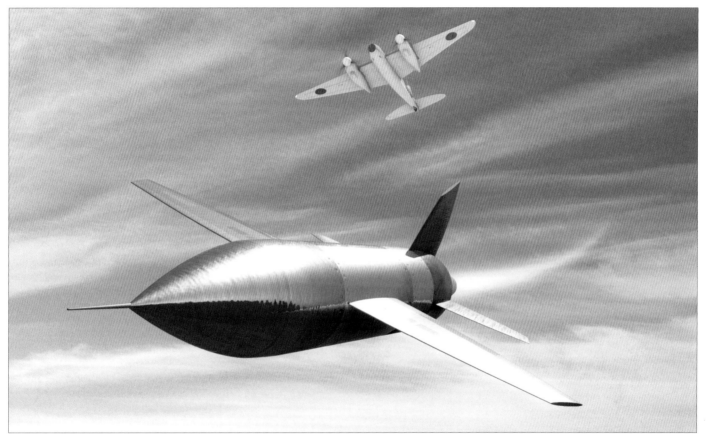

With the Guided Weapons Committee in place and the seven basic requirements on the table, the next stage was to put some hardware into the air. Weapons development invariably follows a set path:

Staff Target – This is what weapon or system the 'Staff' (a military term for the administrators of the armed forces) would like to have in service. General Staff Target (GST) covered Army needs; Air Staff Target (AST) covered the RAF; and the Admiralty Weapon (AW) and later Naval Staff Target (NST) covered the Royal Navy. An example might be: A Surface-to-Air Missile to shoot down M2 bombers.

Staff Requirement – What the Staff would like that weapon or system to do and how it will do it. In the case of our specimen AST: This SAM would need to destroy M2 bombers at a range of 50 miles from the missile launch site and be capable of carrying a nuclear warhead.

Design Study – Industry becomes involved in drawing up airframe proposals and submits these proposals showing how the developer would meet the Staff requirement. For example: The SAM would be powered by twin ramjets, boosted by four rocket motors and use semi-active radar guidance or, if nuclear armed, command guidance.

Prototype – First stage of hardware development, built by the developer and used for trials and testing. A series of scaled test vehicles is designed, built and launched to assess the missile's performance.

Pre-Production – First batch of series production usually used for service trials. A few early examples are handed over to the services to check that the weapons work as stated and that there are no unforeseen problems or teething trouble.

Production – Volume production to meet orders from the service that originally drew up the Staff Target. Weapon enters service and perhaps even sees action.

De Havilland Mosquito B.Mk.XVI (PF604) acts as carrier for the Vickers / RAE Rocket Powered Transonic Aircraft Model (also known as the TR, Transonic Rocket) to investigate pilotless, expendable weapons. Adrian Mann

Much of this book will deal with the design study stage of this process, during which the possible configurations and systems are investigated in various levels of detail. These range from the 'Boy Racer three-view' beloved of the aircraft designers to in-depth parametric studies involving all parties concerned with the design, including the powerplant and systems companies.

Part of this design study process involves testing the aerodynamics and flight characteristics of these designs. Before the days of supersonic wind tunnels and Computational Fluid Dynamics, the designers relied on flight test vehicles. These could be sub-scale analogues or full-scale pre-production examples of the article. In a 1964 lecture to the Royal Aeronautical Society, T L Smith of the RAE defined these as: 'A body used in free-flight to test components, structures, aerodynamics, servo controls, guidance systems and propulsion.' They can range in sophistication from the concrete lumps used in the 1957 Red Shoes launcher development to highly sophisticated, heavily instrumented vehicles such as the recent Australian HyShot and QinetiQ SHyFE scramjet test vehicles.

The simplest test vehicles used in UK weapons development were the ballistic 'shapes' used to prove the aerodynamics of the UK's atomic bomb casings, such as Blue Danube. Painted up with photo calibration markings, these showed that the aerodynamics of the bomb were so good that the bomb flew just below the bomber for a considerable time after release, an alarming prospect for a crew! The upshot of this was the flat front of the Yellow Sun bomb casing.

During World War Two, and immediately after, Guided Weapons development in the UK had been a fairly piecemeal affair and the responsibility of the various Research Establishments and Commands until 1946, when the RAE took overall responsibility for GW development with the creation of the Controlled (later Guided) Weapons Dept.

When it came to guided weapons, the test vehicle gained an importance beyond all previous experience. However, test vehicles are only useful if the effect of the function or component to be tested can be recorded and analysed. Wind tunnels had been used but

only by the analysis of free-flight data could the flight characteristics of guided weapons be assessed. Aircraft builders had always used highly skilled test pilots to test their wares but, as aircraft became more sophisticated, additional methods such as an observer or a second instrument panel, filmed by a movie camera, were used to record flight data. Neither of these methods was applicable to the scaled-down world of guided weapons development. Vickers for example intended addressing this by building a piloted version of its SP.2 Red Rapier flying bomb (or Expendable Bomber) of 1951 to assess its flight behaviour, but ultimately used an unmanned 1/3-scale vehicle.

The first test vehicle for a guided weapon was a full-scale trial of the Ruston Proctor AT on 6th July 1917. The AT climbed rapidly as commanded, but soon turned over on its back and dived into the ground. It was discovered that the trailing aerial had been torn off on launch. An inauspicious start for a guided weapon, but a portent of test vehicles to come.

Initially, ground observation by binoculars, high-speed cameras and kine-theodolites was used on land ranges such as Larkhill in Wiltshire, where the earliest observations of these test vehicles' odd behaviour were made. Observers reported some strange flight characteristics but the developers remained sceptical. Small recording devices, called scratch recorders, were developed to gather data from a number of parameters, such as acceleration, to be recovered for analysis after each flight. This data supported

the ground observations, much to the surprise of the developers. From such devices the 'Black Box' flight data recorder used in modern aircraft evolved.

As the speed and range of test vehicles increased, the test facilities at Larkhill were too restrictive, so it was decided to use the range at Aberporth in Ceridigion on the Welsh coast. As this trials area involved flights over Cardigan Bay, a further problem was that test vehicles fell into the sea. This led to the development of floatation devices to prevent the vehicle sinking, allowing recovery. However these devices were not always successful, leading to the loss of valuable test vehicles and data. This added impetus to the development of radio telemetry.

Today we are surrounded by telemetry, be it the engine RPM and gear selection of a Formula 1 car on TV or the duration of our last call on a mobile phone. All this is possible through advances in sensor and computer technology that would have made the postwar engineers green with envy, allowing masses of flight-test data to be acquired and analysed in the lab.

As the pace of guided weapons development increased in the early 1950s, a more extensive range was required to test long-range Surface-to-Air Missiles, Air-to-Surface Missiles and Ballistic Missiles. Recovery of these to check the condition of components such as ramjet combustors was of paramount importance, so fishing them out of the drink was out of the question. A long-range weapons testing area was required and so the Weapons Research Establishment at Woomera in Australia had been set up in 1947 in response to an early requirement to test a long-range bombardment rocket called Menace. Woomera allowed weapons to be tested to their full potential, tracked over the desert by radar and optical equipment (the weather helping this aspect considerably) and recovery of the vehicle at the end of the flight. The use of high-performance target drones for SAM trials was another benefit of using Woomera's wide open spaces. Over the years Woomera hosted some of the most important milestones in UK weapons development. Interestingly the first test vehicle launched at Woomera (aside from 3in [7.62cm] rockets) was the LPAA (Liquid Propellant Anti-Aircraft), a German Enzian flak rocket captured at the end of the war that was used to test the range facilities.

Having looked at the reasons for test vehicles, let's look at some examples.

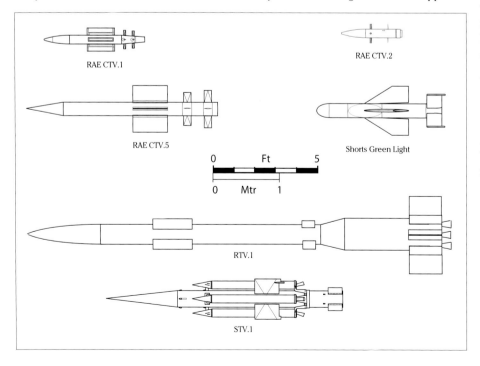

RAE CTV.1

RAE CTV.2

RAE CTV.5

Shorts Green Light

0   Ft   5

0   Mtr   1

RTV.1

STV.1

The main test vehicles used by the Royal Aircraft Establishment and industry during the 1950s.

Long Shot and CTV.1

Component Test Vehicle 1 (CTV.1) had its origins in a beam-riding air-to-air weapon called Long Shot being developed at the end of the war by the Telecommunications Research Establishment. With a diameter of 5in (12.7cm) and a length of 5ft (1.52m), CTV.1 was not powered but boosted by a trio of rocket motors (a solid fuel rocket is called a motor, a liquid fuel rocket is called an engine) for a flight of about ten seconds. Fitted with four rectangular wings, the vehicle possessed separate ailerons and rudders on the rear fuselage in line with the wings. However this configuration led to control problems due to wake turbulence from the wings. CTV.1 was used to test various control systems and develop the recording systems that would become important in future work. CTV.1 was also used for some of the earliest radio telemetry trials, with a five-channel system installed and tested in 1950.

Further work with CTV.1 included command guidance techniques, later applied to SAMs and particularly anti-tank weapons. In all thirteen SAM trials (mainly concerned with 'gathering' the missile into the radar beam) and twenty-six flights for anti-tank weapon development were carried out with CTV.1. A version with moving wings of similar planform to the Bloodhound to investigate polar control was also flown.

LOP/GAP and RTV.1

LOP/GAP evolved from the Admiralty GAP project, but when this weapon was transferred from the Admiralty to the RAE in 1946, the first of a long line of test vehicles was born. Rocket Test Vehicle (RTV) 1 was used by the RAE as the basis of a family of vehicles that throughout the 1950s allowed the UK aerospace companies to develop and build a variety of guided weapons. With a diameter of 9in (22.8cm) and a length of 16ft (4.87m) RTV.1 shared the four rectangular wings of CTV.1, but only had one set of four control fins working differentially to control the vehicle's roll and in pairs for pitch and yaw.

The initial version, RTV.1E, was used to develop beam-riding techniques for SAMs, but a later version, RTV.1Q, was fitted with a warhead and fuzing. It was an RTV.1Q that conducted the first interception of a target drone by a guided weapon in 1954. The somewhat churlish rumour that it was more a case of the Firefly flying into the path of the RTV.1Q rather than the other way round spread quickly around Aberporth!

The problems of recovery over the Aberporth range where most RTV.1 test flights took place was addressed by the develop-

ment of parachute recovery. RTV.1 was fitted with a system that could slow the vehicle down from Mach 1.25 and lower it to the sea, to be picked up by a boat.

A further variant was RTV.1J, used to investigate jet deflection for the vertical launch of ballistic missiles. This was fitted with a Napier NRE.7 engine and gimballed rocket nozzle and stripped of its wings and aerodynamic controls. Steel ballast strips were added to keep the launch acceleration below 1G. This work had particular relevance to the forthcoming Black Knight test vehicle.

CTV.1 and RTV.1 can be viewed as the start point for post-war guided weapons development in the UK. Many of the operational principles and hardware developed for these test vehicles were applied to the first generation of UK guided weapons.

RTV.2 and GPV

As SAM development gained pace, particularly from 1949 on, there was a need for a larger, higher performance test vehicle to run trials of SAM components, particularly homing systems. The RTV.2 was designed by Folland and was much larger than its predecessor. Almost as soon as the RTV.2 project had begun (a few RTV.2 rounds had been fired) there were doubts about Folland's design. In January 1951 the RAE GW Dept said: 'The present design of RTV.2 is admittedly a costly and unversatile vehicle which we feel unable to support as a long term venture, but it has the advantage of being half developed with some of the teething structural problems and boost problems overcome.'

It was decided to redesign the vehicle and hand airframe development to Shorts and

Shorts General Purpose test vehicle just after launch and before shedding its boost rocket motors. Copyright Thales Air Defence

Harland, mainly because the Folland design was too costly to produce. Similar criticism was levelled at Folland for their handling of the Red Dean air-to-air missile.

In Shorts' hands this became known as the GPV (General Purpose test Vehicle, but has also been referred to as the Guided Pilotless Vehicle in some literature). The wider scope of this project was to cover rocket engine development, homing systems, moving wing controls and solid rocket sustainers, amongst others. Elliott Brothers were responsible for the guidance equipment to be used in conjunction with homing systems.

GPV was 26ft 6in (8.1m) long and had a diameter of 17½in (44cm) and was powered by a HTP/Kerosene rocket engine of the KP (Kerosene and Peroxide) series. Eight Demon rocket motors in a wrap-around configuration provided launch boost.

The development teams working on Bloodhound and Thunderbird used GPV to develop homing systems. Elliott Brothers also used the GPV for seeker development under a project called Caravan, using Badger X-band radar 'homing eyes' to investigate factors that affected missile accuracy, such as seeker jitter.

GPV is most noteworthy for its recovery system. This involved two parachutes: the first slowed the vehicle down from supersonic speeds, while the second lowered the vehicle to the sea. Once in the sea, a flotation bag kept the vehicle afloat until it could be recovered by RAF air-sea rescue launch.

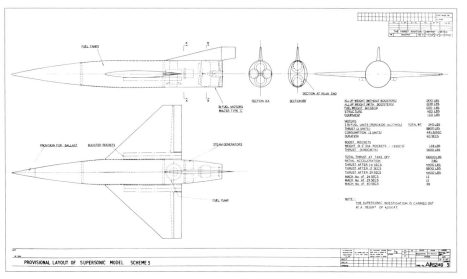

PROVISIONAL LAYOUT OF SUPERSONIC MODEL   SCHEME 5

Fairey Aviation Co Ltd test vehicle to investigate the supersonic flight regime in advance of development of the Delta II.

Fairey Aviation Co Ltd test vehicle to investigate the supersonic flight regime in advance of development of the Delta II.

The CTV Series Develops

Following on from CTV.1 was CTV.2. Used for aileron control and roll stabilisation work, CTV.2 was still 5in (12.7cm) in diameter but was 7ft 7in (2.31m) long including its fixed boost, had much smaller wings at the rear and had the ailerons moved to a forward position. Flares at the wingtips aided observations of the roll stabilisation system.

The next test vehicle in the family was CTV.3, a missile component testbed that was also used for aileron control and roll stabilisation work. This was followed by CTV.4, a seeker testbed used in 1953-1954 for CW radar homing trials for Red Duster (codename for Bristol Bloodhound I) and Red Shoes (codename for English Electric Thunderbird I). CTV.4 also formed the basis of the HTV (Homing Test Vehicle) for the de Havilland Firestreak AAM, which was used for ground trials and boosted by three 5in LAP rocket motors.

The final member of this family was to become the longest-lived. Designed by Frank Hazell of the RAE Aerodynamics Section, CTV.5 Series 1 was another RAE flight-test vehicle originally known as the Cruciform Moving Wing Test Vehicle, CMWTV, and used for high-altitude pitch / roll / yaw control development and in Yellow Feather seeker trials. The CTV.5M version was used to develop polar control systems, later used on Bristol SAMs.

CTV.5 Series 2 had detachable nose cones for testing materials under kinetic heating for hypersonic research related to re-entry vehicles. CTV.5 Series 3 became the Skylark family of sounding rockets that remained in use into the 1980s. Skylark was used for re-entry vehicle development and was even proposed as an ABM (Anti-Ballistic Missile). It was based on a Raven rocket motor and was capable of launching a 150 lb (68kg) payload to high altitudes, and in the early 1960s it could reach 80,000ft (24,384m) when fitted with an additional Cuckoo boost motor.

Aircraft Aerodynamics Testing

As far back as 1903 and the Wright brothers, wind tunnels and models were used to investigate the aerodynamics of an aircraft in flight. Free-flight scale models were also used, particularly for large aircraft such as the Short Stirling and its half-scale analogue, the S.31. In the postwar period high-speed wind tunnels were in short supply, so the companies turned to rocket-boosted scale models. Fairey were particularly active in this field – building the VTO, a half-scale model of Fairey's Delta 1 Vertical Take Off research aircraft. Dating from 1947, the VTO test vehicle was powered by an RAE-developed Beta 1 HTP/methanol hydrazine rocket engine. Interestingly the stability control for the vehicle was sourced from the German V2 rocket weapon!

Also in 1947 Fairey proposed a second series of test vehicles to investigate the delta wing's behaviour in the supersonic flight regime up to Mach 1.5. Schemes 5 and 6 were to use a pair of bi-fuel rocket engines and to be boosted off the ground by a quartet of 3in (7.6cm) rocket motors. Such data would have contributed to the development of the later Fairey Delta Two (see Chapter Twelve).

The test vehicle most familiar to anyone interested in UK aviation was also an aerodynamic model of a full scale aircraft, the Miles M.52. Cancelled in 1946 on the grounds of fear for the pilot's safety, this supersonic research aircraft's configuration formed the basis of a 30% scale model built by Vickers as the Vickers / RAE Rocket Powered Transonic Aircraft Model (also known as the TR, Transonic Rocket) to investigate pilotless, expendable weapons. Powered by a pair of the Beta liquid-fuelled rocket engines mentioned above, the vehicle was launched and controlled from a de Havilland Mosquito B.Mk.XVI (PF604). On 9th October 1948 a TR reached a speed on Mach=1.38, thus proving the supersonic aerodynamics of the full-scale M.52.

Throughout the 1950s and early 1960s instrumented scale models of aircraft, such as the TSR.2, were launched on solid rocket motors and the telemetry transmitted to a ground station until the model's demise in the sea or on the desert floor. Such models were expensive and were soon superseded by computer modelling.

Industry Test Vehicles

These establishment research vehicles were fundamental to the development of guided weapons in the UK. Without them industry would have had to start from scratch and, in the political climate of the early 1950s, this was not what the Government wanted. The RAE test vehicles provided a kick-start to the UK guided weapons developers.

By 1951 industry was getting to grips with the development of their own guided weapons. Armstrong Whitworth, as part of the 502 Group developing the Seaslug naval SAM, was amongst the first to go public with their progress in guided weapons. The 1954 Society of British Aircraft Constructors (SBAC) Farnborough Air Show had Armstrong's Guided Missile Test Vehicle and Avro's Controlled Test Vehicle on display for the first time.

Farnborough proved to be the showcase of choice for guided weapons as well as aircraft. Despite many of the GW-related companies not being obvious members of the SBAC, they still showed off their wares (as long as the Ministry of Supply approved of course). Every company involved in GW development wanted the taxpayer, and more importantly the competition, to know that they were in the field. However, the MoS was reluctant to show off their next generation of weapons and as a result many of the exhibits were actually test vehicles, such as the English Electric tandem-boosted dart, or model from design studies. This practice was bemoaned by Flight's Technical Editor, Bill Gunston, who greeted the appearance of actual hardware at the 1956 exhibition by writing: 'Fictitious mock-ups are happily absent this year, except where they are only incidental to a piece of support or test equipment.'

The Companies Mix and Match

As already mentioned, the companies 'borrowed' various components or even complete vehicles for their own research and development work. This allowed them to concentrate on specifics such as guidance or propulsion systems without the added burden of developing a dedicated control system.

Vickers' Bomb Test Vehicle series is a prime example of this. The BTVs were used to develop the TV-guided Blue Boar bomb and the BTV.1, a 1/3-scale Blue Boar, used the roll stabilisation control system from CTV.2 and CTV.3. BTV.10 was a full-scale test vehicle used for Blue Boar development using the control system from RTV.1.

BTV.10's ultimate use was as a test vehicle for Green Cheese anti-ship missile development. One interesting aspect of the BTV and later Green Cheese trials at Woomera was a full-scale replica of a Soviet cruiser made from chicken wire. Chicken wire, that staple material of outback farms, was as a result in short supply for months, much to the annoyance of the Australian farmers!

De Havilland Propellers used a more or less complete CTV.4 fitted with the Violet Banner Mk.3 Infra-Red seeker as the basis of their Homing Test Vehicle for Firestreak development. This project apparently involved firing HTVs at arrays of radiant electric fires and gas burners set up on Salisbury Plain!

As the industry gained experience of guided weapons, they began to produce their own test vehicles tailored to their particular needs. The main projects for Bristol Aeroplane Company's Guided Weapons Department through the 1950s were the Red Duster and Blue Envoy SAMs, for which they developed the eXperimental Test Vehicle (XTV) series.

The XTVs

No project better illustrates the importance of test vehicles to guided weapons development than the XTV series. Having selected the moving monoplane/over-and-under ramjet configuration for the Red Duster through work in the wind tunnel (see Chapter Four), Bristol embarked on building and flying a series of vehicles to test the various aspects of

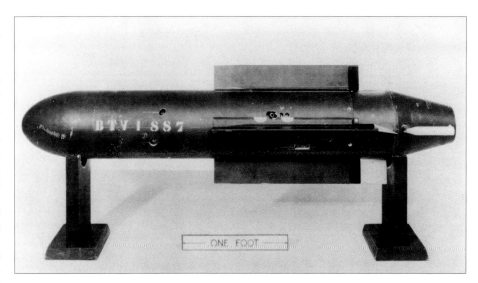

Vickers BTV.1 test vehicle for the Blue Boar TV-guided bomb project. This vehicle used the control system from the RTV.1.

Bristol's XTV.1 (eXperimental Test Vehicle) on the launch rail. Such sub-scale vehicles confirmed that the design was viable and was stable in flight. Bristol Collection via Richard Vernon

Bristol's XTV.3 ready to launch from a modified AA gun mounting. Bristol Collection via Richard Vernon

the design. At the time, the early 1950s, the Cold War was hotting up and a SAGW to protect the forthcoming deterrent was a top priority. The Ministry told Bristol that they could launch as many as they wanted to make progress. Bristol obliged.

XTV.1 was a 1/4-scale model of Red Duster, fitted with dummy ramjets and fixed wings, used to acquire aerodynamic data. It was boosted on rocket motors and proved that the design was aerodynamically sound.

The next vehicle, XTV.2, was a 1/3-scale model, initially without the dummy ramjets but fitted with moving wings, driven by high-pressure air actuators, to prove that the monoplane wing controls were capable of manoeuvring the missile. These sub-scale vehicles were tested on the Larkhill range, but moving to the next phase required a change of venue to Aberporth and, later, Woomera.

XTV.3 was the first of the full-scale vehicles and included dummy ramjets and moving wings. XTV.3 was used to develop the control system. XTV.2 and XTV.3 were launched on rocket motors. XTV.4, again full-scale, was the first of the series to carry working ramjets. Due to the low thrust of the ramjet and the poor performance of the early boost motors in particular, the airframe had to be as light as possible, so the wings and control systems were removed.

XTVs 1 through 4 had proved various aspects of the vehicle. All four variants had a cruciform tail assembly, but the next version, XTV.5, adopted the rectangular tailplanes of the definitive Red Duster. XTV.5 was more or less a fully functioning Red Duster SAM and more than two hundred XTV.5 rounds were fired to develop the ramjets, boost motor configuration and control systems before moving on to the Pre-production eXperimental Red Duster (XRD) for full-blown homing and interception trials.

The XTV programme showed the important role played by test vehicles in the development of a guided weapon. The test vehicles revealed early problems, particularly in the ramjet combustor systems, that would have been difficult to resolve later in the pro-

XTV.6 complete with dummy boosts about to be launched on a tandem boost rocket during the early days of the Blue Envoy project. Bristol Collection via Richard Vernon

XTV.8 comprised the Blue Envoy wing sandwiched between two boost motors to investigate wing flutter. Bristol Collection via Richard Vernon

Bristol XTV.9 for ramjet testing became the BET.9 (Blue Envoy Test) to develop the 18in ramjet for Stage 1¾. Bristol Collection via Richard Vernon

British Secret Projects: Hypersonics, Ramjets & Missiles

The Separation Test Vehicle (STV.1) was used to investigate the behaviour of boost motors when jettisoned and the mechanisms to shed the boosters. Tony Buttler Collection

ject's development life. Telemetry and recoverable vehicles were crucial to this. As Bristol moved forward on the Red Duster XTVs, a new longer-ranged SAM was being developed: Blue Envoy.

XTV.6 and XTV.7 were 1/6-scale models of the Blue Envoy development vehicle launched on a Gosling tandem boost motor. XTV.6 carried dummy boosts to check Blue Envoy's launch characteristics while XTV.7 had no boosts or ramjet pods and was used to check aerodynamic drag of the airframe. XTV.8 was a 1/3-scale model of Blue Envoy's double delta wings sandwiched between two strap-on boosts and used for high-speed flutter tests.

XTV.9 became the BET.9 ramjet test vehicle, while XTV.10 tested Continuous Wave radar seekers on a Red Duster airframe. XTV.11 to 17 were for Bloodhound II development including the new Bristol Siddeley BS.1009 ramjets. Bloodhound III, the Command Guidance, nuclear-armed version called RO.166, employed XTV.18 and 19. XTV.20 was a completely new airframe intended for ABM research.

As a family, the XTVs contributed a significant amount of knowledge to Bristol's Guided Weapons Department, however Bristol Engines was set to become a world leader in a particular field within guided weapons – that of high-speed propulsion.

Propulsion Testing

Running in parallel with the control and guidance systems test vehicle research in the late 1940s and 1950s were the propulsion system test programmes. Guided weapons relied on rocket and ramjet propulsion to provide the high performance required to perform their diverse roles. Ramjets and rockets were not new, but their applications and performance envelopes were, so perfecting them was also a priority.

The bread and butter of the guided weapons developers were solid rocket motors. These were designed by PERME (Propellant and Explosives Research and Manufacturing Establishment) and IMI/SRS (Imperial Metal Industries / Summerfield Research Station). The motor casings them-

selves were built by companies like Bristol Aerojet or English Electric. The IMI/SRS motors were named after dogs such as Basset and Bulldog, whereas the PERME motors were named after birds like Stonechat or Gosling. Some motors for naval weapons were named after famous naval battles, such as Matapan or Cadiz.

Initial trials were made using motors left over from World War Two, such as the 3in (7.6cm) UP motors and the 6in (15.2cm) Swallow rated at 40 lb (18kg) thrust, but as vehicle sizes increased bigger boosts came into use.

Rocket motors were the key to success in the early days of guided weapons, but until their power and reliability improved progress was slow. Low thrust ratings (the highest thrust motor available in 1952 was the 7½in [19cm] Demon, rated at 2,668 lb [1,210kg] thrust) entailed the use of multiple boosts, up

to eight Demons being clustered around the GPV and XTV.3. Of course all these motors added to the drag, reducing acceleration even more, a factor that affected ramjets particularly. The development of more powerful boost motors such as the 10in (25.4cm) Gosling I, rated at 13,230 lb (6,000kg), allowed the XTV.5 to progress Bristol's ramjet design.

Another problem with boost motors was jettisoning them after they had burned out and while the sustainer was running. Tandem boosts, with the boost motor on the rear of the vehicle, posed no problem as they fell away, but wrap-around boosts clustered around the forward fuselage were a different matter. Unless they fell away cleanly they could damage the vehicle. Development of Seaslug included the use of the Separation Test Vehicle (STV) to develop boost separation techniques. Data from this was also applied to the Blue Sky AAM.

Bristol's Jet Test Vehicle (JTV) provided the UK's first supersonic ramjet flight during the effort to develop a ramjet for the Red Duster programme. Bristol Collection via Richard Vernon

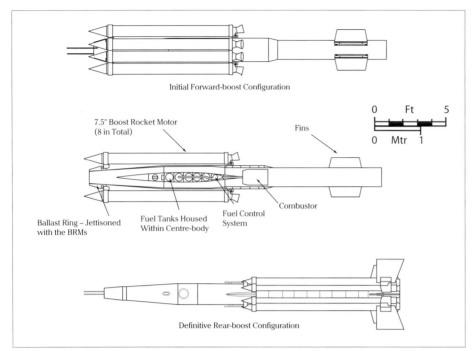

Initial Forward-boost Configuration

7.5" Boost Rocket Motor
(8 in Total)

Fins

0 — Ft — 5

0 — Mtr — 1

Combustor

Ballast Ring – Jettisoned
with the BRMs

Fuel Tanks Housed
Within Centre-body

Fuel Control
System

Definitive Rear-boost Configuration

Reliability has also been mentioned, for example with rocket motors that failed to burn causing vehicles to veer off at launch. This was cured by canting the rocket nozzle to ensure that all of the thrust lines converged at the same point in the vehicle, reducing the effect of asymmetric thrust.

The poor performance of rocket motors forced the guided weapons designers to use rocket engines. Unfortunately the Services, particularly the Admiralty, were not keen to have liquid fuels on their hands. However the availability of rocket motors with adequate thrust was not imminent and the need was urgent, so development continued using rocket engines in lieu of motors. The Seaslug propulsion development team built the Motor Test Vehicle (MTV) to assess various sustainers, including the MTV/H (Motor Test Vehicle / Hot) using methanol and nitric acid and MTV/P(L), for Motor Test Vehicle / Propulsion (Liquid), using RFNA (Red Fuming Nitric Acid) and kerosene in its NK.1 sustainer.

Ramjet Testing
In the interests of developing a GAP, the RAE contracted Bristol Engines to develop a twin-ramjet Jet Test Vehicle. This would be beneficial to Bristol as they were also contracted to develop the ramjet powered Project 1220

SAM, which eventually became Red Duster when the SAM contracts were awarded in late 1949.

JTV was powered by two RAE-developed 6in ramjets with simple combustors that used strontium flares to maintain combustion. Trials did not go well, with boost separation problems and vehicles breaking up in flight revealing the problems of aeroelasticity in small lightweight vehicles. One wag suggested that the JTV was the real Separation Test Vehicle due to its propensity to disintegrate! Aeroelasticity effects were a problem requiring more in-depth research, prompting the likes of Armstrong Whitworth to build and fly a rocket-boosted winged vehicle called Flutter Dart to help with the investigation.

1950 and early 1951 saw changes in boost type and configuration (two Deacon motors in a tandem boost) that allowed JTV1 to fly supersonically in July 1951, the first supersonic ramjet flight to be made in the UK.

Meanwhile down at Pyestock, the NGTE had been working on a larger, more complicated annular ramjet whose combustor used pilot and main burners that employed the knowledge gained from work in the US. NGTE opted for a larger ramjet and contracted D Napier and Son to build the Napier Ram Jet (NRJ).1 and a test vehicle to use it: the RJTV.

D Napier and Son were famous for producing somewhat baroque reciprocating engines (their Sabre and Nomad spring to mind). However these engines were meticulously engineered and superbly finished. Napier, like Wright in the US, had tried to ignore the gas turbine as a passing fancy, but by the late 1940s both companies realised that the gas turbine was here to stay. It has been said that the early centrifugal gas turbines were too simple for Napier to bother about, they were enthralled by the intricacies of piston engines. The complexities and precision engineering of the NGTE's combustor must have appealed, as Napier's engineers produced the first practicable large-diameter ramjet.

The NRJ.1 had a diameter of 16in (40.6cm) and was integrated into the RJTV body, which had a pitot intake and a centre body that served as a diffuser and a fuel tank. Launched

Napier's successful RamJet Test Vehicle with its NGTE-developed NRJ.1 took a world altitude record in the early 1950s after its self-destruct mechanism failed.

An Avro Lincoln was used as a drop aircraft during the development of the recovery system for the Controlled Recoverable Re-usable Test Vehicle (CRRTV). Bristol Collection via Richard Vernon

by eight Demon boosts, the RJTV performed very well, so much so that it gained an absolute altitude record, albeit only as a result of the self-destruct mechanisms failing!

Having got the basics of ramjet design sorted out, a new generation of ramjet test vehicle was required for the Blue Envoy SAM and ramjet-powered stand-off bombs. The NGTE drew up a requirement for a Mach 3 test vehicle and asked Napier and Bristol to tender designs. Following on from the success of the RJTV, Napier and the NGTE had embarked on the RJTV.2, with an integrated Mach 3 to Mach 4 ramjet, assisted by a pair of Mayfly III boost motors.

In 1954 Bristol designed a test vehicle for that speed range which they called the RP.5. This was later known as the Controllable, Recoverable, Reusable Test Vehicle (CRRTV) and was based on the XTV.5. Ramjets work best when tailored to a specific speed regime, so the CRRTV needed a boost to Mach 3. You may recall that boost rocket motors were not particularly powerful and could only boost a vehicle to around Mach 1. CRRTV required boosting to Mach 1.2 where a 16in (40.64cm) 'hack' ramjet took over and accelerated the vehicle to the light-up speed of the 18in (45.72cm) Mach 3 ramjet.

CRRTV would employ the usual parachute recovery system, but since its range meant it would be flown at Woomera and land on the ground, some method of absorbing the impact (even from a parachute descent) was required. The solution was a long spike in the nose that penetrated the earth, absorbing the shock. The flight ended with the CRRTV sticking out of the ground and the parachute billowing in the wind. Tests of the recovery system included airdrops of unpowered CRRTV.1 from Avro Lincoln bombers over the Australian outback.

CRRTV progressed through two variants: CRRTV.2, also known as Bobbin, was intended to test the BRJ.601, a scaled 16in (40.6cm) version of the Mach 3 ramjet. The ultimate version, CRRTV.3 based on the Blue Envoy airframe, was to be used to test a new 20in (50.8cm) ramjet, but it did not progress beyond studies. It was developments in rocket motors that did for CRRTV.3. Blue Envoy was originally intended to use a 20in

An engineer looks over a CRRTV after a drop test from a Lincoln. The impact was to be lessened by the spike penetrating the desert floor, assuming the soil was thick enough. Bristol Collection via Richard Vernon

The Shorts trials team set up for a test launch of the Green Light Test Vehicle (GLTV).
Copyright Thales Air Defence

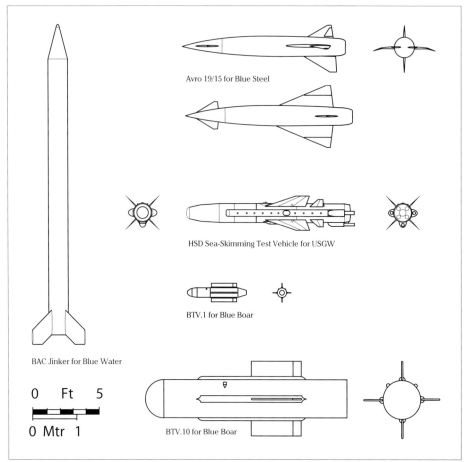

Avro 19/15 for Blue Steel

HSD Sea-Skimming Test Vehicle for USGW

BTV.1 for Blue Boar

BAC Jinker for Blue Water

0   Ft   5

0 Mtr 1

BTV.10 for Blue Boar

Left: **Some of the test vehicles used by industry over the years to pave the way for new designs.**

Opposite page, left: **GW20 Re-entry Vehicle used for ballistic missile warhead tests. In the background is a model of the Black Knight test vehicle used to launch these.**

Opposite page, right: **Further re-entry vehicle testing was carried out using Jaguar and Falstaff test vehicles. Falstaff played a significant part in the Chevaline programme.**

(50.8cm) ramjet because its higher power was required to overcome the drag of the Bulldog boost motors. However, as the Borzoi motor was thinner, generated less drag and was more powerful, the 18in (45.3cm) BRJ.800 ramjet was deemed powerful enough.

BET.9 (Blue Envoy Test), which was used to test combustion systems for the 18in (45.3cm) BRJ.800 Mach 3 ramjet, was derived from the XTV.9. Another member of the Mach 3 SAM test vehicle family was XBE, eXperimental Blue Envoy, a more or less complete missile, analogous to the XRD.

The CRRTV test vehicle series were eventually cancelled, not because the SAM it was intended to aid the development of was scrapped in 1957, but because Bristol Engines had built a ramjet test facility (the High Altitude Test Plant or HATP) at Patchway in 1958. This allowed ramjets to be tested in a similar manner to gas turbines, which reduced the time needed for development as well as limiting the requirement for flight testing.

By 1958 the need for dedicated test vehicles, particularly for propulsion, had more or less disappeared from the guided weapons field. Apart from test vehicles that were more or less prototypes of the next generation of weapons such as the Green Light (for Short's Sea Cat, fired into bales of straw to test the launcher without a range!) or Jinker (for English Electric's Blue Water), the emphasis had changed to materials, systems and aerodynamic testing in support of the UK's future weapons systems.

Further examples of scaled test vehicles for guided weapons development were associated with the Blue Steel stand-off weapon for the V-Force. The 6/5 was a 1/8-scale model of Avro's 48/35 configuration for Blue Steel and was ground launched at Aberporth, the larger 19/15 (a 2/5-scale model) was powered by a Jackdaw rocket motor, rated at 1,480 lb (6.6KN) and dropped from Vickers Valiants. The Jackdaw was unusual in that it was fitted with two blast tubes to emulate the proposed layout of the Stentor rocket engine fitted to the production Blue Steel. The full-scale alloy-bodied Blue Steel test vehicles such as the W.103 were powered by the DH Double Spectre HTP/kerosene rocket engine.

Ballistic Missile Re-Entry Vehicle Trials

Yet again the RAE took centre stage in this, with the companies contracted to produce the hardware. The RAE specified what the particular vehicles were to be used to investi-gate and how the vehicles should be used.

In 1955 Her Majesty's Government committed itself to producing and fielding a Medium Range Ballistic Missisle (MRBM) that became known as Blue Streak. Hand-in-hand with the MRBM was another programme to develop an anti-ballistic missile (ABM) system called Violet Friend.

The two projects would present a considerable challenge to the aerospace industry in the UK. One of the major unknowns was materials, particularly for re-entry vehicles. The problems associated with re-entry vehicles and the interceptors for Violet Friend were that of hypersonic flight. Hypersonic refers to speeds in excess of a Mach Number of 5: Mach Number, in its simplest definition, being a speed divided by local speed of sound. The principal problems of high Mach flight are associated with the thermal effects on the aircraft structure and the air entering any air-breathing propulsion system. Mach 5 is also a point where real gas effects start to occur, with adverse effects on engine performance.

The thermal effects derive from two sources: the friction of air passing over the airframe and 'stagnation' where air is compressed against leading edges, causing its temperature to rise.

Any work on high-speed air vehicles, be they re-entry vehicles or aircraft, would require research work into how materials used for structures and components would react under high temperatures. Some of the earliest tests involved placing samples in the efflux of ramjets in the Bristol HATP, to replicate the heat of hypersonic flight. This however, could not replicate the material's reaction to flight conditions, so test vehicles were required.

Blue Streak was to be fitted with a nuclear warhead housed within a re-entry vehicle (RV). In the late 1950s RV technology was very much in its infancy on both sides of the Atlantic but ballistic missiles were seen as the way forward for nuclear strikes. SAMs had seen off the supersonic bomber threat and so there was a requirement to investigate the behaviour of RVs. The RV designers needed to know how an RV would behave as it re-entered, while the ABM design teams wanted to observe its behaviour to maximise the chance of an interception. Since Blue Streak was still in development and the developers wanted to be able to monitor the RVs on an instrumented range such as Woomera, it was decided to build a small rocket that could loft the RV and allow it to be tracked. This was called Black Knight.

Black Knight
Saunders Roe, usually known as Saro, had a reputation of aviation expertise based on building flying boats. In the late 1940s Saro had flown the Princess 10-engined flying boat airliner, which represented the cutting edge in large aircraft, and by the mid-1950s had also flown the SR.53 mixed-powerplant interceptor prototype. Having experience now in rocket engines, they turned their hand to rockets. The Ministry of Supply had a requirement for a research rocket to test re-entry vehicles for Blue Streak, to be powered by four Armstrong Siddeley Motors (ASM) Gamma engines providing 16,000 lb (71.2KN) thrust at lift-off.

Black Knight's principal role was to act as a test vehicle for the 'Gaslight' trials, used to assess the performance of re-entry vehicles for the Blue Streak MRBM. In order to boost the re-entry velocity of the RVs, the RV was fitted with a Cuckoo rocket motor and mounted inverted in the Black Knight nose cone. On the cancellation of Blue Streak, the use of Black Knight moved from re-entry vehicle research to anti-ballistic missile research. This involved the acquisition of radar and optical data to aid tracking, and therefore the interception, of RVs. A later series of trials using Black Knight, called Dazzle, took place in 1962. Again Black Knight launched the RVs, called GW.20, and ground radar attempted to track them with VHF returns from their wakes. In reality the Dazzle trials were intended to keep the RV design team occupied, and retain its capability to design and build RVs until the Chevaline (described below) programme got under way.

Other tests conducted on Black Knight comprised coatings for hypersonic vehicles, anti-ballistic missile technology and materials development. The last flight of Black Knight was in late 1965, but the rocket was later proposed as a second stage to a Black Prince (Blue Streak Satellite Launch Vehicle, BSSLV) launcher. A further proposal using Black Knight was the 56in (142.2cm) Black Knight that used a Waxwing spherical solid rocket motor as an upper stage.

Chevaline
The Blue Streak project had spawned many of the test vehicle programmes of the late 1950s and early 1960s but it would be a new project that would provide much of the impetus for the test vehicles of the late 1960s and into the 1970s. That project was Chevaline.

A name that appeared in the public domain out of the blue in 1979, Chevaline was a project designed to improve the capability of the Polaris submarine-launched ballistic missile (SLBM) system, while also maintaining a nuclear weapons design team in the UK. Polaris was supplied by the United States and entered service in 1969. Intended to extend the life of the UK's Polaris missiles, the Chevaline project was started soon after the Labour government took power in 1964 and continued until the late 1980s, entering service in 1982.

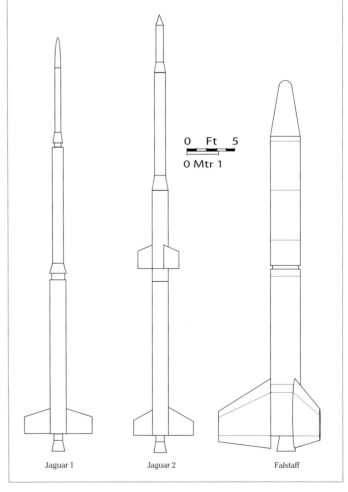

Jaguar 1   Jaguar 2   Falstaff

0 Ft 5
0 Mtr 1

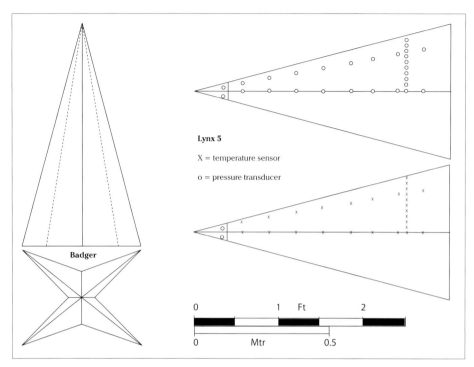

Lynx 5

X = temperature sensor

o = pressure transducer

Badger

0   1   Ft   2

0   Mtr   0.5

RAE free-flight models to investigate the thermal and aerodynamic effects of hypersonic flight included Lynx and Badger. Lynx was instrumented with thermocouples and pressure transducers.

The RAE drew up this design to study the Mach 10+ regime. It is shown here with its boosting system.

Hypersonic Research Vehicles

Throughout the 1960s and 1970s the RAE conducted a major campaign of test flights to assess hypersonic flight. Much of this derived from the ballistic missile-related work of the late 1950s and early 1960s, but was mainly carried out for scientific research. The 'Big Cat' series of test vehicles explored various aspects of the hypersonic regime.

Lynx, boosted by a Raven motor, was a 3ft (0.9m) delta-shaped test vehicle instrumented to measure pressure and thermal effects on a mild steel airframe at Mach 4+. Three models were built and flown: 5 and 8 were 75° deltas, while the 7 was a 60° delta. Panther and Tiger were used for hypersonic research up to Mach 5 and were powered by a Gosling rocket motor.

The RAE used Ranger, powered by a Rook or Gosling rocket motor, for heat transfer experiments carried out at both Aberporth and Woomera. Heat transfer was particularly important in the high-speed flight field because thermal effects were one of the main concerns of the vehicle designers.

In the end the level of hypersonic research activity dropped considerably moving on to mainly lab-based work carried out under a limited budget. The need for test vehicles in this field had in fact all but disappeared.

Another vehicle used to explore aspects of hypersonic flight was the Badger. Powered by a Gosling or Rook rocket motor, Badger was used at Aberporth to free-flight test waverider configurations. Waveriders were developed by Terence Nonweiler, who conceived the idea that an aircraft could ride on its own shockwave. Nonweiler, a highly respected aerodynamicist and Professor of Aeronautics at Glasgow University, saw the waverider as the answer to the problems of hypersonic flight and it is still seen today as the key configuration for this flight regime. The object of the test flights was to investigate pressure regimes and temperature effects at high Mach numbers.

Skylark

As mentioned earlier, Skylark was originally called CTV.5 but, as part of the UK's contribution to the International Geophysical Year (1957), CTV.5 took up a civil guise as the Skylark sounding rocket to carry scientific pay-

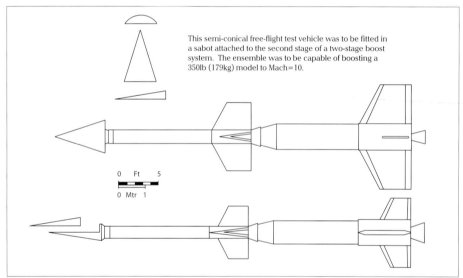

This semi-conical free-flight test vehicle was to be fitted in a sabot attached to the second stage of a two-stage boost system. The ensemble was to be capable of boosting a 350lb (179kg) model to Mach=10.

0   Ft   5

0   Mtr   1

The Chevaline warhead bus is known as the Penetration Aid Carrier (PAC). The PAC has been described as a mini-spacecraft, capable of manoeuvring in its own right and deploying decoys and chaff. The testing of Chevaline components was carried out on the CQ.941/Falstaff test vehicle, with the PAC housed in the bulbous nose of Falstaff.

Falstaff was derived from an RAE test vehicle called Hyperion HRV (Hypersonic Research Vehicle) and used a 36in (91.4cm) diameter Stonechat motor, the biggest solid rocket motor built in the UK, with a Rook or Raven second stage and a Cuckoo third stage. Falstaff was used for hypersonic research with Oberon test vehicles. As you can see the RAE liked to name their vehicles after Shake-

spearian characters. However when the first UK satellite was in the planning stages it was decided that Puck might be misunderstood in communications; consequently the first UK satellite was called Prospero.

While Hyperion tested larger components, a programme to test smaller components and materials was under way using a test vehicle called Jaguar. Later renamed Jabiru to prevent confusion with the SEPECAT Jaguar strike aircraft, Jaguar comprised a Rook first stage, Gosling second and Lobster third stage. Later versions used Goldfinch second and Gosling third stage. A two-stage flight-test vehicle based on Jaguar comprising a Rook booster and Gosling upper stage was called Leopard.

Not all test vehicles flew or swam. This rocket sled was used to test high-speed separation of the Blue Sky / Fireflash AAM. TNA AVIA 54/2239

Whether deliberate or merely humorous, the capabilities of the early guided weapons were somewhat exaggerated. BAE Systems

loads. First launched in February 1957, Skylark initially used a Raven rocket motor but by 1960 a Cuckoo first-stage booster had been added. While other RAE test vehicles were actively involved in military research, Skylark, although proposed as the basis of an ABM, remained a civil project.

Underwater Testing

Not all test vehicles were intended to fly. As we have seen getting the test vehicle into the air in the first place posed a problem that was only solved by improved boosting. When the Hawker Siddeley Dynamics Underwater to Surface Guided Weapon (USGW), later known as Sub-Martel, was being developed, one of the problems was getting it out of the sea. USGW was to be launched from the torpedo tubes in submarines and the difficulty was in getting it to the surface in the correct attitude for a launch. USGW will be covered in Chapter Seven, but it was associated with two separate test vehicles.

The Discharge Test Vehicle (DTV) was used to check the behaviour of the weapon during discharge from the submarine, through its transition to the surface and on to the start of the launch sequence. USGW used a tandem boost comprising five rocket motors as used on the Taildog AAM. Arranged like the five on a dice, the central motor powered the DTV/USGW to the surface, with the TVC controls of the Taildog ensuring that the vehicle breached the surface in the correct attitude.

The second test vehicle used in the USGW project was the Sea-Skimming Test Vehicle (SSTV). The SSTV was a TV-guided Martel airframe fitted with a radio altimeter and sea-skimming control system and launched from the RAE's de Havilland Sea Vixen on the Aberporth range over Cardigan Bay in west Wales. The work carried out using SSTV was used in the development of Active Radar Martel, later known as P3T, which entered service as Sea Eagle.

The Place of Test Vehicles in UK Aerospace History

This chapter has put together only a summary of the most significant test vehicles used in the UK from 1945 until 1980. Without these test vehicles the UK armed forces would have had to wait even longer for their guided weapons

to arrive. The engineers and scientists applied some of the most advanced theories in aerospace engineering to these vehicles to further their knowledge. Just as importantly, the test vehicles provided a wealth of data that could be applied to future developments in high-speed flight, not to mention the work on telemetry and instrumentation that went hand-in-hand with the weapons development. Test vehicles are indeed the forgotten heroes of the aerospace industry.

Why have these test vehicles been described at the start of book on guided weapons and hypersonic aircraft? Simply because none of the missiles and aircraft described in the following chapters would have been possible without them. By pioneering the techniques of high-speed flight and the problems thereof, they provided the foundation upon which the UK aerospace industry, and its engineers and scientists, built its expertise.

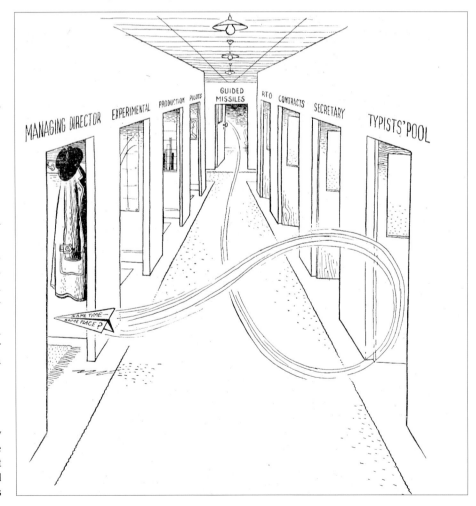

Chapter Three

Air-to-Air Missiles

The GAP committee's list of seven guided weapons described in Chapter One had one glaring omission from the now familiar stable: the air-to-air missile.

While the RPE was looking at Spaniel (see Chapter One) as a ground-launched weapon, modification of the same basic vehicle for airborne use was also being considered. Called Air Spaniel, the weapon was to be fitted to heavy fighters such as the Beaufighter and would home in on the target using a similar photoelectric system to PE Spaniel. Air launch meant that a smaller rocket motor could be installed, allowing a bigger warhead or more electronics. Ultimately Air Spaniel was only slightly more accurate than the original Unrotated Projectile (UP), the guidance system only served to reduce the aiming errors.

Fighter-Controlled (FC) Spaniel superseded Air Spaniel and used command guidance via a radio link. Intended for night fighters, FC Spaniel was to be launched from an aircraft that had been vectored onto the target by Ground Controlled Interception (GCI), standard procedure for a night fighter interception. Once the fighter acquired the target on its Air Interception (AI) radar, in this case a modified AI Mk.VI, the pilot used the 'pilot indication tube' (radar CRT) to adopt a pursuit course and bring the fighter behind the enemy aircraft. Once in position the operator picked up the target, shown as a spot with wings, on his CRT and waited for the range to close to under 2,000yd (1,829m), which would produce an actual flight distance of 3,000yd (2,743m). When in range the Spaniel was launched and showed up on the CRT as a second winged spot. The pilot's role was to maintain the same course for the duration of the intercept.

A pair of Fleet Air Arm Hawker Siddeley P.1154 fighters show the two main roles of the type. Nearest the camera is a fleet defence variant carrying two CF.299 AAMs and the other, a strike fighter, carrying Red Top IR and Blue Dolphin radar guided AAMs. This P.1154 also carries two Tychon air-to surface missiles. Adrian Mann

These 'wings' varied in length in inverse proportion to range, giving a form of perspective view of the interception. The operator guided the Spaniel with a joystick (with the system sending radio commands to the missile) to bring the two spots to coincident range, which was shown on the CRT as both winged spots having the same span. When coincidence was achieved the Spaniel would be detonated either by coincident range fuse or by radio proximity fuse. The Spaniel was uncontrolled during the first two seconds while the rocket motor was burning, so con-

British Secret Projects: Hypersonics, Ramjets & Missiles

trol was only possible during the remaining six seconds of flight, the Spaniel having a speed of 1,150ft/sec (350m/sec) or 784mph (1,262km/h).

Artemis

Spaniels, while an interesting exercise, failed to provide the necessary performance for an effective weapon, particularly in range when launched from the ground. This led to the adoption in late 1943 of a new, air-launched, project called Artemis, under the direction of Flight Lieutenant Benson of the RAE who proposed the name because it was: '...the Greek goddess of chase and death (may the Hun offer continual sacrifice)'.

Benson had been involved in the Spaniel work and opined that by controlling the roll of the rockets, the necessary controls and hardware increased the weight and reduced performance, so complicating the homing process. Also, radio command control of such weapons with short flight times, just six seconds of controlled flight for FC Spaniel, left no time for course adjustment. Lowering this speed to allow more control time turned

Early air-to-air weapons from the basic unguided 3in UP to Little Ben, later known as Long Shot.

Artemis in use. The fighter approaches the target from behind and launches the missile, which flies on a curved path until it acquires the target.

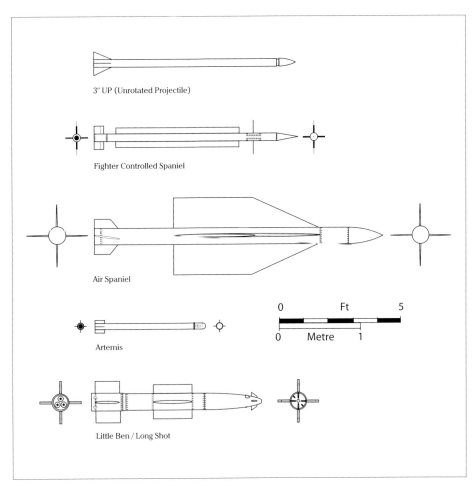

3" UP (Unrotated Projectile)

Fighter Controlled Spaniel

Air Spaniel

Artemis

0   Ft   5

0   Metre   1

Little Ben / Long Shot

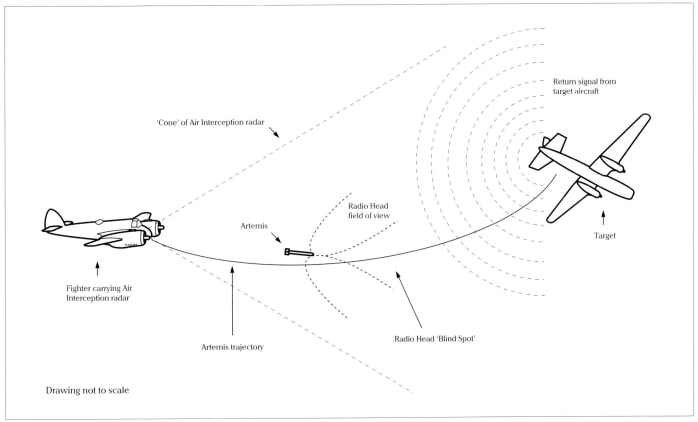

Return signal from target aircraft

'Cone' of Air Interception radar

Radio Head field of view

Artemis

Target

Fighter carrying Air Interception radar

Radio Head 'Blind Spot'

Artemis trajectory

Drawing not to scale

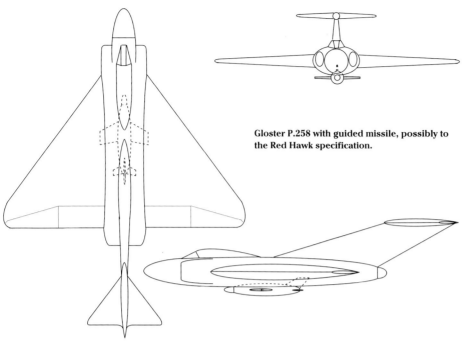

Gloster P.258 with guided missile, possibly to the Red Hawk specification.

ing the warhead and rear-facing radar receivers, with a pair of Stork wrap-around boost motors with canted nozzles that imparted a spin to the weapon. The reason for the wrap-around boosts was the belief that the rocket exhaust from a tandem boost would ionise the air behind the weapon, obscuring the radar signal. The combination accelerated to Mach 2.4 in two seconds and after boost motor burn-out the boosts would separate, leaving the dart to glide on towards its target. At this point the guidance system, using the Swift's E K Coles (EKCO) Radar, Ranging, Mk.2, would take over and direct the weapon. In reality Blue Sky suffered from high drag, high weight and boost separation problems (despite the work carried out with the Separation Test Vehicle). The planned load of four rounds on a Swift was soon cut to two when it was discovered that the missiles placed undue stress on the wings and so restricted manoeuvres.

Against unescorted bombers Blue Sky/Fireflash might have had a slight chance, but what was needed was a fire-and-forget weapon. Two possibilities were considered: Infra-Red homing and active radar homing.

Heat-Seeking Guidance

Infra-red radiation is the heat we feel from a fire or a light bulb. Given the correct equipment this heat can be detected. Originally lead sulphide (PbS) or lead selenide (PbSe) was used as the sensor, this equipment forming the basis of the infra-red homing systems developed for military applications. Early British IR work dated back to 1915 when Prof F A Lindemann, the future Lord Cherwell who later became Churchill's scientific advisor, proposed using IR radiation in warfare.

Between the wars, Lindemann's work formed the basis of a naval communication system as well as an airborne nightfighting device under development by R V Jones, who headed British Scientific Intelligence during World War Two. This work fell by the wayside as airborne radar became the preferred method of nocturnal target acquisition from 1938. Further work was prompted in 1943 by the need to detect German U-boats using their 'schnorkel': a device that, by allowing the U-boats to run their diesel engines without the need to surface, had reduced the effectiveness of anti-surface vessel (ASV) radar. Then, in the postwar scramble for German technology, Air Commodore Roderick

Fireflash on a trials Gloster Meteor. via Tony Buttler

RAF ground crew of No.1 Guided Weapons Development Squadron at RAF Valley fit a pair of Fireflash to a Supermarine Swift. via Tony Buttler

British Secret Projects: Hypersonics, Ramjets & Missiles

Fairey Fireflash trials round on its loading trolley.
Note the boost motor configuration prior to fitting
the canted blast tubes. via Tony Buttler

An early drawing showing a Hawker Hunter F.Mk.1
carrying four Blue Sky. Note rectangular wings on
Blue Sky. Brooklands Museum

Sea Vixen naval fighter carrying a quartet of
Firestreaks. via Tony Buttler

Chisholm found a rather interesting device:
the Kielgerät. This IR detector was the latest
such device to be fitted to Luftwaffe Junkers
Ju 88G night fighters for hunting RAF
bombers. Chisholm, an experienced night
fighter pilot and Senior Staff Officer at 100
Group (the RAF's bomber support and
intruder unit) was well qualified to assess the
potential of the Kielgerät. When used against
Bomber Command aircraft it could detect
engine exhausts up to 4 miles (6.4km) away,
allowing the Luftwaffe's night fighter units to
stalk their quarry undetected until opening
fire.

Jet-powered aircraft generate a great deal
of heat and so, under the right atmospheric
conditions, they present rather good targets
for a weapon guided by an IR seeker. In the
UK research work on IR systems continued
after the end of the war with a variety of new
projects, initially based on the German
research. When it came to using IR as a
weapon guidance system, it had the edge
over radar guidance in that the equipment
was smaller and lighter than that associated
with radar seekers. IR guidance also had the
added bonus of being a fire-and-forget
weapon, unlike Blue Sky's radar system.

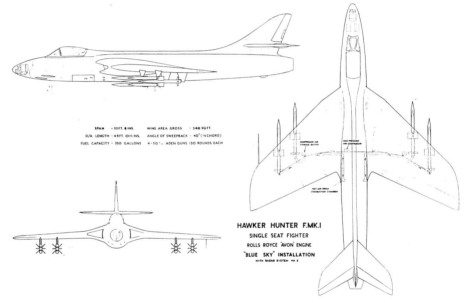

SPAN - 33FT. 8 INS.   WING AREA GROSS - 340 SQ.FT.
O/A LENGTH - 45FT. 10½ INS.   ANGLE OF SWEEPBACK - 40°(¼ CHORD)
FUEL CAPACITY - 330 GALLONS   4 - 30" - ADEN GUNS 150 ROUNDS EACH

HAWKER HUNTER F.MK.I
SINGLE SEAT FIGHTER
ROLLS ROYCE 'AVON' ENGINE
"BLUE SKY" INSTALLATION
WITH RADAR SYSTEM MK 2

OR.1117 and Blue Jay

In November 1951 the Air Staff issued
OR.1117 Issue 1 covering an IR-guided AAM to
be fitted to the RAF's upcoming fighters such
as the Gloster Javelin, while the Admiralty's
AW.274 covered the same weapon for the de
Havilland DH.110, later called Sea Vixen. De
Havilland Propellers (DHP) became the
prime contractor for this and in 1951 began
development of a weapon called Blue Jay.
DHP set up a Guided Weapons Group under
G C I Gardiner as Chief Designer.

Their first project was to be a pursuit
weapon, designed to attack the target from
astern. Seeker development, under the title
Project Metcalf, included work done on
Green Thistle by the TRE, which combined a
lock/follow system with a Kielgerät-based
PbS IR sensor fitted to an Avro Tudor airliner
and, later, an Avro Lincoln bomber. This
seeker borrowed many features from
another pair of MoS/TRE projects called Blue

De Havilland Blue Jay / Firestreak on Lightning.
Note seeker glazing and triangular fuze windows.
via Tony Buttler

Lagoon, a 1950 aircraft detection and tracking system similar to the Kielgerät. Further contribution was made by work on Blue Sapphire and Orange Tartan, which were day/night star trackers for automatic astro-navigation intended for the Blue Moon long-range weapon.

In March 1954 concerns about the PbS sensors' vulnerability to countermeasures prompted the adoption of a Mullard-built Lead Telluride (PbTe) seeker cooled to -180°C (-292°F), with optics by Barr and Stroud. This was also less susceptible to background radiation. Incredible as it may seem, even at this early stage, the methods of reducing the IR signature of jet aircraft were being investigated in conjunction with the NGTE. One particularly successful method was injecting oil into the jet pipes of a Meteor to produce a smoke screen à la Red Arrows!

The result was a seeker for Blue Jay called Violet Banner, which viewed the world through an eight-sided 'sharp pencil' conical window of Arsenic Trisulphide glass produced by ICI. A hemispherical nose (referred to as an 'irdome') was considered but, unlike the conical nose, this was prone to ice accretion. The two rows of triangular windows wrapped around the fuselage were for the IR proximity fuse.

Having commenced flight trials with an unguided test vehicle to prove the configuration, DHP 'borrowed' the Bristol/Ferranti CTV.4 for seeker trials on the range at Larkhill in 1954. This vehicle, boosted on a trio of 5in (12.7cm) LAP (Light Alloy and Plastic) motors, was renamed HTV for Homing Test Vehicle. As described in Chapter Two, trials involved launching the HTV at a bank of gas burners arranged at the far end of the range.

As development proceeded, fully functioning rounds powered by the Magpie I rocket motor were fired. Aircraft trials of Blue Jay test vehicles included ground launches from DH Venom fighters, with the first airborne launch being conducted by a Venom NF.2 at Aberporth in 1955 where it destroyed a Firefly U.8. Later trials were conducted at Woomera using a Canberra and RAAF Avon Sabres.

On entering service with the RAF in 1957, Blue Jay Mk.1 was renamed Firestreak and will be forever associated with early marks of English Electric Lightning and the de Havilland Sea Vixen. For launch the IR seeker was

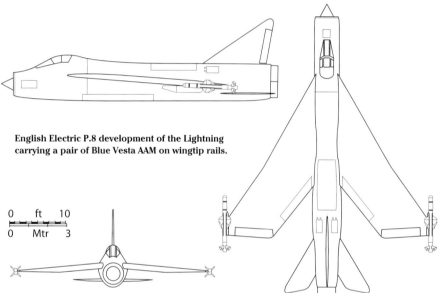

English Electric P.8 development of the Lightning carrying a pair of Blue Vesta AAM on wingtip rails.

```
0       ft    10
0      Mtr    3
```

Artist's impression of the English Electric P.8.
TNA AVIA 53/504

slaved to the aircraft radar: the Ferranti AI.23 AIRPASS (Air Interception Radar And Pilot Attack Sight System) on the Lightning and General Electric Company (GEC) AI.18 on the Sea Vixen. The seeker was cooled by ammonia from an aircraft-mounted refrigeration system. When within range, within 20° either side of the target and with the seeker locked on, an acquisition light indicated that the weapon was ready and the pilot fired the missile. The interceptor would then be free to engage the next target.

Blue Jay Developments

Three basic variants of Blue Jay were developed: Mk.1 with PbS seeker for high-subsonic aircraft such as the Javelin and Sea Vixen. The Mk.2 received a cooled lead telluride (PbTe) seeker and a Magpie II motor. The Mk.3 possessed an increased wingspan of 36in (91.4cm), which ruled out carriage on the Lightning. It also had a lower-power motor, reducing its speed increment to limit kinetic heating, making it suitable for use on supersonic aircraft such as the Avro 720 and Saunders Roe SR.177 at launch speeds up to Mach 1.7 and altitudes up to 65,000ft (18,288m). The Mk.3 also had a minimum launch altitude of 15,000ft (4,572m) rather than the sea level of Mk.1 and 2. Only the Mk.1 entered service in the end, effort moving on to the next member of the Blue Jay family, the Mk.4. The Saunders Roe SR.177 and Avro 720 were being developed to meet Air Staff OR.337 (Specification F.177) and Admiralty requirement NA.47 for

The de Havilland Blue Jay series and successors.

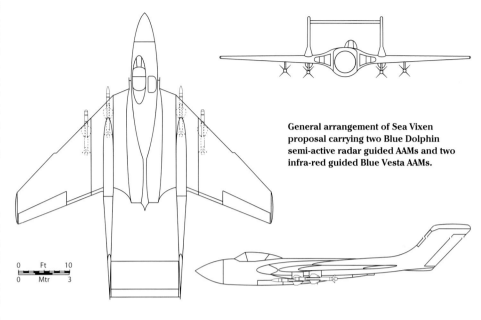

General arrangement of Sea Vixen proposal carrying two Blue Dolphin semi-active radar guided AAMs and two infra-red guided Blue Vesta AAMs.

an interceptor powered by a DH Gyron Junior turbojet and a DH Spectre rocket engine. It was intended to climb rapidly under dual power to intercept high-speed Soviet bombers with Blue Jay Mk.4, and then return to base under turbojet power. The aircraft project was cancelled in 1957 when the Red Duster SAM programme began to show promise but Blue Jay Mk.4 carried on.

Even before entering service, Firestreak's limited capability was under review. A new requirement for a collision-course weapon for the F.155/OR.329 supersonic interceptor was issued as OR.1131 in 1955. DHP began

development of Blue Jay Mk.4, later renamed Blue Vesta, which was intended to arm the new supersonic fighter, the Fairey Delta III being selected. This Fairey design was a large two-seater powered by a pair of DH Gyrons and two DH Spectre rocket engines. Blue Vesta was to be launched from a Mach 2.5 aircraft and, with a new continuous rod warhead, would provide all-aspect capability against Mach 2 targets. Modifications for higher speeds included solid steel wings with 'Mach tips': forward-swept trailing edges to prevent flutter in the Mach cone. Enlarged swept rudders were also fitted with 'Mach

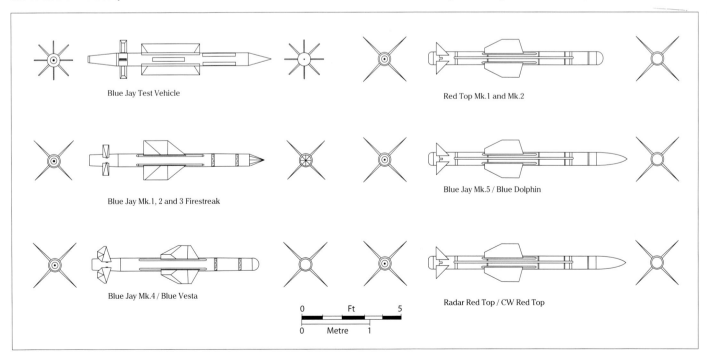

tips'. The Violet Banner seeker (using cooled PbTe) was further improved to increase the angle of view to 60° and provide all-aspect collision-course homing but the RAE Guided Weapons Department considered that Blue Vesta '…would have little value if used with F.155'.

This was due to the range of the weapon and the closing speed of launch aircraft and target. As no contract was forthcoming by late 1956, much of the activity on Blue Vesta ceased but some work was continued at a reduced level and would contribute to the next generation of IR weapons. (Note that the Fairey Delta III was also earmarked to carry the radar-guided Vickers Red Hebe, which will be described shortly.)

Known as Blue Jay Mk.5 from August 1956, a radar version of the Mk.4 to meet OR.1117 (Issue 3) with a Continuous Wave (CW) semi-active radar seeker was also proposed for use by the Fleet Air Arm's Sea Vixens as an alternative to the American Sparrow 3. The Lightning and the Sea Vixen used pulsed radars, with only the Sea Vixen's AI.18 suitable for the addition of a CW illuminator. Fitting the Lightning's AI.23 with the CW illuminator would be prohibitive, so the Mk.5 was to be a naval affair since CW provided better performance at low level. In the end problems with signal polarisation (which reduced range) and interfacing the CW and pulsed radars on the Sea Vixen saw an end to Blue Jay Mk.5, which was to be resurrected as Blue Dolphin in November 1957.

Ultimately the F.155/OR.329 heavy interceptor was cancelled in the 1957 Defence Review, taking with it the need for a Mach 2.5 air-to-air missile like Blue Vesta. However Blue Vesta was not alone.

The Radar Homers – Vickers' Big Hitters

At this point we turn to the development of the radar-guided weapons that followed on from Blue Sky. Beam riding was not suited to the air-to-air role, even against the large piston-engined bombers it was intended to counter such as the Tu-4 *Bull*, the Tupolev copy of the Boeing B-29 Superfortress. As mentioned above, keeping the radar beam on the target for the missile flight time placed the launch aircraft in a vulnerable position.

The original Red Hawk studies had called for a weapon with all-aspect, all-weather performance and by 1951 this was still under consideration. The Air Staff and RAE also decided that the technology had advanced sufficiently to address the full Red Hawk specification and to this end invitations for designs were distributed to industry. These called for an active radar homing weapon with a big warhead, with the MoS colour code Red Dean registered in May 1951.

One problem with Red Hawk and Red Dean, identified at the early stages of development, was range. Rocket power, as discovered by the SAGW developers, left a lot to be desired in the propellant and range stakes, so like their SAGW colleagues, the AAGW designers turned to ramjets. In 1953 the RAE performed a design study for a pair of ramjet-powered AAGWs, one of which was to meet the requirement for Red Dean, by having active radar guidance and a large warhead. These studies used twin podded ramjets with twist-and-steer controls.

One benefit the RAE identified was that, as the ramjets used kerosene, they could be fed with fuel from the aircraft tanks; in addition the ramjet thrust could contribute to that of the aircraft's engines. The RAE based their

interceptor study on an Armstrong Whitworth AW.166 (a competing design to the Bristol 188 research aircraft) with the ramjets helping to raise this type's maximum level speed to Mach 2.25. However, the drag of the ramjets reduced this to Mach 1.9 and the ramjets required a minimum speed for launch in the region of Mach 1.3. Therefore a boost rocket motor would be required anyway, adding 50 lb (22.7kg) to the weight of the missile and so Red Dean would be rocket-powered.

Red Dean

Folland Aircraft Ltd had been involved in the design of the RTV.2 test vehicle and this led to development work on a large air-to-air guided weapon, with designer W E W 'Teddy' Petter tendering a proposal for an active homing missile in mid-1951. Petter, formerly Chief Engineer at English Electric Aviation, had designed the Canberra and Lightning and joined Folland in February 1950 having become disillusioned with the direction that fighter development had taken, that of ever-increasing size and weight.

Problems with the E K Coles guidance system, compounded by the same weight and cost increases that plagued the RTV.2, meant that Red Dean development did not go well. This, combined with Petter's apparent lack of enthusiasm for the weapon, preferring to work on his lightweight fighter concept that became the Folland Midge, saw the end of Folland's involvement with Red Dean. The Air Staff had chosen Folland on the grounds that Petter, with an excellent track record at English Electric Aviation, would be fully involved in the programme. Petter wrote to the Air Staff, explaining the situation and how he did not think that Folland was a suitable company to work on a large GW project. The Air Staff took no time considering the circumstances and cancelled the contract in November 1951 – no doubt the cost over-runs and problems with the RTV.2 were fresh in their minds. Oddly enough a similar accusation of taking his eye off the ball had been levelled at Petter during the development of Westland's Whirlwind in the late 1930s.

With a reputation for being 'dictatorial, difficult, brilliant, eccentric and intense', the uncharted waters of guided weapon development no doubt appealed to the brilliant and intense side of Petter's nature. However the hard reality of this nascent field was probably not to the taste of the dictatorial and difficult aspects of his disposition.

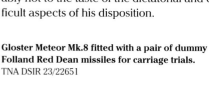

Gloster Meteor Mk.8 fitted with a pair of dummy Folland Red Dean missiles for carriage trials.
TNA DSIR 23/22651

British Secret Projects: Hypersonics, Ramjets & Missiles

Vickers' Red Dean

Vickers of Weybridge essentially took over where Follands left off. Vickers' Red Dean weighed in at around 600 lb (272kg) and was powered by a Propellant and Explosives Research and Manufacturing Establishment (PERME)-designed Buzzard 10in (25cm) rocket motor rated at 6,750 lb (30kN). Vickers' studies commenced in July 1952, with a development contract being placed in March 1953. Red Dean was intended to arm the day and night fighter developments of the Meteor, but would not fit these types due to ground clearance constraints. Consequently the missile was thereafter destined for the Gloster F.4/48, which became the Javelin, and the de Havilland DH.110. The official issue of the requirement, OR.1105 (or AW.281 for the Admiralty), was made in June 1955 and called for an 'Active radar homing all-round attack weapon system operating on collision course tactics.'

By this time, problems with the guidance system had caused delays and increases in size and weight. Operation with the Javelin was out of the question, Red Dean's in-service date on that type having slipped, and the weapon was now being developed to arm the Gloster Thin-Wing Javelin to meet F.153. The weapon's original hemispherical nose, installed to simplify seeker design, was replaced by an ogival radome and the tail fins replaced by swept items with 'Mach tips'.

What ultimately became Vickers' Type 888 development for Red Dean was fitted with a GEC X-band active radar seeker, which could be switched to semi-active if necessary. Development commenced with a 40% scale model, Weapon Test Vehicle WTV.1, used for ground-launched trials, boosted by three Demon motors. The full-sized WTV.2 series was also ground-launched, with wire recorder telemetry systems, prior to embarking on an air-launch programme. Red Dean was now 16ft 1in (4.9m) long and weighed in at 1,330 lb (603kg) with a 100 lb (45.3kg) warhead. It was a monster. With the increase in size Red Dean was powered by a more powerful 10¾in (27.5cm) Falcon rocket motor rated at 14,000 lb (62.3kN). Despite the bigger motor, Red Dean had a surprisingly short range of less than four nautical miles (7.4km). Part of the reason was the size because it had grown from its original 600 lb (272kg). The poor performance of the seeker dictated the

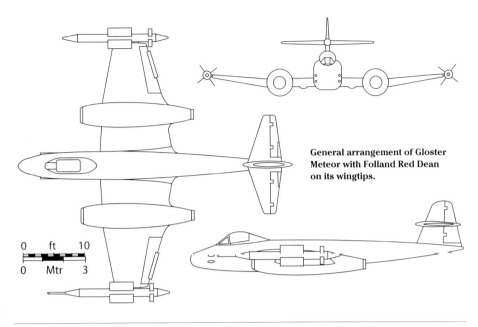

General arrangement of Gloster Meteor with Folland Red Dean on its wingtips.

large warhead, GEC being criticised for their lacklustre implementation of the guidance system; however this criticism did not come from H H Gardner, the head of Vickers GW who '…was very pleased with GEC's work on this project'.

Elliott Brothers also carried out research on an active Q-band seeker for Red Dean under the name Dingo. The GEC seeker was fitted to a WTV.4C and the fuze in the WTV.4E for captive flight trials on an AI.18-equipped Canberra. Trials of WTV.4D/P test vehicles included launch from a Canberra to prove the aerodynamics and autopilot. The second flight test saw an almost-catastrophic failure when the WTV.4 remained attached to the pylon for three seconds after the motor was fired due to a wrongly oriented shear pin. This almost caused the loss of the launch aircraft as it yawed and flick rolled through 400°

Wind tunnel testing of scale model Red Dean and its separation from the trials Canberra. Note the net to prevent objects entering fan.
TNA AVIA 6/19645

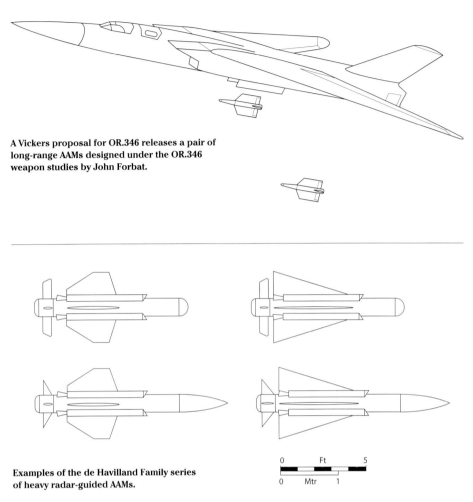

A Vickers proposal for OR.346 releases a pair of
long-range AAMs designed under the OR.346
weapon studies by John Forbat.

Examples of the de Havilland Family series
of heavy radar-guided AAMs.

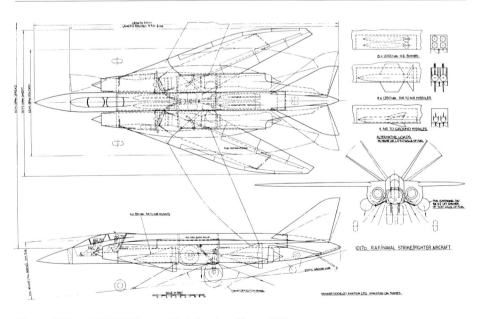

Hawker Siddeley APD.1017 shown with delta-winged heavy AAM,
possibly one of the 'Family'. Brooklands Museum

future when the Sea Harrier appeared almost
twenty years later?

By June 1959 ten Red Top trials rounds,
with the Firestreak-style irdome, had been
fired and fully guided trials using a Canberra
were due to start in early 1960, with development trials using a Lightning starting in September 1961. Service entry of Red Top (the
MoS colour code surviving as the official service name) was in 1964 on the Sea Vixen
Mk.2s of 899 Squadron, Fleet Air Arm and on
Lightning F.3s of No.74 Squadron RAF. Red
Top's influence on the Lightning was not just
on its capability, it changed the shape of the
aircraft. Lightning F.3 and F.6 fitted for Red
Top needed additional fin area to maintain
stability, producing the square top fin characteristic of these types.

A longer-range Red Top Mk.2 was proposed, fitted with a MAFI/RFNA (Mixed Amine
Fuel One/Red Fuming Nitric Acid)-fuelled
rocket engine, possibly the de Havilland Spartan. This may also have formed the basis of a
longer-ranged Radar Red Top that could have
been in service by 1968 if development had
been authorised.

Red Top and Firestreak remain the only
AAM of wholly British design to enter front-
line service, finally retiring with the Lightning
in 1988.

The Groundwork for AST.1193

Apart from TSR.2, in the early 1960s there was
only one other high-performance aircraft in
the pipeline for the UK: a replacement for the
Sea Vixen under AW.406 and its RAF equivalent, OR.356. Types proposed for this were the
Hawker P.1154, a supersonic VTOL fighter for
the Fleet Air Arm that UK industry had hoped
would be a generation ahead of the forthcoming US types. The other aircraft was the
Vickers Type 581, a four-engined variable
geometry type derived from Barnes Wallis'
Swallow studies. An air-to-air missile for
these types was set out under Admiralty
requirement GDA.103, with the RAF requirement covered by AST.1193, calling for a
medium range (<60miles / 96km) radar-
guided weapon.

The previously described Mk.2 Red Top
with liquid fuel rocket and Radar Red Top
seeker may have fulfilled this, but this would
not meet the range requirements. Such a
weapon was also seen as incompatible with
the new generation of aircraft and AI radars.
The Navy were adamant that longer range
was required from radars (90 miles / 144.8km
was quoted) and missiles destined for aircraft
in service by the early 1970s.

To complement these new aircraft Vickers
proposed a totally new semi-active AAM with

British Secret Projects: Hypersonics, Ramjets & Missiles

low aspect ratio wings carrying twist-and-steer controls. Designed by John Forbat, this missile was to be powered by a solid boost/sustain rocket motor giving a range in the order of 35miles (55.5km). The flattened fuselage was 8in (20.3cm) deep and 16in (40.6cm) wide and tapered forward to an 8in (20.3cm) circular section where the continuous rod warhead and radar seeker were fitted. The missile was 12ft (3.65m) in length with a span of 6ft (1.8m).

Since the missile was designed for internal carriage in a weapons bay, the ventral and dorsal fins were folded for stowage. The OR.346 aircraft weapon bay was only 4ft (1.2m) deep, up to four of the 700 lb (317.5kg) weapons were to be stacked side-by-side with the tail fins folded flush with the fuselage and one wing projecting from the bay. For launch the missile was released from the bay, the fins deployed, the rocket engine fired and the seeker picked up the radar signal reflected off the target.

These new Vickers AAMs met a similar fate to Red Dean and Red Hebe, cancelled for want of a launch aircraft.

Hawker Siddeley Dynamics' Family
Vickers was not the only company proposing a heavy AAM. From 1959 de Havilland had been carrying out design studies for a heavy, long-range AAM under the title 'Family'. Each Family comprised a variety of planforms and configurations within a weight range. For example, Family 5 ranged in weight from 500 lb to 1,500 lb (227kg to 680kg), used a pair of solid metal wings and had four tailplanes.

A monoplane configuration allowed bigger wings, which conferred improved performance at high altitude and permitted carriage on aircraft where ground clearance was an issue, such as the Vickers Type 582. Twist-and-steer control was used in this monoplane configuration, which also allowed internal stowage on the Vickers Type 581 and Hawker P.1017 variable geometry naval aircraft to meet OR.346, issued in March 1959, for a strike aircraft with a secondary interceptor role. A proposal to use Airborne Early Warning (AEW) aircraft (a modified Vickers Type 582 was suggested) as the illuminator for a semi-active Family was dismissed as nonsense given the state of the UK's AEW technology, as personified by the Avro Shackleton AEW.3 with its recycled US radars in an obsolete airframe.

The air-launched SAMs. Swapping from one role to another was not as easy as it first looked. Guided weapons were becoming ever more distantly related.

The Family was to be powered by four solid boosts and a packaged MAFI/RFNA rocket similar to that proposed for Red Top Mk.2. This engine would sustain the Family weapon at Mach 4 after solid booster burn-out, hence the solid metal wings and steel structure to withstand the kinetic heating.

Yet again diversification pops its head above the parapet, with the Family being considered as a surface-to-air missile by the use of bigger solid rocket boosters. Quite apt really, as the Family were rather large, up to 15ft (4.57m) long, with fuselage diameters ranging from 12 to 15in (30 to 37.6cm). Their span, however, was restricted to 4ft (1.22m) to fit the OR.346 aircraft weapon bays. The Family, like its Vickers contemporaries, was cancelled in 1962 when its mount was cancelled. By April 1962 joint requirement OR.356/AW.406 was issued to replace the Hawker Hunter and de Havilland Sea Vixen respectively. These would need a new air-to-air weapon.

AST.1193 – The Submissions
With the change of focus to OR.356/AW.406 the weapon designers also had a new joint requirement for an air-to-air weapon: OR.1193/GDA.103. While de Havilland Propellers proposed an air-to-air missile (AAM) as a surface-to-air missile (SAM), Bristol and the 502 Group (led by Armstrong Whitworth) proposed quite the reverse for OR.1193. As ever, industry attempted to get more out of existing systems by giving them additional roles. In February 1961 Bristol Guided Weapons (by now part of BAC – the British Aircraft Corporation) proposed using a version of their SIG-16 SAM (designed for the SIGS programme, Small ships Integrated Guided weapon System, to replace Seaslug which is described in Chapter Four) as an AAM for the Sea Vixen and the aircraft being developed under AW.406/OR.356.

SIG-16 used a solid rocket motor sustainer with a cluster of seven boost motors in a tandem configuration. Capable of launch from aircraft at speeds up to Mach 2.5, this posed a problem for SIG-16. Constructed from light alloy, its airframe could not withstand speeds above Mach 3.5: a speed it was likely to reach after launch from a supersonic aircraft. This was to be solved by the control system selecting the appropriate number of boosts to be fired on launch. The central motor would fire to boost the missile clear of the aircraft before the main boosters were fired, with between one and six firing to produce an appropriate thrust level to boost the missile to a maximum speed of Mach 3.5. A further solution to this was to use a controllable rocket engine that would cut out when Mach 3.5 was reached. Despite all of this SIG-16 had a range of only 14 miles (22.5km), a range that was also a concern to the SIGS committee dealing with the naval SAM. There was one more problem associated with a modified SAM: the rocket exhaust gases contained highly acidic material, such as hydrochloric acid; which the aircraft engineers certainly didn't want on their airframes and, particularly, in their engines.

When the SIGS programme evolved into the 502 Group's CF.299 and adopted a Bristol Siddeley Odin ramjet rather than a rocket as a sustainer, this was also submitted as an

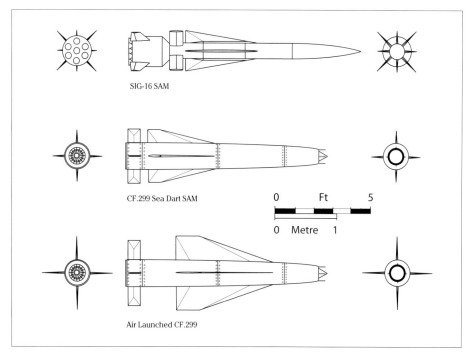

SIG-16 SAM

CF.299 Sea Dart SAM

0   Ft   5

0   Metre   1

Air Launched CF.299

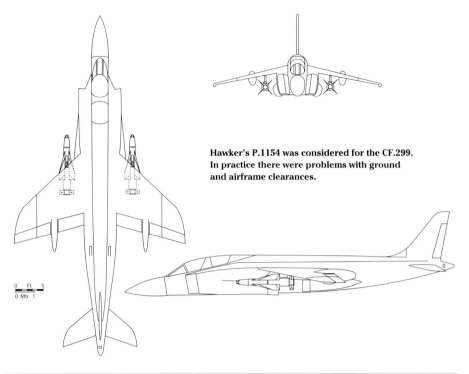

Hawker's P.1154 was considered for the CF.299. In practice there were problems with ground and airframe clearances.

lag' with the ramjet intake requiring undisturbed air flow.

However the clincher was that CF.299's powered range would far exceed the guidance range available due to low power of the P.1154 radar and lack of sensitivity in the CF.299 interferometer homing system. CF.299 used a polyrod interferometer antenna with four antennae arranged around the intake lip, leaving the intake centre-body to maintain airflow to the ramjet, which limited the seeker size. An interferometer homing system compares the signal strength received by each of the four antennae of the polyrod seeker and manoeuvres the missile until the signal strength on each is equal, indicating that the target is dead ahead. In summary, its legs were too long and it was too short-sighted, so would not meet the requirement. In the end, the Director of the RRE, Robin Aspinal, said that: '...the CF.299 SAGW was one of the least favoured starters'.

AAM for AST.1193 with the caveat that it required the correct AI radar system. The reason for the adoption of ramjet power was range, with the Navy rubbing their hands at the prospect of a 45 mile (72km)-capable AAM for the Sea Vixen and Combat Air Patrol variant of the Buccaneer. However, the prospects of long-range interceptions and active homing missiles were dashed by the realisation that a) the aircraft radars were not capable of such feats and b) the missile could not carry a big enough seeker dish.

The Admiralty considered CF.299, but concluded that the problems encountered were not worth resolving since the P.1154 would carry Red Top anyway. Mounting CF.299 on P.1154 would have posed problems with ground clearance since it had larger wings than the SAM, spanning 3ft 10in (1.17m). Its attachment to P.1154 would be restricted to the inboard pylons, limiting warload to two rounds. Admirals were also critical of its weight, 750lb (340.1kg) in AAM guise, and restricted manoeuvrability due to 'incidence

Modifying an existing SAM for air-launch looked simple on paper, especially from the SAM designer's point of view, but as SIG-16 and CF.299 showed, there was more to it than bolting the weapon onto an aircraft. One problem was carriage on the P.1154 (as noted above only the inboard pylons were usable) and while Bristol claimed the Vickers Type 581 could carry two SIG-16 rounds internally, Vickers disagreed, saying only one could be accommodated. Internal carriage was the preferred option for CF.299 due to drag from the ramjet intake, which would otherwise require an aerodynamic fairing and attendant jettison system.

By March 1963, air-launched CF.299 was scrapped, but plans were afoot to fit a Canberra, serial WH660, with the CF.299's GEC A5 seeker and recording equipment to perform airborne trials against air and surface targets. However by late 1964 this programme had been restricted to work related only to SAM development.

Becalmed in the Doldrums
In late 1962 the UK had no radar-guided AAMs in the pipeline and eyes were being cast across the Atlantic. As of April 1963 Sparrow III was in the frame for AST.1193/GDA.103, albeit with some British modifications for use on RAF aircraft.

In the summer of 1963, Hawker Siddeley Dynamics (HSD, as DHP was now known) was back on the scene with a semi-active, pulsed radar guided Red Top. Meanwhile in Wythenshawe, Ferranti was working on a new pulsed Doppler seeker head that could be fitted to Red Top. While this was wel-

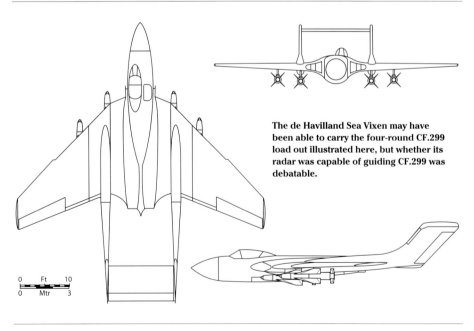

The de Havilland Sea Vixen may have been able to carry the four-round CF.299 load out illustrated here, but whether its radar was capable of guiding CF.299 was debatable.

British Secret Projects: Hypersonics, Ramjets & Missiles

comed by the Ministry, they were uncertain as to the future of P.1154, due to the realisation that a) economies must be made in the defence budget and b) it was technologically 'difficult'. Such difficulties included resolving differences between the Royal Navy and RAF on radar types, development of the Bristol Siddeley BS.100 engine and a basic lack of commonality on what was to be a common airframe. The Royal Navy Fleet Air Arm (FAA) had opted for the McDonnell Douglas F-4K Phantom II in February 1964, with the RAF version of P.1154 being cancelled in February 1965 in favour of the F-4M Phantom.

By early 1965 the received wisdom in the RAF was that Radar Red Top would not match the capabilities of future aircraft and radars, in fact British AAM development was in the doldrums. The only AAMs that had entered service were the Firestreak/Red Top line and, as for radar-guided weapons, it appeared that S/Ldr Poole had been prescient. AST.1193 had lapsed and US missiles had prevailed, with the purchase of Sparrow and Sidewinder for the newly acquired F-4 Phantoms.

A New Hope
A fresh start was required and the powers-that-be actually appear to have acknowledged this. This saw the issuing in May 1965 of Specifications WE.565, covering structures, aerodynamics and performance, and WE.566, covering guidance and control. Further to this, by August 1966 the RAE had produced a discussion paper acknowledging the faults of the past and assessing the current status of the business. The RAE described how AAM, AI radar and aircraft were interdependent and subsequently, without a long-term policy, it was impossible to draft targets and requirements. This in turn led to a lack of direction in the research field. Possible collaboration with the French was dismissed, as they would demand authority over design and specification to meet their requirements. The RAE expressed a fear that the UK industry could lose all expertise in this field without continuing research. Unsurprisingly this paper was stamped 'SECRET, U.K. EYES ONLY'!

The RAE and the Ministry saw a need for renewed research into guided weapons and their associated systems. They feared radar expertise, particularly AI, would be lost to the Americans, with AEW radar seen as particularly vulnerable.

So, what was the outcome of all this? Inevitably, Sparrow and Sidewinder had been purchased as a job lot for the RAF and FAA Phantoms and the Lightning soldiered on with Red Top, and even Firestreak, until retirement in 1988. Sparrow and Sidewinder were the obvious solution for the Phantom and had been constantly improved since their inception in the late 1940s. The Sparrow had been S/Ldr Poole's benchmark in his no-holds-barred analysis of the UK's guided weapons back in 1956 and, to come up to scratch, Sparrow was procured.

The RAE was of the opinion that there would be no need to develop a new AAM for use in the 1970s. However, when the Phantom/Sparrow/Sidewinder combination was due for replacement in the late 1970s, British industry should have new weapons available. The main stumbling block was the lack of a long-term coherent policy for such weapons, and without addressing this there would be little or no point in continuing major research and development programmes. Low level work would continue until there was a solid requirement laid out for Sparrow/Sidewinder replacements in the late 1960s.

By the time the RAF and RN had received their Phantoms (F-4M and F-4K respectively, which the RAF would initially use for ground attack) the Sparrow was looking a touch jaded. Having progressed through the beam-riding Sparrow I and the active Sparrow II, the semi-active Sparrow III was the version that became most widely used. However in the Vietnam theatre, the Sparrow, as the saying goes, wasn't having a very good war. Unreliable under harsh conditions, limited launch envelope, slow to warm up (the need to warm up electronics has disappeared in the digital era) and indifferent at short range, Sparrow wasn't delivering. To be fair, the rules of engagement imposed by US policy, for example the visual identification of targets before engagement, failed to utilise Sparrow's capability. S/Ldr Poole's pertinent observations on American systems being more susceptible to electronic countermeasures than British systems were also apparently correct. By the mid-1960s, as Sparrow was entering RAF service, this susceptibility became an issue and provided the impetus that British industry needed.

Sky Flash – A Sparrow Re-hatched
Air Staff Target 1219, calling for a radar-guided medium range AAM, was issued in January 1972. This was to provide all-weather, all-aspect interception against low and medium altitude targets with snap up/snap down capability and was to be used by the forthcoming MRCA Air Defence Variant and its AI radar to meet AST.395. MRCA, the Multi-Role Combat Aircraft, was the development designation for the UK/German/Italian variable geometry aircraft that became Panavia Tornado. The Air Defence Variant (ADV) was the British-developed fighter version, which entered service with 29 Squadron in early 1984 as the Tornado F.2 and became the F.3 after a systems and engine upgrade in 1985. The AI.24 radar for the ADV was developed by Marconi and entered service as the Fox-hunter.

A US Navy McDonnel Douglas F-4J launches a Hawker Siddeley Dynamics XJ.521 Sky Flash during trials in the United States. The XJ.521 trials were considered to be the most successful in guided weapon history. HSD via T Panopalis

Close-up view of the underside of a McDonnell Douglas F-4 Phantom showing the semi-recessed mountings for Hawker Siddeley's XJ.521 Sky Flash.

Sweden's Sky Flash were carried by the SAAB JA 37 Viggen, which could carry two on wing pylons. Tony Buttler

If available, AST.1219 was also to be used by the RAF's F-4M Phantom force when they transferred to the air defence role. Although Warsaw Pact strike, reconnaissance and ground support aircraft were the primary targets for AST.1219, some capability against high-altitude types such as the MiG-25 *Foxbat* reconnaissance aircraft was preferred. An in-service date of the late 1970s was stated and, interestingly, the Air Staff specified that the weapon must use the existing semi-sub-merged mountings on the F-4 Phantom. The Air Staff obviously had something in mind.

The solution to this was to apply some of the expertise that S/Ldr Poole had praised on the Sparrow. As related earlier, back in 1963 the Sparrow III had been considered, with modifications, for AST.1193 on the P.1154. However AST.1219 was to be semi-active and used the newly developed inverse monopulse radar seeker. Extensive experi-ence of such systems included its use in the Lightning F.1's AIRPASS radar. Monopulse radar uses four overlapping beams, with each beam coded independently. With the target dead ahead, the set outputs a zero voltage due to the four beams cancelling each other out.

Oddly enough S/Ldr Poole's 1956 forecast that GEC wouldn't get a second chance was the one that turned out to be incorrect. The company did get a second chance and made a pretty good fist of it. GEC and the RAE had been looking at such radars and seekers since the early 1960s and by 1969 had been given the go-ahead to develop an inverse monopulse seeker for the Sparrow AIM-7E-2. The so-called Dogfight Sparrow, this had been developed to meet the needs of the Vietnam theatre. However, despite its shorter range, the E-2 was also deemed acceptable for the European theatre. After a feasibility

study based around the E-2, the Air Staff issued the requirement, ASR.1219, in January 1973 and this project was given the Ministry of Aviation reference number XJ.521.

The prime contractor for XJ.521 was Hawker Siddeley Dynamics, with Marconi Space and Defence Systems (as the GEC guided weapons division had become) developing the I-band seeker. By December 1977 the new missile had sailed through its tri-als, in one of the most successful develop-ment programmes in UK guided weapons history. New electronics also allowed quick-reaction launch at higher 'G', using an Angli-cised version of the AIM-7 Sparrow's Aerojet Mk.52 boost-coast motor made by Bristol Aerojet called Hoopoe. A new active radar fuze developed by Thorn EMI gave the missile a very high one shot/one kill capability.

The weapon produced from ASR.1219 and XJ.521, originally to be called 'UK Sparrow', soon acquired the name Sky Flash. Carried by the RAF's Phantoms from 1978, Sky Flash's first 'kill' was by a 29 Sqn Phantom FGR.2 against a Gloster Meteor drone in August 1979. Sky Flash proved superior to the US equivalent, the AIM-7M, in both low-altitude performance and in its resistance to elec-tronic countermeasures (ECM). It also proved particularly potent in tackling targets approaching at high speed, a scenario the Air Staff Requirement had identified as critical for the defence of the UK.

Although slightly longer, Sky Flash was practically identical to the Sparrow, only the rectangular panels for the EMI fuze on the for-ward fuselage identify them as Sky Flash. Black spots were added to the wings to ease identification until Sparrows were retired with the last of the Phantoms in October 1992.

When the Tornado F.2 and later F.3 entered service, its primary armament was a

quartet of Sky Flash semi-recessed under the fuselage. In operation the Sky Flash was pushed clear of the aircraft for launch by a Frazer-Nash ejection system and homed in on the target under semi-active guidance pro-vided by a J-band illuminator that was part of the AI.24 Foxhunter, the I-band radar devel-oped for AST.395. In Swedish service Sky Flash was known as the Rb.71 and the Swedish Air Force's SAAB JA 37 Viggen inter-ceptors each carried two.

The ultimate service version of Sky Flash was fitted with a boost-sustain Hoopoe motor using base bleed technology. This improved the snap-up performance of Sky Flash against targets at higher altitude, especially important when used with the Tornado. The boost-sus-tain motor from the AIM-7F had been sug-gested but this motor, although having the potential to double the missile's range, was 8in (20.3cm) longer than the Hoopoe, which meant that the four-missile load-out require-ment could not be met due to the Tornado's forward semi-recessed mountings being unusable.

BAe Dynamics also worked to develop Sky Flash specifically for the Tornado ADV, under a programme called Improved Sky Flash. BAe Dynamics conducted a Kinematic Upgrade that reduced drag through aerodynamic mod-ifications and upgraded the control system.

Sky Flash's main competition came from the US AIM-120 Advanced Medium Range AAM or AMRAAM, an active radar weapon with mid-course update that entered service with US forces in September 1991. AMRAAM was ordered for the Royal Navy's BAe Sea Harrier F/A.2 and, with a foot in the door, AMRAAM with its long range and active seeker could have replaced Sky Flash on the RAF Tornados. To address this, BAe Dynam-ics worked on Sky Flash Mk.2 to meet

ASR.1233. Also known as Active Sky Flash (or Rb71A in Sweden), this had a Thomson CSF-designed active seeker and inertial mid-course update. Active Sky Flash, with modifications including thinner wings and a tapered rear fuselage, was intended to arm the Tornado F.3 and SAAB JAS 39 Gripen.

In lieu of Active Sky Flash, the RAF did purchase AMRAAM and this was earmarked for the Tornado as part of the Capability Sustainment Programme (CSP) that also adapted the type to carry the Advanced Short Range AAM (ASRAAM). The AI.24 Foxhunter radar was modified with a datalink to provide mid-course updates for the longer range US missile, with the first upgraded Tornado F.3 entering service in late 1998. Despite the CSP, the F.3 only had limited capability with AMRAAM, and so continued with Sky Flash until a further upgrade in 2002. The latter also integrated the MBDA Air Launched Anti-Radiation Missile (ALARM, described in Chapter Seven) with the Foxhunter radar to produce the Tornado EF.3, in service from 2003 with XI(F) Sqn.

The problem with Active Sky Flash (also known as Sky Flash Mk.2) was no doubt weight, tipping the scales at 460 lb (208kg) against AMRAAM's 345 lb (156.5kg). As ever, each pound or kilo shaved off All-Up-Weight (AUW) improves performance, so perhaps the choice of AMRAAM really was down to saving 460 lb (208kg) in AUW for a four-missile warload. 16th December 1999 saw the first launch of an AMRAAM by a Tornado on a UK test range.

Other types that could have used Sky Flash were the Hawker Siddeley Brough-designed HS.1207, and the Kingston-designed Harrier development, HS.1205. These projects, the first a conventional design, the second a VSTOL fighter, were part of the research carried out in the 1970s for new fighters that eventually led to Eurofighter Typhoon. Interestingly the McDonnell Douglas F-15 was also proposed as an alternative to the Tornado ADV and would have been armed with Sky Flash.

Further Developments and the Road to Meteor

Developments on the Sky Flash theme included Active Sky Flash Tail Control, later known as S225X. This designation carried on a tradition of naming guided weapons after the development location, S225X being the project's postbox at Stevenage. The MoD had issued Requests for Proposals to SR(A).1239 covering Future Medium Range AAM (FMRAAM) in 1995. Active Sky Flash had been proposed to the RAF as a stopgap pending full

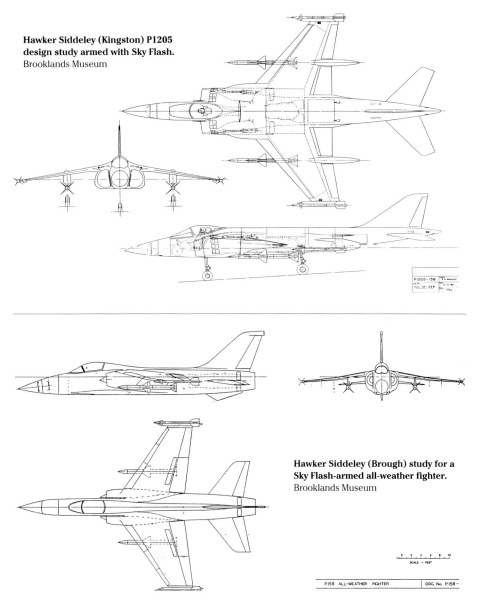

Hawker Siddeley (Kingston) P1205 design study armed with Sky Flash.
Brooklands Museum

Hawker Siddeley (Brough) study for a Sky Flash-armed all-weather fighter.
Brooklands Museum

development of S225X, but AMRAAM was purchased instead. S225X used a boost-coast-boost rocket motor in a slightly smaller diameter airframe, it dispensed with the wings and used tail fins for directional control. S225X with a dual-mode radar and IR seeker formed the basis of the BAe Dynamics bid for Staff Requirement SR(A).1239. The original requirement stated that FMRAAM should have a range in the order of 80nm (150km), so the next step was to increase the range with the now traditional use of a ramjet.

A ramjet-powered Sky Flash variant had been proposed to the Swedes as the RB73, so work carried out on this was transferred to the S225X, becoming S225XR. Meantime wings had re-appeared on S225XR and the result was the MBDA Meteor, selected for

SR(A).1239 in May 2000. However, by 2003 the wings had gone again and the original S225XR wingless configuration was reinstated and this will enter service as the Meteor. Power is provided by a variable flow ducted rocket ramjet, fed by a pair of prominent intakes and ducts on the flanks.

Intended for use on the Eurofighter Typhoon with its CAPTOR radar, Meteor confers beyond-visual-range interception capability; 62 miles (100km) on the Typhoon. The SAAB JAS 39 Gripen, Dassault Rafale and the Joint Strike Fighter are other types destined to use Meteor, and the Gripen was used for test firings of the Air-Launched Demonstrator (ALD) during 2006.

Finally, Sky Flash was proposed as a naval SAM, with the 'Sky' prefix changed to 'Sea' for a box-launched SAM for small warships. No

Hughes' unsuccessful bid for the Future Medium Range Air-to-Air Missile to SR(A).1239 based on the AIM.120 AMRAAM.

MBDA Meteor AAM carried by a SAAB JAS 39 Gripen. Interestingly another of the unsuccessful candidates for SR(A).1239, the MRAAM, is on the adjacent pylon. via Tony Buttler

customers were forthcoming for this. In the late 1990s Meteor was proposed as the basis of an air-launched anti-tactical ballistic missile system, with Typhoon as the launch platform.

A Memorandum of Understanding

What probably did for the active Sky Flash Mk.2 was a document drawn up in 1980 between the UK, USA, Germany and France. This Family of Weapons Memorandum of Understanding outlined the need for a medium-range weapon, which would be the American AIM-120 AMRAAM, and a new close-range weapon to be developed in Europe as the AIM-132 ASRAAM. Suffice to say the basic understanding was that the US missile would become the standard medium-range weapon (no doubt becoming the NATO standard in time) and the European missile

the short-range weapon for the countries that had signed up. In due course the former case came to fruition but the latter did not, and it was to be a long drawn out process.

Taildog and ASRAAM

In addition to the Sparrow's woes in the Vietnam theatre, US forces, being forced into dogfights, were finding that they lacked an effective short-range weapon. The AIM-9 Sidewinder did not perform particularly well at very close range and the F-4 Phantom pilots could only watch as their Sidewinders were out-manoeuvred by the enemy's agile MiGs. Gun fighters like the Vought F-8 Crusader and even the Republic F-105 Thunderchief fighter-bomber were using their internal cannon to score kills against the MiG-17 *Fresco* and MiG-21 *Fishbed* types of the North Vietnamese AF. The Phantom, designed as a mis-

sile platform from the start, carried no cannon until the addition of the SUU-16 (ram-air driven) or SUU-23 (electrically driven) Vulcan Gatling gun pod in May 1967.

Unlike an internal gun, the Vulcan pod tended to be inaccurate due to recoil forces affecting the pod's alignment. With nothing else available, the RAF also fitted their Phantom FGR.2s with the SUU-16/SUU-23. The ministry recognised the need for a small, agile dogfight weapon that could be carried by aircraft that lacked the target acquisition systems of the Phantom and Lightning. To this end the Air Staff drew up AST.1218 in 1970.

HSD responded with a small 110 lb (50kg), 6ft (2m) long, 6.3in (16cm)-diameter weapon called Taildog. Taildog was to be highly manoeuvrable and capable of engaging targets between 273yd (250m) and 2,187yd (2,000m), a true dogfight weapon. In fact Tail-

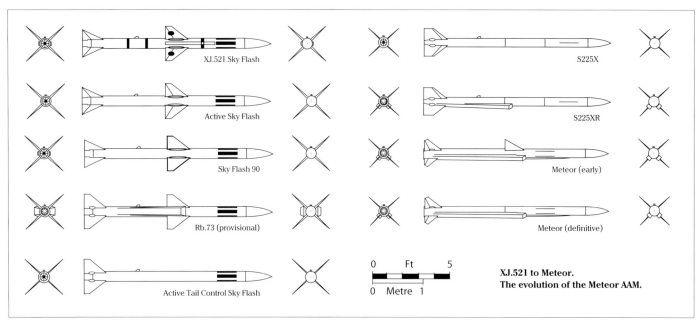

XJ.521 Sky Flash

Active Sky Flash

Sky Flash 90

Rb.73 (provisional)

Active Tail Control Sky Flash

S225X

S225XR

Meteor (early)

Meteor (definitive)

XJ.521 to Meteor.
The evolution of the Meteor AAM.

The trials crew of a de Havilland Sea Vixen pose with a pair of Hawker Siddeley Dynamics Taildog AAMs. Taildog led to the latter SRAAM and ultimately to ASRAAM. HSD via T Panopalis

dog was described as something between a bullet and a missile. The weapon's manoeuvrability was to be achieved by Thrust Vector Control (TVC) and a control system using Acceleration Vector Navigation (AVN). Summerfield Research Station developed a new motor with TVC, the E577, for Taildog trials that used four semaphore spoilers (six had also been tested), which were essentially deflector vanes in the solid motor exhaust. These flicked in and out of the efflux to direct the thrust up to 10° off axis, thereby turning the missile. However the semaphore spoilers proved troublesome and were replaced by a moving dome deflector. Yet again, the mix'n'-match so characteristic of UK weapons development saw this motor used in the tandem boost for the CR.137 Sub-Martel anti-ship weapon described in Chapter Seven.

AVN was more suited to a TVC weapon at short ranges where rapid changes in direction were required. The only aerodynamic surfaces were six folding fins on the rear fuselage allowing Taildog to be launched from tubes, protecting the weapons from the environment prior to launch. In further ground tests Taildog was fired from tubes attached to a rotating ground rig to simulate launches at high 'G'.

Taildog proved that such a weapon could be produced and on this basis the MoD endorsed Taildog to meet a new Staff Requirement for a Sidewinder replacement, ASR.1222, with the project adopting the Ministry of Aviation reference number QC.434 in January 1972.

Taildog had shown the bright promise that typified the rare jewels in British guided weapon development programmes. QC.434 built on the Taildog experience and, as ever, a series of test vehicles were built. The Design And Demonstration Model (DADM) series were more or less prototypes of the final weapon. The project also acquired a name, SRAAM for Short Range Air-to-Air Missile – unimaginative perhaps, but SRAAM did exactly what it said on the tin. SRAAM came in two versions, the -75 and -100, both slightly larger than Taildog: 8ft 11in (2.7m) long and 6½in (16.5cm) in diameter. Development progressed, with air firings of the DADM with fixed fins being carried out from a Hawker Hunter in 1974.

During these firings more problems arose with the TVC, which caused the round to fly off course. This prompted a change to the

Hawker Siddeley HS1184-7 'Skewdog' armed with a pair of QC.434 AAMs in an angled tail installation reminiscent of the German 'Schrage Musik' of World War Two. Brooklands Museum

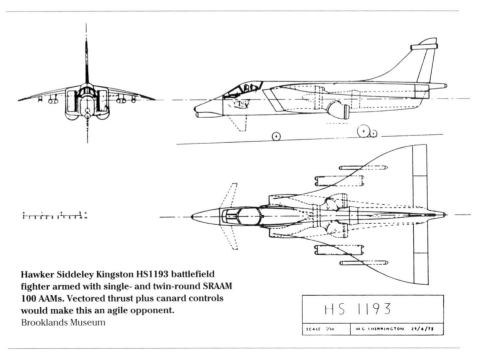

Hawker Siddeley Kingston HS1193 battlefield fighter armed with single- and twin-round SRAAM 100 AAMs. Vectored thrust plus canard controls would make this an agile opponent.
Brooklands Museum

Hawker Hunter XG210 launches an AATV from a twin round pod during trials for SRAAM / QC.434. HSD via T Panopalis

MBDA's ASRAAM on the wing pylon of a Eurofighter Typhoon. via Tony Buttler

TVC system with the adoption of a swivelling nozzle on the solid rocket motors and roll control via motor exhaust bleeds.

SRAAM, like Taildog, was to be pod mounted on almost any aircraft with a free pylon, with the fire control system on the pod support. The pods had doors fore and aft that opened for launch with the missile acquiring the target almost immediately and, courtesy of the TVC and AVN, it could make violent turns onto an intercept path. One famous case involved the missile barely missing the Hunter launch aircraft; such was the rate of the turn.

With such agility it was surprising that Hawker Siddeley coupled SRAAM with the highly agile HS.1193. This handsome study, drawn up by M G Cherrington, combined a shoulder-mounted ogival delta wing with a Pegasus-derived engine using reheat in the single jet pipe and plenum chamber burning in the front nozzles. Not content with this, the HS.1193 carried a pair of canards and a vertical stabiliser under the nose. This configuration would allow the HS.1193 to carry on in forward flight while pointing the aircraft nose at an angle to the flight path! Carrying six SRAAMs, this would make for a highly manoeuvrable dogfighter.

Once again, SRAAM spawned a family of weapons studies. The main thrust was for a maritime SAM called SHIELD (SHip Installed Equipment for Low-air Defence), which is described in Chapter Four and SAMM-10, a helicopter-launched anti-ship weapon described in Chapter Seven. Other studies included Skewdog, which mounted a pair of SRAAM at 45° in the rear fuselage of a Harrier variant called HS.1184-17. Another Harrier study, HS.1184-16, featured a rear gunner in the tail armed with SRAAMs! Curiously, rearward firing of AAMs had been discussed in 1969 between the Air Staff and the Ministry of Technology with the HS.1184-16 being one possible solution.

SRAAM continued from strength to strength until 1974, when the entire project was relegated to technology demonstrator status, with low-level activity keeping the project ticking over. The first guided launches occurred in 1977, but unfortunately that was the year that the MoD decided to adopt the all-aspect Sidewinder, the AIM-9L. However, in 1980, with the signing of the multinational Memorandum of Understanding, SRAAM (as a BAe Dynamics programme) was well placed to meet the short range AAM requirement.

BAe Dynamics joined forces with the German company BGT (Bodenseewerk Geräte Technick) to develop this short-range weapon. Hughes also played a part in looking after the American interests in what they called the AIM-132. On the British side the MoD drew up AST.1234 to cover development of this new missile. Other bids for AST.1234 included the Israeli Python 4 and Matra Marconi's MICASRAAM, probably the only serious competitor. Both of these used aerodynamic controls, and in doing so had higher drag and therefore shorter ranges than SRAAM (which also extended its range by having the body providing lift).

First to go on the AIM-132 project was TVC control, four aerodynamic controls being adopted instead because there was no need for SRAAM's tube launcher. The MoU had stated that the new missile must be compatible with existing Sidewinder launchers, thus releasing the designers from size constraints. Having decided on the configuration, and with a Staff Target in place, the companies got on with development of the weapon now being called ASRAAM.

Then the Berlin Wall came down. In late 1989 the Soviet Union began its withdrawal from Eastern Europe and, within a new united Germany, the air force of the former East Germany was absorbed by the Luftwaffe. With this merger came some of the Soviet Union's best equipment, namely the MiG-29 *Fulcrum* and its weapons suite, which included a missile called AA-13 Archer, an IR dogfight weapon. The Germans and the rest of NATO were impressed by its performance, so much so that the German Defence Ministry pulled out of ASRAAM in favour of developing a weapon based on the Russian missile, to be called IRIS-T.

Air-to-Air Missiles

Missile	Length ft (m)	Diameter in (cm)	Span ft (m)	Guidance	Propulsion
Fireflash	9.3 (2.8)	6 (15)	28.1 (0.7)	Beam riding	2 x boost motors
Firestreak	10.4 (3.2)	8.75 (22.2)	29.4 (0.75)	IR	Rocket Motor
Red Top	11.5 (3.5)	8.75 (22.2)	35.75 (0.91)	IR	Rocket Motor
Red Dean	16.1 (4.9)	12.5 (31)	4.5 (1.14)	Active radar	Rocket motor
Red Hebe	17.5 (5.3)	15 (38)	6 (1.8)	Active radar	Rocket motor
Sky Flash	12 (3.66)	7.9 (20)	3.3 (1)	Semi-active radar	Rocket motor
SRAAM	8.9 (2.7)	6.5 (16.5)	Flip out fins	IR	Rocket motor
ASRAAM	8.9 (2.7)	6.5 (16.5)	1.6 (0.45)	Imaging IR	Rocket motor
Meteor	11.9 (3.6)	6.7 (17)	22.3 (0.56)	Active radar	Ramjet

By 2002 the guided weapon interests of the UK, France and Italy had been amalgamated into a consortium called MBDA (Matra, BAe Dynamics and Alenia) to look after guided weapons development in response to the mergers that had occurred in the USA. One of MBDA's main products is ASRAAM, whose development has been protracted, with the 1993 in-service date slipping to 2003.

In service ASRAAM uses a Remus motor and is fitted with an Imaging Infra-Red seeker that sees the world not as the bright blobs of old but as an image of its quarry, allowing targeting of specific parts of the aircraft for maximum damage. It can be carried by the new generation of aircraft such as the Typhoon and Gripen amongst others.

Three variants of ASRAAM have been proposed. The first was SRARM, Short Range Anti-Radiation Missile, which was for use as a self-protection weapon for strike aircraft to meet a seven-nation and NATO requirement, including the UK's ASR.1240. This requirement lapsed and the RAF received the BAe ALARM to meet ASR.1228. Next came the bizarre VSRAAM (Very Short Range AAM) that lacked a warhead and depended on kinetic energy for its lethality. The third proposal, Typhoon (not to be confused with the aircraft of the same name), was an anti-armour weapon based on the ASRAAM airframe with a millimetric wave radar seeker to meet SR(A).1238, eventually met by Brimstone. The air-to-surface weapons are described in Chapter 7.

The ultimate version of ASRAAM is the Planned Production Improvement Programme P3I-ASRAAM which, to provide better agility 'off the rail' uses TVC. Taildog had chased its own tail. And caught it.

Helicopter vs Helicopter

One other AAM that has been developed in the UK is ATASK. As ever this showed how a weapon designed for a specific role could be switched, with modification, to another. The modified Starstreak SAM, for use by attack helicopters such as the Westland AH-64 Apache, was called Helstreak initially but later renamed ATASK (Air-To-Air StarstreaK). The US Army held trials in 1991, with the rationale for the laser-guided Starstreak being that laser guidance allowed its use against targets with low IR signature, such as helicopters

with suppressed exhausts. Later trials against airborne targets in 1998 proved the concept. The weapon is housed in a two-round pod and is integrated with the Apache's Target Acquisition and Designation System. Starstreak is described in Chapter Four.

Conclusion

The weapons evolved from Blue Jay are still the only wholly UK designed and built AAMs to enter front-line service. Thankfully, being designed to counter Soviet bombers, they were never used in anger. The large AAMs at Vickers appear at first sight to border on the ludicrous, but this was an extremely secretive endeavour in a technical *terra incognita* requiring massive investment in new equipment and acquisition of new techniques. Teddy Petter appeared to acknowledge this from an early date and relinquished Folland's interest in guided weapons. Threats changed without warning and with changing threats came changing policy. Through innovation and ingenuity, British engineers and scientists overcame the official stumbling blocks of budget constraints and policy muddle to meet the requirements. Unfortunately these requirements were never clear enough to give them a decent crack of the whip.

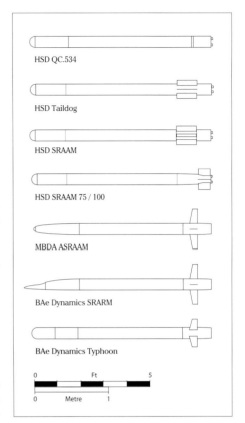

HSD QC.534

HSD Taildog

HSD SRAAM

HSD SRAAM 75 / 100

MBDA ASRAAM

BAe Dynamics SRARM

BAe Dynamics Typhoon

0   Ft   5

0   Metre   1

The evolution of ASRAAM from Taildog to SRARM, with provisional drawing of the anti-tank Typhoon.

" *Seen anything of a guided missile . . . ?*"

De Havilland's in-house magazine tended to make light of the guided weapons development programmes. The expressions of the characters, particularly the driver, suggest that a 'misguided weapon' was a regular occurrence. BAE Systems

Chapter Four

Missiles Against
the Aircraft Threat

At the end of the war a new Guided Anti-air-craft Projectile (GAP), Great Triumph, became the focus of the RAE's work after Ben had been cancelled. The first post-war study evolved out of Great Triumph and was called Howler. This could be viewed as the starting point of post-war anti-aircraft missile development in the UK and, as it moved from research establishment project to Ministry of Supply development programme, it acquired a rainbow code – Red Hand. Red Hand was later split into land-based and naval versions, mainly due to the stabilisation problems of launching from a pitching and rolling vessel.

These Red Hand studies being carried out under the auspices of the MoS looked promising, but the Admiralty still wanted a weapon

that they could launch from a destroyer so continued with Seaslug. A 1948 MoS proposal to rename Seaslug as Red Slug was met with indifference from the Admiralty so they decided to carry on with Seaslug and leave the Army and Royal Air Force to develop their own weapons. It is these land-based weapons that will be examined first.

Defending the Deterrent

In the Introduction we saw how UK postwar defence policy was based on the possession of the nuclear deterrent. Since this was to be dropped by the medium bombers of the V-Force, a means of defending the V-Force and its bases was required. This was originally to be a task for the Army, but the RAF

A British Army PT.428 battery intercepts an incoming squadron of MiG-17 ground-attack aircraft. Adrian Mann

soon took over the defence of its bomber bases.

By late 1946 the Red Hand GAP studies had led to a study for a land-based GAP called Red Heathen with a range of 57 miles (91.7km). Red Heathen was more or less a longer-range Seaslug, but the range requirement was too ambitious.

The Army also had a requirement for a GAP to defend its formations in the field, which meant mobility. So by the end of the 1940s two land-based GAPs were required: a static weapon to defend the V-Force and a mobile weapon to defend the Army. A further study into long-range defence by guided weapons to OR.202 began in 1945 and was known as the Green Water study. This concluded that long-range weapons, such as an RAE study called Rover for a pilotless interceptor with a range of 150miles (241.4km), were not feasible at the time (1952) and that shorter, 20 mile (32km)-range weapons would present a better prospect for success. In the light of this development the Red Heathen requirement was altered, reducing the range requirement to 20 miles (32.2km).

In fact it was hoped that an integrated air defence system of the type that had protected the UK in World War Two would also be applicable to the guided weapons era. With new radars, guided weapons and communications in the pipeline some method of implementing this was required. Thus was born the Stage Plan.

Staged Air Defence

The postwar air defence of the UK has had a variety of incarnations. The 1948 ROTOR plan involved a massive investment in bunkers and operations centres (52 stations were planned). It was still based around gun-based defences, as were the Nucleus and later Igloo Plans. From the point of view of guided weapons systems, the Stage Plan is significant since it recognised the need for integrated air defence systems and the development of radars and missiles in parallel. In 1949 a series of conferences were held and over the next couple of years the Stage Plan took shape. A total of three stages were planned.

Stage 1 – Based around the Orange Yeoman early warning radar, the Stage 1 Surface-to-Air Guided Weapon (SAGW) was drawn up around the 1953 requirement OR.1124. This involved the introduction of SAGWs to protect the UK's nuclear deterrent, the V-Force, and the British Army in the field. As already noted, the range would be 20 miles (32km).

The first project to meet OR.1124 was the English Electric Aviation Red Shoes. This mobile, rocket-propelled missile used the Yellow River pulsed Target Illumination Radar (TIR). Red Shoes initially used a liquid-fuelled rocket engine, but because the Army (like the Navy) was not keen on having dangerous rocket fuel around, this was replaced by a solid rocket motor as soon as their development allowed. Red Shoes entered service with the British Army as Thunderbird I in 1959.

A second SAGW was also being developed for Stage 1. This was Red Duster, which had a somewhat convoluted gestation. The Bristol

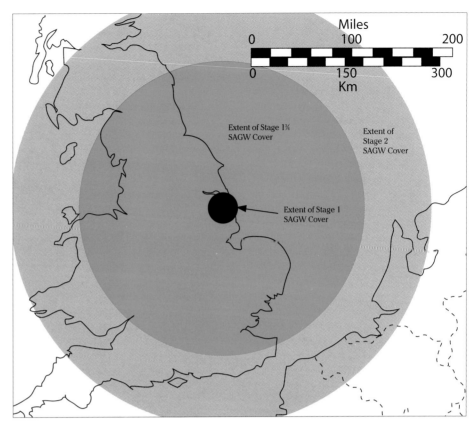

Using RAF North Coates as a reference point, the extent of the SAM coverage of the various stages is apparent.

The IM-99 Bomarc ramjet-powered, long-range SAM was proposed for Stage 2. Its range was deemed excessive, but its use of pulsed radar was unacceptable for European service.
Tony Buttler Collection

Aeroplane Co had been asked to develop a SAGW as an alternative to the Armstrong Whitworth Seaslug naval weapon after de Havilland had declined the task on the grounds of having too much work on their hands. Bristol embarked on this work under the title Bristol Seaslug, but it was soon shelved in favour of a research project to assess the performance of ramjet propulsion, with an eye to producing a longer-ranged SAGW in the future. This became Red Duster and, like Red Shoes, it used pulsed target illumination radar and a quartet of Gosling boosts.

Stage 2 – The Blue Label (AMES Type 84) radar formed the basis of this stage along with the SAGW to meet OR.1137. This was very ambitious and was to extend air defence coverage over the main population centres of the UK, replacing the heavy anti-aircraft guns that had provided such cover since the war. A 200-mile (321km) range guided weapon combined with high power radars and a limited anti-ballistic missile capability was called for.

The missile was to be capable of command guidance and active terminal homing using a CW seeker with passive homing on jamming available.

The resulting Green Sparkler was to be ramjet powered and use a guidance system that was under development by Marconi. The American IM-99 Bomarc missile was also suggested for Stage 2, but it was thought that its range (300+ mile / 483km) was excessive and that its pulsed radar would make it vulnerable to electronic countermeasures in the European theatre. This was an odd observation given that the US and the UK were defending against the same Soviet threat, but British radar specialists such as S/Ldr Poole of OR.18 were convinced that US radars were more susceptible to countermeasures.

Why did we need a SAM with a 200-mile (321km) range? When these requirements were drawn up, the only method for delivering a nuclear weapon was an aircraft such as the V-bombers. These took time to scramble, but also required time to arm the bombs. One of these bombs, Violet Club, required 40 minutes to arm because the safety device, 133,000 ball-bearings, had to be removed. Long-range SAGWs could by that time deal with massed raids, so picking off incoming bombers at long range bought the V-Force time.

Stage 3 – didn't get past the discussion phase and was intended to deal with threats up to 90,000ft (27,432m) and speeds of Mach 4. Very ambitious, but it was quietly dropped as the ICBM threat became more credible.

The Bomarc was not the only missile prone to jamming. The pulsed radars of the Stage 1 SAGW were not only susceptible to ECM but possessed poor low-altitude performance, which as time progressed would become a necessity.

So, given that Stage 1 had short range, poor ECM resistance and indifferent low-level performance plus the realisation that Stage 2 was years away from service, a pair of additional stages were to be added: Stages 1½ and 1¾.

... and the Vulgar Fractions

Stage 1½ – Recent developments had shown that Continuous Wave (CW) radar could solve the ECM and low-level deficiencies of Stage 1, so Stage 1½ evolved to address these. This resulted in OR.1145, met by Green Flax, a renamed Red Shoes with a CW seeker using the Ferranti Indigo Corkscrew TIR. At some point the paperwork was lost and as a security measure the name was changed to Yellow Temple. A further name change, to VR.725 (the Ministry of Aviation reference number), was applied after the Ministry of Supply was dissolved. This version, using the Green Ginger radars, entered service as Thunderbird II.

Stage 1¾ – Service Acceptance Trials of Bristol's Red Duster for Stage 1 had shown rather poor performance, so the RAF cancelled its order for Red Duster and ordered Thunderbird II instead. This wasn't such a major blow to Bristol as might be imagined, because they still had the Stage 1¾ weapon to develop. For some time Red Duster had been viewed as a development tool for this longer-ranged weapon to

meet OR.1146, calling for a 150-mile (241km) range SAGW with mid-course update and semi-active terminal homing using CW radar.

Bristol Guided Weapons' Stage 1¾ SAGW used a new design of ramjet and a CW radar guidance system that was probably built around the Orange Toffee radar set and a mid-course correction system called Brahms. Another guidance method was home-on-jamming that allowed the missile seeker to lock on to the source of CW jamming in the target and use this for guidance.

While Stage 1½ was Red Shoes with a new homing system, Stage 1¾ was a different beast altogether. The RAE had been looking at a long-range, high-speed manned interceptor since the days of the Green Water study, but by 1954 this was seen as too difficult and, following on from a study called Rover, the pilotless interceptor was back under consideration. The RAE began looking at such a weapon in detail under the name Project Q, initially using the RTV.1 to prove the theory. It was soon obvious that the only way to gain such range was by powering the weapon with ramjets. Gas turbines would be too heavy and the received wisdom was that a SAGW needed a speed of 1.5 times that of its target, that is Mach 3 to intercept a Mach 2 bomber, turbojets could not operate at such speeds. A ramjet was the only option and the only company with sufficient ramjet experience was Bristol. Interestingly one other powerplant was suggested for the Stage 1¾ SAGW, the turbo-rocket. Parametric studies soon showed that there was no real advantage in using turbo-rockets and, to overcome slower acceleration at launch, bigger boosts would be required, so ramjet power prevailed.

Bristol used the Red Duster as a basis for a Mach 3 Stage 1¾ SAGW, but used much of the data from the RAE's Project Q. Many of the aerodynamic studies for this had been carried out by Diettrich Kuchemann. Kuchemann was a German aerodynamicist who, during the war, had worked at the Deutsche Versuchsansalt fur Luftfahrt at Brunswick and, after the war, at RAE Farnborough. He believed that the delta was a stable planform for a high-speed aircraft. Such a wing also allowed a much stronger structure to cope with aeroelasticity, reduced drag and improved cruise performance. Bristol began development of a twin-ramjet powered 150-mile (320km) range Mach 3 SAGW called Blue Envoy, which will be described shortly.

Blue Envoy was cancelled in 1957, but the work was not entirely wasted, as we shall see below.

So, having had a general snapshot of post-war air defence SAGW development until

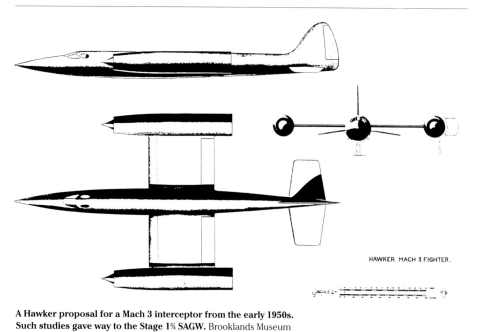

HAWKER MACH 3 FIGHTER.

A Hawker proposal for a Mach 3 interceptor from the early 1950s. Such studies gave way to the Stage 1¾ SAGW. Brooklands Museum

1960, perhaps a more detailed look at the weapons themselves is required. In reality only two programmes were on the go and these start out with 'the fortyniners'.

The Fortyniners

This name was applied to the engineers who began development of Surface-to-Air Guided Weapons (the new name for GAPs) in 1949. Two different weapons were to be developed by industry and the two companies selected to carry this out were English Electric and the Bristol Aeroplane Co.

Any missile arising from the Red Heathen study could not have achieved its range requirement when powered by just rocket motors so Bristols were tasked with developing a 20-mile range SAGW powered by ramjets, with a guidance system by Ferranti. This weapon, Project 1220 (the project office was in Room 1220 apparently) was to be developed as a proof-of-concept vehicle but also to form the basis of a SAGW that would fulfil OR.1124. This would later be called Red Duster. Various configurations were tried out with much of the testing being done by scale models in wind tunnels. Integrated designs along the lines of the US Bumblebee test vehicle were examined, but this would need a large single ramjet, while the ramjets currently under development were 6in (12.7cm) and 7¼in (18.3cm) in diameter. Ramjet power

is related to capture area with larger ramjets generating more thrust, at the time large ramjets were posing a problem for developers so smaller ramjets, used in multiple installations, were preferred.

A four-winged type with four 10in (25.4cm) ramjets, called the Multi Ram Jet Weapon (MRJW) 410, was rejected as underpowered, as was the MRJW 214 with two 14in (35.6cm) ramjets. However, the MRJW 214 used the monoplane configuration of Brakemine (see Chapter One) combined with over- and under-ramjet positioning. This configuration would remain with the Red Duster/Bloodhound series throughout its lifespan, because the simpler manoeuvres available under polar control kept airflow to the ramjets within inlet limits. Ramjets are particularly susceptible to changes in airflow incidence at the intake, which severely affect thrust levels.

Following the selection of the basic configuration, a series of scaled eXperimental Test Vehicles, the XTVs, were constructed and flown. As described in the chapter on Test Vehicles, these proved the basic aerodynamics of Red Duster and were used to prove the propulsion and control systems. The next

step was a series of firings of more or less complete missiles, the XRD-1 (eXperimental Red Duster), as part of Red Duster's Service Acceptance Trials (SATs). XRD-1 was, to put it bluntly, useless. Problems with the guidance electronics and flameouts with its BRJ.2/5 ramjet during manoeuvres plagued the test flights. A major re-think was needed, particularly on propulsion and electronics.

A switch from valves to transistors solved the electronics problems. Bristol's Ramjet Department at Patchway scrapped the flare-ignited ramjet and adopted the NGTE two-stage burner system that had been developed for the Napier Ramjet Test Vehicle (RJTV). The solution to the flameouts during manoeuvring was a grid placed in the intake. This straightened the airflow and kept a steady flow regime in the inlet. The result was the BRJ.3, BRJ.4 and later BRJ.5 series of ramjets, which were fitted to the XRD-2.

The BRJ.5 became known as Thor and a further series of SATs showed that the Red Duster could now be taken into RAF service. It was given the name Bloodhound after the hunting dog: '…that could seek out its enemy and ultimately pull it down'.

Bristol investigated numerous configurations for Red Duster. This, the MRJW.410, used four 10in ramjets. Bristol Collection via Richard Vernon

Having decided on the monoplane with over and under ramjets, Bristol Aircraft began development in earnest. This is an XTV.2 ready for launch. Bristol Collection via Richard Vernon

Ideal for monitoring guided weapon tests, WRETAR cameras could take 100 frames per second with a 186° field of view. In these images an XRD.2 is about to impact a target drone. Bristol Collection via Richard Vernon

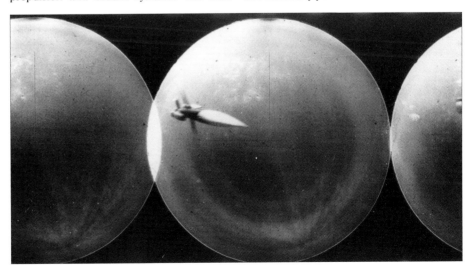

Bloodhound with all four Gosling boost rocket motors at full power. Boosting the missile to Mach 2 in around four seconds, the point the ramjet can begin operating. Author's collection

A late example of Red Shoes, known as Thunderbird I, on display at the Farnborough Air Show. Built by English Electric it entered service with the British Army in 1958.
Tony Buttler Collection

By 1962 the Continuous Wave radar-equipped version of Red Shoes had had at least three more names before being called Thunderbird II. This example is set up in the field.
Tony Buttler Collection

The Luton Thunderbird

Meanwhile, the other team looking at a Stage 1 SAGW was English Electric's Navigation Control Project that had been set up in 1949 as a cover for guided weapon development at Luton. English Electric were particularly concerned with the needs of the Army, a mobile

SAGW, which became known as Red Shoes. Scale models of the Luton Test Vehicle were test flown on solid rockets to prove the aerodynamics, but the full-scale D3 series was powered by a Napier NRE.11 HTP/kerosene rocket engine because a suitable solid motor sustainer was not available. When the

Airedale sustainer motor was available, the D4 series was used for test flights. Guidance development, as with Red Duster, was carried out using Shorts Guided Pilotless Vehicles (GPV) as test vehicles.

Being a mobile weapon Red Shoes would be set up in tactical situations, for example unprepared fields, leading to ground erosion when the boosters fired. This caused problems with reloading, but the erosion scars could also be seen on reconnaissance photos and might reveal the battery's position. Such scars had revealed the nature of the German Messerschmitt Me 262 and Me 163 fighters' method of propulsion to British Scientific Intelligence during World War Two. After

British Secret Projects: Hypersonics, Ramjets & Missiles

numerous tests with the 'Flying Brick', a concrete shape boosted by four rockets, a blast mat was developed in an attempt to prevent this ground erosion problem.

On entering service in 1958, Red Shoes was named officially Thunderbird I and deployed with the British Army of the Rhine to replace the 3.7in (9.4cm) anti-aircraft guns of the Royal Artillery.

While Red Shoes was being developed, progress was also being made on an improved homing system. The Stage 1 SAGW was to use a semi-active pulsed radar 'homing eye', which was applied to Bloodhound I and Thunderbird I; but as Thunderbird would be used at low level the Continuous Wave (CW) radar system would provide better performance. The programme to develop a CW Red Shoes (the Stage 1½ SAGW) was renamed Green Flax, however the paperwork was compromised through a security leak and the project was renamed Yellow Temple.

Blue Envoy

At this point we return to Bristol and the development of Stage 1¾, Blue Envoy. Bristol had pondered fitting a CW homing system to Red Duster, but were becoming more involved in the Stage 1¾ SAGW. Blue Envoy was intended to intercept incoming Mach 2 bombers carrying stand-off weapons before they came within launch range of the UK. It was also intended for installation aboard warships to provide a carrier group with area defence.

The double delta designed by Kuchemann, with 75° sweep on the inboard and 42° on the outer wing, was selected and a series of test vehicles (XTV.6 to XTV.9) was used to explore the aerodynamics for the delta-winged SAGW. One of the problems shown by this and wind tunnel testing was disruption of the airflow to the auxiliary intakes. After much analysis by Roy Hawkins of the RAE Aero Dept, this was cured by the extension of the leading edge along the fuselage with a sweep of 82°. In the 1980s these would be called Leading Edge Root Extensions (LERX) but back in 1955 they were merely strakes. The

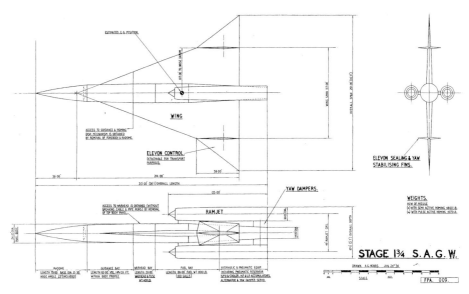

Initial trials for the Stage 1¾ SAGW project involved sub-scale models such as this XTV.6 boosted by a tandem boost motor. Bristol Collection via Richard Vernon

General arrangement drawing of Blue Envoy in its original guise as the Stage 1¾ SAGW. Rolls-Royce Heritage Trust via Roy Hawkins

Desktop model showing Blue Envoy's original double delta planform. via Richard Vernon

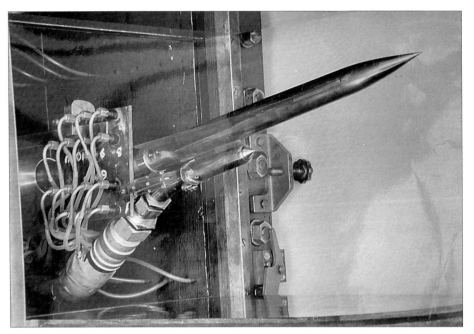

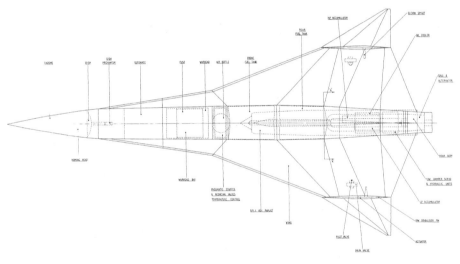

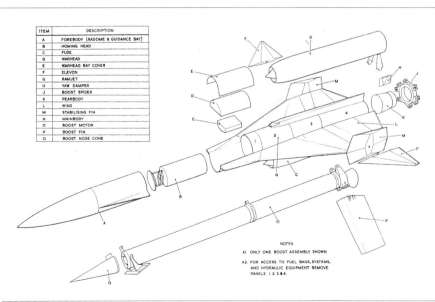

ITEM	DESCRIPTION
A	FOREBODY (RADOME & GUIDANCE BAY)
B	HOMING HEAD
C	FUZE
D	WARHEAD
E	WARHEAD BAY COVER
F	ELEVON
G	RAMJET
H	YAW DAMPER
J	BOOST SPIDER
K	REARBODY
L	WING
M	STABILISING FIN
N	MAINBODY
O	BOOST MOTOR
P	BOOST FIN
Q	BOOST NOSE CONE

NOTES

A1. ONLY ONE BOOST ASSEMBLY SHOWN

A2. FOR ACCESS TO FUEL BAGS, SYSTEMS,
AND HYDRAULIC EQUIPMENT REMOVE
PANELS 1, 2, 3 & 4.

Roy Hawkins – aerodynamicist and ramjet development engineer. Rolls-Royce Heritage Trust, Bristol Branch

Wind tunnel model used to investigate the modifications to Blue Envoy's planform. Bristol Collection via Richard Vernon

The definitive planform for Blue Envoy. The strakes along the forward fuselage changed the location of vortices to ensure adequate airflow to the auxiliary intakes. Rolls-Royce Heritage Trust via Roy Hawkins

Diagram showing the main components of Blue Envoy. Note the size of the warhead bay that was intended to accommodate a 'special' warhead, possibly the Blue Fox nuclear device. Rolls-Royce Heritage Trust via Roy Hawkins

result was a planform not unlike the SAAB Draken, except that on Blue Envoy the outer wings formed elevons for polar controls. Polar control (also known as Twist and Steer) allows two surfaces to be used to control the vehicle. The surfaces act differentially as ailerons to rotate the vehicle along its line of flight, and then they act together as elevators to 'raise' the nose. Thus the aircraft 'twists and steers' towards the target.

Hawkins had been seconded to the RAE Aero Dept in 1945, at a time when German aerodynamicists like Kuchemann were being brought over from Germany. He joined Bristol Engines in 1956 when ramjet development for Bloodhound and Blue Envoy was under way and immediately became involved in applying his aerodynamic expertise to ramjet combustor development.

To provide the Mach 3 speed and 200-mile (321.8km) range, Bristol's Ramjet Dept developed the BRJ.800, an 18in (45.7cm) ramjet that used the NGTE combustor system. This allowed the pilot and main combustors to be used for the acceleration and climb. Once in the cruise phase, the main combustor was shut down and only the pilot combustor used. A temperature sensor in the airframe controlled the thrust levels and therefore speed, ensuring that the temperature of the stainless steel airframe did not exceed 327°C (620°F / 600°Kelvin).

However, by late 1956 doubts were being raised about the viability of the Stage 1¾ SAGW. Construction of the stainless steel airframe would be, as the Bristol 188 high-speed research aircraft proved, rather difficult. The role of the missile itself was also called into question, initially by the Navy, who had had their fingers burnt with Seaslug. Blue Envoy was far too big for the new generation of smaller warships and, because it had to be

assembled before launch, would not have had a very high rate of fire. The RAF also doubted that Blue Envoy would have much use in a conflict at a time when the high-flying supersonic bomber was being replaced by the low-level transonic strike aircraft. In this role Blue Envoy's long range would have been superfluous, if not a hindrance, because its minimum range would be in the region of 10 miles (16km), close to the low-altitude radar horizon of a ship. Blue Envoy was cancelled in April 1957 in the Defence White Paper, one of the many guided weapons projects cancelled in Defence Minister Duncan Sandys' review – despite his reputation as being a lover of missiles.

This caused consternation at Bristols. After being informed of the cancellation, Don Rowley was quoted as saying, 'When Blue Envoy was cancelled we [Bristol Guided Weapons Division] were on our beam-ends: that was

our most dangerous period. I can remember Bloodhound II being invented in a taxi outside Ferranti's office.'

Based on information from Bristol and Ferranti on a CW Red Duster, OR.1169 was drawn up to more or less match the weapon hatched in the back of the cab. In the end Bristol did fit a CW homing system to Red Duster (called at various times 'Super Bloodhound', 'Red Duster Series 3A', 'Red Duster 1½' and '1½ Duster') and applied the BRJ.800 series combustor modifications to the Thor ramjet, to produce what ultimately became known as QF.169 and, when entering service in 1965 with Blue Anchor radar, Bloodhound II. One of the finest SAGWs of the Cold War era, it served with the air forces of Great Britain, Singapore, Sweden and Switzerland. It was finally retired from the RAF in 1991, but soldiered on in Switzerland to be withdrawn after almost thirty years in service.

The final result of the Red Duster and Blue Envoy programmes – QF.169 Bloodhound II.

British area defence SAMs since 1956.

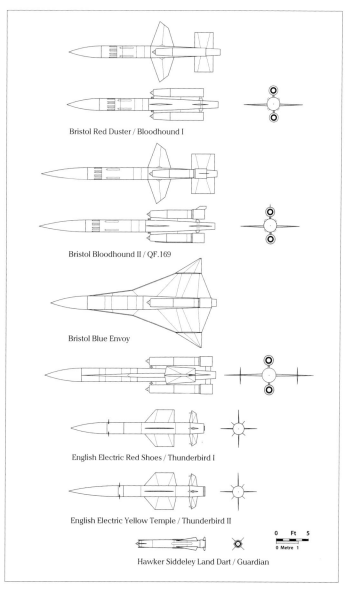

Bristol Red Duster / Bloodhound I

Bristol Bloodhound II / QF.169

Bristol Blue Envoy

English Electric Red Shoes / Thunderbird I

English Electric Yellow Temple / Thunderbird II

Hawker Siddeley Land Dart / Guardian

Nuclear Warheads and Air Defence

Before moving on to the next generation of SAGWs produced in the early 1960s (by this time the American term Surface-to-Air Missile, or SAM, had been adopted) let us take a look at the use of nuclear warheads on anti-aircraft missiles.

Nuclear warheads, in the context of air defence, are usually seen as a means of intercepting bomber formations. This is not strictly true, however, because all the formation needs to do is to increase the separation between individual aircraft to reduce attrition. Back in the early 1950s nuclear weapons were too large to allow guided weapons to lift them to altitude. However, plans were afoot to use Javelin and Lightning interceptors to toss Red Beard tactical nuclear weapons into bomber formations.

By the late 1950s warheads had become small enough to fit into missiles, with OR.1140 outlining a 24in (61cm)-diameter warhead weighing 300lb (136kg) for use on Blue Envoy. A fission warhead called Blue Fox (later renamed Indigo Hammer) with a yield of 5 to 10 kilotons was in development for SAGW use.

When applied to SAGWs, nuclear warheads were really required for use against single aircraft, the reason being that an incoming supersonic aircraft and an intercepting missile would have closing speeds in the region of Mach 4-5. These speeds meant conventional warheads, and in particular their fuze systems, would not react quickly enough, the SAGW would overshoot and explode harmlessly behind the target. A warhead with a bigger blast effect was required to counteract this overshoot, in other words a nuclear device.

Having grasped victory from the jaws of defeat with Bloodhound II, the same team at Bristol was now tasked with fulfilling a new requirement, OR.1166, for a nuclear-armed SAM: this would become Bloodhound III.

Referred to by Bristol as Red Duster Series 3A, but officially as RO.166, the new variant was fitted with a new Command Guidance system. Through improved BS.1009 Thor ramjets and bigger boosts, RO.166 possessed longer range and the ability to carry an Indigo Hammer nuclear warhead (designed to OR.1167). Command Guidance was the preferred system for the nuclear-armed missile due it being controlled from the ground and therefore less likely to, in the words of the Director (Guided Weapons), 'go astray'. Bloodhound III utilised the new Argus computer and a pair of Yellow River radars, one to track the missile and the other to track the target.

Command Guidance was also seen as a step towards the Anti-Ballistic Missile (ABM) capability that had been laid out in the original Stage 2 requirement, OR.1137. Bloodhound III was cancelled in 1960, but some of the modifications found their way into further improvements to Bloodhound II. The main reason for the cancellation of a UK nuclear-armed SAM was the lack of sufficient fissile material for the warheads. The production capacity of the UK's reactors was insufficient to meet the needs of both the nation's nuclear deterrent and the SAMs. The greater priority accorded to deterrent meant that defensive systems didn't have a look in.

Two more versions of Bloodhound were studied. The first, Bloodhound IV, was intended to replace Thunderbird II in the British Army. This was a mobile version based on the experience of the Swedish Air Force, whose *modus operandi* was mobile, dispersed operations for their Bloodhound IIs. Bloodhound 21 was a proposed export derivative with degraded ECCM facilities but was not proceeded with.

View of a Bloodhound II battery with Blue Anchor radar in the background. Bloodhound III (RO.166) would have required a second radar and data link to provide command control.

Defending the Fleet – SAMs for the Navy

As shown in Chapter One one of the driving forces behind GAP development had been the Admiralty who wanted to defend their ships against airborne threats. The focus of that effort was a beam-riding weapon called Seaslug. Developed by Armstrong Whitworth, Sperry Gyro and General Electric as Project 502, references to Seaslug can be traced back to 1946, perhaps even 1943. It was more or less cancelled at one point in favour of the US Terrier SAM in the mid-1950s, but it finally entered service as GWS.1 in 1962.

Initially liquid fuelled (Kerosene and Red Fuming Nitric Acid because the Navy didn't like the idea of liquid oxygen and petrol on their ships) with a tandem boost, due to size constraints Seaslug soon evolved into a solid-fuelled, wrap-around boost configuration. HMS *Girdleness* (a converted World War Two Liberty Ship) had served as a trials platform for the system from 1956 to 1961. The first Royal Navy Seaslug-armed County Class destroyer, HMS *Devonshire*, was commissioned in November 1962. Seaslug's problem was that the launcher and handling system took up a lot of space on board, mainly due to the missiles being stowed horizontally. To address this issue, Vickers proposed a more compact twin launcher, but this went no further than wooden models shown in a Vickers brochure.

Two versions of Seaslug eventually entered service: the Mk.1 was to intercept high-altitude threats, particularly bombers, while the Mk.2 had improved low-level capability and a limited surface-to-surface role. This role wasn't limited to anti-ship as a Seaslug was used to destroy an Argentinian radar station in the Falklands War by laying the missile guidance beam on the enemy radar and having the Seaslug fly along the beam. A dedicated anti-ship version called Blue Slug did not progress beyond the design study stage.

The New Generation of Naval SAMs

By 1957 the Royal Navy was shrinking, both in the number and in the size of its vessels. Only eight County Class destroyers were eventually acquired and Seaslug was a large system whose capability was somewhat limited. Its intended replacement (Blue Envoy) had been even larger, but was incapable of intercepting the new threat from low-level naval strike aircraft.

The Navy was changing, with guided weapons replacing the anti-aircraft guns (such as the STAAG – Stabilised Tachometric Anti-Aircraft Gun with six 40mm Bofors and the 5in [12.7cm] dual-purpose gun) that had been developed in the years before World

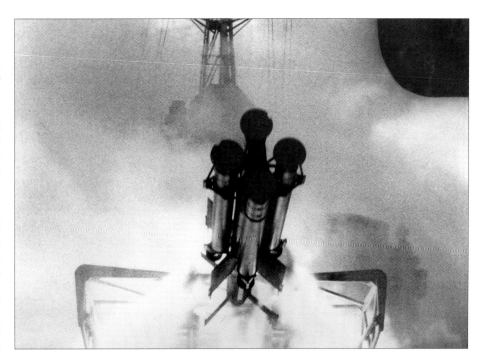

War Two. Two roles were envisaged: a long-range, (50miles / 80.5km) area defence missile and a close-range point defence weapon.

For the long-range weapon a study called New Naval Guided Weapons System was under way from 1958 to replace Seaslug. Becoming known in the trade as NIGS and by the MoA as WA.726, this was to counter a Mach 3 target flying at 70,000ft (21,336m) and intended to arm the next-generation CVA.01 aircraft carriers. The preferred bidder, the Project 502 team of Armstrong Whitworth, Smiths and Sperry, were intending to update Seaslug and include new technology.

Bristol had not been asked to tender for

Seaslug launch with the four boost motors at full chat – a spectacle indeed. This photo was taken on trials ship HMS *Girdleness*. TNA ADM 263/201

At the receiving end, a Firefly drone has a near miss with a Seaslug. Had a warhead been fitted, the target would have been destroyed. TNA ADM 263/201

NIGS, but had got wind of this important project through unofficial channels. Somewhat put out, the company investigated two configurations. The first, using Bloodhound II experience, was a tailed delta with over and under ramjets similar to Blue Envoy, but with a tandem boost. Like its predecessor, it was

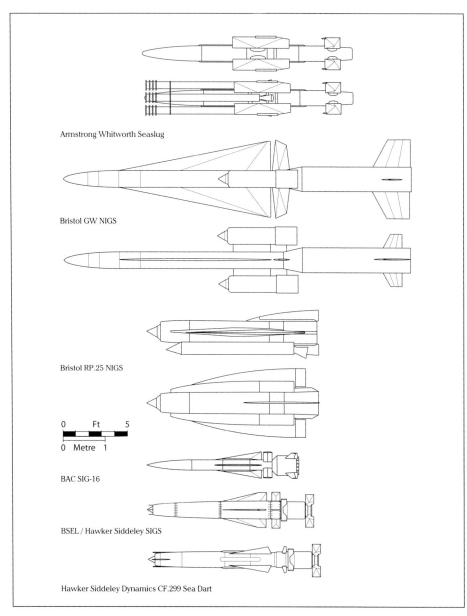

Armstrong Whitworth Seaslug

Bristol GW NIGS

Bristol RP.25 NIGS

0 Ft 5

0 Metre 1

BAC SIG-16

BSEL / Hawker Siddeley SIGS

Hawker Siddeley Dynamics CF.299 Sea Dart

British naval area defence SAMs. Most noteworthy is the reduction in size for more or less the same capability.

SIGS – Small ships Integrated Guided weapon System – was to be handled like a round of gun ammunition using hoists and rotary magazines.

dismissed as too big at 26ft 7in (8.1m) long including boost, so a fully revised submission was made. Strangely enough, Bristol tendered a completely new SAM for NIGS called 'Large PT.428' to address these size concerns. Two and a half times larger than the British Aircraft Corporation PT.428 (being developed for the Army and described later in this chapter), Bristol's Large PT.428 used semi-active homing, but policy and requirements were changing once more.

NIGS carried on until 1961, but prior to this the Navy had indicated that it required a SAM that was both effective and capable of storage and handling like gun ammunition. Apparently the Admiralty were quite taken with the BAC PT.428 SAM, but it didn't have enough range, even with a tandem boost, nor was its beam-riding guidance deemed suitable for naval applications. The requirement was filled by SIGS – the Small ship Integrated Guided weapon System.

The two main players in the SIGS contest were the Project 502 team and Bristol Aeroplane Co's GW Department under David Farrar. BAC initially proposed SIG-16, a small solid rocket-powered weapon with a tandem boost, but its range of 16 miles (25.7km) was deemed too short to be of any use in the intended area air defence role. Ramjet power was necessary to meet the range, so Bristol GW looked to the Bristol Engines Dept for a suitable power unit.

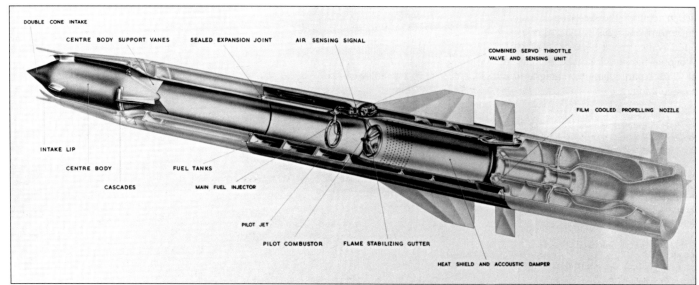

DOUBLE CONE INTAKE
CENTRE BODY SUPPORT VANES
SEALED EXPANSION JOINT
AIR SENSING SIGNAL
COMBINED SERVO THROTTLE VALVE AND SENSING UNIT
FILM COOLED PROPELLING NOZZLE
INTAKE LIP
CENTRE BODY
FUEL TANKS
CASCADES
MAIN FUEL INJECTOR
PILOT JET
PILOT COMBUSTOR
FLAME STABILIZING GUTTER
HEAT SHIELD AND ACCOUSTIC DAMPER

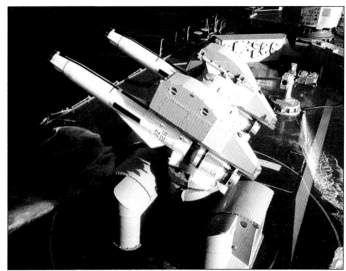

The second Bristol GW submission for SIGS was called RP.25 (Ramjet Project 25) and featured a Gothic arch delta wing and an integrated BS.1001 ramjet. Boosted by a pair of rocket motors mounted on the underside, RP.25 was to have a powered range of almost 50 miles (80.5km), a ceiling of 110,000ft (33,528m) and a maximum speed of Mach 4. Interestingly one of the drawbacks of this configuration was the effect of the airframe structure on the warhead, producing zones of limited effectiveness around the missile. As the warhead exploded the missile's airframe, particularly in the plane of the wings, absorbed the blast and much effort was put into solving this.

The Admiralty approved of the design study, but wanted the 502 team to have design authority. The requirement had called for the new weapon to be handled like traditional gun ammunition, which precluded the use of large wings. The design was altered to produce a sleek weapon with a pitot intake, which acquired the Ministry of Aviation reference number CF.299 in 1962. Although developed by the Project 502 team, Bristol Guided Weapons had much influence on the design of CF.299, particularly the integrated ramjet configuration.

Eventually named GWS-30 Sea Dart, CF.299 entered service with the Royal Navy in 1973 and performed well in the 1982 Falklands War. The ramjet it used was the BS.1003 Odin and the missile was boosted by a Chow solid rocket motor when launched from a twin rail launcher. Initially deployed on the Type 82 destroyer HMS *Bristol*, Sea Dart became the main weapon of the Type 42 'Sheffield Class' fitted with two launchers per ship, fed from a circular magazine holding 22 rounds. The ships were fitted with a pair of Type 909 target illumination radars, which allowed a high rate of fire and great accuracy.

In the 1970s a variant with improved propulsion and guidance was in development. Called Sea Dart II, it used more compact integrated circuitry that allowed

increased fuel capacity as well as Thrust Vector Control (TVC) on the Chow booster. TVC allowed the missile to perform manoeuvres 'off the rail', reducing its minimum range and conferring the ability to engage targets from all directions. John Nott, Minister of Defence in the first Thatcher Government, cancelled this in the 1980 Defence Review, although some recent improvements have significantly improved Sea Dart's already formidable performance (these remain classified).

One interesting variant of Sea Dart was Sea Daws 100, which used a simplified launcher. Listed as the main weapon of the air defence destroyers proposed as follow-on to the Type 82 destroyers, Sea Daws 100 used a launcher with a single rail rather than the twin rail of the standard system.

Sea Dart round in the Bristol Collection. In the foreground is a four-round box launcher for the Guardian land-based variant.

A Sea Dart launcher with two rounds ready to fire. Fitted to the Type 42 air defence destroyers and the Illustrious Class aircraft carriers, GWS-30 Sea Dart provided air defence of a battle group.
Crown Copyright/MOD

A GWS-30 Sea Dart launch is a spectacular sight as the Chow rocket motor boosts the missile to a speed where the Odin ramjet can produce thrust.
Crown Copyright/MOD

CF.299/Sea Dart also formed the basis of a couple of land-based SAM systems proposed by Hawker Siddeley Dynamics (HSD). In the early 1960s HSD proposed replacing the Army's Thunderbirds and the RAF's Bloodhounds with a mobile, box-launched CF.299 called Land Dart. Land Dart was intended to fill a NATO requirement for a tactical SAM. HSD lobbied hard for Land Dart, explaining that if CF.299 became a tri-service weapon, its adoption as NATO's standard weapon would follow. This came to naught as the improved (and cheaper) VR.725/Thunderbird II would enter service just prior to any Land Dart being available. Ultimately the American Hawk missile filled that NATO requirement.

By the late 1970s the General and Air Staffs were drawing up GAST.1210 for a Bloodhound II replacement. HSD proposed its CF.299-derived Guardian SAM system that used the Plessey GF75 Panther radar as the TIR. Again this went no further than design studies and the Bloodhound was finally retired from RAF service in 1991 leaving the UK without any medium-range SAM defence. As ever the threat changed, in fact it disappeared, with the collapse of the Warsaw Pact.

Short-Range Naval Air Defence
As we saw in Chapter One, Admiralty interest in such weapons first stirred in 1943 thanks to the need to defend against German glide bombs such as Fritz-X and the Hs 293 guided missile. Although these studies led ultimately to Seaslug, a further series of studies were undertaken to defend the fleet against anti-ship weapons.

In the immediate post-war period the only weapon available for fitting to ships was the RAE's Ben, in its beam-riding radar guise. Ben's limited capability was soon overtaken by developments based on the RAE's test vehicle programmes and this led to the Popsy studies.

Popsy A was a subsonic close-in defence SAGW for small ships designed to the 1948 requirement GD 81/48, but first mentioned back in 1946. The Popsy A airframe was based on the CTV.1 test vehicle. Popsy A used a semi-active Q-band seeker for use against glide bombs similar to Fritz-X and Vickers' Blue Boar, plus any putative Russian guided weapons based on the German Hs 293.

Popsy B was a supersonic development for small ships such as the new Royal Navy frigates designed at the war's end and was intended for use against transonic aircraft. To be in service by 1957, Popsy B was an extension of the Popsy A project to deal with aircraft threats as well as the guided bombs. It used a semi-active Q-band seeker in an airframe derived from the Long-Shot test vehicle. Interestingly, Popsy was in competition with a gun-based system called Direct Acting, Close Range (DACR, in current parlance, a close-in weapons system) as the main defence for small ships. The gun-based proposal comprised a sextet of Oerlikon 34mm cannon on a Scarecrow V mount. This competition was to be repeated in the 1980s after the Falklands War when such a system was found lacking on Royal Navy ships.

The entire Popsy project was cancelled in 1950, but another interesting aspect of Popsy was that it could be bolted on to merchant

ships, with the weapons controlled from a 'command ship'. Therefore each vessel in a convoy could be better protected by its own defences, without the need to fit every ship with the fire control system. This aspect of Popsy re-surfaced in the Falklands War where a valuable asset, such as a carrier, had to have its close escort acting as 'goalie'.

A further development was Mopsy, also known as Popsy-Meteor, a US/UK SAGW for small ships to meet GD.165/55. This used a US Meteor AAM airframe with the Popsy Q-band seeker head and was to be installed on warships and merchant ships.

By 1953 the threat had changed from guided bombs to supersonic missiles and aircraft, so a new requirement appeared and a study called Orange Nell was drawn up. Orange Nell was to be small enough to fit on a frigate and capable of dealing with threats from 1970 onwards. Obviously a protracted development programme, à la Seaslug, was expected!

The study was built around a requirement to defend against a supersonic missile in the same class as Fairey's Green Cheese anti-ship missile. With a maximum range of 5.7 miles (9.1km) Orange Nell was to be capable of engaging the target down to a minimum of 1.1 miles (1.8km). Ideally the interception should take place at 1.7 miles (2.7km). This requirement dictated the need for transonic performance, with Mach 1.2 being most likely. A reaction / dead time of ten seconds from acquisition to launch was anticipated, if the missile was already 'warmed up' (one forgets about warming up electronics in the digital age!) and ready to go.

Orange Nell was designed around an S-band 'volume scanning' target acquisition radar with an X- or Q-band Continuous Wave illuminator for the missile's semi-active seeker. The weapon would be capable of lock-on prior to launch, but the preferred technique was searching for the target after launch.

As proposed, Orange Nell was to carry a 100 lb (45.3kg) blast/fragmentation or continuous rod warhead. The twin-rail launcher would replace a 5in gun turret and would include a magazine with forty missiles stacked vertically in two concentric rings.

However, the old problem of dealing with the warhead, first encountered with the Kamikaze, soon reared its ugly head again. Since anti-ship missiles are designed to pen-

A Green Light Test Vehicle for the Seacat programme streaks away from its launcher. Tracking flares are attached to the tail fins.
Copyright Thales Air Defence

British Secret Projects: Hypersonics, Ramjets & Missiles

Seacat mounting on a Royal Navy vessel. These mounts carried four rounds, but a three-round mounting was also available.
Copyright Thales Air Defence

Tigercat, the land version of Seacat, could be set up quickly and provided air defence to mobile forces. Copyright Thales Air Defence

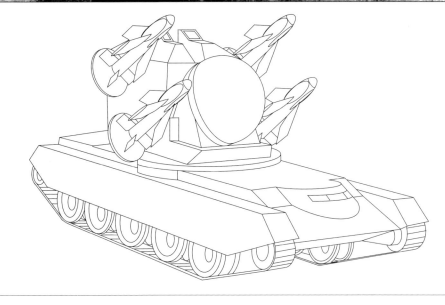

Shorts studied a mobile version of Tigercat mounted on a modified Centurion tank chassis.

etrate a ship's armour, they are somewhat robust structures (see the warhead for Red Angel) and the best way to deal with them is by a direct hit. Given a miss distance of 20ft (6m) a blast warhead would perhaps damage the missile airframe and guidance system but the warhead could still carry on to damage the target ship.

The destruction of an attacking missile appeared more difficult than initially thought so the preferred solution was to attack the launch aircraft before it could release its missiles, which was the domain of the Seaslug. Orange Nell was therefore cancelled in 1957.

Meantime, Shorts had been looking at a basic replacement for the 40mm Bofors gun. Under a study called Green Light, Shorts developed a lightweight, optically-guided SAM that could intercept attacking low-level aircraft at short range. Using SXA-5 and SXA-7 test vehicles based on the Malkara anti-tank missile, Shorts developed what became known in service as the Sea Cat. Mounted on a four-round trainable launcher, and boosted by a Sealyham rocket motor, Sea Cat had a range of 4 miles (6.4km).

Sea Cat began sea trials in 1962 and entered service with the Royal Navy shortly afterwards. It also became a considerable export success and performed well in the Falklands War, claiming eight Argentinian strike aircraft. A land-based version on a towed launcher, called Tigercat, was also fairly successful, serving with the RAF Regiment as well as many overseas users. Shorts also intended mounting the Tigercat on a Centurion tank chassis as a mobile air defence vehicle. An anti-ship version called Hellcat, to be launched from helicopters or Air Cushion Vehicles, was not proceeded with.

Beating the Sea-Skimming Missile

Having scrapped Orange Nell, there was still a requirement for a point defence weapon for use against anti-ship missiles, surface launched as well as air launched. In 1962 Shorts proposed a supersonic Sea Cat II, a more or less completely new design using the same launcher, but this progressed no further

Conventional Launch
Seawolf Missile (Mock Up)

than studies. Also in 1962 the Admiralty issued requirement GD.302 for a study called Confessor, to produce a short-range weapon to engage the next generation of anti-ship missiles, including the sea-skimming types that were on the cards.

Confessor led to the adoption of a 1967 BAC proposal known by the Ministry of Aviation Reference Number PX.430, but better known as Seawolf. Originally mounted in a six-box trainable launcher, Seawolf employed a Blackcap boost/sustain rocket motor.

Using the experience of the PT.428 project (described later in this chapter), Seawolf used radar guidance with a TV back-up using IR flares on the missile, with a command link to the missile. The guidance system used differential tracking whereby the radar tracks the target and the missile (via aerials on the fins) with the system bringing the two tracks together for an intercept. The system can handle two missiles at the same time.

Later developments included a vertical launch installation based on a 1968 Royal Navy study called 'Sinner' (every confessor must have a sinner) and this resulted in the development of GWS-26 Vertical Launch Seawolf, which has an additional Cadiz boost motor with TVC. VL Seawolf has been fitted in a block on the foredeck of the Royal Navy's Type 23 frigates.

Seawolf not only destroyed missiles, it was also capable of intercepting shells. A story did the rounds about a warship captain, having fired a 4½in shell at Seawolf trials ship HMS *Penelope*, being heard announcing on the RT 'Oh look, we shot down your missile!' as the Seawolf hit the shell.

Later developments of Seawolf included SCADS (Shipborne Containerised Air Defence System) for installation on merchant ships or naval auxiliaries and VM40, a lightweight version using the Dutch Signaal STIR radar. Under a design study called SAM.3, Seawolf formed the hardware of a BAC land-based air defence study called Landpax, with the missile being called Landwolf. This was to meet the same GAST.1210 requirement as HSD's Guardian to supplement or replace Blood-

Seawolf, developed as Confessor and PX.430, provided Royal Navy ships with defence against sea-skimming missiles and aircraft at close range.

A GWS-25 Seawolf SAM (developed as Confessor and PX.430) leaves the six-round launcher on a Type 22 Broadsword Class frigate.
Crown Copyright/MOD

Caught by a high-speed camera, a GWS-26 Vertical Launch Seawolf, developed as Sinner, emerges from its silo on a Type 23 destroyer.
Crown Copyright/MOD

British naval point defence SAMs since 1945.

hound II. However, Bloodhound soldiered on into the 1990s and remained a potent weapon to the end.

An enlarged version of Seawolf with a bigger warhead was called XPX.430 and was proposed for the abortive SAM.72 study. This was a feasibility study for a medium-range SAM conducted in 1972 that foundered on the lack of an RAF requirement for such a SAM and the need for international co-operation on the project, which was not forthcoming.

While the likes of Seawolf could defend ships down to frigate size (the first warships with Seawolf were the 4,000 ton [3628 tonne] Type 22 Broadsword Class and the broad-beam Leander Class) there was also a need for air defence of smaller vessels and for 'bolt-on' defensive systems. The US had a track record of using modified air-to-air missiles (AAMs) as SAMs on US Navy ships, with a modified AIM-7 called Sea Sparrow (which was Seawolf's main competitor) being fitted to a variety of ships. BAe had proposed a naval SAM version of the XJ.521 Sky Flash AAM called Sea Flash in the mid 1970s, but this system was still too large for small ships.

From the early 1970s HSD had been pursuing the development of a dogfight AAM called QC.434. A successor to Taildog, its story is fully covered in Chapter Three; suffice to say it became the subject of a naval air defence study called SHIELD.

SHip Installed Equipment for Low-air Defence (SHIELD), was an HSD study for a SAM system to protect small ships from low-altitude threats, particularly sea-skimming missiles. The Admiralty had produced Naval Staff Target NST.6452 as a Sea Cat replacement for ships too small to carry GWS.25 Sea Wolf and even for vessels as small as 200 tons (181 tonnes).

The initial research comprised a passive IR detection system called Montana with box launchers holding modified QC.434 missiles. Modifications included increasing the IR seeker sensitivity by a factor of five. The system worked automatically, with the launchers slaved to the incoming threat prior to launch of the missile. Later proposals included vertical launch, particularly relevant when QC.434 already possessed thrust vector control. The passive detection system was to be based on the Montana surveillance system developed for warships by ASWE. SHIELD went no further than project studies, as an alternative close-in defence system would carry the day in the post-Falklands War era.

The newest generation of Naval SAM is the MBDA PAAMS (Principal Anti-Air Missile Sys-

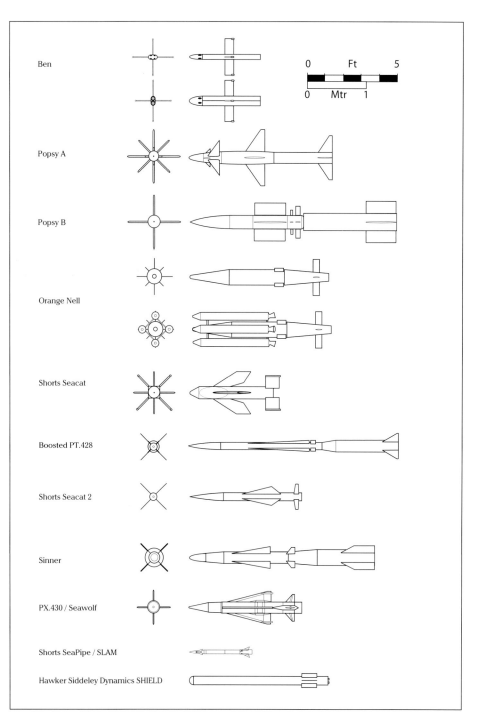

tem) derived from the studies for the late 1980s Support Defence Missile System (SDMS). Short-range point defence and a longer-range area defence version are in development for the Royal Navy's forthcoming Type 45 destroyers. Interestingly they use a control system called Piff-Paff, where rockets mounted on the flanks of the missile provide the turning force, which is not dissimilar to that used on Continued Thrust Spaniel of 1941 – so there is nothing new under the Sun!

All of the systems described above are guided weapons, however there were alter-

native methods for defending ships at close range. During World War Two various unguided anti-aircraft rockets were developed such as the 3in (7.6cm) Unrotated Projectile and SAR (Surface-to-Air Rocket) series. This appeared in 2in (5cm) and 3in (7.6cm) variants before the war and a 5in (12.7cm) version carrying an AA shell followed in 1947. It had a ceiling of 53,000ft (16,154m) and was effective if it hit the target.

Such systems were resurrected in the 1970s, possibly as a result of similar work being done in France. Sea Fox, was a shipborne anti-aircraft system firing salvoes of unguided rockets in a similar manner to the Z-batteries of World War Two. In truth however, this type of air defence system had had its day, due to the advent of radar-directed gun systems such as the potent 30mm Goalkeeper and 20mm Phalanx, both in service with the Royal Navy. These solved the warhead destruction problem by 'shredding' the incoming weapon with depleted uranium projectiles. The CIWS radar tracks the target and directs the fire at it until the radar return disappears. Yet again we see ambitious, if not novel, UK weapons systems, being beaten by a more basic, some would say traditional, system – the gun.

Defence of the Army in the Field

The Stage 1 SAGWs had given the services practical experience of using guided weapons; Stage 1½ had turned this experience and improved hardware into a viable weapon. The Army had taken their Thunderbirds into the field, but it wasn't a replacement for the 40mm Bofors guns that had provided low-level defence for so long. By the late 1950s the threat to the Army came in the form of low-level transonic strike aircraft, such as the Soviet MiG-17 *Fresco* and Sukhoi Su-7 *Fitter* fighter-bombers, rather than high-altitude supersonic bombers. Throughout the

1950s there was an ongoing project to replace the Bofors gun called Red Queen. This was a twin-barrelled 42mm weapon designed by Oerlikon and its rate of fire was up to 450 rounds per minute fed from a large circular magazine on the left side of the gun. However, the ultimate replacement for the Bofors proved to be another Bofors: the updated L70 fitted with the Yellow Fever fire control equipment. This solution was somewhat unsatisfactory and was lambasted in the press.

In NATO armies the day of the anti-aircraft gun appeared to be over, but the US with its M163 Vulcan Air Defence System and the German Army with the Gepard flakpanzer have continued to use guns for mobile air defence. Britain had at least two attempts to produce a gun-based air defence vehicle. The first was Falcon, an Abbot self-propelled gun chassis with a Vickers turret carrying a pair of Hispano Suiza 30mm cannon. Doubts about its ammunition capacity saw the Falcon off.

The second was Marconi's Marksman to GST.3822, which used a pair of Oerlikon 30mm cannon and a Series 400 radar on a turret that could be fitted to a variety of main battle tanks, such as the Chieftain, although it was only ever used by the Finnish Army on their Russian-built T72s! In the end the British forces stuck with SAMs for air defence and apart from small arms and some captured

SkyGuard gun systems, this is still the case. So let us examine the evolution of the Army's SAM defences.

By 1960 the Army had identified a need for an all-weather, low-level, anti-aircraft guided weapon with better mobility than the Thunderbird. Described as mobile, Thunderbird II was better considered as transportable since it had to be moved as a 'convoy' and its Green Ginger radar system (the AMES Type 88 and the AMES Type 89 Height Finder, known to the troops as Noddy and Big Ears) had to be set up and missile launchers deployed before use. This was not a good recipe for mobile warfare and made the system vulnerable to attack by the new generation of Soviet strike aircraft.

In 1959, having failed with the dual role anti-tank / anti-aircraft Orange William, the General Staff decided that the time was ripe for a new self-contained mobile SAM system to replace the Bofors L70 gun. Vickers Guided Weapons at Weybridge commenced design of what they called the Light Anti-Aircraft (LAA) system. In due course LAA was transferred to the newly formed BAC Guided Weapons division at Stevenage who turned it into a classic.

Vickers' Light Anti-Aircraft system was to be installed in an all-terrain truck and capable of rapid deployment.

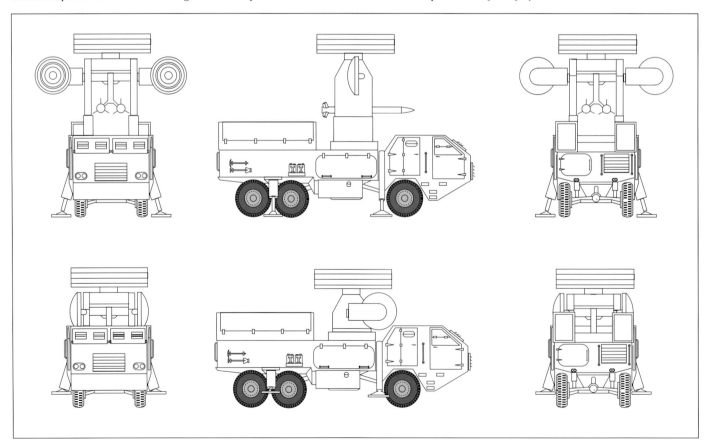

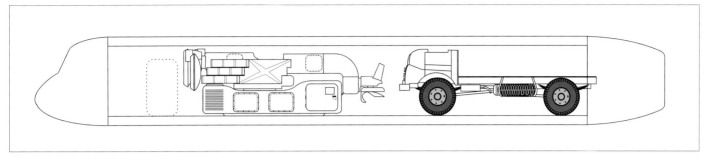

PT.428 – A Missed Opportunity

In 1960 came the result, a mobile all-weather SAM to be developed by BAC and called PT.428. The eighteen-round fire unit was capable of what was called 'blindfire' (operating in the dark and bad weather) and was to be carried on a Bedford RL truck with good off-road performance. It could be off-loaded and set up in a short time or, given the right ground conditions, used mounted on the truck and be ready to fire in sixty seconds. Installation on a tracked launcher was also proposed, and with hovercraft all the rage in the 1960s, some brochures showed it installed on them as well. Air-portable and with a high rate of fire, BAC had high hopes for PT.428 with sales to other NATO allies in mind, particularly the Americans. The PT.428 system was formidable and its performance would have exceeded anything else in the pipeline, but it relied on some very advanced computer technology.

Across the Atlantic the US Army did have a similar requirement to supplement their HAWK (Homing All the Way Killer) weapons, which were similar to the Thunderbird II in capability and operation. As well as keeping an eye on PT.428, the US Army was looking at a General Dynamics system called Mauler, a mobile, low-altitude missile with similar capability.

The specification for Mauler was not as extreme as that outlined for PT.428, plus it was to be much cheaper, thanks to the economies of scale associated with a US Army order. The UK MoD looked at the two projects and decided that PT.428 was far too ambitious, far too expensive, and would not meet the expected capability. This is still the official line but Solly Zuckerman, Scientific

The RAF expected to have the Fairey Rotodyne in service by the mid-1960s, so PT.428 was to be sized to fit within its hold, as seen from the diagram, the Bedford truck also fitted – just.

BAC's PT.428 – the TSR.2 of the British guided weapon industry. This was to be a self-contained launcher system capable of transport on a medium truck, under a helicopter or within a Fairey Rotodyne.

Adviser to the MoD from 1960, states otherwise in his autobiography 'Monkeys, Men and Missiles': 'My own view, which I made perfectly clear, was that Blue Water should go. While I recognized that PT.428 was highly ambitious from a technical point of view, it made more sense to spend such money as was available on a weapon system that had some obstensibly military purpose rather than one which I thought had none.'

Zuckerman suspected a stitch-up by the Defence Staffs: 'In those days there was a certain amount of back-scratching in these matters, with "Buggins" knowing his turn would come.'

The Army could not have funding to develop both PT.428 and the Blue Water nuclear SSM (described in Chapter Nine), so PT.428 was cancelled in December 1961 to protect Blue Water and the MoD opted to buy

Mauler. This was also cancelled in 1965 because Mauler turned out to have problems meeting the US Army requirement. It has been suggested that Mauler was merely a spoiler, hatched to kill off PT.428, but the $200 million spent on Mauler makes for a very expensive spoiler! PT.428 is an example of what Sir Frank Cooper, MoD Permanent Secretary, described as 'over-optimism' at best and 'arrogance' at worse in the capabilities of weapons systems under development by UK companies. Yet another attempt by British industry to leapfrog the Americans had come to nought.

Attention has been drawn to the advanced computers needed to operate PT.428. It has since been suggested that the required computing technology was achievable, particularly at Ferranti, and had in fact been surpassed by the time PT.428 was cancelled.

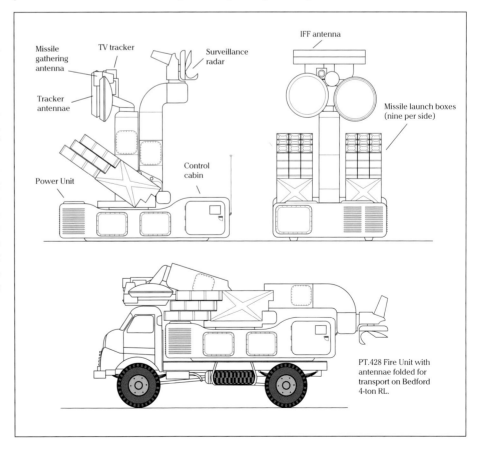

PT.428 Fire Unit with antennae folded for transport on Bedford 4-ton RL.

Rapier – *A Light Slender Sharp-Pointed Sword for Thrusting Only* (OED)

Having decided that PT.428 was unaffordable and with Mauler cancelled in the US, in 1962 the General Staff and the Air Staff issued a joint requirement (GASR.3132) for a cheaper clear-weather optically tracked SAM system for the Army and RAF Regiment. As usual, having had their fingers burnt and knowing how the MoD worked, BAC had been working in the background on such a system as an off-shoot of PT.428.

This was a six-round PT.428 launch unit with optical tracking, which became known by the company as Sightline. As the GASR.3132 requirement was firmed up, and it changed from a cheaper PT.428 to a completely different system, the name Defoe was applied to the project. Defoe later acquired

the Ministry of Aviation reference number ET.316, and the official name Rapier. As development proceeded it soon became clear that Rapier was a particularly effective weapon and, despite its small size and warhead, could destroy strike aircraft. Much of this effectiveness was due to Rapier having an impact fuse and so it was better described as a 'hittile' rather than a missile.

But why call it Rapier? In fact a precise, thrusting weapon more than adequately describes ET.316. BAC originally wanted to call the weapon Mongoose, after the small carnivore with a reputation for tenacity and speed when killing bigger foes. However, during a board meeting at BAC the question of what to call more than one Mongoose arose. Mongeese? Mongooses? Mongii? Nobody knew, so the name Rapier was suggested and adopted.

An even simpler (and cheaper) wholly optical version of Sightline/Defoe was also considered to meet a requirement for a clear-weather optical weapon (GASR.3134) but it was decided that a picket radar was required to give advance warning to the crews, as had been specified in GASR.3132. The surveillance radar for Rapier, installed on top of the launcher, would warn the crew of an incoming threat and identify it as enemy via an IFF system. The controller then slewed the launcher in the direction of the threat, allowing the optical tracker to pick up the target. Interestingly such a radar, called Green Bacon, had been considered for the Bofors guns back in the mid-1950s, but was cancelled in 1957 because trials had shown that it only gave one second advanced warning over 'the Mk.1 Eyeball'. The state of the art had obviously progressed.

No sooner had the development of the clear-weather version of Rapier been started than the all-weather requirement from PT.428 was re-assessed (due to Mauler's cancellation). The Staff considered that weather conditions in Western Europe would degrade the capability of an optical tracking system for much of the time, so it issued GASR.3362 in 1965 to add blindfire capability for ET.316 by using a Q-band radar system, designated DN.181 and developed by Marconi.

Many versions of Rapier have been developed over the years, such as Darkfire fitted with an electro-optical system configured for night and bad-weather use with a six-round launcher, improved radar and an IR tracker. Another variant, Laserfire, was a clear-weather, pallet-mounted, simplified Rapier system using a new Racal Possum surveillance radar and laser tracking. With shades of PT.428, it was to be mounted on a Bedford truck and dismounted for use in static defence, but Laserfire failed to win any orders. The Advanced Rapier for the US Army's DIVAD (Divisional Air Defence) requirement was to involve a turret-mounted Rapier system with eight Rapier SAMs and a 25mm Hughes Chain Gun mounted on a Bradley IFV.

The ultimate development is Rapier Field Standard C to GASR.3732, incorporating a new tracker, proximity fuze (for use against UAVs) and all earlier improvements into the

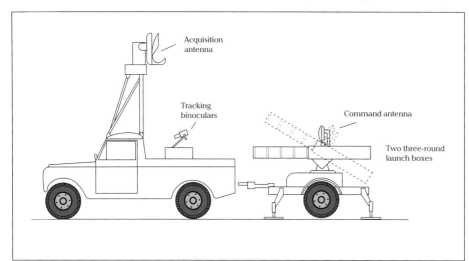

BAC PT.428 lightweight launcher and Land Rover. This may have formed the basis of Sightline, the system that ultimately became Rapier.

BAC ET.316 mobile SAM. Ultimately became Rapier, a very successful weapon with a multitude of variants. This is the basic fire unit with four rounds. BAC via author

British Secret Projects: Hypersonics, Ramjets & Missiles

Rapier 2000 missile. Mounted on a new trailer with integrated power supply, FSC uses the Dagger surveillance radar and Blindfire targeting radar and allows multiple engagements. Rapier FSC has been optimised for desert use and exported under the name Jernas: an Arabian falcon in its hunting prime.

Rapier became very successful, entering British Army and RAF Regiment service in 1977, and saw action in the Falklands War. The weapon also came full circle with the development of Tracked Rapier, which saw the system on a turntable mounted on an RCM 748 armoured vehicle. Designed for the Shah of Iran, the British Army took over the order after the 1979 Islamic Revolution and Tracked Rapier was in service from 1983 until 1995, including deployment in the 1991 Gulf War. Perhaps Tracked Rapier showed what PT.428 would have been like, in other words, deadly. However, it is doubtful that PT.428 could have provided such performance, as

Tracked Rapier had benefited from a revolution in electronics and miniaturisation. In fact PT.428 is possibly the classic example of British over-ambition. PT.428 was to guided weapons what the TSR.2 strike aircraft was to the British aircraft industry in the 1960s: an attempt to jump a generation that stumbled and fell.

Shoulder-Launched Developments – MANPADS

If Rapier was an example of cutting your coat to match your cloth, the early development of shoulder-launched SAMs was more a case of serendipity.

In 1964 Shorts submitted a brochure to the MoD covering a test vehicle called Blowpipe that they hoped could form the basis of a man-portable SAM. Blowpipe had been developed as private venture using the optical guidance technology used in the Sea Cat, rather than the infra-red seekers of the con-

BAC's Rapier SAM as it leaves its launcher. Based on the ET.316 work from the early 1960s, Rapier can trace its lineage back to the Vickers LAA of the mid 1950s. Tony Buttler Collection

temporary US Redeye and Soviet SA-7 Strela missiles. The General Staff was very interested and the Navy's Lord Mountbatten positively enthusiastic, but the RAF was sceptical of the Army's aircraft recognition skills and demanded an integrated IFF system. Adopting optical guidance meant it could be used against approaching aircraft, rather than 'tail-chasing' after the threat had passed overhead, and against targets with lower IR signatures such as helicopters. Unfortunately there was no current requirement for such a weapon, so General Staff drew up a Staff Target for a Unit Self-Defence Surface-to-Air Weapon that would be known as Dagger. To Shorts' consternation, rather than write the Staff Target to match the known capabilities

A Royal Marines Commando with a Shorts Blowpipe shoulder-launched SAM. Such weapons give small units some defence against attack aircraft and helicopters. Copyright Thales Air Defence

SLAM Submarine Launched Air Flight Missile on a test stand. SLAM may or may not be in service with the Israeli Navy, the only customer for SLAM. Copyright Thales Air Defence

of the system, Blowpipe didn't meet the document as issued! After much revision, the Blowpipe test vehicle did meet Staff Target NGST.3156.

When the Staff Target moved to the requirement stage as NGSR.3156 and Blowpipe became funded by the MoD, the Ministry of Aviation registration number RF.268 was assigned. Initially to be called Dagger by the Army, in line with the trend towards naming missiles after cold steel, the test vehicle name Blowpipe was adopted when it entered service. Blowpipe was developed as a shoulder-launched, man-portable SAM (now called MANPADS – MAN-Portable Air Defence System) for the British Army and used a separate acquisition package that clipped onto the missile launcher, reducing the weight and complexity of the missile itself.

After an initial boost provided by a Blip ejection rocket motor to clear the tube and deploy the fins, a Crake sustainer motor provided the thrust to accelerate the missile to Mach 1.5. Brought into the operator's line of sight automatically, the missile was optically tracked during its flight. Guidance commands from a thumb-operated joystick were transmitted by radio via a datalink transmitter housed in the acquisition package. Aerodynamic control was by twist-and-steer, using the fins on the nose.

Blowpipe was another success story for the UK missile business, with export sales to countries such as Argentina, Canada and Portugal amongst others. It also found its way to the Mujahadin fighting the Soviets in Afghanistan in the 1980s, who apparently preferred to use it against vehicles while keeping their American Stinger missiles for airborne targets!

As with other SAMs, the addition of 'Sea' to the name signified development of a naval version. Shorts studied a version of Blowpipe called Seapipe, which was intended to provide defence against anti-ship missiles. Optical tracking was considered superior for intercepting low-altitude missiles, as radar tracking would suffer from clutter. However, a somewhat more devious naval application for Blowpipe was drawn up…

Maritime patrol aircraft had long been the scourge of the submarine, ever since World

British Secret Projects: Hypersonics, Ramjets & Missiles

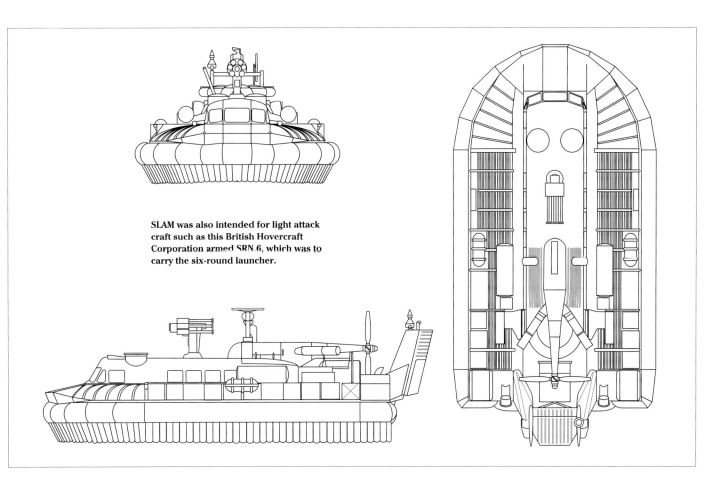

SLAM was also intended for light attack craft such as this British Hovercraft Corporation armed SRN 6, which was to carry the six-round launcher.

War Two when aircraft sank around 36% of U-boats lost to enemy action. By the 1960s improvements to battery technology and the use of nuclear propulsion meant that subs no longer spent long periods on the surface charging their batteries. However, new technologies such as the Magnetic Anomaly Detector, Autolycus diesel exhaust sniffer fitted to Shackletons, and new IR linescan techniques, based on the Yellow Duckling IR wake detector tested from 1953 to 1956, gave aircraft a chance to hunt down submerged submarines. Another threat to submarines was the use of passive and active sonobuoys to pinpoint submerged submarines prior to attack with depth charges or homing torpedoes.

How could a submerged submarine defend itself against such threats? The answer lay in a shadowy 1968 Vickers project called SLAM. The Submarine Launched Air-flight Missile used the Blowpipe in a six-round launcher that was fitted to a retractable mount installed in the conning tower of a submarine. The SLAM system was fitted to the 'A' Class submarine HMS *Aeneas*, was tested successfully

Blowpipe's replacement was Javelin, which used laser guidance instead of radio command.
Copyright Thales Air Defence

The Starstreak HyperVelocity Missile forms the basis of a few air defence systems. The photograph shows Starstreak fitted to an Alvis Stormer armoured fighting vehicle.
Copyright Thales Air Defence

A snapshot of the land-based surface-to-air missiles studied since the early 1950s. Only the last five reached service.

saying 'Here I am!'. Every ASW asset in the area would be on the trail and eager for a kill, probably with a nuclear depth charge or two. Submariners would no doubt be rather sceptical of SLAM, after all they do pride themselves on being elusive.

As well as proposals for fitting to hovercraft as an air defence system, Vickers' literature shows SLAM in use against ships as well as aircraft, so perhaps the Mujahadin weren't the first to suggest using Blowpipe against surface targets.

By the 1980s Blowpipe was becoming a bit long in the tooth and finding the going tough against opposition such as the new generation of portable SAMs like the US Stinger and Soviet SA-14 Gremlin. An upgraded version called Javelin was developed, but this still used the datalink. Since a radio command link could be easily jammed, and still eschewing the use of infra-red, Shorts opted to modify Javelin to use laser guidance. The clip-on guidance package was replaced by a laser system and the result was Starburst,

and was ready for operations by 1972. It was never officially adopted by the Royal Navy, but was fitted to a trio of Vickers-built Gal class submarines of the Israeli Navy and is possibly still in use.

SLAM's lack of success was probably due to Shorts not really understanding the ethos of the 'Silent Service'. Using a weapon with a range of 2 miles (3.2km) to shoot down an anti-submarine type would be tantamount to

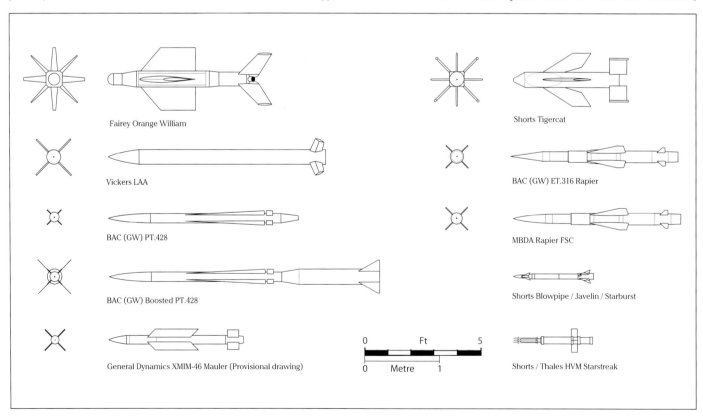

Fairey Orange William

Shorts Tigercat

Vickers LAA

BAC (GW) ET.316 Rapier

BAC (GW) PT.428

MBDA Rapier FSC

BAC (GW) Boosted PT.428

Shorts Blowpipe / Javelin / Starburst

General Dynamics XMIM-46 Mauler (Provisional drawing)

0   Ft   5

0   Metre   1

Shorts / Thales HVM Starstreak

which replaced Blowpipe and Javelin in British forces service.

Changing threats and the use of laser warning systems meant that aircraft, and particularly helicopters, could take evasive action and avoid a hit by Starburst. Shorts' solution was to decrease the flight time of the missile, which meant a missile with hypersonic performance, and the result was Starstreak (also known as the HVM, Hyper-Velocity Missile). Starstreak used three high-density darts that flew towards the target at speeds in excess of Mach 4, before penetrating the airframe and exploding.

Shorts faced stiff competition in the HVM field from a BAC Guided Weapons missile called Thunderbolt. Similar in size and performance to the Shorts weapon, Thunderbolt used a quartet of gas jets to provide control: a technique harking back to the earliest Spaniel and Ben guided anti-aircraft projectiles from the 1940s. Thunderbolt carried no warhead, but used a tungsten penetrator that also allowed it to be used against lightly armoured vehicles.

All of the above missiles can be fitted to a LML (Lightweight Multiple Launcher), a stand carrying three rounds and fitted with an IFF interrogator or the Thorn EMI ADAD (Air Defence Alerting Device). Starstreak/HVM is also in service in an eight-round turret mounted on an Alvis Stormer APC, replacing Tracked Rapier in providing mobile air defence for the Army. A helicopter-launched Air-to-Air Starstreak (ATASK in the US) for the Army Air Corps' Westland Apaches is called Helstreak. Thales recently revealed Thor, an integrated vehicle-mounted launcher and fire control system using Starstreak to perform the force protection role on rapid reaction operations.

Drone Interceptor

One further type of air defence system, hearkening back to the days of Green Water and Rover, was a Hawker Siddeley Dynamics design study from the early 1970s for an unmanned interceptor.

This was a small canard delta-winged aircraft powered by a single Roll-Royce Spey turbofan, fed by a pair of box intakes on either side of a nose housing an air intercept (AI) radar, possibly related to the AWG-12 of the F-4M Phantom. The aircraft was to be fitted with a dorsal pylon for a single HSD Sky Flash semi-active AAM and a pair of AIM-9C Sidewinders or HSD SRAAM IR-guided AAMs mounted on wingtip pylons.

The drone would be launched under command guidance and directed towards the incoming threat. Once in AI radar range the

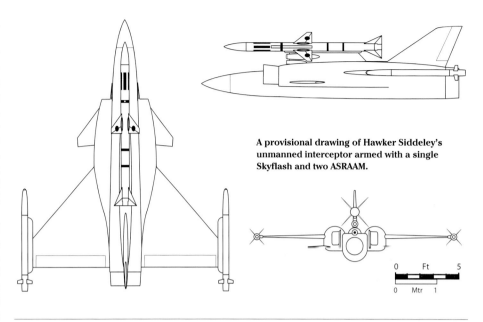

A provisional drawing of Hawker Siddeley's unmanned interceptor armed with a single Skyflash and two ASRAAM.

radar would illuminate the target and launch the Sky Flash. Alternately the target could be illuminated by a TIR on the ground. Further targets could be intercepted using the SRAAMs. Presumably the interceptor was to be fitted with a two-way data link and control system to enable it to be controlled by a pilot on the ground via a TV camera fitted in the dorsal pylon.

This concept was later reprised in the late 1980s as the Unmanned Fighter Aircraft (UFA). Powered by a Rolls-Royce Adour turbofan and carrying a pair of AMRAAM and a pair of ASRAAM, the UFA was launched and recovered from an articulated truck which also housed the guidance system. UFA spawned a large family of what are now called UCAVs, but details remain sketchy.

Conclusion
Surface-to-air missile development in the UK never followed a clear-cut path, all three services had irons in the fire by the war's end, but

from these 'hobby' programmes the aerospace companies felt their way through the 1950s by trial and error to reach maturity in the 1960s. As ever, muddle over the threat, changes in defence policy and financial austerity dictated what eventually came into service. Many of these programmes, such as PT.428, showed the bright promise that accompanied numerous UK aerospace projects; however when it came to practical application this same bright promise was unfulfilled. Watered down for economic reasons, PT.428 sired Rapier, leading to export success for UK industry.

Bloodhound, the child of the 'Fortyniners', soldiered on until the 1990s, despite at least two attempts to replace it with Sea Dart derivatives. But there is an interesting postscript to the Bloodhound story. One Bloodhound derivative, Blue Envoy, probably had the most surprising influence on British aircraft design, because its planform became the basis of Concorde's ogival delta wing.

Surface-to-Air Missiles

Missile	Length ft (m)	Diameter in (cm)	Span ft (m)	Guidance
Brakemine	6.6 (2.0)	10.5 (0.26)	2.75 (0.83)	Beam rider
Seaslug I	19.75 (6)	16.1 (41)	56.6 (1.4)	Beam rider
Bloodhound I	22.1 (6.75)	21.5 (0.55)	9.3 (2.83)	Semi-active radar
Bloodhound II	25.4 (7.75)	21.5 (0.55)	9.9 (2.83)	Semi-active radar
Blue Envoy	26.25 (8)	24 (0.6)	16.4 (5)	Semi-active radar
PT.428	8.2 (2.5)	5 (12.7)		Beam rider
Rapier	7.4 (2.2)	5.25 (13)	1.25 (0.38)	Beam rider
Sea Dart	14 (5.25)	16.5 (42)	3 (0.91)	Semi-active radar
Seawolf	6.25 (1.9)	7.1 (18)	1.9 (0.56)	Beam rider / optical
Sea Cat	58.3 (1.48)	7.5 (19)	2.2 (0.65)	Optical
Thunderbird	20.8 (6.3)	20.75 (0.53)	5.3 (1.6)	Semi-active radar
Blowpipe	4.6 (1.4)	3 (0.07)	0.9 (0.27)	Optical
Starstreak (dart)	1.3 (0.4)	0.9 (0.02)	0.18 (54)	Laser

Chapter Five

Air Defence –
The Ballistic Missile Threat

RAF Flying Shield anti-ballistic missile carriers in the patrol circuit over the North Sea. One of the carriers has just released its missile which, having jettisoned its booster, is about to intercept a Soviet re-entry vehicle. Adrian Mann

The Boeing AL-1, BMD / Son of Star Wars, SDI / Star Wars and Safeguard were all American anti-ballistic missile (ABM) systems investigated during the last thirty years. To continue the family tree analogy, we could also talk about Star Wars' long-lost British great-grand-fathers: Violet Friend and the Airborne Carrier ABM systems.

Britain first discussed defence against the German V-2 weapons (known by the code-name Big Ben) in the late war years. Initially British scientific intelligence had believed that the V-2 carried a radio guidance system that could be jammed, basing this on the remains of a V-2 that had been recovered from Sweden in June 1944. Unfortunately this

had been a test vehicle for the German Wasserfall SAM and as such carried radio guidance equipment. In fact the V-2 was a ballistic missile and fell to Earth without the need for a guidance system other than to keep it stable during launch and give it a nudge in the right direction – to the West.

It may come as a surprise that the earliest ABM weapons were the humble bomb, machine gun and cannon. Radar had shown that the V-2 was travelling at around 3,000mph (4,828km/h) before impact, a speed that made interception impossible, so the primary counter to Big Ben was to attack the launch sites. The first attempt to shoot down a V-2 in flight was made as an example climbed past a USAAF Consolidated B-24 Liberator bomber and one of the waist gunners took a pot shot at it. A more famous attempted interception dates from February 1945 and involved RAF Spitfire XVIs of 602

Squadron on a dive-bombing operation over Holland. F/Lt Raymond Baxter's flight saw a V-2 climb out of the forest. Baxter's Number 3, a Scotsman called 'Cupid' Love, opened fire but, luckily for him and the rest of his flight, he missed.

Defence against 'V2-type' weapons was given a high priority in UK defence planning in the immediate post-war period and it wasn't too long before a plan to deal with this threat was drawn up. However in the late 1940s there wasn't much that could be done about ballistic missiles, so interest in defending against them waned. They could be detected by radar but this provided little practical information apart from an indication of the impact area.

Ballistic Missile Defence Basics
Before examining the weapon systems and project studies, a quick look at the problems posed by ballistic missiles would be helpful.

A Ballistic Missile in flight passes through three phases:
1. Launch and boost
2. Exo-atmospheric flight with re-entry vehicle (RV) separation and decoy / Penetration Aids (Pen-Aids) deployment
3. Re-entry and detonation

Phase 1 interception was impossible in the 1950s, the sensors being too primitive and the launch sites too far away. Interception in Phase 2, with the problem of identifying a specific radar return as an RV amongst the clutter of boosters and shrouds, would need a lot of missiles. The figure of 'thousands' was being bandied about in the research studies. The longer the system had to analyse the incoming targets (which might comprise decoys as well as booster components and the warhead re-entry vehicle) the higher the probability of identifying the re-entry vehicle and intercepting it. The problem had some urgency, as these RVs would be carrying nuclear warheads.

As the assemblage enters the denser atmosphere at the end of Phase 2 the light-weight decoys, such as balloons, slowed down while the heavier RVs decelerated much less. This density sorting allowed improved target discrimination.

In Phase 3, below 200,000ft (60,960m), the fire control system should have a reliable enough track on a confirmed warhead re-entry vehicle to allow a successful interception. The system would have approximately fifteen seconds to intercept the RV before impact/detonation. In practice the RV should be dealt with at heights above 50,000ft (15,240m) in case the warhead was primed for air-burst, but this would not always be possible. Another reason is that the interceptor will have a nuclear warhead and it would be bad form to create collateral damage in the area you claim to be defending. This reduced the effective interception window to eleven seconds.

A successful ground-based Phase 2 interception system required a system with loiter (or, in 1950s parlance, lurk) and side-step capability. In Phase 3 a fast-reacting system with a very fast missile, such as the US Sprint, was required.

The Initial Threat and Response

In the mid-1950s the analysts and planners believed that from 1960 the UK would be under threat of attack by Medium and Intermediate Range Ballistic Missiles (MRBM and IRBM). In fact these were to be the missiles that would trigger the Cuban Missile Crisis, such as the 750 mile (1,200km)-range R-5

(NATO designation SS-3 *Shyster*) launched from Eastern Europe or the 1100 mile (1,700km)-range R-12 (NATO designation SS-4 *Sandal*) launched from the Soviet Union. The UK had weathered attack by ballistic missiles in the late war years when the Wehrmacht had launched its V-2 rockets at London, so the memory of the lack of defensive capability was still fresh in the planners' minds. Given the situation, a research programme was set up to counter such threats and in 1954 the Ministry of Supply placed study contracts with the English Electric Co and Marconi to develop a defence against ballistic missiles. By February 1955 Air Staff Target AST.1135 for defence against ballistic missiles had been drawn up. As the programme grew, the other main players in the SAM business, Bristol Aircraft Ltd and Ferranti Ltd, became involved and the entire programme was given the rainbow codename Violet Friend.

Integrated Defence

The Violet Friend programme (referred to as 'interim' in contemporary accounts) was initiated in early 1957 and was to be integrated with the guided weapons then under development, such as the Stage 1 Surface-to-Air Guided Weapons (Bristol's Bloodhound and English Electric's Thunderbird). It was hoped that this integration would provide a 'simple' defence against all airborne threats from 1963.

To expedite the interim system's entry into service, existing hardware or hardware in the later stages of development was to be used as far as possible. This would also allow the programme to be cancelled at minimal cost if a more complex threat evolved before the system was deployed. The system was required to handle up to six ballistic missile engagements at a time; each missile requiring dedicated tracking radars.

A quartet of radars would be utilised for each engagement: an early warning radar, the AMES Type 85 Blue Yeoman; an AN/FPS-16 boost tracking radar; a second AN/FPS--16 warhead tracker; and finally an AMES Type 83 Yellow River for the Bloodhound. The AN/FPS-16 was a US-built, three-dimensional, missile-tracking radar that would become the mainstay of UK guided weapons trials at Aberporth and Woomera. The AN/FPS-16 was capable of tracking very small high-speed targets and is still in use around the world for this purpose today.

The Blue Yeoman early warning radar would be located in East Anglia, possibly at RAF Watton, and the warhead-tracking AN/FPS-16 radars would be sited in Holland, in the south near Terneuzen and in the north on the island of Terschelling. The rationale

Violet Friend – the concept. Using radars sited in eastern England and The Netherlands, the system would detect, track and destroy incoming Soviet warheads.

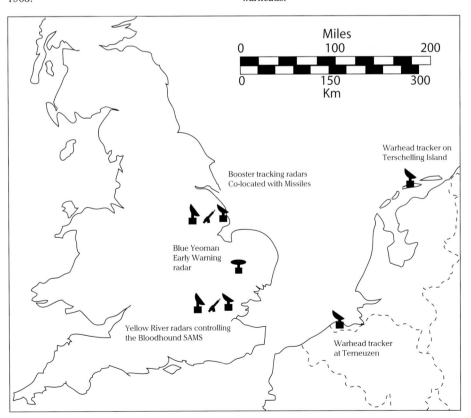

Warhead tracker on Terschelling Island

Booster tracking radars Co-located with Missiles

Blue Yeoman Early Warning radar

Yellow River radars controlling the Bloodhound SAMS

Warhead tracker at Terneuzen

Miles
0   100   200

0   150   300
Km

behind this was that the target's conical-shaped re-entry vehicle had a very small frontal radar cross-section, so it was thought that a radar transmitting from the side as the warhead flew overhead had a better chance of tracking the re-entry vehicle. These locations also allowed improved missile tracking and targeting information for the interception system. Further AN/FPS-16 radar sets would be sited in the interception area in Eastern England to track the boosters. These would be co-located with the missiles at sites such as Coltishall, Felixstowe and Strubby.

Violet Friend in Action

Blue Yeoman would detect the MRBM as it rose above the radar horizon. The booster-tracking AN/FPS-16 would then be directed onto the booster to follow its target. It was assumed that the MRBM's warhead would remain close to the booster until the re-entry process began and, being a bigger radar target, could be used to give clues to the warhead location.

The warhead-tracking AN/FPS-16 would use the booster-tracker information to acquire the warhead and track it until it came within the engagement envelope of the Bloodhound. RV trajectory and speed data

would be fed to the missile guidance computer and the Bloodhound would be launched and guided to its target. The Bloodhound would intercept the RV in the altitude range 30,000 to 40,000ft (9,144 to 12,192m), hopefully before the warhead was armed.

However the Ministry of Supply considered that the development of a UK ABM system would cost as much as the Blue Streak MRBM project (see Chapter Nine): that is, between £160 and 200 million. Consequently, the Violet Friend project was terminated in 1962.

The Bloodhound, which in its Mk.2 Series 3A guise was also known as Bloodhound III, would have been armed with a nuclear warhead, typically the Indigo Hammer lightweight device then in development for such applications. Bloodhound III was developed with Command Guidance and a nuclear warhead and was seen as a better solution to the ABM problem, with the anti-aircraft role being a second string to its bow for use against reconnaissance and stand-off electronic warfare (EW) aircraft.

Bristol developed a dedicated ABM version of Bloodhound under the designation Project 29, with bigger ramjets and modified wings and tail. However Bloodhound III, being a 'simple solution', would not have been up to

the job of defending against ballistic missiles equipped with decoys and what became known as Penetration Aids (Pen-Aids), which required target discrimination. Studies had shown that interception during Phase 3, post discrimination, offered the best odds for interception. This would need a dedicated ABM rather than a modified SAM.

The solution to this Phase 2 / 3 discrimination problem required a high-speed missile. Initially Bristol hoped to use the CTV-5 Series 3 Skylark, but a further Bristol study, Project 36, was for a custom-built ABM based around the RAE's Missile 8 studies. Both of these missiles featured high-speed boost (Mach 10 was quoted) with the ability to lurk and side-step.

There was one rather mundane but important stumbling block that was found during the research into a Phase 2/3 ABM, the missile would be most effective when used with a trainable launcher. Studies had shown that a launcher capable of moving the missile, weighing in the region of 10,000 lb (4,536kg), in azimuth and elevation at high enough rates would consume as much electrical power as a small steel rolling mill!

However by June 1965 all ABM work was suspended, as a result of the Government-commissioned Penley report of 1962. Pre-

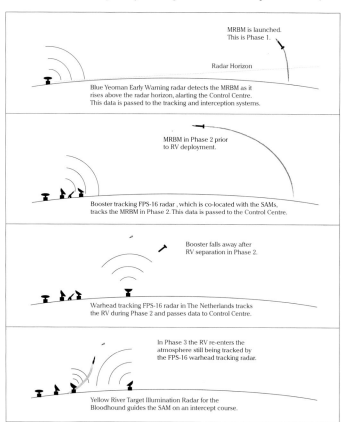

Violet Friend in action. Each stage of the interception, although utilising different sensors at widely spread locations, was handled by a central command centre.

Bloodhound I and II. The Mk.I is the light-coloured example. Both early and late Marks were intended for ABM work, with the Mk.II being upgraded with Command Guidance and a nuclear warhead to become the Mk.III RO.166.

British Secret Projects: Hypersonics, Ramjets & Missiles

pared by Dr W H Penley of the Radar Research Establishment this identified a lack of progress and no prospect of a viable system for ten years. As a result AST.1135 was cancelled and the work reduced to a test vehicle programme, with the XTV.20 as the intended test vehicle.

The Last Kick of the Match

A final look at missile defence was made in the late 1960s when the Land Dart (Sea Dart for the Army) was proposed as a weapon for use against tactical missiles such as the Soviet FROG (Free Rocket Over Ground), but this came to naught. The Americans had tested their Hawk SAM against tactical ballistic missiles such as MGR-1A Honest John. Having been informed of the American success in this, the British considered the Land Dart to be ideal, as it possessed longer range, higher speed and better guidance. The only negative aspect would be the Land Dart's warhead, considered too small to be lethal against a ballistic missile. This may have added further impetus to the development of a nuclear warhead for Sea Dart.

The Flying Shield Concept

Another study, in fact paper exercise is probably more accurate, was carried out in the late 1950s at the RAF Technical College at Henlow. Their approach was to mount the ABM on a flying platform. As has been discussed already missiles were the weapons of choice, but target discrimination is a major problem for any ABM system. Without a clearly identified target, much of the defensive capability would be squandered on destroying decoys, shrouds and spent boosters.

In addition the very fast Mach 10 missiles, as Bristol Aircraft had discovered with its Project 36/Missile 8, posed particularly thorny problems. A loiter capability in a surface-to-air missile isn't particularly feasible, so an ABM-armed aircraft would fit the bill.

By launching an ABM from an aircraft flying at high altitude, the reaction time was reduced by cutting out the climb through the densest portion of the atmosphere. This also allowed more time for warhead discrimination and thereby reduced the number of missiles required to deal with an attack. A force of 250 platforms was deemed sufficient to protect RAF V-Force and USAF Strategic Air Command bases, there being no plans to defend population centres and the so-called 'Vulnerable Areas'. This would require an ABM force deployed at a series of bases around the V-Force main and dispersal fields of eastern England.

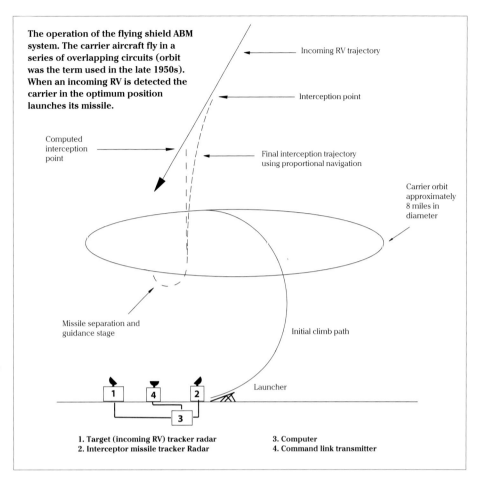

The operation of the flying shield ABM system. The carrier aircraft fly in a series of overlapping circuits (orbit was the term used in the late 1950s). When an incoming RV is detected the carrier in the optimum position launches its missile.

Incoming RV trajectory

Interception point

Computed interception point

Final interception trajectory using proportional navigation

Carrier orbit approximately 8 miles in diameter

Missile separation and guidance stage

Initial climb path

Launcher

1. Target (incoming RV) tracker radar
2. Interceptor missile tracker Radar
3. Computer
4. Command link transmitter

HM Government's war plans hinged on a period of 'escalating tension' with a surprise Soviet attack being unlikely. Consequently this period (two weeks was the best guess) would allow preparation for war so that, if the balloon did go up, the defences would be ready.

These unmanned ABM platforms or carriers would climb to 40,000ft (12,192m) and enter an 8 mile (12.8km)-radius circular holding pattern, or orbit, flying at a speed of 385kt (713km/h). A series of overlapping orbits would provide an umbrella for the V-Force bases and each carrier was to maintain its orbit for forty-five minutes, after which it would be ditched, missile and all, in the North Sea. Wasteful? Indeed, but it was the time of the Trip Wire: any sign of aggression on the part of the Soviet Union would be met by a nuclear response. A nuclear attack on the United Kingdom would be all-out, so an all-out defence was required. To overcome the possibility of a false alarm a disturbing method of verifying the attack was proposed – to allow the first warhead through. Sounds incredibly rash, but when you have one shot at defence, launching on a false alarm could actually leave the country defenceless.

When an incoming RV was identified, the fire control system selected the carrier in the best position for interception and commanded it to launch its missile.

The ground system required three radars (four if you include Ballistic Missile Early Warning System, BMEWS) to control an interception.

1. A warhead tracker radar
2. A carrier guidance set
3. An interceptor guidance / tracker radar

The Flying Hardware

The business end was to be a pilotless aircraft carrying an ABM. Launched from fixed ramps, this aircraft could be held at immediate readiness and a swept, tailless design was considered ideal as a launch platform. While no aircraft company is mentioned by name, the study illustrated in the MoS paper bears the hallmarks of Armstrong Whitworth. AWA was in the forefront of flying wing research in the UK, having flown its AW.52 family of research aircraft.

The missile would be tucked under the rear of the vestigial fuselage but the clever aspect of this design involved the change in centre of gravity (CoG) as the missile was launched. With the missile on board the CoG is close to the wing's centre of lift, but at sep-

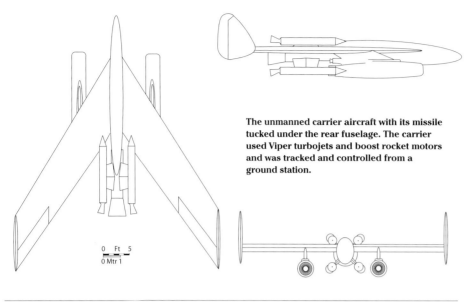

The unmanned carrier aircraft with its missile tucked under the rear fuselage. The carrier used Viper turbojets and boost rocket motors and was tracked and controlled from a ground station.

0 Ft 5
0 Mtr 1

aration the CoG moved forward, causing the carrier to pitch downwards. This was accompanied by the firing of a pair of rocket motors that pushed the carrier away from the manoeuvring missile. The system allowed only 0.3 seconds between missile release and the moment it started the violent flip manoeuvre that would point it towards the incoming target.

The missile carrier was to be powered by a pair of reheated turbojets, with the Bristol Orpheus being suggested. However, to get the combination to take off and to allow it to climb to the 40,000ft (12,192m) orbit altitude in the specified two minutes, rocket boosters were also required. While not in the Lightning class, this would be a respectable rate of climb for an aircraft weighing in at 20,000 lb (9,072kg) without the boosters.

Liquid-fuelled rocket engines were considered as boosters, but the complexity and need for maintenance precluded their use for long-term alerts. The RAF would have enough trouble maintaining the few liquid-fuelled rocket engines on the Blue Steel missiles that entered service in 1961. Pre-packaged types were also considered, but this technology was too immature for the timescale of the project.

One solid rocket motor to be considered was the Saluki. This interesting motor was a 24in (61cm) two-stage boost/sustainer intended for English Electric's Blue Water surface-to-surface missile. The Saluki (or its Phoenix replacement) would have been ideal, providing the high thrust to launch the aircraft from its ramp and cutting back to power the climb. A burn time of eighty seconds was required after which the turbojets would power the combination to its orbit altitude.

The Sharp End

As stated already, the advantage of air-launch is that reaction times are reduced. By being launched at 40,000ft (12,192m) the missile could dispense with the large booster that would normally be required by a ground-launched missile. However, it wasn't a simple reduction in booster size. Launching from an orbiting aircraft required some rapid, and agile, manoeuvring that entailed the application of thrust vector control. The missile would be manoeuvred from its horizontal position under the carrier to the vertical, followed by a turn onto the correct heading for interception. In fact the study outlined a requirement for the missile to turn through 180° (to tackle threats aft of the launcher) in two seconds, this initial 'flip' being powered by four wrap-around rocket motors.

Even after the initial flip the missile had some complex manoeuvres to perform. The main booster would take over for the acceler-

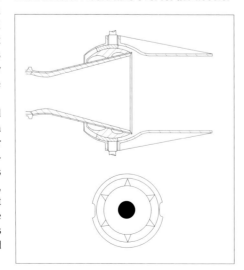

In the absence of aerodynamic control in the early phase, high agility for the ABM was to be provided by a gimballing nozzle on the sustainer motor. This cross-section shows how the nozzle operated.

ation into the intercept climb but the aerodynamic controls would not provide sufficient turning moment at the low post-separation speeds, so a means of using rocket power for directional control was investigated.

The simplest method of directing the thrust of a rocket was to fit vanes in the nozzle, as used by the V-2. However, these could not provide the speed nor the magnitudes of turn required. A better method was to gimbal the rocket combustion chamber and nozzle or place a hydraulically-driven collar around the nozzle. In summary the launch sequence was:

1. Release missile
2. Carrier pitches nose-down and fires rocket motors to push itself away from the missile.
3. Missile manoeuvre motors fire to flip the missile into a vertical attitude.
4. Missile main boosters fire and the guidance system drives thrust-vectoring collar to place missile on correct interception heading.
5. Missile accelerates towards target reaching Mach 6 and detonates its warhead 500yd (457m) ahead of the incoming RV.

Stages 1 to 4 were to take 2.5 seconds.

A nuclear warhead, such as Indigo Hammer, would be fitted to take advantage of what was known as the R1 effect. A re-entry vehicle is, by design, a rather robust piece of kit. Blast and heat might knock the RV about a bit, but the serious damage was to be inflicted by 'R1', a neutron flux designed to disrupt the RV's physics package. Recent research by nuclear weaponry historians suggests that the R1 effect would have been too short-lived to cripple a warhead, so the intention was to envelop the RV in the fireball. Why trigger the warhead 500yd (457m) ahead of the RV? As with SAMs, the main reason for using nuclear warheads on ABMs is that the preferred guidance method is command guidance. This relies on the missile being 'flown' to an interception position via a command link from the ground, which also controls detonation. Since the missile was not homing in on its quarry, a warhead with a greater sphere of lethality is required.

Would it have worked? ...probably as well as any of the project studies carried out in the Cold War. Like many British weapons programmes, this system was way ahead of its time. It would have been complicated and rely on a level of computer and communications technology that would not be available

The hardware of the various Anti-Ballistic Missile studies undertaken since 1950.

for decades. The study ends with the writers describing the post-attack world where the defence has been successful and the unused machines, having ditched in the North Sea, are recovered so the fissile material in their warheads can be used for peaceful purposes in power stations.

As a postscript to the air-launched ABM story, serious consideration was given to a 1997 German Air Staff proposal to use a modified Eurofighter Typhoon (such as the big-winged version proposed for the RAF's SR(A).425 Future Offensive Aircraft requirement) as a launch platform for an ABM version of the Meteor AAM.

Steel Rain

One other approach to the ABM problem harks back to the days of the anti-aircraft gun. A 1960 UK/Canada air defence and ABM system project study called Helmet attempted to simplify missile defence even further. Explosive pellets were to be fired into the path of incoming RVs. As a result an airborne 'helmet' was to be placed across the sky in a belt between 50,000 and 125,000ft (15,240 and 38,100m) altitude to counter an incoming ballistic missile attack. Studies showed that to give a 95% chance of destroying an American Atlas ICBM the system required one hundred guns per mile of front with a calibre of 10in (25.4cm) firing at six rounds per minute! The tonnage of metal falling from the sky from a one-minute barrage could be up to 100 tons (91 tonnes)! No doubt this rain of steel was preferable to an exploding nuclear weapon.

Alerting the Defences

All of the above proposals would have relied on some kind of early warning to initiate the interception process. Prior to 1964, when the US Ballistic Missile Early Warning System (BMEWS) began operations at RAF Fylingdales, the UK research establishments examined a couple of ways to provide early warning of a missile approach.

In 1957 Bernard Lovell had used the radio telescope at Jodrell Bank (later named in his honour) to track the Soviet satellite Sputnik I and the following year it was proposed that the radio telescope be modified to provide early warning under a project called Verify. Lovell, having been involved in radar development at the Telecomunications Research Establishment (TRE) during the war, was enthusiastic but would like the involvement in Verify to be kept under wraps because the radio telescope was a civilian scientific pro-

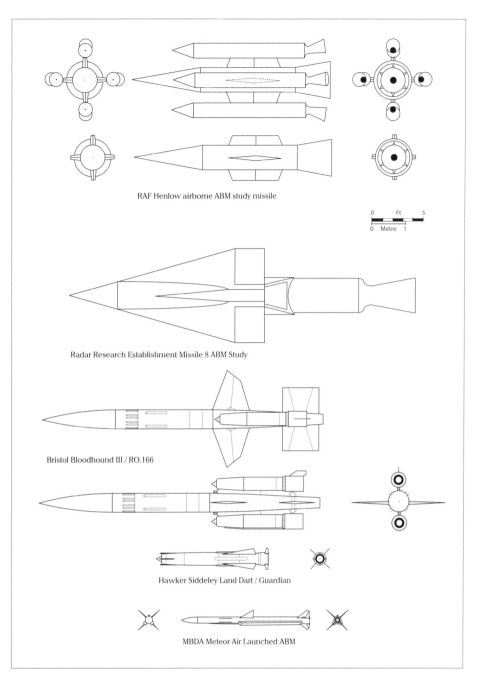

RAF Henlow airborne ABM study missile

Radar Research Establishment Missile 8 ABM Study

Bristol Bloodhound III / RO.166

Hawker Siddeley Land Dart / Guardian

MBDA Meteor Air Launched ABM

ject. Verify involved the addition of an RAF department at Jodrell Bank to collate and analyse the data from the radio telescope.

In addition Verify worked in tandem with an ongoing RAE project called Zinnia that from 1962 collected data on Russian ICBM firings. Zinnia was a high-frequency back-scatter radar whose main purpose was develop methods of detecting missiles and aircraft beyond the radar horizon. Both Zinnia and Verify fell by the wayside as the Ballistic Missile Early Warning System (BMEWS) came into operation.

Thus ended UK's interest in active defence against ballistic missiles. In fact Britain's role would continue as a picket for US systems and

it looks like continuing to be so in the future.

In a summary report on ABM systems in general, Theodore Von Karman, the aerodynamicist and highly respected analyst, summed it all up in a single sentence: 'Whoever solves the ABM puzzle first will have a considerable advantage'.

The British aerospace industry has had a couple of attempts at solving Von Karman's puzzle but, despite some promising starts, the pace of technological development and defence policy overtook them. In due course the UK would rely solely on deterrence through the deployment of the American-designed Polaris submarine-launched ballistic missile system.

Chapter Six

Airborne Anti-Tank Weapons

One lesson learned during World War Two was that armoured fighting vehicles (AFVs) were vulnerable to air attack. The Royal Air Force, Russian Air Force and the Luftwaffe learned this very quickly and equipped their ground-attack aircraft with heavy cannon to attack tanks from above and behind. Next on the scene was the 3in (7.6cm) unguided rocket, used particularly effectively by the RAF's Typhoon fighter-bombers in the last year of the war, the battle of the Falaise Gap being its most famous exploit. The Wehrmacht's armoured divisions feared air attack more than anything, restricting their movements to night-time and bad weather.

The unguided rocket projectile lived on, with the 3in (7.2cm) RP of the 1944 Typhoon replaced by the 68mm SNEB (Société Nouvelle des Etablissements Brandt) rocket on the Hawker Hunter and McDonnell Douglas Phantom of the 1960s. Such rockets are still in use, with the RAF now using the Canadian

CRV.7 for ground-attack work. Anti-tank work needed something different. There were two approaches: the sniper rifle and the shotgun.

Modern anti-tank guided weapons (ATGW) are being equipped with what is called 'top attack'. As with the air-launched weapons of World War Two, these allow a smaller warhead to be used against the thinner armour on the upper surfaces of AFVs. Top attack warheads for ground-launched ATGWs have only really appeared since the 1980s, requiring such ATGWs to carry a heavier punch.

The evolution of the helicopter gunship, particularly in the anti-tank role, saw the General Staff issue GST.3334 in March 1966. This target, for a post-1975 anti-tank missile for helicopters to replace the French SS-11, led to a Swingfire development called Hawkswing (also called Air-Strike Swingfire by BAC). Swingfire, a BAC weapon based on original work by Fairey as Project 12, was a wire-guided heavy ATGW that was normally

Hawker Siddeley P.1239 Versatile SABA aircraft attack a Soviet armoured formation and its helicopter support with Merlin smart mortars, 30mm cannon and HVMs. Adrian Mann

mounted on armoured vehicles and has been very successful in this role.

Proposed for use on the Westland Lynx anti-tank helicopters for the Army Air Corps, Hawkswing would give the Army Air Corps considerable clout. The Lynx could carry up to six rounds and used a roof-mounted sight. Modifications included additional equipment for airborne launch and a newly developed sustainer motor, the Somme, giving longer range. However, after an evaluation of Hawkswing, the US TOW and Franco-German HOT weapons, the TOW was selected for the Lynx. This was later developed in the UK as FITOW, with improved top-attack capability. The main problem with Hawkswing was its slow launch speed that made the missile susceptible to deflection by the helicopter's rotor downwash.

There are two methods by which an aircraft can destroy tanks. The first is by direct attack with a guided weapon (the sniper rifle). Until recently, this was the domain of the dedicated anti-tank helicopter or ground-attack aircraft. The alternative shotgun approach was exemplified by the cluster bomb.

Armoured formations are easiest to tackle before they begin their movement across the battlefield. Attacks on choke points, such as the Fulda Gap in Germany, or forming-up areas in the rear were the targets of choice for the nuclear-armed tactical ballistic missiles of the 'tripwire' days of the 1950s. This changed with the adoption of Flexible Response whereby, rather than immediate nuclear retaliation, a Soviet attack was to be met by conventional warfare in the first phase but there was always the chance of fighting 'escalating' to a nuclear exchange. As a result of this doctrinal change in 1967, it became the job of the fast strike aircraft to attack such Soviet formations. Their weapon of choice was the cluster bomb, such as the Hunting Engineering BL.755 that was procured to replace the SNEB rocket.

Everything went well with the cluster bomb until it was actually used in combat in the face of heavy air defences. The BL.755 had to be delivered at fairly low level to maintain an effective concentration of the 147 bomblets as they were released. This proved to be a problem when heavy losses of Panavia Tornado strike aircraft in the 1991 Gulf War prompted a change to medium altitudes to fly above the effective ceiling of Iraqi anti-aircraft artillery (AAA) fire. Delivery from medium altitudes spread the bomblets around the target area causing a lot of collateral damage, which

included dead civilians. A major row erupted over this, compounded by the fact that any unexploded bomblets acted as anti-personnel mines.

At this point you may be wondering why a cluster bomb, that most indiscriminate of weapons, is in a book on guided weapons. The solution to all this was to fit the BL.755 with a radar altimeter / proximity fuse to ensure that the bomblet dispenser did not open until the most effective altitude was reached, thus concentrating the bomblets to greatest effect. This was now called the RBL.755.

The other reason for the heavy losses in 1991 was that the aircraft had to overfly the target and was thus vulnerable to ground fire. Some stand-off capability was needed, requiring a guided weapon, which is why BL.755 is pertinent to this story.

Back in 1966 Hawker Siddeley Dynamics had proposed the Cluster Martel. This mated the AJ.168 TV Martel airframe (see Chapter Seven) with many of the components of Hunting's BL.755. To allow ejection of the bomblets at the appropriate altitude, the radar fuse from the WE.177 nuclear bomb was to be used. However, the Air Staff considered this a complete waste of time and effort for what was basically a powered cluster bomb and so BL.755 entered service as a free-fall bomb.

The Sniper Rifle Approach

Using cluster bombs against armoured formations was perfectly acceptable, but what about single tanks or formations too close to friendly troops to allow cluster bombs to be employed? The Air Staff duly formulated a Staff Target, AST.1227, to replace the BL.755 with a guided weapon.

In the late 1970s HSD and BAC proposed modifications of existing designs to AST.1227. HSD modified the SRAAM air-to-air missile (see Chapter Three) for ground attack, but IR guidance was deemed unsuitable for air-to-ground use due to possible countermeasures. BAC GW offered an air-launched laser-guided version of the Rapier called Sabre. This added a Martin Marietta laser seeker from the US Copperhead or the Swedish RB.83 ASM (UK / Swedish co-operation was not only on AAMs) plus an armour-piercing warhead to the Rapier airframe. Sabre used ground designators or the strike aircraft's Ferranti LRMTS (Laser Ranger and Marked Target Seeker) for targeting. On the nationalisation of the aerospace companies to form British Aerospace in 1977, Sabre was selected for development. With an 80% hit rate and up to ten rounds on an aircraft, such as the Harrier/Jaguar replacement to meet AST.403, Sabre was considered superior to cluster weapons. Also considered for use on the Lynx helicopter in lieu of Hawkswing, and as an anti-gunship weapon, Sabre looked like a very capable weapon. Alas, like many promising British weapons, technology had overtaken it by dispensing with the laser.

One interesting application for Sabre could have been the Wide Speed Range Aircraft. This 1960s Ministry of Technology project laid out a need for an aircraft with higher performance than a helicopter but retaining its agility and VTOL capability. Westland and Hawker Siddeley investigated WSRA, with an eye to a mid-1970s service entry, but the entire programme became a victim of cost cutting.

The hunt for a smart cluster bomb continued and Hunting Engineering came up with

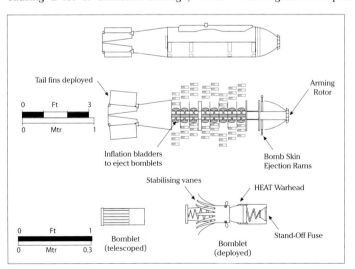

The Hunting BL.755 cluster bomb carries its anti-tank sub-munitions in a series of bays within the bomb body. On being released, the bomb skins fall away and gas pressure inflates a series of bladders to eject the spring-loaded bomblets, which extend to deploy stabilising vanes and a stand-off fuse.

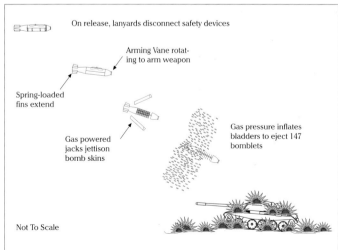

The HEAT warhead is effective against armoured and soft-skin vehicles, with pattern dispersion proportional to the weapon's release altitude. The RBL.755 adds a radar altimeter to delay bomblet release and reduce dispersion.

Hawkswing, also known as Air Strike Swingfire, is seen here mounted on Westland Lynx XW839 in September 1974. Hawkswing was found to be too slow and with insufficient range for helicopter use. Avia Press via Elfan Ap Rees

MBDA Brimstone. Often accused of being a Hellfire copy, Brimstone shares only its configuration with the American weapon. The innards are entirely different and Brimstone is intended for launch from high-speed attack aircraft.

the VJ.291, a guided anti-armour cluster bomb. Targeting information was provided by the aircraft navigation system allowing stand-off attacks on targets offset from the aircraft track. VJ.291 had folding cruciform wings at the rear coupled with nose-mounted cruciform canards. It dispensed dual-purpose submunitions, each with a sensor that detonated them on impact with a vehicle. If a submunition landed on the ground it functioned as a 'minelet'.

With an eye on developments in the USA, the Air Staff was well aware that what was required for the 1980s was a smart weapon, and so AST.1227 was cancelled in 1981. By this time Millimetre Wave (MMW) radar had been developed, providing higher resolution for target identification to allow more accurate targeting. This was the way ahead and, after considerable deliberation, the Air Staff issued AST.1238 in 1981, which later was to become SR(A).1238, for an air-launched anti-armour weapon.

Hellfire and Brimstone

The Gulf War of 1991 emphasised the need for a stand-off anti-armour weapon, and so this was placed at the top of the requirements list. The RAF's low-level doctrine had been found wanting, mainly due to being too specialised in the deep strike / counter-air role rather than anti-tank and a re-visit to AST.1227 was required.

The RBL.755 was an interim solution, but a dedicated weapon was still called for. The weapons companies leapt at the chance to

develop their ideas and a major competition commenced, with five main bids.

The Thomson Thorn TAAWS (Thorn Anti-Armour Weapons System) was another variation on the BL.755 theme, based on BL.755 but with each bomblet having a rocket motor. TAAWS received scant attention from the Air Staff and was dismissed as yet another cluster weapon. (This type of weapon was now becoming somewhat 'politically incorrect'.) Hunting Engineering came up with a new approach with SWAARM (Smart Weapon Anti-ARMour weapon), based on the German Daimler Benz Aerospace Mehrzweckwaffe-2 that also formed the basis of the DWS-39 dispenser for the Swedish Air Force's new SAAB Gripen fighter. SWAARM resembled a small, unpowered cruise missile with a pivoting wing on the fuselage underside. When the nose-mounted IR sensor detected a target, a MMW radar-equipped SADARM (Sense and Destroy ARMour) submunition was dispensed to engage it. A similar design from Texas Instruments called Griffin-38 also failed to meet the requirement, almost certainly due to its lack of range and speed, principally because it was unpowered.

That left two bidders, both proposing missile variants to meet the requirement. BAe Dynamics hoped to win the competition with a weapon called Typhoon. Not to be confused with the Eurofighter, the Typhoon guided weapon was based on the ASRAAM air-to-air missile, but fitted with the warhead from the Euromissile Trigat.

The winner was the GEC-Marconi bid; the AAAW (Advanced Anti-Armour Weapon) that utilised a Hellfire missile-style airframe with a UK developed 94GHz MMW radar seeker and motor. This AAAW, renamed Brimstone and offering an autonomous, all-weather, day/night capability, represented a quantum leap in the RAF's armoury.

Currently being developed and built by MBDA, Brimstone has been accused of being a copy of the US Hellfire, but apart from the basic configuration, it is in fact a new design. Brimstone is intended for launch from all levels and at all speeds, particularly by high-speed aircraft. A strike aircraft can launch its entire warload of Brimstones into a target area and each missile will select individual targets and destroy them.

Capable of launch from fast jets, helicopters, vehicles and fixed ground installations, Brimstone brings a new lethality to any vehicle capable of carrying it. While not discussed specifically, Brimstone would no doubt be an ideal weapon for the future Unmanned Combat Air Vehicles (UCAV).

Minicas and SABA

One other anti-tank system, and its proposed use, requires discussion, Merlin. Starting off as a BAe Dynamics private venture anti-tank mortar bomb with MMW radar terminal guidance, its development began in 1981 under the name MORAT (MORtar, Anti-Tank). The round was fired from a standard 81mm mortar and as it reached its apogee the MMW seeker was switched on and began to scan the area below the weapon. The seeker would identify moving targets amongst the ground clutter but if no moving targets were detected, static targets would be identified instead and then the seeker would guide the Merlin to impact. Merlin allowed infantry to have a beyond-visual-range, indirect fire method of dealing with armoured formations.

Anti-Tank Weapons

Missile	Length ft (m)	Diameter in (cm)	Span ft (m)	Guidance
Swingfire / Hawkswing	3.5 (1.1)	6.7 (17)	15.3 (39)	Wire / command
Sabre	7.7 (2.3)	5.25 (13.3)	15 (38)	Laser
Merlin	2.9 (0.9)	3.2 (8.1)	–	MMW radar
Brimstone	5.9 (1.8)	7 (18)	13 (33)	MMW radar

Control is by four fins on the nose that are deployed at the same time as the seeker is switched on, orienting the round into its search attitude. Initial flight is stabilised by six folding tailfins that flip out as soon as the round exits the mortar tube.

This concept generated sufficient interest from the MoD to have them draw up GST.3954 in 1983 and even provide funds. However, the MoD withdrew funding to return Merlin to a private venture status.

Merlin had yet another, rather devious application that could turn a basic ground-attack aircraft into a smart tank-killing machine.

In the late 1970s Hawker Siddeley Aviation at Kingston was working on design studies for a small, lightweight ground-attack aircraft to meet a 1970 specification (AST.396) that was called Minicas (Mini Close Air Support). As ever, the Staff Target had but one simple objective – knocking out Soviet armour as it charged across the North German Plain. By the 1970s the use of nuclear weapons was the last option, conventional means were preferred. Smart weapons were in their infancy so rockets, guns and cluster bombs were the weapons of choice, to be delivered by swarms of small Minicas aircraft.

The Minicas design studies produced a variety of configurations for small single-seater types with dorsal-mounted engines, usually the Rolls-Royce RB.199 turbofan or the Viper turbojet. One of these, the HS.1194, sported a canard and a variable incidence 'Kasper Wing' (that allowed slow speed by producing strong lift-generating vortices) with endplate fins and a rotary augmenter for the RB.199 turbofan. These subsonic (typically Mach 0.75) aircraft had an all-up-weight around 10,000 lb (4,536kg) of which around 700 lb (317.5kg) was weapon load.

One rather handsome shoulder-winged design (handsome for a role not normally associated with good looks) was the HS.1196. This sported the typically Hawker curved tips to the wing and tail surfaces that were mated to a beaver-tailed fuselage carrying a Rolls-Royce Viper turbojet which, to protect it from ground fire, was housed in a dorsal pod. Apart from a ventral 30mm ADEN cannon, rockets and cluster bombs, the HS.1196 could carry four QC.434/SRAAM missiles for use against helicopters and enemy ground-attack aircraft.

Minicas fell by the wayside, as such ideas do; only to be re-invented in 1987 in another guise as the Small Agile Battlefield Aircraft (SABA). Hawker Siddeley Aviation was convinced that highly manoeuvrable lightweight aircraft were ideal to give ground support for troops, especially if they had some STOL capability. The Harrier had shown how such

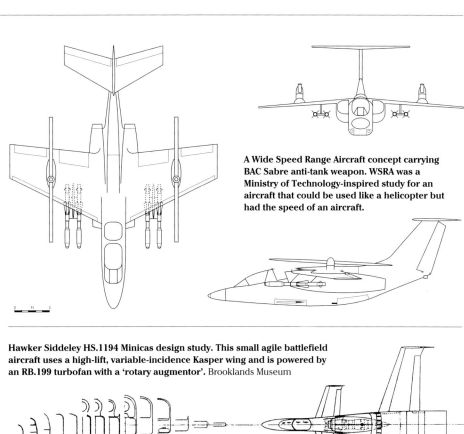

A Wide Speed Range Aircraft concept carrying BAC Sabre anti-tank weapon. WSRA was a Ministry of Technology-inspired study for an aircraft that could be used like a helicopter but had the speed of an aircraft.

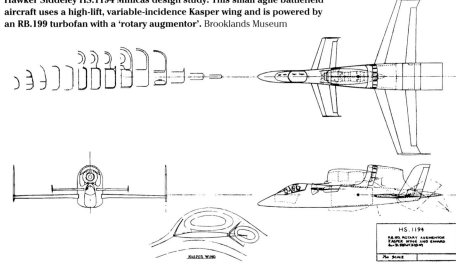

Hawker Siddeley HS.1194 Minicas design study. This small agile battlefield aircraft uses a high-lift, variable-incidence Kasper wing and is powered by an RB.199 turbofan with a 'rotary augmentor'. Brooklands Museum

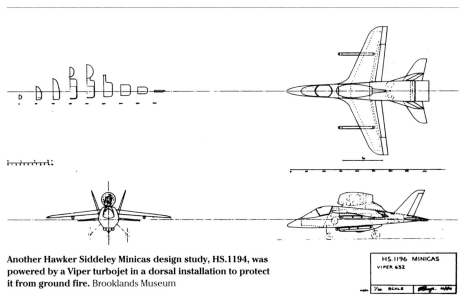

Another Hawker Siddeley Minicas design study, HS.1194, was powered by a Viper turbojet in a dorsal installation to protect it from ground fire. Brooklands Museum

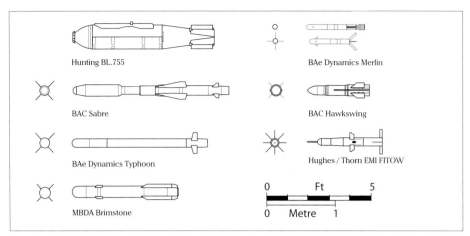

Hunting BL.755

BAe Dynamics Merlin

BAC Sabre

BAC Hawkswing

BAe Dynamics Typhoon

Hughes / Thorn EMI FITOW

MBDA Brimstone

0   Ft   5

0   Metre   1

a type could perform, deployed close to the Forward Edge of the Battlefield Area (FEBA in the jargon of the era).

Hunting Engineering's VJ.291 anti-armour cluster bomb had used a guided dispenser to fly over the FEBA, but HSA put the VJ.291 submunition to use in one of its SABA studies. The HS.1239, 'Versatile SABA' was a squat, shoulder-winged aircraft whose weapons were carried in a removable dorsal module. Amongst the weapon fits, which could include a turret with an Oerlikon KCA 30mm cannon, was a dispenser for the VJ.291 or HB.872 minelets and a magazine holding fourteen Shorts

Hypervelocity Missiles, later known as Starstreak or its BAe competitor, Thunderbolt.

The HS.1239's modular payload system allowed a wide variety of roles. One intriguing application was battlefield surveillance, with a radar system and 8ft 4in (2.54m) diameter rotodome fitted. This was intended to be a successor to the CASTOR system then under development for the Army. Given that the HS.1239 was a single seater, some means of datalinking the radar picture to a ground station must have been intended.

Of most interest and relevance to this chapter was the intention to fit the HS.1239 with a

module carrying 72 tubes firing modified Merlin guided mortar bombs. One of the modifications was no doubt a rocket booster, due to the heavy recoil associated with a mortar and its effect on the airframe. The HS.1239 was most definitely a very nasty piece of work, capable of wreaking havoc on Soviet armour formations as they poured through the Fulda Gap but, like most design studies, it elicited little official interest.

Conclusion

The destruction of tanks from the air by fixed wing aircraft was, literally, a hit and miss affair. Only in the 1980s with the development of millimetre wave radar seekers did it become possible to destroy a tank with a single round. Helicopters suffered from the need to remain in a vulnerable position while the weapon was guided to its target, a factor in the acquisition of FITOW rather than Hawkswing. Laser guidance for types such as Sabre helped, but required a designator on the ground or in the air. In the heat of a battle some degree of stand-off for an autonomous weapon is required and a missile such as Brimstone meets this need. Aircraft weapons for use against tanks have come a long way from the 3in rocket.

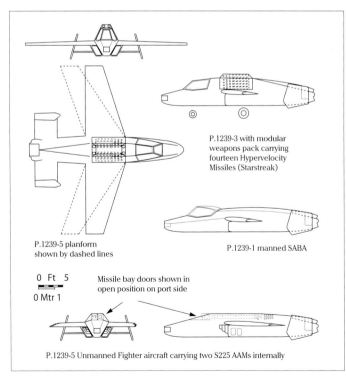

P.1239-3 with modular weapons pack carrying fourteen Hypervelocity Missiles (Starstreak)

P.1239-5 planform shown by dashed lines

P.1239-1 manned SABA

0 Ft 5
0 Mtr 1

Missile bay doors shown in open position on port side

P.1239-5 Unmanned Fighter aircraft carrying two S225 AAMs internally

SABA – Small Agile Battlefield Aircraft – in this instance the Hawker Siddeley P.1239 with modular weapons system. An unmanned version carrying S225X AAMs was also considered.

The various SABA weapons modules including Castor (Corps Airborne Stand Off Radar) that was to provided a 'God's Eye View' of the battlefield.

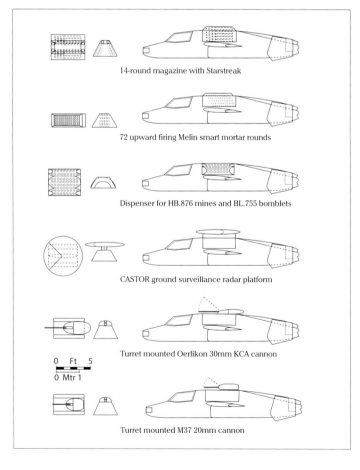

14-round magazine with Starstreak

72 upward firing Melin smart mortar rounds

Dispenser for HB.876 mines and BL.755 bomblets

CASTOR ground surveillance radar platform

Turret mounted Oerlikon 30mm KCA cannon

0 Ft 5
0 Mtr 1

Turret mounted M37 20mm cannon

Chapter Seven

Air-to-Surface Guided Weapons

Guided weapons development in the UK can be traced back to the first test vehicles under development at the end of World War Two and in the immediate postwar era. While many of these test vehicles attempted to establish the flight rules and control techniques for guided weapons others, particularly for surface-to-air guided weapons (SAGWs), were aimed at a specific goal – a functioning weapon.

One weapon type that appears to have benefited indirectly from this work was the air-to-surface Weapon, and particularly the anti-ship missile. Traditionally 'Torpedoes let in water, Bombs let in air', but by the end of the War rocket weapons, both guided and unguided, had entered the fray. The post-war development history of such weapons has been largely ignored yet the research into SAGWs over the years has been looked at in depth; but how did UK forces come to field such world-beating weapons as ALARM, Sea Eagle and Sea Skua?

Air-to-surface weapons can be split into three distinct classes:
- Anti-ship weapons – ranging from an unguided rocket to a sophisticated guided missile.
- Short-range air-to-ground weapons – from cluster bombs for use against troop and vehicle formations to anti-radiation missiles for air defence suppression.
- Stand-off weapons – usually for strategic use with nuclear warheads.

The initial emphasis was towards anti-ship weapons for use against the surface units of the Soviet Navy. During the Second World War, because it was mainly restricted to coastal submarine operations, the Soviet Navy had played but a minor part in the conflict. However these operations were very successful in disrupting German supply routes to the Eastern Front, particularly to East Prussia. Their most widely known action was the January 1945 sinking of the *Wilhelm Gustloff*, a cruise liner being used to evacuate

A Bristol Type 175 maritime patrol aircraft launches a variant of the Fairey Sea-Skimmer anti-ship weapon at a Soviet battle group in the North Atlantic. Adrian Mann

refugees in the Baltic Sea. This saw the greatest loss of life in any single maritime incident.

The Cold War saw the Soviets move on to build a new 'Blue Water' navy designed to counter the UK and particularly the US carrier task forces that had the run of the world's oceans. This navy grew apace in both numbers and technology, with a large submarine fleet posing a threat to the convoys that would supply and reinforce the European theatre should the Cold War turn hot.

Historically the Royal Navy was tasked with maintaining the trade routes to Britain and in the 1950s the new generation of Soviet warships posed a threat to that trade (albeit military traffic more than commercial) therefore the Navy would need a new generation of anti-ship weapons to allow it to continue its trade protection role.

Anti-Ship Weapons in 1945

The Royal Air Force (RAF) and Fleet Air Arm (FAA) ended the Second World War with five means of attacking enemy warships:

Bombs – the gamut of free-fall bombs from the 250 lb (113.4kg) general-purpose bomb to the 12,000 lb (5,443kg) Tallboy as used against the German battleship *Tirpitz*. Generally the 1,000 lb (453kg) medium capacity bomb was the weapon of choice, mainly due to its availability, but 2,000 lb (907kg) armour-piercing bombs were also in use.

Torpedoes – principally the 18in (45.7cm) diameter air-dropped torpedo. These were going out of fashion in the late 1940s, due to the vulnerability of the inbound aircraft carrying it to air defences. However the torpedo continued to be used in anti-submarine warfare.

Guns – depending on the target, every calibre was employed, from the .303 machine gun to the 57mm (6-pounder) Molins gun on the Tsetse variant of the de Havilland Mosquito (much favoured for attacks on U-boats). Like the air-dropped torpedo, guns fell from favour as the attacker had to get in close to engage its target.

Rocket projectiles – the 3in (7.62cm) 60 lb (27kg) RP-3 (Rocket Projectile) was a favourite with Coastal Command Bristol Beaufighters and Consolidated Liberators. Aimed to impact just short of the target's hull, these were used with great effect against small ships, particularly flak-ships and submarines.

Unorthodox – These could be lumped in with bombs and included Highball and Johnny Walker. Highball was a spherical weapon based on the principle of the Upkeep bouncing bomb used in Operation Chastise in May 1943 to breach German dams. The only Highball unit, No.618 Squadron, was working up on Mosquitoes to move to the Far East theatre at the war's end. Application of Highball to the de Havilland Hornet piston fighter was in hand after the war, possibly for the Sea Hornet variant. Johnny Walker was even more unusual, being a 6ft (1.82m) cylinder containing 100 lb (45.4kg) of Torpex explosive and a hydrogen tank. Described as a 'hopping mine', it worked by using a buoyancy chamber that was flooded and blown repeatedly by the hydrogen held under pressure in the tank. This caused the weapon to rise in the water column, drift, and then sink until such time as it struck a solid object and exploded. Used (not particularly successfully) against the *Tirpitz*, it was unpopular with aircrew because of its hydrogen tank. The standing order was to jettison Johnnie Walker as soon as its carrier aircraft came under attack.

Unguided Rocket Projectiles

Due to the nature of the weapon, torpedo-carrying aircraft were required to fly straight and level, at low altitude, well into the gun-defended zone around the target. This was generally acknowledged to be 3,000yd (2,740m) for radar-directed AA guns at the war's end. Rocket projectiles allowed the launch aircraft to take some evasive action on a faster run-in to the target. The 3in (7.6cm) RP was deemed fine for use against 'soft' tar-

gets such as submarines and destroyers, but a more heavily armed and armoured cruiser or battleship required something with a bit more clout…

Uncle Tom

Not dissimilar to the US Tiny Tim, Uncle Tom, designed to meet Air Staff Operational Requirement OR.1009, was an 11½in (29.8cm) diameter, 9ft (2.74m) long rocket projectile, powered by a sextet of 3in (7.6cm) rocket motors. It may have been a larger development of a rocket projectile based on the 7.2in (18.3cm) howitzer shell powered by three rocket motors and tested on some Supermarine Seafangs, the final piston-powered successor to the Spitfire. Uncle Tom was intended for the anti-ship/anti-submarine role on aircraft such as the Mosquito, or later, the Blackburn Firebrand. Trials were conducted at A&AEE Boscombe Down using an American Grumman Avenger and a Mosquito. The most obvious feature of Uncle Tom was its four large fins, which were essential to give directional stability

In 1941 it had been discovered (quite by accident) that by aiming short and having the rocket enter the water at a shallow angle, the weapon would arc upwards in the water and strike the target below the waterline. A further benefit of this phenomenon was that this provided a much larger 'virtual target' to aim at and these underwater ballistic effects would re-appear in the development of later weapons. The prime reason for underwater hits, as has been pointed out in the past by historian John Keegan, was that water transfers shock more effectively than air, an effect that helped 617 Squadron breach the Ruhr dams in 1943.

Uncle Tom unguided rocket during trials on a Mosquito. TNA DSIR 23/17581

The Virtual Target – the underwater dynamics of a rocket allowed a greater margin for error in launch.

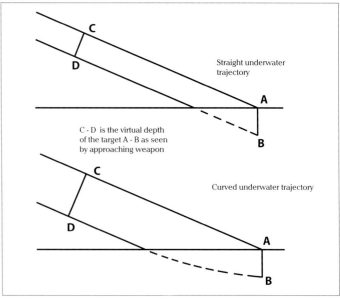

Straight underwater trajectory

C - D is the virtual depth of the target A - B as seen by approaching weapon

Curved underwater trajectory

Red Angel

An indirect development of Uncle Tom, Red Angel replaced the former's large fins with six flip-out fins and also had more powerful rocket motors. These would provide the higher velocity required for Red Angel's main role – that of piercing the armour of large surface vessels. A close look at a photograph of Red Angel reveals a nose not unlike that of an engineer's centre-punch, capable of punching its way through the deck armour of Soviet cruisers such as the 1950s Sverdlov Class. Red Angel could be used for 'dry hits' on the decks and superstructure, or for 'wet hits' under the waterline armour belt using the technique described above. Five or six such hits were considered ample to cripple a cruiser.

Red Angel was to arm the latest strike aircraft of the Fleet Air Arm, such as the Westland Wyvern, and was tested on this aircraft at Lake Alwen in 1954. Red Angel was a brute: 10ft 9in (3.28m) long, a diameter of 11¼in (28.58cm) and weighing in at 1,055 lb (478kg), 88 lb (40kg) of which was explosive. Delays to the project included stability problems, when the fins deployed 'sluggishly' at low temperatures, and rocket motor misfires. There was also some debate on whether the rocket exhaust would burn the aircraft's dive brakes or flaps and whether these would need to be deployed for launch in the first place.

Top left: **Red Angel on a Westland Wyvern S.4 during firing trials at Lake Alwen.** Fred Ballam, Agusta Westland

Top right: **Side view of Red Angel showing its armour-piercing warhead, rocket nozzles and flip-out fins.** Fred Ballam, Agusta Westland

Bottom: **Uncle Tom and Red Angel showing how much had changed in such short a time at the end of the war. Delays to Red Angel were primarily due to the flip-out fins sticking at low temperatures.**

All this meant that the development of guided weapons overtook Red Angel. The number of Royal Navy carriers was being reduced and so many naval flotillas would lack air support. To take on the Soviet Navy such flotillas would need to carry a weapon that could outrange the 6in (152mm) guns of the Sverdlov class cruisers. Only a ship-launched missile could fill that role in the absence of aircraft. The solution was to be Blue Slug, an anti-ship version of the Seaslug surface-to-air missile fitted with Red Angel's armour-piercing warhead.

A guided development of Red Angel to meet OR.1057 may have been called Nozzle, but Red Angel's main problem was its short range of 5,000yd (4,572m), which would bring the launch aircraft well within the range of a target warship's air defences.

Guided Weapons

By 1943 Allied forces had come under attack by German guided weapons such as the visual command guided Fritz-X and Hs 293. Having seen their effect on capital ships and how difficult they were to counter (the Italian battleship *Roma* was sunk and the British HMS *Warspite* damaged enough to put her out of action), the Admiralty and Air Staff were impressed. Of course, they had to have one of their own. The following year the Japanese unleashed the Kamikaze. In the light of this, the Admiralty began looking for similar weapons (not, of course, the Kamikaze!) and began development studies for guided weapons, initially anti-aircraft weapons as related in an earlier chapter, but thoughts soon turned to anti-ship weapons. The main driver was to keep the attacking

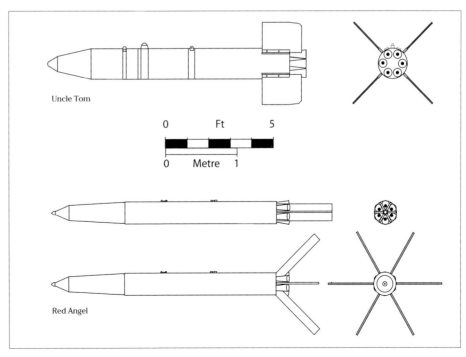

Uncle Tom

0   Ft   5

0   Metre   1

Red Angel

aircraft out of range of the target's gun defences while delivering enough ordnance to disable, if not sink, the target. In fact at an Admiralty meeting in May 1954 the Director (Gunnery Division), Commander Johnstone, highlighted the need for guided weapons as the existing bombs and unguided rockets: '...were suicidal in delivery against modern AA gunnery'.

The RAE had studied a glide bomb with a 250 lb (113kg) warhead as far back as 1918, but the end of the Great War saw that project put on ice. It was dusted off in the mid-1930s, as the basis of a winged torpedo called the Toraplane. After some tests with Beauforts and Swordfish, the project was terminated.

The initial post-war studies included what became known as the Z-series, which were almost certainly based on the same principle as the German L10 Friedensengel winged torpedo. This diverse family included the Zeta, Zonal and Zoster rocket-boosted winged torpedoes and would have flown at 500kts (925km/h) before diving into the sea just outside the defended area to home in at 60kt (111km/h) as a high-speed torpedo. Zoster was an air-launched version of Zonal while, to meet OR.1058, Zeta evolved into Pentane: the Vickers/Whitehead Mk.21 air-dropped 21in (53.3cm) torpedo. A further variation on this theme was Bootleg, designed to meet OR.1060; a rocket-powered torpedo that was to be tossed into the target area by Bristol Brigand piston-engined bombers fitted with a specially designed sight to meet OR.1015. However, the Admiralty wanted a weapon for use against land targets as well, so it gave up on Bootleg and converted this to an air-launched homing torpedo, BA-920, and the land attack version was quietly dropped.

Given the difficulties in achieving such performance goals, the Z-series was cancelled as being far too ambitious, after a lot of time and effort, not to mention money, had been spent on what were unrealistic goals. Such abortive attempts at quantum leaps in technology are a recurring theme in the story of UK guided weapons. Another factor was the possibility that an anti-torpedo weapon had been developed by the Soviets.

Journey's End and Blue Boar
In the last year of World War Two the weapon of choice for use against capital ships, after its employment against the *Tirpitz*, was the 12,000 lb (5,443kg) Tallboy bomb. The problem was that to be effective against such a vessel a bomb, even as large as this one, needed a direct hit. At the end of the war Barnes Wallis at Vickers (the designer of Tallboy) was working on the Line Controlled Tall-boy, a version that used radio command guidance while the bomb was modified with enlarged tail fins plus vertical fins on the nose. These were fitted with spoilers that could be flicked out to control the bomb in azimuth; hence the name as the line the bomb followed could be controlled. Unfortunately these control surfaces only provided 50% of the azimuth change required.

The Luftwaffe's guided weapons had included television guidance where a camera in the bomb transmitted an image of the target to the launch aircraft, which allowed it to be guided via radio command. The first British foray into this technology came from the Admiralty but was superseded by a weapon suggested by Lord Cherwell, Churchill's scientific advisor, and Brigadier Jeffries of the General Staff. This Cherwell/Jeffries anti-ship bomb was intended for use against the Japanese, but with the end of the war it assumed the name Journey's End. This TV guided bomb used a circular scanning TV system with final control coming from a single-shot 'bonker' rocket motor rather than the spoilers of the Line Controlled Tallboy. Of limited capability, Journey's End was declared obsolete in 1947. However it laid the foundations for the next generation of TV-guided glide bomb, Blue Boar.

Blue Boar
Blue Boar was worked up by Vickers against the 1947 requirement OR.1059, which covered the control of heavy bombs. Initially intended as an anti-ship weapon, its size governed the types that could carry it and so it became a weapon for the Valiant strategic bomber.

Originally called Project G, Blue Boar was derived from the Journey's End studies but differed by having flip-out wings spanning 62in (1.57m) that carried the aerodynamic controls. The standard Blue Boar was 17ft 6in (5.3m) long with a diameter of 32in (81.3cm) and weighed in at 5,000 lb (2,270kg).

Many Blue Boar components came from other projects such as the control system from the RTV.1. It employed a 40° glide angle which allowed the bomber a degree of stand-off, 25miles (46km), that was probably just enough to ensure a target defended by heavy AA or early SAGWs would not need to be overflown.

The OR.1089 TV guidance system used a television scanner with a field of view of 27.5°. The test programme included trial drops over the Aberporth range of a 1/3-scale model called BTV.1. BTV.3 to 6 were used to develop the control systems and TV equipment while other, full-scale, control system test vehicles included the BTV.10 with fixed wings and BTV.11 with flip-out wings.

A proposal to guide Blue Boar by radar using the NBC/H2S bombing system (Navigation and Bombing Computer with H2S ground mapping radar) to interrogate a transponder in the weapon was dismissed, there being no perceived gain in accuracy over conventional bombing with NBC/H2S. This, combined with the extra equipment required, meant that this proposal went no further than a study.

Blue Boar was cancelled because it was too heavy for naval aircraft and, probably more importantly, its TV guidance was of limited use due to cloud cover, despite Vickers' assertion that blind-bombing techniques could be used until the bomb fell through the cloud (there is a lot of cloud over Russia in the winter). The RAF was also concerned about the use of countermeasures to jam the guidance signals.

However, the work was not wasted and the casing was later used for the initial trials of the Green Cheese anti-ship missile. Standard Blue Boar was a rather large weapon, but its 10,000 lb (4,536kg) version was 22ft (6.7m) long, with a wingspan of 78in (1.98m) and a diameter of 40in (101cm).

Three other versions were proposed, first Extra Large Blue Boar had a diameter of 53in (134.6cm), was 22ft 6in (6.86m) long and weighed in at 13,700 lb (6,214kg). It was proposed that this bomb should carry additional equipment to allow the control of a number of standard Blue Boars and act as a Master Bomb with the entire stick flying in formation towards the target. Ambitious stuff!

Special Blue Boar, as the epithet 'Special' suggests, carried a nuclear warhead and was intended to replace the Blue Danube free-fall bomb, providing some degree of stand-off for the V-bomber. Utilising the Extra Large Blue Boar airframe, Special Blue Boar would use the same physics package as the Brown Bunny nuclear land mine, which was also based on the Blue Danube device.

The third version was a small 1,000 lb (454kg) model that shared the same aerodynamics as Blue Boar and was to be used for training. This was 8ft 4in (2.54m) long and had a diameter of 15in (38cm). This round leads to an unusual aspect of Blue Boar development, the need for a target to practise on. As a result a dummy cruiser was built out of chicken wire on the Woomera range!

Another guided bomb project in the works was Yellow Sand. Described as a homing bomb, this may have been a development based on the German Fritz-X, with a guidance system by EMI and controls by Smiths. Glide bombs could provide adequate stand-off range if launched high enough by types such as the Vickers Valiant, but not if launched from carrier strike aircraft such as the Fairey Gannet. This prompted the main effort to be placed in the development of a more sophisticated weapon – Green Cheese.

Green Cheese

Originally known as the Fairey Project 7, Green Cheese was developed in the mid-1950s to meet OR.1123 and was intended for use by RAF Valiants. It was also prepared to a January 1954 Royal Navy requirement, AW.319, for carriage by Fairey Gannets, but ultimately on the Navy's forthcoming aircraft to Specification M.148 and NA.39. The M.148 submissions included the Hawker P.1108 and the Blackburn B.103, the latter eventually winning the competition to become the Buccaneer. The target for Green Cheese was the new Sverdlov Class cruisers entering service with the Soviet Navy.

From the off, the differing launch conditions of these aircraft cast doubts on a joint requirement. The Ministry had great hopes for Green Cheese, indeed Brigadier John Clemow, Director (Guided Weapons Projects) and later to become Chief Engineer (Weapons) for Vickers-Armstrong, hoped

that the weapon had: '...reached a stage where a missile was no longer regarded as a tiresome appendage and a nuisance to the aircraft designer'.

By now the reader will be well aware that many early guided weapons developed by the UK companies 'borrowed' components from other projects. Green Cheese is a classic example of this, comprising a shortened 5,000 lb (2,268kg) Blue Boar casing fitted with the GEC radar seeker from a Vickers Red Dean air-to-air missile. The Blue Boar glide bomb suffered from high drag so, to improve the glide angle for Green Cheese, the wings were cut back to reduce drag.

Further plans to reduce drag involved tapering the tail; however this reduced the volume available for electronics. Fairey gave up on the glide bomb idea and after examining different rocket motor types, fitted a cut-down Smokey Joe boost/sustainer motor (used on the Thunderbird SAGW) to provide the correct 30° glide angle for the ultimate version.

Two versions were envisaged, a fixed wing version to OR.1123 producing 'dry hits' for the RAF Valiant, which could carry up to four of the weapons externally. The version for the Navy to AW.319 for 'wet hits' with flip-out

Brigadier John Clemow, a great believer in guided weapons, became Chief Engineer of Vickers Guided Weapons after a spell as Director (Guided Weapons Projects) at the MoS. via John Forbat

Vickers Blue Boar series included test vehicles and the formation-flying Extra Large Blue Boar.

The development of Green Cheese saw a couple of configurations investigated. A scrap view shows the problem with the Fairey Gannet.

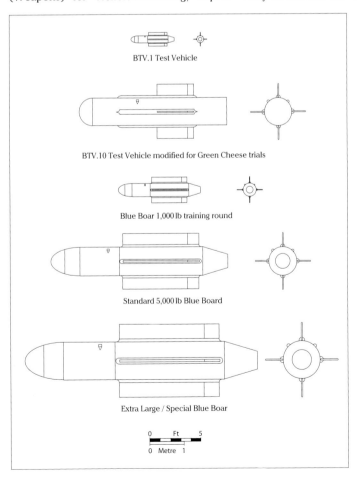

BTV.1 Test Vehicle

BTV.10 Test Vehicle modified for Green Cheese trials

Blue Boar 1,000 lb training round

Standard 5,000 lb Blue Board

Extra Large / Special Blue Boar

0   Ft   5
0   Metre   1

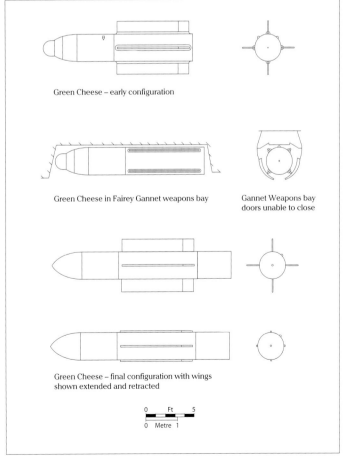

Green Cheese – early configuration

Green Cheese in Fairey Gannet weapons bay

Gannet Weapons bay doors unable to close

Green Cheese – final configuration with wings shown extended and retracted

0   Ft   5
0   Metre   1

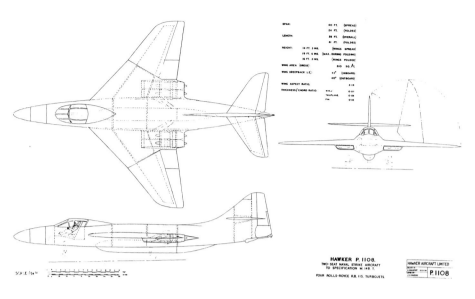

SPAN: 40 FT. (SPREAD)
                               24 FT. (FOLDED)
LENGTH: 58 FT. (OVERALL)
                               51 FT. (FOLDED)
HEIGHT: 14 FT. 3 INS.   (WINGS SPREAD)
              19 FT. 6 INS.   (MAX. DURING FOLDING)
              16 FT. 3 INS.   (WINGS FOLDED)
WING AREA (GROSS):   510 SQ. FT.
WING SWEEPBACK L.E.:   45° (INBOARD)
                               40° (OUTBOARD)
WING ASPECT RATIO: 3.16
THICKNESS/CHORD RATIO: WING: 0.07
                          TAILPLANE: 0.06
                          FIN: 0.05

HAWKER P. 1108.
TWO-SEAT NAVAL STRIKE AIRCRAFT
TO SPECIFICATION M.148.T.
FOUR ROLLS-ROYCE R.B. 115. TURBOJETS.

HAWKER AIRCRAFT LIMITED
P.1108

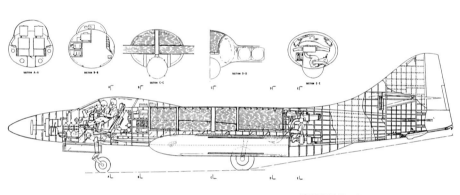

Cutaway of the P.1108 showing Green Cheese with
its flip-out wings stowed for carriage.
Brooklands Museum

HAWKER P.1108.
TWO-SEAT NAVAL STRIKE AIRCRAFT
TO SPECIFICATION M.148.T.
FOUR ROLLS-ROYCE R.B.115. TURBOJETS.

HAWKER AIRCRAFT LIMITED
P1108.

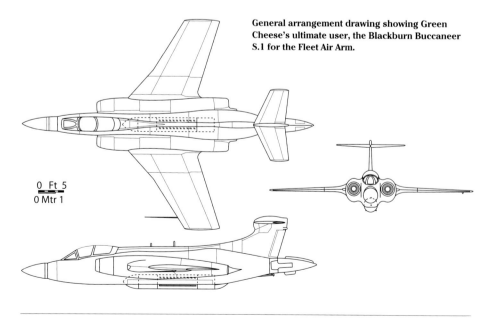

General arrangement drawing showing Green
Cheese's ultimate user, the Blackburn Buccaneer
S.1 for the Fleet Air Arm.

0 Ft 5
0 Mtr 1

**The Hawker P.1108 was intended to carry the
Green Cheese anti-ship weapon in a semi-recessed
mounting. As can be seen from the general
arrangement drawing it required a rather large
aircraft to carry it.** Brooklands Museum

wings/control surfaces allowed internal carriage in the weapons bays of the Gannet and
Buccaneer. However internal carriage in the
Gannet meant that some form of extending
launch rail was required to lower the missile
out of the bay, allowing it to acquire the target. This added weight and complication to
the entire system. In the end the requirements were merged to produce a weapon
with flip-out wings for the Buccaneer that was
carried in the rotating weapons bay.

Targeting of the weapon was to be controlled by the ASV-21 radar that was being
developed for Buccaneer and this would provide initial targeting data for the Green
Cheese seeker. An early proposal to use the
missile's seeker as a target-acquisition radar
was dropped, again due to the need to
expose the weapon prior to launch. Green
Cheese's active homing seeker, which
allowed a 'launch and leave' delivery, was
being developed by GEC and EMI. It was
based on their X-band seeker for Red Dean,
but with an enlarged dish.

A semi-active seeker was proposed but this
would require the target to be illuminated by
the launch aircraft's radar, thereby making
the aircraft vulnerable to attack by the target
ship's defences. The missile itself would be
vulnerable to ship defences (the Orange Nell
anti-missile system had been drawn up
specifically to counter weapons such as
Green Cheese) so it was proposed to fit a
'jinker' to make the missile perform a random
weave manoeuvre during its attack.

Green Cheese was to hit the water at an
angle of 40° (after motor burn-out the glide
angle would have steepened) a distance of
150ft (45.2m) from the target ship. The impact
would shear off the radome to leave an
angled surface that forced the missile
upwards under the ship to impact under the
waterline, producing a wet hit. To ensure that
the missile hit the water rather than the ship
itself (the strongest reflector) the seeker was
to be given 'squint'. However, it was pointed
out that the angle of squint was dependent on
the range to the target, so the squint would
need to change as the missile approached
the target. Having dismissed the squint, the
Staff decided that the missile should dive at a
predetermined distance from the target. Both
suggestions were dismissed as adding complication to the homing system and a conventional anti-ship warhead was adopted. All

British Secret Projects: Hypersonics, Ramjets & Missiles

that this discussion produced was delay and cost escalation.

Weighing in at 3,800 lb (1,724kg), Green Cheese was too heavy to be carried by the Fairey Gannet. Even if the Gannet could carry Green Cheese, its weapons bay doors couldn't close. This carriage problem was compounded by the need for Gannet to enter the area defended by the target's AA weapons prior to launch. The Admiralty graciously dropped the requirement for use by the Gannet, but it must have led to some serious questions at Fairey as to why their GW department had developed a weapon that a Fairey aircraft could not carry. The Admiralty had also raised doubts about Green Cheese's ability to sink a major ship, due to its shallow angle of impact.

Green Cheese showed promise, but was essentially scuppered by cost and weight over-runs, not to mention being overtaken by another Fairey project, the Sea-Skimmer. Fingers were also pointed to delays in the trials caused by reliability problems with the RAF Washington piston-engined bomber used for test drops. By March 1955 the writing was on the wall for Green Cheese and it was finally cancelled in 1956.

The ultimate version, with improved capability, was called Cockburn Cheese, named after the Principal Director of Scientific Research (Guided Weapons), PDSR(G), Dr

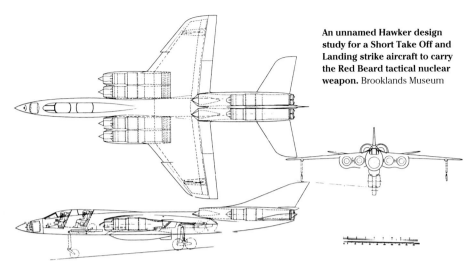

An unnamed Hawker design study for a Short Take Off and Landing strike aircraft to carry the Red Beard tactical nuclear weapon. Brooklands Museum

Robert Cockburn. This was intended to be in service from 1962. The replacement for Green Cheese was called Green Flash, which had a Red Beard nuclear warhead. This was dropped due to the Atomic Weapons Establishment's (AWE) desire to have a common warhead for Green Cheese, Blue Water and for the Bloodhound III.

In the nuclear role Green Cheese was replaced by a Red Beard 15/25-kiloton nuclear weapon carried by the Navy's Super-

marine Scimitars and Blackburn Buccaneers. To avoid engagement by the defences, this weapon was to be tossed at the target using the Low Altitude Bombing System, LABS, and remained in service until the late 1960s.

Hawker STOL aircraft attack a Soviet battle group with Red Beard weapons delivered by the Low Altitude Bombing System. This role, carried out by Supermarine Scimitars, replaced Green Cheese on its cancellation in 1956. Adrian Mann

Sea-Skimmer

Early in the Green Cheese programme Fairey suspected that it wasn't going anywhere and so had a parallel project called Sea-Skimmer up its sleeve. As the name suggests, this was a sea-skimming anti-ship missile, which was powered by a Rolls-Royce Soar sustainer engine and was proposed for the same OR.1123/AW.213 requirement as Green Cheese. Sea-Skimmer looked like a small aircraft, but used twist-and-steer controls.

Sea-Skimmer's X-band seeker was intended to be locked onto the target before launch and it would fly just above wave-top height, with the final approach being a bunt onto the deck of the ship. This bunt attack was thought to have a more lethal effect than the shallow dive of Green Cheese.

The Rolls-Royce Soar sustainer turbojet required thirty seconds running-up time prior to launch so the launch aircraft's Air to Surface Vessel (ASV) radome had to be retracted, thus blinding the launch aircraft for this period. This was a particular problem on aircraft such as the Avro Shackleton whose ventral radome was mounted aft of the weapons bay.

The missile used mid-course guidance, with a terminal homing phase using radar. The Admiralty considered Sea-Skimmer to have a better chance of sinking a large ship than Green Cheese, due mainly to the angle of its terminal dive. The additional range allowed by the turbojet sustainer, greater than 40 miles (64km), and the mid-course guidance also appealed to the Admiralty, especially since it would keep the Gannet out of harm's way. However Sea-Skimmer was cancelled due to guidance problems, particularly with the mid-course guidance system, but also due to the time taken to launch from a Shackleton. Unfortunately, in selecting the Shackleton as its maritime patrol aircraft, the Air Staff had rejected the Bristol 175MR proposal (based on the Britannia airliner) that could use Sea-Skimmer with ease, carrying one under each wing. In addition the 175MR ASV radar was housed in a chin mounting.

In the end, the conventional anti-shipping role was filled by Royal Navy Scimitars fitted with the American Martin Marietta AGM-12 Bullpup missile acquired under OR.1173/GDA.5. This was very much a stopgap, so a better solution was required.

Into the Sixties

By 1960 the prospect of new types such as the TSR.2 strike aircraft, the OR.357 maritime reconnaissance type and the project to meet OR.356 for the Navy (the Hawker P.1154 supersonic V/STOL aircraft) led to the drawing up of OR.1168 and GDA.101. Weapons such as Bullpup had to be launched in a dive towards the target, taking the aircraft into the target's air defence zone, particularly SAMs. The OR.1168/GDA.101 weapon was to be a tactical air-to-surface weapon that allowed the launch aircraft to remain well out of the range of future enemy defences, preferably at low altitude. While not specifically a requirement for an anti-ship weapon, it could of course be used as such, as outlined in the Admiralty's GDA.101.

The full list of targets included bridges, buildings, parked aircraft and ships. Against ships the weapon was required to disable the air defences of large units and sink smaller vessels such as submarines, while a further requirement to destroy radars and vehicles was also included. The destruction of radars called for a homing capability, which in the terminology of the time was called a radar buster but today is better known as an anti-radiation missile.

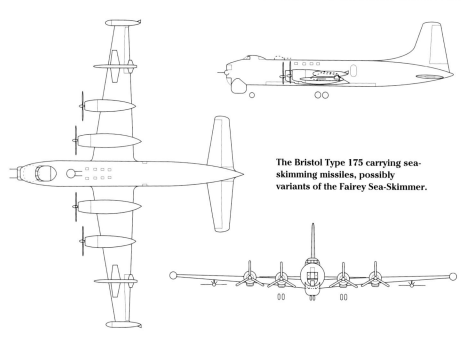

The Bristol Type 175 carrying sea-skimming missiles, possibly variants of the Fairey Sea-Skimmer.

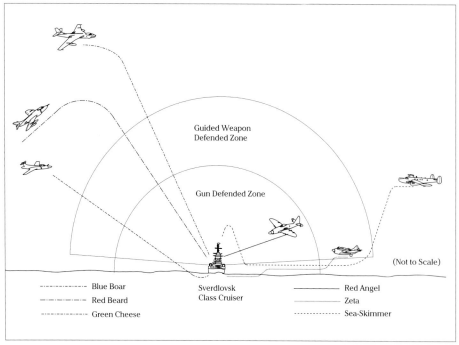

Guided Weapon Defended Zone

Gun Defended Zone

(Not to Scale)

- - - - - - - Blue Boar
- · - · - · - Red Beard
- - - - - - - Green Cheese

Sverdlovsk Class Cruiser

- - - - - - - Red Angel
- - - - - - - Zeta
- - - - - - - Sea-Skimmer

The various attack profiles of the anti-ship weapons of the 1950s with their platforms.

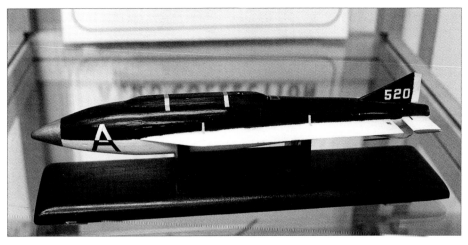

Bristol's Momentum Bomb that formed the basis of the Tychon ASM. Bristol Collection

Unlike the toss-bombing manoeuvre, Barnes Wallis' Momentum Bomb allowed strike aircraft, such as TSR.2, to avoid engagement by low-altitude air defences.

Bristol Guided Weapons proposed a weapon called Tychon, which has also been described as a powered version of the Momentum Bomb. Developed by none other than Barnes Wallis at Vickers Aircraft, the Momentum Bomb was conceived to attack targets while the strike aircraft remained below the radar horizon. The unpowered weapon was fitted with small wings or long strakes with a symmetrical aerofoil section and a basic tail unit. The beauty of the Momentum Bomb was that it did not require the attacker to climb before weapons release, unlike the standard toss/loft bombing manoeuvre.

The strike aircraft flew over the target at low level and released the bomb at a predetermined point down range of the target. After release, the elevators commanded the bomb to enter a climb that became ever steeper and turned into a loop. At the top of the loop the elevators reversed and commanded the bomb into a gently sloping flight path to the target on the reciprocal bearing to the aircraft flight path, that is, behind the aircraft. Being unpowered the Momentum Bomb relied on the momentum from its launch and low-drag shape to carry it to the target.

To attack targets off the aircraft's ground track, Wallis suggested that the aircraft performed a turn onto a bearing whose reciprocal took the Momentum bomb onto the target.

For Tychon, its modular design was the key to flexibility. With seeker modules including TV-guided or anti-radiation and payloads such as a nuclear warhead or a reconnaissance package, the modules were to be assembled for specific roles. Canberras were to carry a single round, V-bombers and Buccaneer a pair, but TSR.2 could carry four. The design was to be suitable for future types including the Vickers Type 581 Swallow strike aircraft and 'sub-orbital bombers'. As ever, alternative roles were outlined, including a rocket-boosted tactical surface-to-surface weapon launched from trucks or Seaslug mounts on ships. Tychon didn't really appeal to the Air Staff or the Admiralty and lost out to one of those Anglo-French programmes that were all the rage in the early 1960s. OR.1168, later retitled AST.1168, was to become quite a political weapon.

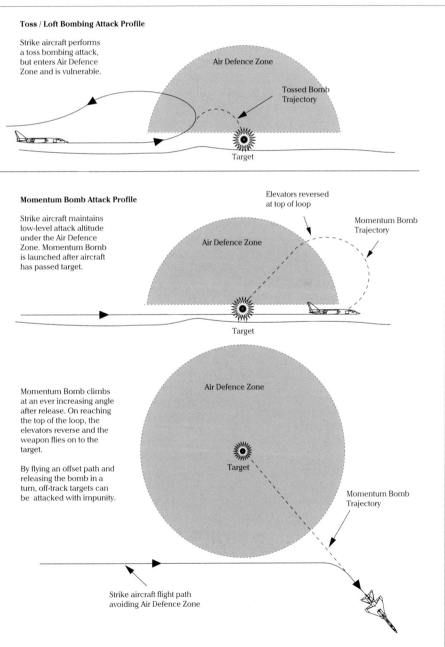

Toss / Loft Bombing Attack Profile

Strike aircraft performs a toss bombing attack, but enters Air Defence Zone and is vulnerable.

Air Defence Zone

Tossed Bomb Trajectory

Target

Momentum Bomb Attack Profile

Strike aircraft maintains low-level attack altitude under the Air Defence Zone. Momentum Bomb is launched after aircraft has passed target.

Elevators reversed at top of loop

Momentum Bomb Trajectory

Air Defence Zone

Target

Momentum Bomb climbs at an ever increasing angle after release. On reaching the top of the loop, the elevators reverse and the weapon flies on to the target.

By flying an offset path and releasing the bomb in a turn, off-track targets can be attacked with impunity.

Air Defence Zone

Target

Momentum Bomb Trajectory

Strike aircraft flight path avoiding Air Defence Zone

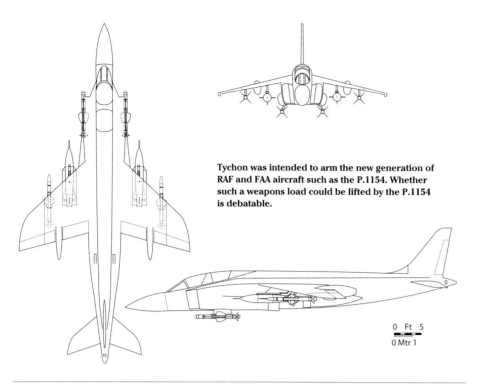

Tychon was intended to arm the new generation of RAF and FAA aircraft such as the P.1154. Whether such a weapons load could be lifted by the P.1154 is debatable.

0 Ft 5
0 Mtr 1

Martel

One of the earliest of joint Anglo-French projects AJ.168, later called Martel, stemmed from a de Havilland air-to-surface weapon study called RG10 and the French Matra R630 anti-radiation missile. RG10 was a cruciform-wing design to be carried internally with two of its wings folded for stowage. Amongst the aircraft types considered for RG10 was the Hawker Siddeley APD.1017 designed to meet the 1963 M.232 strike aircraft specification that led to the Buccaneer Mk.2.

The RAF requirement OR.1168 was issued in 1962 and called for a missile with anti-radar and TV-guided variants. The Air Ministry was concerned that going it alone on this weapon would lead to delays and cost, to the point that the Under Secretary of State at the Air Ministry, writing in October 1962 to the Deputy Chief of the Air Staff Air Marshal Sir Ronald Lees, stated: 'I believe, however, that we would get a simpler and cheaper weapon by teaming up with the French, and it would have an enormous advantage of having as much RAF operational thinking built into it. If you agree with me, it would be of great assistance to us if you could let me have an exhortation to get on with the job as quickly as possible on an Anglo-French basis. I am most anxious not to fall behind in producing this weapon for the TSR.2 and subsequently the P.1154.'

A month later, using politics as a tool to progress the project, discussions with the French Government on a missile to OR.1168 began. France and Germany had already begun development of the AS.30 into the conventional AS.33 and nuclear AS.34 air-to-surface missiles but neither met the British requirement. The French and British were keen to have an anti-radiation missile (ARM), in which Matra took the lead, developed as the AS.37 with an Avions Marcel Dassault AD.37 passive seeker. What the British really wanted was an air-to-surface missile, with both weapons using a common basic airframe.

By early 1963 de Havilland Propellers, by this time named Hawker Siddeley Dynamics, embarked on a TV-guided version of the AS.37, with the Ministry of Aviation giving it the reference number AJ.168. After examining the TV guidance work done for Blue Boar, Marconi was tasked with the development of the seeker and datalink pod.

The missile transmitted a video picture of the target back to the launch aircraft via the datalink, the same method pioneered in World War Two by the Germans. A joystick was used to adjust the flightpath and commands passed back to the missile via the datalink. At longer ranges Martel was guided over a series of landmarks until the target entered the field of view. Altitude was maintained by reference to a barometric altimeter.

AJ.168 had a total weight of 1,200lb (545kg), of which 330lb (150kg) was the semi-armour piercing warhead. With a length of 13ft 6in (4.1m) and a diameter of almost 16in (40cm) it was a sizeable weapon.

The AJ.168 was fitted initially with a Pheasant boost rocket motor, but a Basilie motor, in common with the AS.37, replaced this. The Cassandra sustainer gave the AJ.168 a range of 37 miles (60km) and a speed of Mach 0.9.

Now named MARTel (Missile, Anti-Radiation, Television), AJ.168 entered Royal Navy service in October 1973 on the Buccaneer S.Mk.2, which needed major work on its wings to accommodate up to four weapons, to become S.Mk.2D. The RAF's S.Mk.2Bs were Martel-capable off the assembly line, but aircraft transferred to the RAF from the Fleet Air Arm lacked this capability until BAC modified them as the 'Interim S.2B'. Proposals to fit it to the McDonnell Douglas Phantom came to nought as this was thought to be a duplication of the Buccaneer role.

The Hawker Siddeley Nimrod, another proposed carrier, was wired and fitted for Martel but never flew with it operationally. However, having the wiring in place proved fortuitous when Nimrods were fitted with Sidewinder AAMs during the 1982 Falklands War for self-defence purposes.

Various variants of Martel were proposed including a nuclear-armed version called Megaton Martel, while Cluster Martel fitted with a bomblet dispenser was pooh-poohed by the Ministry as being a waste of time. However, one variant that did prosper was Active Radar Martel, which features in the next section.

The RAF was never really happy with Martel, finding its capability somewhat disappointing. One grumble was the need to carry the separate datalink pod, which occupied one of the Buccaneer's four wing pylons and restricted the war load to three rounds.

In a confidential 1970 memo on the future of guided weapons the following appears: 'Martel – this has been a disappointing weapon. Costs have risen sharply…and of course the TV missile is vulnerable to ground defences. However, there is no feasible alternative stand-off missile and we must proceed with our present commitment for 200. It is debateable whether we should place a further supplementary order, but we have several months to weigh this up.' Obviously Martel didn't have too many fans at the Air Staff.

Sea Eagle

A range of 40 miles (65km) would still place a launch aircraft within range of the air defences of a Soviet battlegroup, particularly if that aircraft had to fly high enough to maintain datalink contact with the missile. The solution was to provide longer range and a different homing system, and in the early

Right: **Martel evolved via de Havilland design study, the RG.10 and the Matra AS.30.**

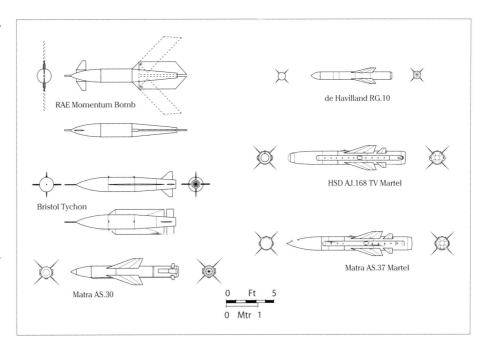

RAE Momentum Bomb

de Havilland RG.10

Bristol Tychon

HSD AJ.168 TV Martel

Below: **TV Martel seen on a trial de Havilland Sea Vixen ready for a trials flight over the Aberporth range.** BAE Systems via Tony Buttler

Bottom left: **A de Havilland Sea Vixen is made ready for a test launch of a TV-guided AJ.168 MARTel. The nozzles of the boost and sustainer motors can be clearly seen in the rare rear view.**

Matra AS.37 Martel

Bottom right: **Close-up of a TV Martel showing the TV seeker in the nose.**

Matra AS.30

0   Ft   5

0   Mtr 1

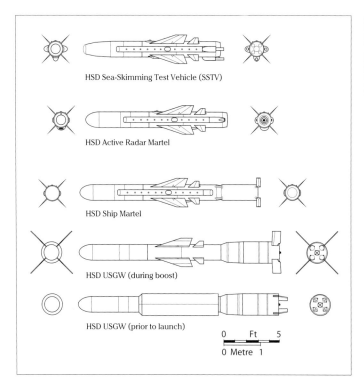

HSD Sea-Skimming Test Vehicle (SSTV)

HSD Active Radar Martel

HSD Ship Martel

HSD USGW (during boost)

HSD USGW (prior to launch)

0　　Ft　　5

0　Metre　1

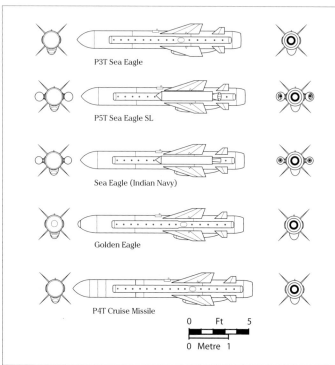

P3T Sea Eagle

P5T Sea Eagle SL

Sea Eagle (Indian Navy)

Golden Eagle

P4T Cruise Missile

0　　Ft　　5

0　Metre　1

Under Sea Guided Weapon (USGW) also known as CR.137 was a submarine-launched weapon based on Martel.

BAe Dynamics Sea Eagle and its variants. Also shown are provisional drawings of Golden Eagle and the P4T cruise missile.

The Hawker Siddeley Dynamics Sea Skimming Test Vehicle that was used for CR.137 and later P3T (Sea Eagle) trials. Its Martel lineage is obvious.
HSD via T Panopalis

Hawker Siddeley Buccaneer XK527 of the Aircraft and Armament Experimental Establishment carries a full complement of Sea Eagle trials rounds.
HSD via T Panopalis

1950s Fairey addressed the range problem with its Sea-Skimmer study. As noted above Sea-Skimmer was sunk by guidance problems, but for attacking ships this would become the method of choice.

Extra range could be provided through the use of a gas turbine, while the guidance problem could be addressed by an autonomous weapon using a programmable seeker with active radar for terminal guidance. HSD had commenced studies on a weapon called Underwater to Surface Guided Weapon (USGW), also known as CR.137, to meet a June 1969 requirement for a submarine-launched, sea-skimming anti-ship missile. One of the spin-offs from this project was an air-launched test missile called the Sea-Skimming Test Vehicle (SSTV). By the early 1970s the problems attendant on introducing sea-skimming capability had been cracked.

The rocket-powered SSTV was a minimum-change AJ.168 airframe that used a Honeywell radar altimeter, a Sperry-Rand developed GK.352 sea-skimming control system and a telemetry system. Test firings were conducted at Aberporth with a de Havilland Sea Vixen fighter providing the launch platform and chase. The requirement called for the SSTV to fly as low as 2m (6ft 6in) in calm seas, but in a tactical sense altitudes less than 50m (164ft) were considered to be sea-skimming, with 4m (13ft 1½in) being the goal. This work was applied to USGW and to a proposed Ship-Martel, but on cancellation of these projects it was transferred to another HSD project called Active Radar Martel.

By the early 1970s there was a need to update the anti-ship weapons available to the UK forces and ASR.1226 was drawn up in response to this. The initial proposal from HSD was Active Radar Martel, essentially a stretched AJ.168 fitted with a GEC Marconi active radar seeker and a gas turbine sustainer. This failed to elicit interest, but studies for a new anti-ship weapon began in 1973 under the designation P3T. This built on the Active Radar Martel work and eventually, on entering service on the Buccaneer in 1985, P3T acquired the name Sea Eagle.

Sea Eagle was a sea-skimming, long-range weapon designed for air launch from fast jets. As such it needed no booster and used an air-breathing Microturbo TRI-60 gas turbine to provide a range of almost 70 miles (112km). Totally autonomous after launch, its guidance was undertaken by an inertial navigation system (INS) with active radar used in the terminal phase, making it a true 'fire and forget' weapon.

The guidance system can be programmed to provide a variety of attack profiles allowing

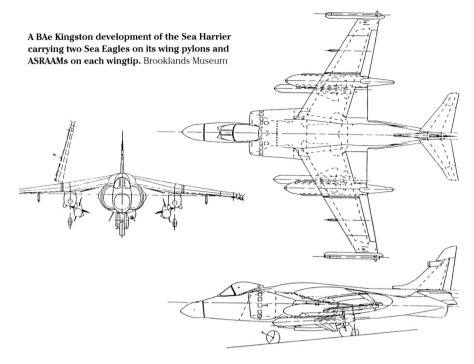

A BAe Kingston development of the Sea Harrier carrying two Sea Eagles on its wing pylons and ASRAAMs on each wingtip. Brooklands Museum

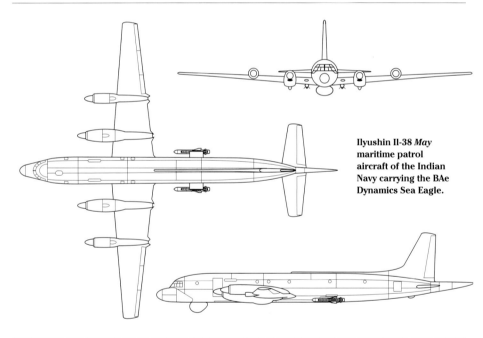

Ilyushin Il-38 *May* maritime patrol aircraft of the Indian Navy carrying the BAe Dynamics Sea Eagle.

the launch aircraft to stay out of harm's way. Buccaneers and Tornados, with no need for a datalink pod, could carry four Sea Eagles, the Sea Harrier two. However Sea Eagle has also been tested on Hawker Siddeley/BAe Hawks (a single round) and Indian Air Force SEPECAT Jaguars (two). Perhaps the strangest carriers of the Sea Eagle are the Indian Navy's Soviet-designed Ilyushin Il-38 *May* and Tupolev Tu-142 *Bear* maritime reconnaissance aircraft. The Il-38 carries the Sea Eagle, fitted with a pair of Wagtail rocket boosters, on fuselage pylons just aft of the wing. These boosters are used on any low-speed platforms including Westland Sea King helicopters (also used by the Indian Navy).

Variants of Sea Eagle included the P5T, later called Sea Eagle-SL. This was launched from a box mounted on the deck of a warship and boosted by the Wagtail motors. The longer-ranged Golden Eagle from the early 1980s, with an imaging infra-red seeker and a datalink, was intended as a cruise missile but went no further than a paper study.

A Royal Navy Lynx, armed with a ½in (12.7mm) heavy machine gun and a BAe Dynamics Sea Skua, is well armed to counter fast patrol boats and small boats on suicide missions.
Crown Copyright/MOD

A Royal Navy Lynx HAS. releases a BAC (GW) CL.834 Sea Skua over the Aberporth range in 1980.
BAE Systems via T Panopalis

The solution came in the shape of the French Nord AS-12. This was a wire-guided weapon so it was not vulnerable to counter-measures and had a range of 6km (3.7 miles), keeping the launcher out of gun range. The AS-12 was fitted to Westland Wasp and Wessex helicopters and is credited with disabling the Argentinian submarine *Santa Fe* in the 1982 Falklands War.

By the mid-1960s it had become obvious that FPBs would be fitted with lightweight SAMs, such as HSA's SHIELD, that could out-range the likes of AS-12. The answer to this was to increase the range again, allowing the launch platform (usually a ship-borne heli-copter) to remain at a safe distance. Such a weapon would also need a dedicated target-ing radar in the helicopter, as visual guidance would not be possible.

Project studies began in the late 1960s, with Naval Staff Requirement NSR.6624 drawn up in 1969. Hawker Siddeley proposed to meet this with their SRAAM-derived SAMM-10, but the Admiralty chose a clean-sheet design from the British Aircraft Corporation Guided Weapons division. Development of this weapon started in 1972 under the Ministry of Aviation reference number CL.834. This was to be mounted on the Westland WG.13 heli-copter, later named Lynx, which was to replace the Westland Wasp and to carry four CL.834s on stub pylons. Target detection and illumination for the semi-active seeker was to be provided by a radar developed by Ferranti to meet Requirement NSR.6449. This radar may have been called Blue Tit during its development phase, but once in service this was renamed Sea Spray.

CL.834 entered Royal Navy service in 1982, and was named Sea Skua. Compact in size at 2.85m (9ft 9in) long and weighing 145kg (345 lb), of which 20kg (44 lb) is a semi-armour piercing warhead, Sea Skua is more than adequate for dealing with FPBs.

Having detected the target, the Lynx releases the weapon and a Redstart booster motor accelerates the missile to flight speed. The Redstart is wrapped around the blast tube of the Matapan sustainer, which powers the missile towards the target at low level, using a radar altimeter to maintain a sea-skimming profile.

Sea Skua – Scourge of the Fast Patrol Boat
While the aforementioned weapons were intended to deal with larger warships, the Royal Navy had a requirement for a weapon to destroy Fast Patrol Boats (FPB). Having seen how the Egyptians had used Soviet Osa Class missile boats against the Israeli Navy in the Six-Day War of 1967, the Admiralty was concerned that their warships were also at the mercy of such craft.

Shorts proposed Hellcat, an air-launched version of Seacat, to be carried by small ship-board helicopters such as the Westland Wasp. The Hellcat system comprised a pair of standard Seacat SAMs, a mounting frame with launch rail on each side of the helicopter cabin and a gyro-stabilised sight. Guidance used optical tracking and a radio command link. Shorts' rationale was that Hellcat's use of the standard Seacat allowed savings to be made in spares and maintenance, but the Seacat's 3.5km (2.2 miles) range would put the helicopter within range of the target's guns. This was particularly relevant because the Osa FPBs also carried a pair of turret-mounted twin 30mm guns, with a range of 5km (3.1 miles). Something with longer legs was required.

British Secret Projects: Hypersonics, Ramjets & Missiles

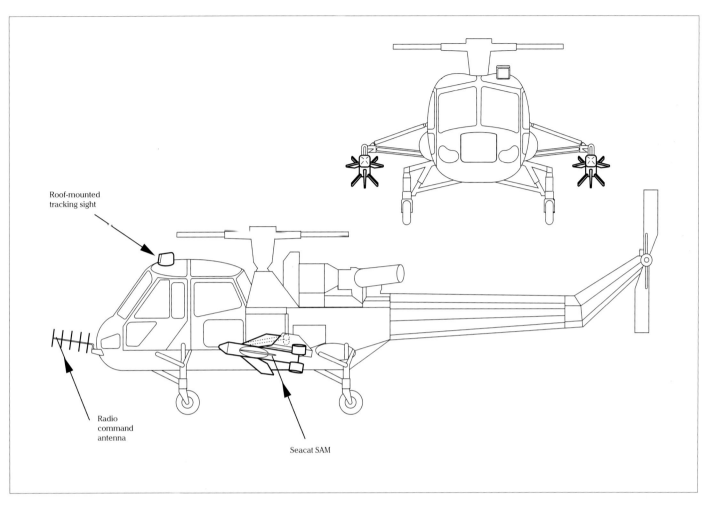

Roof-mounted
tracking sight

Radio
command
antenna

Seacat SAM

**Provisional drawing of the Shorts Hellcat system
fitted to a Westland Wasp naval helicopter.**

**Specialist weapons include Anti-Radiation Missiles
(ARM) that armed the RAF. Also included is an
ASRAAM variant called SRARM.**

Sea Skua became combat proven during
the Falklands War and two Gulf Wars and has
provided considerable export success, being
fitted to German Kriegsmarine Sea King helicopters and Turkish Navy Agusta Bell
AB.212s, as well export Lynx. It can also be fitted to maritime patrol aircraft, such as the de
Havilland Canada Dash 8. To complete the
circle, a surface-launched version for Fast
Attack Craft is also in service, turning it into
the sort of threat it was originally developed to
counter!

Anti-Radiation Missiles
The American experience in Vietnam had
shown that aircraft would become increasingly vulnerable to air defences. IR-guided
ground-based defensive weapons could be
countered by passive means such as flares
and suppression of heat sources, but radar-

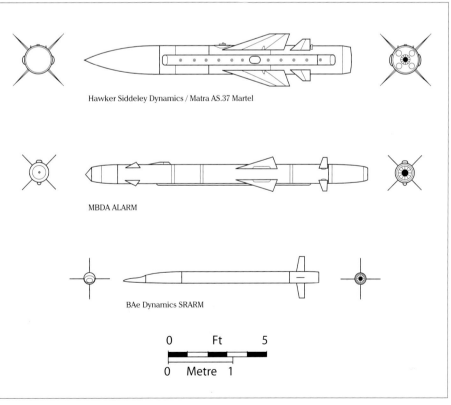

Hawker Siddeley Dynamics / Matra AS.37 Martel

MBDA ALARM

BAe Dynamics SRARM

0   Ft   5

0   Metre   1

On display at the Bristol Collection, the offset nose profile of the SRARM can be seen. Changing requirements saw the self-defence anti-radiation missile cancelled.

guided guns and missiles needed a more active measure. Jamming was possible, but this allowed the enemy radar to 'live to fight another day', so its destruction had to be the answer. The missiles developed to counter radars became known as anti-radiation missiles or ARMs.

Dealing with hostile radars was old hat to the RAF, right back to the Second World War, but the service monitored the USAF's activities in Vietnam with considerable interest. The initial American response was to dedicate fighter bombers such as the North American F-100 Super Sabre 'Iron Hand' to attack the missiles and radars with bombs and rockets but, as the conflict in Vietnam escalated and more modern Soviet hardware and additional advisers arrived, the toll on US aircraft grew. In response the USAF set up the Wild Weasel system, using the F-100 initially but ultimately the Republic F-105F Thunderchief in the Suppression of Enemy Air Defences (SEAD) role (in other words these aircraft were tasked with the destruction of enemy radars).

Thunderchief also came with some new weapons, the Shrike and Standard ARMs. The AGM-45 Shrike had appeared on the scene in

1962, looking like an enlarged AIM-7 Sparrow AAM, and remained in the USAF inventory until 1992. The AGM-78 Standard Anti-Radiation Missile, based on the RIM-66 Standard naval SAM, allowed longer range attacks than the Shrike. Standard and Shrike worked by locking on to the radiation emitted by the hostile radar and flying towards the source of its emissions, eventually hitting and destroying the radar.

As previously noted the British were never really enamoured with the Franco/British AS.37 Martel, They preferred to use the US Shrike in the Falklands war, which worked on the same principle. However, it could be countered by the simple expedient of switching off the radar. This prompted the Americans to develop a new ARM, called the AGM-88 High Speed Anti-Radiation Missile (HARM), which relied on high speed to defeat this tactic. HARM entered service in 1984, replacing the Standard ARM.

The British had other ideas. Well aware of this switch-off-the-radar tactic, the Air Staff decided that a different approach was required. Rather than have a dedicated SEAD type, such as the F-105F, it decided that any aircraft should be able to carry an ARM for

self-protection against hostile air defences.

In 1978 Staff Target AST.1228 was drawn up for an advanced defence suppression weapon for the Tornado GR.Mk.1. In response to this and the subsequent Requirement, BAe Dynamics developed a missile that it called ALARM (Air Launched Anti-Radiation Missile) and this was selected in preference to the US HARM in 1983.

ALARM is a self-contained fire-and-forget system, with an added loiter capability conferred by a parachute. Initially powered by the Bristol Aerojet Nuthatch rocket motor, development problems led to this unit's replacement with a Bayer Chemie Bayard motor. While the problems with Nuthatch were being dealt with, test flying continued using a Linnet motor from the Red Top AAM.

ALARM can operate in two modes. The first is direct attack at high speed towards the target in the traditional manner and the second allows the weapon to loiter. Loiter mode is intended to deal with the radar being switched on and off and in this mode ALARM will climb to a higher altitude on launch. If the target radar shuts down, the missile will deploy a parachute and descend slowly until the radar switches on. However, given that the radar operators probably know that an ARM has been fired, they will be expected to keep the radar shut down for an extended period which allows the strike aircraft to fly past unmolested. If the radar is switched on, the missile will lock on to the radar's ground location and then fire its motor again to attack the target even if the target is immediately switched off again. This stop/start requirement proved to be the main difficulty during the development of the Nuthatch rocket motor.

With a length of 4.3m (14ft 1¼in) and a weight of 265kg (584 lb), ALARM can be carried by any aircraft pylon and is a favoured weapon for the Tornado GR. Mk.1 and Mk.4 Interdictor Strike (IDS) variant. Despite eschewing the dedicated SEAD aircraft in the past, the RAF has recently integrated ALARM with the Tornado F.Mk.3 to produce the Tornado EF.Mk.3. ALARM itself was upgraded under a mid-life update to meet SR(A).1247 in the 1990s.

Despite accusations of unnecessary complexity due to its loiter mode, ALARM is credited with being highly effective against difficult targets. During the 1999 'Allied Force' offensive in Kosovo, Luftwaffe Tornado ECR,

Air-to-Surface Missiles

Missile	Length ft (m)	Diameter in (cm)	Span ft (m)	Powerplant	Guidance
Blue Boar	17.5 (5.3)	32 (81)	5.2 (1.6)	Glide	TV radio
Green Cheese	15 (4.5)	32 (81)	5.2 (1.6)	Rocket	Active radar
Martel	12.7 (3.9)	15.75 (40)	4 (1.2)	Rocket	TV / Radar
Tychon	11.7 (3.6)	18 (48)	3 (0.9)	Rocket	TV / Radar
ALARM	14.1 (4.3)	8.8 (22)	2.4 (0.72)	Rocket	Radar
Red Angel	10.75 (3.28)	11.25 (28.6)	–	Rocket	None
Sea Eagle	13.6 (4.14)	15.8 (40)	4 (1.2)	Turbojet	Active radar
Sea Skua	8.2 (2.5)	9.8 (25)	2.3 (72)	Rocket	Semi-active radar
Hellcat	58.3 (1.48)	7.5 (19)	2.2 (0.65)	rocket	Optical

British Secret Projects: Hypersonics, Ramjets & Missiles

USAF Wild Weasel F-16s and US Navy EA-6B Prowlers attempted to destroy a Serbian air defence radar with HARM. After one hundred attempts, the RAF was called in and the radar was destroyed with a single ALARM.

ALARM and HARM were however too large to be carried by small strike aircraft. As a result, under a multinational programme that included the USA, a small self-protection ARM was to be developed to meet ASR.1240, for use against airborne radars as well as air defence radars. BAe Dynamics used the SRAAM airframe as a basis for this and produced a very odd-looking weapon with an offset nose. It was named SRARM for Short Range Anti-Radiation Missile, but the project foundered when the USAF withdrew in 1987.

Smart Weapons

Despite having been around since the late 1960s, US Paveway laser-guided bombs (LGB) first 'exploded' on the public stage when footage of them being guided through Baghdad windows was released in January 1991. In fact, what the Iraq War footage showed was basically old hat because the RAF had used Paveway LGBs to great effect during the Falklands War. Indeed, the Argentinian surrender was prompted by a Forward Air Controller declaring, in clear on the radio, that the Command Post in Port Stanley was designated and ready for a Paveway attack by Hawker Siddeley Harrier GR.3s. The RAF's Paveways and Pave Spike designators had been acquired to meet ASR.1220, and the later ASR.1229, a requirement covering LGBs for use by the Buccaneer. This combination performed sterling work in the 1991 Gulf War and proved to be the Buccaneer's swan song.

While the creation of these freefall 'smart bombs' had been left to the Americans, GEC/Marconi had embarked on the development of a laser-guided air-to-surface missile called AGM-500. For some reason this weapon's development was most closely associated with the United Arab Emirates, who became the first customer and called the weapon Al Hakim. Available in two variants, the AGMs are categorised by warhead weight: the AGM-500 with a 500 lb (226.8kg) warhead and the AGM-2000 with a 2,000 lb (907.2kg) warhead. The AGM series can be carried on aircraft such as the BAe Hawk.

GEC/Marconi (who became part of MBDA) developed the rocket-powered AGM-500/ 2000 series into the PGM (Precision Guided Munitions) family. The major changes were to the seeker: PGM-1A is a semi-active laser seeker, PGM-2 is TV-guided and PGM-3 uses infra-red imaging. The A suffix denotes the 500 lb (226.8kg) warhead while the 2,000 lb (907.2kg) warhead is identified by the B label.

The RAF was offered variants of the AGM, including one called Pegasus, developed jointly by BAe and Marconi in the 1990s to meet the SR(A).1242. This was unofficially known as Lancelot. However, the Air Staff were not particularly interested in these weapons, preferring to acquire US weapons such as the improved Paveway with added GPS guidance for use in bad weather. A further development, Centaur, replaced the Pegasus' rocket motor with a gas turbine to produce a stand-off weapon to meet ASR.1236.

Conclusion

As ever, the UK companies had to deal with changing threats, requirements that were sometimes preposterous, and the perpetual advance of technology. The concepts that were considered in the 1950s such as sea-skimming and TV-guidance systems would only come to fruition in the late 1960s and reach maturity in the 1970s as advances in computing and electronics made these systems compact enough to fit in a reasonably sized airframe. Despite the various abortive attempts to develop an effective anti-ship missile over four decades, the UK industry (in the shape of BAC and HSD) ultimately produced world-beating weapons in Sea Eagle and Sea Skua.

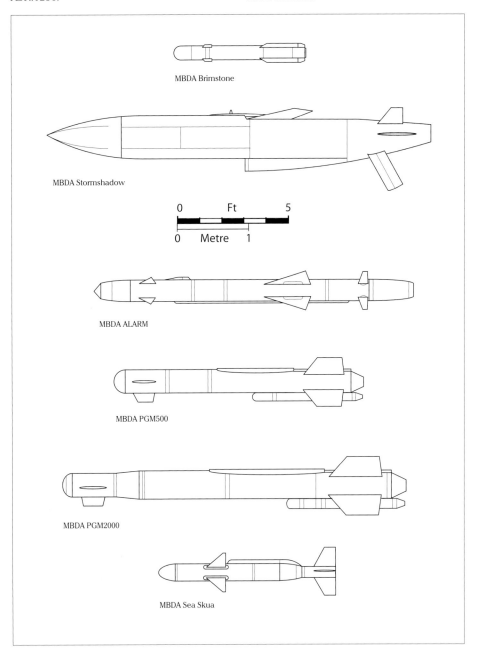

MBDA Brimstone

MBDA Stormshadow

0   Ft   5

0   Metre   1

MBDA ALARM

MBDA PGM500

MBDA PGM2000

MBDA Sea Skua

Current British Air to Surface Missiles.
All are in UK service apart from the PGM series.

Stand-Off Weapons

On the night of 30th March 1944, RAF Bomber Command conducted a major raid on the southeast German city of Nuremberg. This mission saw one of the biggest air battles in history as the bomber stream progressed across Europe. Of 779 aircraft on the raid, 96 were lost, the greatest loss of aircraft in a single mission, leaving a trail of burnt-out bombers from Belgium to Southern Germany.

The Nuremberg raid had shown how an effective air defence system could function under ideal conditions. Luftwaffe Nacht-jagdgruppen (night fighter units) tore into the bomber stream and 82 aircraft were lost on the outward leg of the raid. The RAF was only saved from a similar mauling on the return journey by the need for the night fighters to land for refuelling and re-arming. Bomber

Command had suffered its greatest defeat of the war and experienced the havoc that could be wreaked on a bomber force when the air defences gained the upper hand.

The V-Force

The intended *modus operandi* of Bomber Command's aircraft in the post war era was to be high speed and high altitude. This prompted the issuing of OR.199 for what became the English Electric Canberra and OR.229 for the Medium Bomber that became the Avro Vulcan and Handley Page Victor. By flying high and fast, the intention was to fly well above the gun defences of the Soviet Union and too fast for the defending fighters to catch up. This, of course, paid little heed to the development of guided weapons.

A Vulcan B.2 Phase 6 fires an air-launched Polaris missile. Polaris was suggested as a replacement for the cancelled Skybolt in 1961. Adrian Mann

In 1954 Bomber Command was preparing for the arrival of the V-bombers, the Vickers Valiant first, with the Vulcan due to come into service in mid-1960. Members of the Air Staff, many of whom had been involved in Bomber Command's wartime operations, became increasingly concerned about the V-bomber's ability to survive in Soviet airspace. Intelligence estimates advised that the capability of the PVO-Strany (the Soviet air defence organisation) was improving rapidly and would continue to do so for the foreseeable future. These improvements would have made a strike on Moscow, the cornerstone of UK

The map of the Nuremberg Raid 30th/31st March 1944.

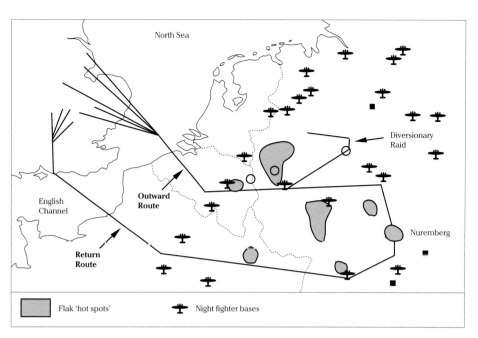

North Sea

Diversionary Raid

English Channel

Outward Route

Return Route

Nuremberg

Flak 'hot spots'   Night fighter bases

deterrence, a very hazardous activity indeed.

Air Ministry papers in The National Archives dating back to 1950 show that the Ministry had commissioned studies into bomber losses, with a view to fitting the V-bombers with defensive armament. The Avro Vulcan, which would become the mainstay of Bomber Command and the succeeding Strike Command, depended on altitude and speed to perform its mission. Unlike the American Strategic Air Command's Boeing B-47 and later Boeing B-52 aircraft, the V-bombers did not possess defensive armament, nor was there a long-range escort fighter in the McDonnell F-101 Voodoo mould in the offing for the RAF. The prospect of a repetition of the Nuremberg raid must have weighed heavily on their minds.

The Pattern of the Future Offensive

One paper, titled 'The Pattern of the Future Offensive', based its conclusions on three different scenarios, each built on an analysis of wartime operations and post-war exercises. The first analysis was based on an RAF night fighter exercise called 'Dagger' that involved de Havilland Mosquito fighters operating against Avro Lancaster and Avro Lincoln bombers. The results were extrapolated to take account of the different performance of the replacement jet-powered V-bombers and produced a loss of 22%, which would be reduced to 7% by the use of Radio Counter Measures (RCM).

The second study used information gathered during the night fighter defence of the United Kingdom against the Luftwaffe from mid-1942. This period covered the Baedeker raids and Operation Steinbock, producing a loss to the German Kampfgruppen of 5%.

The third case analysed the losses inflicted by the Luftwaffe on Bomber Command during raids on Germany in the period from September 1943 to October 1944. This was a period when the tactics of both sides had reached maturity and the Nachtjagdgruppen reached a peak of efficiency. A loss of 2% was to be expected based on this analysis, but Bomber Command raids invariably involved 700-plus aircraft, plus the support activities of 100 Group.

Another factor to be considered was that, in all three situations, the bombers were fitted with defensive armament. This, and the technological differences in speed and manoeuvrability of the future aircraft, would no doubt have had some effect, but may have cancelled each other out. The standard World

War Two procedure when a bomber was under fighter attack was to execute a corkscrew turn, a violent manoeuvre for a Lancaster but impractical in a Vulcan flying at penetration speed.

The conclusion, when all the factors were taken into account was that the loss rate for a 100 aircraft on a deep penetration of the Soviet Union, using the best RCM, would be in the order of 5 to 10%.

This figure, being based on a 100-aircraft raid, would have varied in proportion to the number of bombers in the force with a raid of fifty aircraft suffering 8% loss while a force of ten aircraft would suffer 21% losses. Increasing the size of the bomber force was thought unlikely to produce a reduction in losses.

However, these statistics related to night operations only. Daylight operations would see the loss rate increased to 29% for a 100-aircraft raid, purely due to the increased number of day fighters available. Another caveat in the report was the probable improvement in the quantity and quality of Soviet radar and fighter capabilities that would undoubtedly occur in the future. A loss rate of 10 to 20% for a 100 aircraft mission was to be expected by 1957.

This report must have confirmed the fears of the Air Ministry, but with so much expenditure already sunk into the V-bomber force and an urgent need for Britain to present a credible deterrent, what could be done to improve the situation?

The authors summarised their findings in a simple graph showing how the air defences of the Soviet Union would improve and how the RAF's future equipment would fare against it. Essentially the V-Force would be

vulnerable to guided weapons after 1960, but by using decoys and stand-off weapons their effective career could be extended to 1965 at least. Ballistic weapons would provide the credible deterrent after that.

Fitting defensive armament may have been reassuring to the crews, but it added weight and complexity that was better used for radio countermeasures equipment. Flying faster and higher looked promising and the mid-1950s requirement for a Mach 2.5 reconnaissance aircraft for the V-Force was now under way, so why not modify that as a bomber? The original recce requirement, R.156 and OR.330, was supplemented by RB.156 and OR.336 for the bomber. Avro's 730 project was selected to fulfil both, but in time this would also be vulnerable.

Another proposal involved a converted flying bomb called Blue Rapier, whose development is covered in the ballistic missile chapter. Blue Rapier was to act as a decoy recreating the feint raids and jamming activities of Bomber Command's 100 Group units of World War Two. Low-level attacks had worked for both sides during that conflict, the 'tip and run' raids by the Luftwaffe, and various RAF operations such as the Dam Busters raid, so these were also considered. The final proposal, the one that came to fruition, was fitting the V-bombers with a stand-off weapon.

Stand-Off Weapons

Stand-off (with a hyphen according to the OED) describes any weapon launched against its target at long range. Under that definition an unguided rocket such a Red Angel could be described as a stand-off weapon,

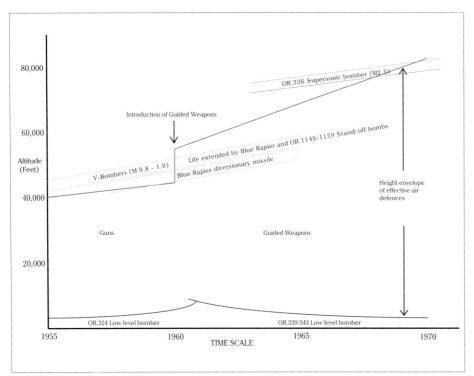

but it isn't. Strictly speaking, it should mean any guided weapon that can be launched against its target while allowing the launch aircraft to remain well outside the enemy's air defence zone. In the 1950s true stand-off weapons were described as powered bombs; with the term stand-off, possibly under American influence, coming into use in the 1960s.

As related in the previous chapter, some degree of stand-off was afforded by the Blue Boar guided bomb. While its ability to be released from 25 miles (46km) away might

Left: **The Air Ministry drew up a diagram showing how it saw the future of attacks on the Soviet Union.**

Below left: **The RAE Controlled Weapon Department's thoughts on powered bomb configurations.**

Below right: **Avro's powered bomb test vehicles included scale models 6/5 and 19/15 plus the full scale 48/35. The Stage 3 extended range weapon is also illustrated along with the definitive service Blue Steel.**

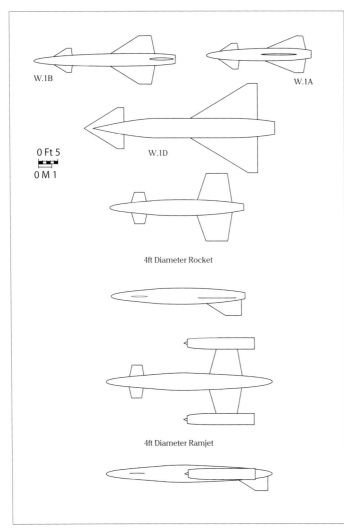

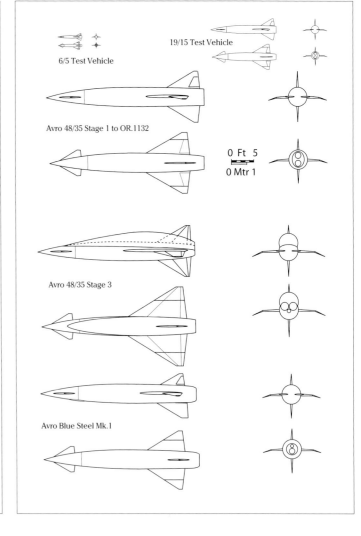

have been sufficient for a gun-defended target, targets with surface-to-air guided weapon (SAGW) defences demanded a bit more respect.

The main problem with such weapons in the 1950s was, as ever, guidance. The basic idea of a stand-off weapon was for its carrier aircraft to launch it and then return to base or carry on to another objective, leaving the weapon to fly to the target. Some means of autonomous guidance was required, not only to guide it to the target but also to tell it where that flight would begin. Such equipment only became available with the development of Doppler (such as Blue Silk) and inertial navigation systems in the late 1950s. A further less problematic factor was powering the weapon with a propulsion system capable of sufficient range to keep the launch aircraft outside the ever-increasing range of the SAGW. The chapter on SAGWs describes the flip side of this problem.

As can be seen from the Air Ministry's graph, up to 1960 there was a zone of lethality from 1,000ft to 40,000ft (305m to 12,192m) where the PVO-Strany was at its most effective. The V-bombers flew above this zone but post-1960 would be vulnerable again. That left the airspace up to 1,000ft (305m) more or less immune from anti-aircraft fire due to the minimum range of SAGWs, short warning times and slow tracking of AA guns. The Air Staff sought to exploit this by issuing a requirement, OR.314/Spec. B.126T, for a low-level bomber. This was superseded in October 1953 by OR.324, which also laid out a need for a stand-off weapon to further increase the survivability of the OR.324 aircraft. This weapon, called Red Cat, was to meet a separate November 1953 requirement called OR.1125. Handley Page and Bristol produced design studies for Red Cat, which was to possess a stand-off range of 20nm (37km). The aircraft and weapon were to be in service by 1962.

Bristol Aircraft was the preferred company to build this aircraft, tendering its Type 186 to B.126 and OR.234. Bristol's idea was to have the weapon mounted dorsally in a semi-recessed weapon carrier. The rationale for pick-a-back carriage was that, since the bomber was at low level, the weapon should go upwards. Prior to launch Bristol's Red Cat was to be raised into the airflow on hydraulic jacks, it would then be released and, on firing its solid rocket motor, fly off towards the target. Bristol's weapon was a monoplane with an elliptical body and stubby wings that folded upwards to allow semi-recessed carriage, dropping into place on launch. Any concerns regarding tail clearance were

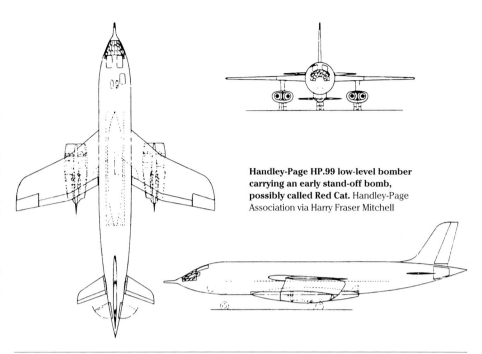

Handley-Page HP.99 low-level bomber carrying an early stand-off bomb, possibly called Red Cat. Handley-Page Association via Harry Fraser Mitchell

addressed by fitting the 186 with a butterfly tail.

Handley Page also featured a semi-recessed weapon station for its more conventional Red Cat on the HP.99 bomber submission. However HP opted for ventral carriage for what resembled a small, rotund, swept-wing aircraft with normal fin and tail surfaces, power being provided by a rocket motor.

A V Roe tendered the Avro 721, powered by four Napier NP.172 turbofans, one variant of which, in a departure from convention, was a two-stage machine with a twin-boom slip-plane carrying a ramjet-powered bomber in the initial phases of flight.

As already discussed, guidance was the problem and considerable effort was expended in the UK and in the US to develop a suitable guidance system for OR.324 and Red Cat. A Doppler navigation system called Green Hammock was under development as was a terrain-following radar but the technology involved was not mature enough to be practicable. A clue to this was the inclusion in the requirement of 'in-flight electronic servicing'. This, compounded with the difficulties involved with low-level ingress to a target (on the Dams Raid 617 Sqn had lost two out of nineteen Lancasters from flying into power lines), meant that OR.324 went no further and was withdrawn in 1954.

The RAE's Powered Bomb

In the early 1950s, the RAE's Controlled Weapons Department studied a powered guided bomb to provide, by 1960, a weapon

with the following aims: prolong the life of the V-bombers, carry a fusion warhead and be immune from interception, jamming and interference. These objectives required a balance between the diameter of the missile, governed by the size of the Atomic Weapons Research Establishment (AWRE) Orange Herald or Green Bamboo warheads, and their installation on the V-bombers. The bomb's guidance required a self-contained inertial navigation system that was under development by Elliott Brothers and its propulsion needed to make possible speeds in excess of Mach 3. An Operational Requirement covering the above, OR.1132, was issued by the Air Staff on 3rd September 1954.

To minimise the effect on the V-bombers' performance, internal or semi-recessed carriage was preferred, but this governed the size of the weapon. Any missile with a diameter greater than 40in (102cm) could not be carried by the Vickers Valiant, while the maximum size for the Avro Vulcan and Handley Page Victor was 50in (127cm). AWRE could not guarantee any dimensions for the forthcoming fusion weapons, a fact that muddied the waters for a long time, so the RAE produced the 'W' series that covered a variety of weapon configurations and fuselage diameters. Based on these studies, RAE decided that it alone should have control of the powered bomb's development, but the Ministry of Supply thought otherwise.

In late 1954, on canvassing the V-bomber companies for their views on the powered bomb, the Ministry noted that Handley Page was 'most enthusiastic' about it, Vickers was

Blue Steel with an RAF technician to provide scale. Its size is readily apparent. TNA AIR 29/3452

A kinetheodolite photograph of an Avro Vulcan over the Woomera test range about to release a Blue Steel. via Brian Wetton

A Blue Steel trials round drops away from a Victor before lighting the Stentor rocket engine. via John Saxon

tract G/Proj/6220/GW35A was placed on 4th May 1955. There was one additional caveat: the Ministry stressed the need for the weapon to be carried on all V-bombers, not just Avro's products. However, this last condition soon fell by the wayside when the development potential of the Vickers Valiant was deemed limited, so the new requirement only covered carriage of the OR.1132 weapon on Vulcan and Victor. In fact only B.2 versions of these aeroplanes would actually receive the missile, having been developed with it in mind.

Blue Steel

In late 1955 Avro's Weapons Research Division, under the leadership of Chief Engineer R H Francis, commenced development of the weapon to meet OR.1132. Armstrong Siddeley was to develop the liquid-fuelled rocket engine, Elliott Brothers the inertial navigation system and AWRE was in charge of the warhead. The Ministry of Supply applied the codename 'Blue Steel'. This would stay with the weapon on service entry with the RAF and possibly alluded to the weapon's stainless steel construction. For its shape Avro selected one of the RAE's rocket-powered canard delta configurations and named it 48/35.

As usual in a guided weapon project, a series of test vehicles was built to speed development. These included the 2/5th-scale 19/15 (powered by the Jackdaw solid rocket motor) for air launch trials from a Vickers Valiant and the ground launched 1/8th-scale

'very enthusiastic' but Avro, apart from its aerodynamicist, '...was uncooperative'. An odd observation since all three companies had carried out studies based on the RAE's configurations. Avro, looking to extend the life of its 730 supersonic reconnaissance bomber to OR.330, had done most work on the 100nm (185km) missile. Handley Page was of the opinion that a 100-mile range was inadequate and proposed a 500nm (926km) range ramjet-powered weapon. Despite HP's forward thinking (which was vindicated long before the decade was out or the OR.1132 weapon had reached service), the Ministry and RAE dismissed the idea, mainly because Elliott Brothers' inertial navigation system was found to be inaccurate at ranges in excess of 100nm due to gyro drift.

On paper, Vickers was most likely to get the job because of its previous work on Blue Boar

(Chapter Seven) and Red Rapier (Chapter Nine), but the RAE thought that Vickers lacked leadership in the project area. Vickers advised that it could do the job in two years less than Avro – if the RAE provided help. The Ministry was convinced that a contractor unconnected with V-bomber production should build the powered bomb, but RAE thought not. As stated above, RAE wished for complete control of the project from the off, but the Ministry did not entertain this idea.

So why did Avro get the job? As noted already the company had done a lot of 'under the counter' work on a powered bomb and this private venture work swung it. Also, RAE was on Avro's side from the start because six of the design team were ex-RAE employees! So, having decided to give design authority to Avro, a company with no track record in guided weapons, a Ministry of Supply con-

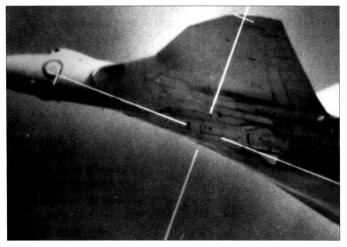

6/5 free-flight model. Avro also proposed the use of one of their 'delta wing fighters' (possibly the mixed powerplant 720 rocket fighter carried aloft by a Vulcan), as a manned test bed for guidance and systems trials.

Avro saw the Blue Steel development programme progressing in four stages. Stage 1 would weigh in at 13,000 lb (5,895kg), be capable of Mach 2.5 to the required 100nm (185km) range and was powered by a single Armstrong Siddeley (AS) RB.9/2 two-chamber engine, the predecessor of the Stentor. This engine used a large 16,000 lb (71.2KN) thrust chamber for boost and a smaller 4,000 lb (17.8KN) thrust chamber for cruise. The 16,000 lb (7,256kg) Stage 2 came next with increased speed and range, Mach 4.5 and 240nm (444km), and power from an improved AS RB.9/2 two-chamber engine.

The long-range Stage 3 was to be a boosted version, with a detachable dorsal fairing carrying two RB 9/2 large chambers and extra fuel for boost and a single 4,000 lb (17.8KN) thrust small chamber for cruise. This had a much larger wing and weighed 25,000 lb (11,338kg), but it did have a range of 450nm (833km). Stage 4 was to be launched from the Avro 730 supersonic bomber and came in A and B versions with a launch taking place at Mach 2.5. The 18,000 lb (8,163kg), 40ft (12.2m)-long model A had a range of 600nm (1,111km); while the 26,000 lb (11,791kg), 50ft (15.2m)-long model B had 900nm (1,667km).

What these different versions show is that even in early 1956 (and as Handley Page had predicted from the off), Avro foresaw the need for ever-increasing stand-off range. Indeed Avro was suggesting that a completely new delta flying wing with a range of 1,000nm (1,852km) be adopted, but the Ministry stuck to its guns and insisted that Avro proceed with Blue Steel to meet OR.1132.

Avro did as it was told. The 6/5 vehicles were ground-launched at Aberporth, but these trials were soon suspended due to a lack of break-up system on the vehicles, the first of many delays that would plague the entire project. Avro decided that the final missile, designated W.100, would be fabricated in AF.520 stainless steel to cope with the thermal effects of Mach 2.5 cruise. On the other hand the vehicles to be used for systems trials, the twin Spectre-powered W.102, W.103 and W.104 which were Mach 2 limited, would be constructed in aluminium alloy by Gloster Aircraft at Hucclecote. W.104 was to be a recoverable vehicle but, after it was realised that its development would delay the programme, this item was dropped. The final test vehicle, W.105, was a fully functional weapon fabricated in stainless steel, but carrying test equipment instead of a warhead.

Even before embarking on full-scale W.100 construction, Avro was having problems with the fabrication of the 19/15. The company had gambled on using the experience gained from the steel construction of its 730 reconnaissance bomber to alleviate any problems with Blue Steel. After the 730 had been cancelled, Blue Steel took up the challenge of stainless steel fabrication and the team had to learn the processes from scratch. Costs and delays began to mount, so Avro applied for

Handley Page Victor carrying an Avro Blue Steel. The Victors gave up this role before the Vulcan as the Polaris system's deployment approached. The Victors took on the tanker role. TNA DEFE 7/1716

monetary help from the US in the form of Mutual Weapon Development Program (MWDP) aid. Bear in mind that this was 1957, less than two years into the project and before a full-scale vehicle had even flown. The MWDP board declined the application on the grounds that Blue Steel was obsolete!

Francis et al had believed that the fabrication side would be the easiest part of the project. However, they rightly foresaw problems with the inertial navigator, particularly with gyro wander. Elliotts' navigation system continued to fail, even after sourcing highly precise gyros from Kearfott in the USA, and this delayed both the test flights and entry into service. It must be remembered that inertial navigation was in its infancy at this time – long before the solid-state revolution ushered in by the transistor. In the end Elliotts' system was made to work and eventually formed the basis of many systems used in the 1970s and 1980s.

The Blue Steel powerplant proved to be the least problematic area of development. The fuels, HTP and kerosene, were Britain's propellants of choice, having been used in manned and unmanned projects since 1945. Armstrong Siddeley developed the RB.9/2 engine, which used a large chamber to produce 16,000 lb (71.2KN) of thrust to boost the missile to 70,000ft (21,336m) and Mach 2.5, before the smaller 4,000 lb (17.8KN) thrust unit took over to perform the cruise part of the

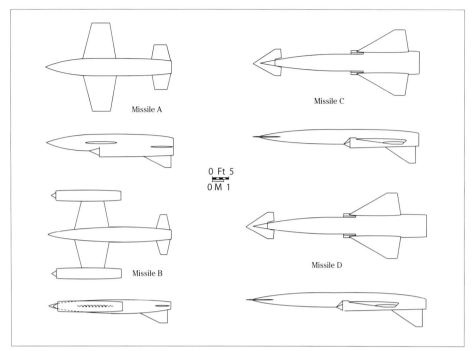

Missile A

Missile C

0 Ft 5

0 M 1

Missile B

Missile D

The RAE Controlled Weapon Department's thoughts on long-range powered bomb configurations to meet OR.1149.

flight. This engine formed the basis of the Stentor 101 in the operational Blue Steel, with 24,000 lb (106.8KN) thrust for the large and 6,000 lb (26.7KN) for the small chamber.

The first W.100 round was finally launched over the Aberporth range in July 1960. A series of test flights at the Woomera range in Australia was planned as part of what became Blue Steel's slow progress from initial study to operational service. Given the delays with the W.100 and later W.105 test vehicles, it was decided to air freight the weapons to Australia, rather than transport them by ship. Since the fastest means would be the Vulcans

and Victors that had been developed to carry the weapon, these types got the job, and thus was born operation Blue Ranger. Flight trials at Woomera also began in July 1960 (the date Blue Steel was originally supposed to be in service) and continued until the end of 1964.

Blue Steel, Avro's W.100 with Stentor 101 engine and Red Snow warhead (a British version of the US W28 warhead) was given 'emergency operational capability' in August 1962, with full release to service not forthcoming until February 1963. By this time the weapon was undoubtedly obsolete. Soon afterwards the V-Force was forced to begin

operating at low level and Blue Steel was consequently modified for low-altitude launch.

Why did Blue Steel survive in a time when missile and aircraft projects were being cancelled? With hindsight, Blue Steel would have been a prime candidate for the Sandys Axe in 1957. Perhaps its money-pit characteristics were not obvious at that time, but maybe the fact that it was the only option in nuclear deterrence made a difference. Sandys had after all been appointed to cut defence costs by substituting a credible deterrent for costly conventional forces. The remainder of this chapter will show how, despite numerous attempts, a replacement for Blue Steel was not available. The RAF soldiered on until 1969 with a weapon that the Americans had considered obsolete in 1957.

A More Ambitious Requirement

By 1956 intelligence reports indicated that the Soviets were developing SAGWs and that the V-bombers would have to enter the air defence zones to launch Blue Steel. Obsolete or not, Blue Steel would be the only game in town until the Blue Streak MRBM was deployed in 1962 (in fact, more realistically, until the mid-1960s). Blue Steel, even through the rosiest tinted glasses, would indeed be obsolete by 1964. Something with a bit more range was required.

Blue Steel's main drawback was its limited range. The Americans had indicated that they would contribute to a 'more ambitious' standoff weapon, so then in May 1956 Air Staff came up with a new requirement designated OR.1149. This called for a range of 1,000nm (1,852km), with the last 100nm (185km) to be flown at low level. Ambitious? Certainly. Achievable? Probably not. Another complication was guidance, with inertial systems suffering from excessive gyro drift over such a long range. This gyro drift produced inaccuracy so another navigation method such as Yellow Lemon, a Doppler system, was required.

First proposals for OR.1149 came from the RAE with a series of design studies, A to D. All were to be launched from Vulcan and Victor, with Missile A having a conventional layout with an Olympus 21R providing the power. Missile B shared the configuration of the A, but with de Havilland Gyron Junior turbojets on each wingtip.

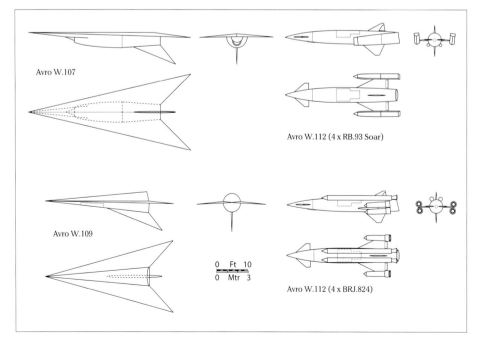

Avro W.107

Avro W.112 (4 x RB.93 Soar)

Avro W.109

0 Ft 10

0 Mtr 3

Avro W.112 (4 x BRJ.824)

The various Avro proposals for OR.1149.

The most interesting, and the study to which most effort appears to have been applied, was a twin de Havilland Gyron Junior powered canard delta called the '1000-mile range flying bomb'. This came in two versions, Missile C and Missile D. Both shared the same basic airframe with an 18ft (5.5m) wingspan, however Missile C was 46ft (14m) long while Missile D was 50ft 6in (15.4m) long. The longer fuselage allowed Missile D to house additional fuel for reheat use during the entire flight, unlike Missile C that only used heat in its acceleration stage.

Avro, with their Blue Steel Mk.1 experience, had already proposed increasing the fuel volume in that missile to improve its range. This was deemed unacceptable, but Francis and his team bounced back and were in the van when it came to tendering with their Z-series for use by Victor and Vulcan. Z.1 took a Blue Steel airframe and coupled it with a de Havilland Gyron Junior supersonic turbojet, while the Z.12 fitted two Bristol BRJ.1000 32in (81.3cm) ramjets to the Blue Steel. Bristol Engines called this work RP.2 (Ramjet Project 2), but the combination was deemed underpowered and lacked range and altitude performance. To counter this, the Z.16 was fitted with a pair of Rolls-Royce RB.93 turbojets on each wingtip. Bristol also carried out work on RP.5 (called Z.20 by Avro); this employed a pair of BRJ.851 19in (48.3cm) ramjets in the same mountings as the BR.93s.

Avro also proposed some larger 'clean sheet' designs, such as the Gyron Junior-powered W.107 and the Stentor rocket-powered W.109, based on their 1956 longer-ranged Blue Steel delta proposal. Both types used highly swept delta wings, with the W.107 having a conical fuselage, the upper half of which formed a jettisonable fuel tank. The rocket-powered W.109 also posed structural problems since to achieve the range requirement it had to cruise at Mach 5.

Carrying this series of Avro's larger weapons, particularly the W.110 that used a Gyron Junior and two Armstrong Siddeley Gamma rocket engines, may have posed ground clearance problems for the Handley Page Victor. This was due to the weapon's underslung engine installations and so, in the end, Avro opted to use the basic Blue Steel with wingtip engines.

The Z.20 became the W.112 with a stretched Blue Steel fuselage, but its four ramjets were underpowered, thereby reducing range and speed. The obvious solution of adding two more engines was considered, but instead it was decided to use English Electric's 'Split Wing' ramjet, which comprised a

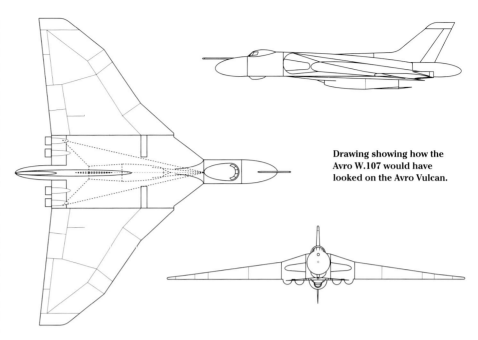

Drawing showing how the Avro W.107 would have looked on the Avro Vulcan.

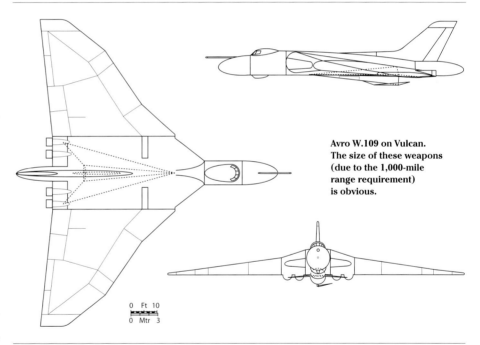

Avro W.109 on Vulcan. The size of these weapons (due to the 1,000-mile range requirement) is obvious.

series of ramjet burners integrated into the wing structure. This project was taken over by English Electric and evolved into what they called the P.10D.

Meanwhile at Weybridge, Vickers were keen to gain the OR.1149 contract. By deploying the design team from the cancelled Red Rapier (a flying bomb project to be described shortly), Vickers proposed to meet OR.1149 with a turborocket-powered weapon called the Type 569. However Vickers soon discovered that turborockets (an engine whose low-speed thrust is produced by employing rocket-driven turbomachinery) lacked the

power for acceleration while suffering from high specific fuel consumption. Acceleration could be improved with solid boost motors, but fuel consumption and its impact on range could only be solved by changing the powerplant. Bristol Engines carried out a project study (RP.4), aimed at fitting the BRJ.1000 30in (81.3cm) ramjets to the Type 569, but eventually Vickers opted for turbojets. The Type 569 was of conventional layout, with engines on the wingtips. Unfortunately, for centre of gravity reasons, it had to be loaded without fuel and then fuelled in flight from the carrier aircraft's tanks.

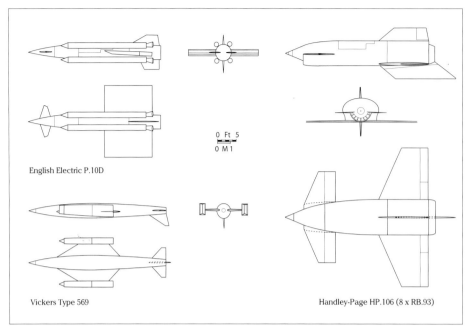

English Electric P.10D

Vickers Type 569

Handley-Page HP.106 (8 x RB.93)

0 Ft 5
0 M 1

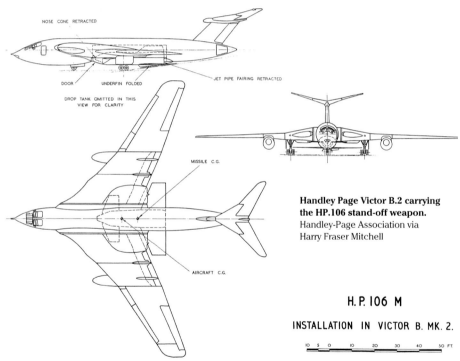

NOSE CONE RETRACTED

DOOR   UNDERFIN FOLDED   JET PIPE FAIRING RETRACTED

DROP TANK OMITTED IN THIS VIEW FOR CLARITY

MISSILE C.G.

AIRCRAFT C.G.

Handley Page Victor B.2 carrying the HP.106 stand-off weapon.
Handley-Page Association via Harry Fraser Mitchell

H. P. 106 M
INSTALLATION IN VICTOR B. MK. 2.

10 5 0   10   20   30   40   50 FT

In late 1956 Handley Page, not known for their guided weapons, produced a design study called the HP.106 to OR.1149 that was novel in a couple of ways. Firstly it had a squat fuselage holding a pair of DH Gyron Junior turbojets fed by a chin intake. Secondly it used diesel fuel because the denser diesel provided greater range as a result of reduced boil-off at the higher temperatures experienced during the cruise. To allow it to fit into the V-bomber's weapons bay, the HP.106 had a retractable nose cone.

OR.1159 – Back to the Drawing Board

Ambitious from the outset, OR.1149 was causing problems for the developers. The Ministry was asking awkward questions about range (or rather the lack of it) and in-service dates. Only the P.10D and the HP.106 met the requirement, but the former would suffer a prolonged engine development and the latter used an unusual fuel (for the RAF at any rate). In addition neither could be used on a Victor fitted with rocket assisted take-off (RATO) gear.

By October 1957 the emphasis had switched to an early service entry and ease of weapon carriage. Avro and its W.112 were back in the competition. The Air Staff also took a rational look at how the OR.1149 tenders had fared against the requirement. In short, apart from English Electric Aviation and Handley Page, the companies had difficulty meeting the range requirement. Addressing the range problem would take longer, with 1964 looking like the realistic deployment date. A weapon with a reduced range would be ready sooner, so OR.1149 was withdrawn and in May 1958 was replaced by OR.1159 and Specification UB.200. This saw the range requirement reduced to 600nm (1,111km) and the low-level phase deleted. A new megaton-yield warhead was also defined, with OR.1160 (issued in June 1958) covering that.

The new weapon could be based on the existing Blue Steel, so Avro automatically led the field. There would be no problems installing the missile in the V-bombers and the existing airframe could be used with minimal changes, speeding up the development. From this Blue Steel Mk.2 was born, with the Mk.1's Stentor rocket motor replaced by a fuel tank, a pair of BRJ.824 18in (47.7cm) ramjets on the wingtips, and two dorsally mounted Gosling boost rockets. This, the definitive Blue Steel Mk.2, carried the Avro designation W.114.

Skybolt

By mid-1959 the USAF had committed to Weapon System WS.138A, the Douglas Skybolt air-launched ballistic missile. Ongoing delays with Blue Steel Mk.1 continued to concern the Air Ministry and MoS, who began to have doubts about Avro's ability to bring the weapon to operational status (never mind the Mk.2 which they saw as diverting effort away from the Mk.1). The Air Council concluded that Skybolt would be available before Blue Steel Mk.2 and hence studies for the integration of Skybolt on both the Victor and Vulcan were under way by August 1959. The main stumbling block was the warhead for Skybolt. Britain lacked a lightweight (700lb/318kg) nuclear warhead at that time and buying a US warhead was: 'incompatible with Her Majesty's Government policy of Independent Deterrent'.

However the AWRE claimed that they could produce such a lightweight warhead (possibly to OR.1161 for a small 500lb /

This rare drawing shows how Blue Steel Mk.2 would have been loaded into the weapons bay of the Vulcan. via Tony Buttler

Sketch of the Victor patrol bomber. Note the additional wingtip tanks to improve endurance on a sortie. via Tony Buttler

This graph shows the improvement Avro hoped to achieve with Blue Steel Mk.1A. The Ministry was unimpressed

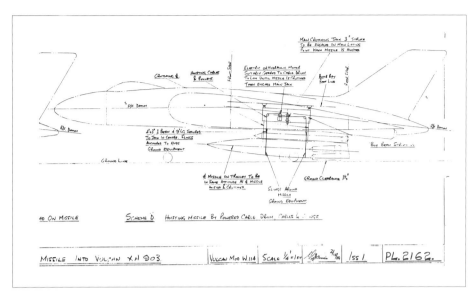

226.8kg megaton device) by the time Skybolt was ready for service in 1963/1964.

So, the options were a) continue with OR.1159, or b) buy Skybolt and fit a British warhead, or c) improve Blue Steel.

Hugh Francis wrote to the Under Secretary at the Ministry of Aviation on the 21st of October 1960 outlining Avro's proposals for Blue Steel. The simplest improvement to Blue Steel, to reduce its vulnerability to SAMs, was to make it 'jink': change course continually. At this point the Controller of Guided Weapons and Electronics (CGWL), Steuart Mitchell, wasted no time and stepped into the discussion. In a letter dated 24th October 1960, he noted that jinking had been tried '…to avoid murdering Meteor pilotless targets during Seaslug trials we have tried to "jink" Meteors at the optimum moment during the approach of Seaslug missiles. The effect is very limited and would have no result whatsoever against a [defensive] nuclear-headed SAGW'.

Therefore more complicated improvements to Blue Steel were considered including the Mk.1S with the Skybolt warhead, TSR.2 strike aircraft navigation suite and internal rearrangement to increase fuel capacity.

There was also the Mk.1A, which was the Mk.1S fitted with wing tanks. In addition a new smaller (4,500lb / 2,041kg) solid rocket-powered weapon was suggested by Avro for the TSR.2 and Buccaneer. The W.130 was described as a general-purpose weapon that was also capable of ground launch as a two- or three-stage SSM. This proposal appears to have infuriated the CGWL. In the same letter he states: 'I do not know what requirement the "small general purpose tactical weapon" version of Blue Steel is intended to meet. I would state firmly however that if there be such a requirement it be analysed in the customary way by the Ministry, (sic) and the various possible ways of meeting it should be examined. To buy a pig in a poke out of an Avro sales brochure would, in my view, be inexcusable. Let us see this requirement if it exists, and have it competently analysed by our own resources. I am sure CA (Controller, Aircraft) would agree.'

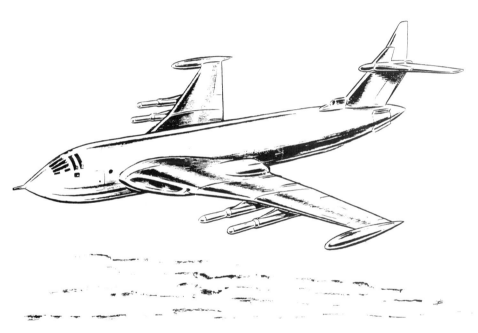

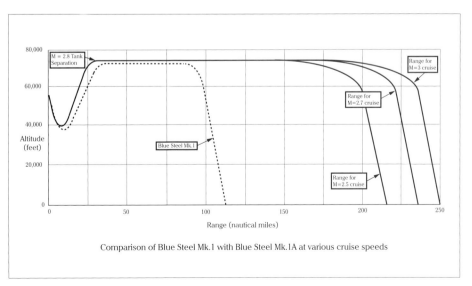

Comparison of Blue Steel Mk.1 with Blue Steel Mk.1A at various cruise speeds

In November 1960 the Director General of Guided Weapons development wrote to the CGWL and described the W.130 as a '...nebulous proposal that amounts really to a Meccano set of weapons...and suffers from all the drawbacks of Meccano set arrangements...'. What the DG/GW meant was that the weapon comprised bits and pieces rather than the discrete deterrent that was required. Avro had not finished improving Blue Steel, particularly its range. The company also suggested the Mk.1* with a four-chamber Bristol Siddeley PR.41 engine to increase speed (and hence range) to Mach 4. The PR.41 was also shorter than the Stentor, thus freeing up extra space for fuel. To produce extra power, Avro wanted to use hydrazines as the fuel and 95% High Test Peroxide (HTP) to produce the oxidant. Given that fuelling Blue Steel on the ground was already fraught with risk from HTP, the mere suggestion of hydrazines, a poisonous rocket fuel that would need to be imported from the USA, took the Air Staff and Ministry aback. Avro pointed out that the hydrazine would be carried in sealed capsules inserted into the missile. Avro also suggested the Mk.1*KG, which used a new kerosene-fuelled engine.

Yet again the Air Ministry and the MoD took a hard look at Avro's activities and by January 1960 had concluded that Avro should concentrate on Blue Steel Mk.1. Avro continued to propose improvements, prompting the Minister of Defence, Harold Watkinson, to say: 'The aim was to get the best improvement in performance for the Mk.1 at a reasonable cost, and (he) did not want the project to be tied to any particular range.'

In due course the Ministry scrapped Blue Steel Mk.2 and in December 1959 withdrew OR.1159. They also decided to go for Option B (Skybolt), with the added incentive that Skybolt would also replace the more vulnerable Blue Streak MRBM discussed shortly.

Technology had progressed in the late 1950s to a point where a nuclear-powered submarine capable of carrying and launching ballistic missile was feasible. This allowed a credible deterrent to be maintained out of reach of an enemy pre-emptive strike. The US had developed such a system (called Polaris) and in December 1962 opted to purchase Polaris as the UK future deterrent. However it would not be in service before 1969, so the Douglas Skybolt would be in service pending delivery of Polaris.

OR.1182 – Third Time Unlucky

Although committed to Skybolt and with the necessary modifications to the Victor and Vulcan under way, the Ministries were under no illusion that Skybolt would enter service. Douglas had been having problems with the weapon and there was a possibility, despite their assurances, that the Americans would cancel it. The other spanner in the works was the belief that ballistic missiles would be vulnerable to anti-ballistic missiles (ABM) systems that the Soviets had under development. In short the deterrence story had come full circle: subsonic bombers were again the delivery vehicle of choice, but kept out of harm's way by long-range stand-off missiles.

As insurance, the Air Staff drew up OR.1182 for a new stand-off weapon that was to be in service on V-bombers by 1966. Issued on 10th January 1961, OR.1182 called for a 1,000nm (1,185km) range, Mach 3 performance at high altitude, and high-speed (Mach 2) terrain-following at low level for the last 100nm (185km).

Avro went back to the drawing board and drew up the W.140, capable of Mach 3 at 70,000ft (21,336m) and Mach 1.5 at sea level. It was to be powered by a single Rolls-Royce

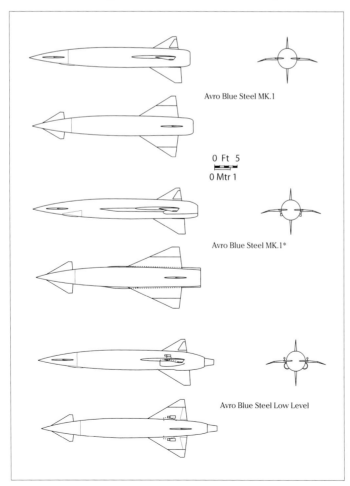

Avro Blue Steel MK.1

0 Ft 5
0 Mtr 1

Avro Blue Steel MK.1*

Avro Blue Steel Low Level

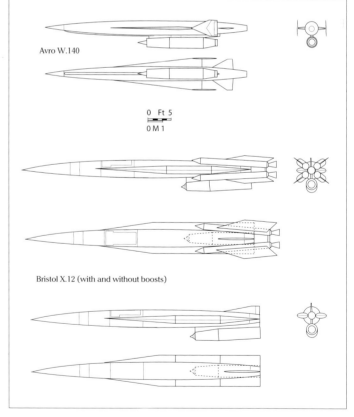

Avro W.140

0 Ft 5
0 M 1

Bristol X.12 (with and without boosts)

Left: **Numerous Blue Steel Mk.1 proposals from Avro.**

Above: **The two main proposals for OR.1182: Avro's W.140 and BAC's X.12 stand-off weapons.**

British Secret Projects: Hypersonics, Ramjets & Missiles

RB.153 turbojet rated at 6,850 lb (30.5kN) thrust dry and 11,645 lb (51.8kN) with reheat. The Air Staff was unimpressed by the W.140, indicating that it was too slow both at altitude and at low level. Avro countered this by claiming that terrain-following flight was easier at Mach 1.5. However the most concern was voiced about the range, initially 580nm (933.4km), which caused consternation, but this was later improved to 950nm (1,529km).

Bristol was very experienced in long-range, high-speed flight, having developed the Blue Envoy SAM. The company had also had significant input into the propulsion systems of the OR.1149 and OR.1159 tenders and using this expertise it produced the X.12. Previously called Pandora, the X.12 was powered by a BRJ.824 18in (45.7cm) ramjet, the X.12 would have been capable of Mach 3 at altitude and, with changes to airframe materials, Mach 4 if required. Its low-altitude performance would be in the region of Mach 2.8, which Bristol pointed out aided survivability no end, guided by a version of the Forward Looking Radar from TSR.2. Unfortunately X.12 was heavy at 15,000 lb (6,804kg), which restricted the number of missiles the V-bombers could carry as well as reducing their range. The Vickers VC-10 transport could carry four X.12 as far as 1,470nm (2,722km), but Avro and Handley Page were working on variants of the Vulcan and Victor with increased all-up weights to meet the range and carriage requirement. However, even a Victor B.2 Stage 3 could only manage 755nm (1,398km) with four X.12 aboard. With full British participation in Skybolt from March 1960, OR.1182 would not be required and so the latter was dropped in late 1961.

Having seen the way the wind was blowing, the British Aircraft Corporation at Stevenage proposed a British alternative to Skybolt. The X.12B was an air-launched ballistic missile, essentially a three-stage solid rocket version of the X.12 armed with a variant of 'Steven', the AWRE nickname for the Anglicised version of the Mk.47 Polaris warhead. Launch aircraft was to be the VC-10, for reasons already described, but official interest was not forthcoming. That was about to change.

On 19th December 1962 Skybolt was cancelled by the Kennedy administration. Having already cancelled the Blue Streak and allowed OR.1182 to lapse, the British Government was left without a credible deterrent. Blue Steel Mk.1 was given an 'Emergency Operational' status in August 1962 but, as had been realised years before, it was not the answer. The US government offered Skybolt to the UK for development but Her Majesty's

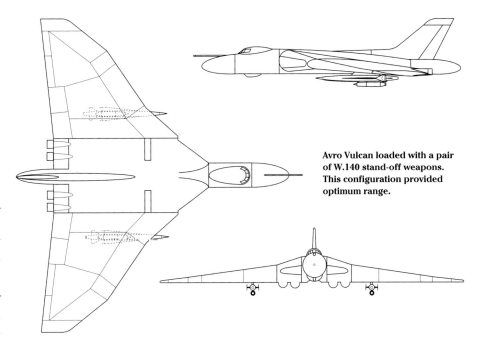

Avro Vulcan loaded with a pair of W.140 stand-off weapons. This configuration provided optimum range.

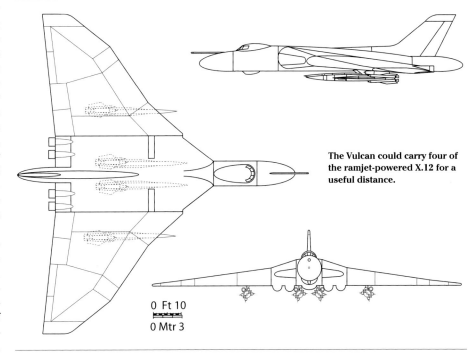

The Vulcan could carry four of the ramjet-powered X.12 for a useful distance.

0 Ft 10
0 Mtr 3

Government declined. They had committed to Polaris as the future 'credible deterrent' and could not afford to develop both.

However, committing to Polaris had been on the understanding that Skybolt would be available pending operational deployment of the Resolution Class missile submarines that would carry Polaris, estimated to be from 1969. No Skybolt meant there was a gap in strategic capability and this had to be filled.

The impression gained from the departmental correspondence lodged in The National Archives at Kew is one of panic, or as

near to panic as the British Civil Service gets. A paper dated 2nd January 1963 lists various proposals, including improved ECM and free-fall bombs for the V-Force, stretched Blue Steel, AJ.168 with a nuclear warhead, extended range TSR.2 (SSR.2 perhaps?) and a silo-launched, two-stage Black Knight. None of these were really up to the job: Blue Steel was still not fully operational and Black Knight was too short-ranged. The call went out for tenders for a 'gap filler' deterrent. The RAE GW Dept bore most of the brunt of this and rose to the challenge.

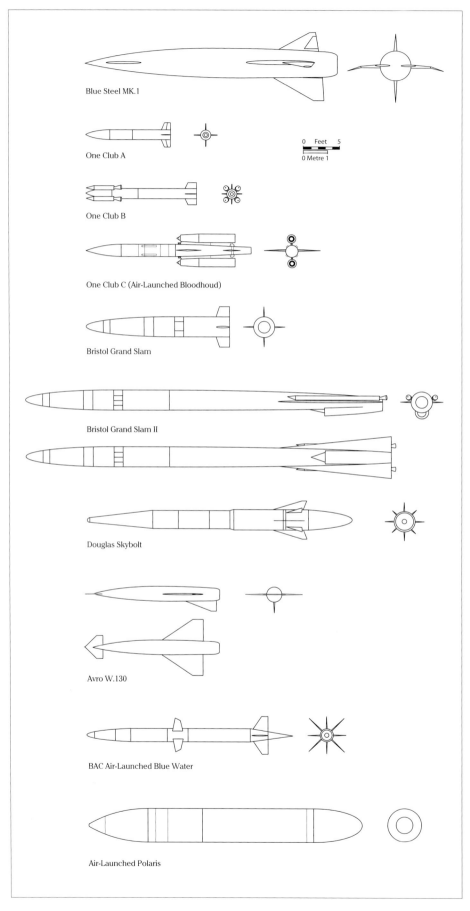

Blue Steel MK.1

One Club A

One Club B

One Club C (Air-Launched Bloodhoud)

Bristol Grand Slam

Bristol Grand Slam II

Douglas Skybolt

Avro W.130

BAC Air-Launched Blue Water

Air-Launched Polaris

0   Feet   5
0 Metre 1

Stop Gaps and Gap Fillers – The Dash for Deterrence

Over the years the RAE and the Air Staff had reached the startling conclusion that a stand-off weapon with a range between 60 and 400nm (111 and 740km) was a waste of time. They wanted a small 25nm (46.3km)-range missile that could be launched from TSR.2 or Buccaneer as well as the V-bombers or a larger, long-range weapon for the V-bombers. The RAE declared that a Blue Steel capable of low-level launch was not what was required.

BAC's Guided Weapon Department at Filton proposed a trio of Gap Fillers, named One Club A, B and C.

One Club A was the simplest, taking the new lay-down bomb, to the August 1959 requirement OR.1177 (which became known as WE.177A), and adding a Raven rocket motor. This unguided weapon was to be carried internally and launched from TSR.2 and Buccaneer strike aircraft. The B model was essentially the same but with four Linnet III rocket boosters and a lifting body warhead that acted as a glide bomb. The C model was a Bloodhound SAM, modified for air launch from a Vulcan with a range of 25nm (46km). The Staff liked One Club A and proposed launching it with a few concrete-headed decoys to saturate the defences.

De Havilland, fresh from losing Blue Streak as a weapon (see next chapter), proposed two designs. The first was a short-range, air-launched ballistic missile called Hatchet. Powered by a Foxhound motor from Seaslug, its range was 55nm (102km) when launched from TSR.2. The second DH study, RG.17, weighed in at 4,600 lb (2,086kg), was 19ft (5.8m) in length and had a diameter of 28in (71.1cm). RG.17's range was 120nm (222km), or 200nm (370km) if toss-launched from TSR.2. The RAE dismissed DH's RG.17 as 'too sketchy'.

BAC at Filton also looked at larger weapons. Two were proposed: Grand Slam (unrelated to the World War Two weapon) and Grand Slam II for the longer-range mission. The former was a 100nm (185km) range rocket-propelled toss bomb to be launched from TSR.2, while the latter definitely did not fall within the RAE's size category. Grand Slam II took the toss bomb and added extras. With a launch weight of 32,000 lb (14,515kg) and a length of 50ft (15.2m), Grand Slam II could only be carried by the V-bombers. Its 1,300nm (2,408km) range was achieved by flying at Mach 3 for the first 500nm (926km) at

The various studies for a 'gap filler' weapon to equip the V-Force.

high altitude, descending to low level and Mach 2 for the next 700nm (1,296km) before pitching up to toss the Grand Slam onto the target from 100nm (185km). Power for the weapon would be provided by an integrated BS.1013 ramjet fuelled by a high-density/low-volatility fuel such as Shelldyne, then under development for high-speed ramjets.

Other proposals included air-launched versions of the American Polaris and Pershing ballistic missiles, but it was the airborne application of a British weapon that received most attention. BAC Stevenage submitted a proposal for an air-launched, extended range version of the Blue Water surface-to-surface missile (SSM). The Staff considered this the most viable design of the lot, especially when coupled with TSR.2 as the launch aircraft.

Avro were noticeably absent from this dash for deterrence. In 1964, with Blue Steel in service and Polaris not too far off, a new proposal appeared: SLAM – Supersonic Low Altitude Missile. This was submitted by Shorts, Elliots and Rolls-Royce and used a Blue Steel layout, TSR.2 navigation system and an RB.153 turbojet. Described by Air Cdr J H Hunter-Tod of the Ministry of Aviation as a 'souped-up low-level Blue Steel', it seemed rather more feasible than BAC's Grand Slam II, but would be vulnerable to Soviet fighters. SLAM was dismissed in late 1964, but earmarked for future resurrection to extend the life of TSR.2.

In the end the RAF soldiered on with the Vulcan and W.105, the production version of Blue Steel, both modified for low-level operations. 1968 saw the drawdown of Blue Steel when the first patrols by the Polaris-equipped Resolution Class submarines slipped out of Faslane and down the Firth of Clyde. Blue Steel disappeared from the Victor's armoury the same year, with the last Vulcan/Blue Steel sorties ending the missile's career in December 1970. The V-Force swapped its Blue Steels for the WE.177B, a parachute-retarded gravity bomb that used the ZA.297 warhead derived from the UK Skybolt RE.179 warhead. Known in service as 'Bomb, HE, 950lb MC', the WE.177 was also carried by Panavia Tornado GR.1s and had been withdrawn from service by August 1998, ending the RAF's nuclear capability.

There was one more attempt to produce a stand-off weapon dating back to 1972. TASM (Tactical Air-to-Surface Missile) was designed to meet what became SR(A)1244 for a WE.177 replacement. Martin Marietta's bid was based on their AQM-127 Supersonic Low Atitude Target (SLAT), Boeing's on the AGM-131 Short Range Attack Missile (SRAM II)

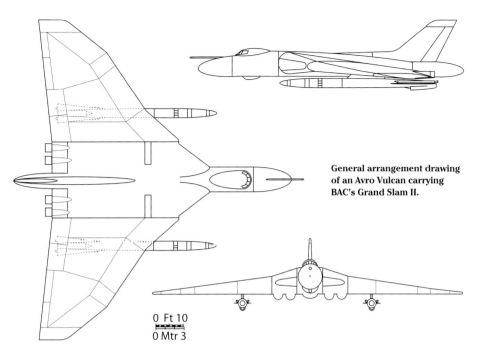

General arrangement drawing of an Avro Vulcan carrying BAC's Grand Slam II.

0 Ft 10
0 Mtr 3

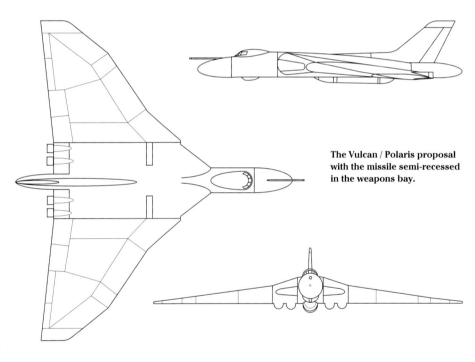

The Vulcan / Polaris proposal with the missile semi-recessed in the weapons bay.

and Aerospatiale's on the Air-Sol Longue Portée (ASLP). Deemed too expensive for a UK company to develop, TASM was cancelled in 1993.

Stormshadow

The RAF lacked a stand-off weapon until the introduction of the MBDA Stormshadow in 2003. With the growing interest in Air Launched Cruise Missiles in the USA through-

out the 1970s, BAe Dynamics proposed a cruise missile version of Sea Eagle to be developed under the designation P4T for Tornado. This solicited little interest and was cancelled in 1981.

The following year NGAST.1236 was drawn up and led to the LRSOW (Long Range Stand-Off Weapon) in conjunction with the US and West Germany. By 1986 this had become a seven-nation project called MSOW (Modular

Stand-Off Weapon), but the UK and the US withdrew in 1989. As a consequence of this withdrawal, the Staff Target lapsed.

Having been mauled flying low-level attacks on Iraqi airfields in January 1991, the RAF began detailed studies for an air-launched cruise missile to allow targets such as heavily defended airfields to be attacked. In 1993 a revamped SR(A).1236 was issued covering a Conventional Air-launched Stand-Off Missile (CASOM). Seven tenders were submitted including P31, a turbofan-powered derivative of the Texas Instruments AGM-154 Joint Stand-Off Weapon (JSOW), itself a derivative of the Israeli Popeye and the AGM-109 Tomahawk. From BAe Dynamics came REVISE, MANTIS and the Al Hakim-derived Pegasus in conjunction with Marconi.

BAC's Grand Slam II in a mocked up image from a Bristol Siddeley brochure. Bristol Collection via Richard Vernon

As BAC's TSR.2 development progressed, a plethora of design studies for stand-off weapons to arm it appeared. Apart from the W.130 and Vickers Momentum bomb, all of these were RAE proposals.

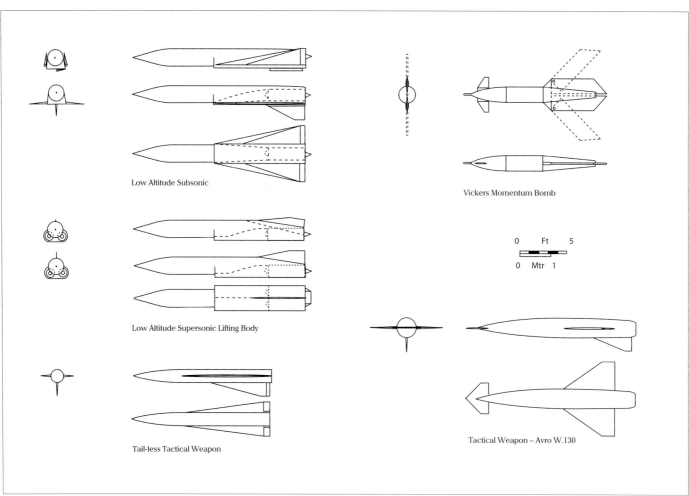

Low Altitude Subsonic

Low Altitude Supersonic Lifting Body

Tail-less Tactical Weapon

Vickers Momentum Bomb

0 Ft 5
0 Mtr 1

Tactical Weapon – Avro W.130

The main contender was SCALP EG, a Matra design based on the Apache anti-run-way sub-munition dispenser. After the merger of Matra, BAe Dynamics and Alenia into MBDA in 1996, development of SCALP EG to meet SR(A).1236 started in earnest, with the contract being awarded in 1997. The name Stormshadow was selected and the weapon entered service in 2002, in time to be used by 617 Squadron's Tornados in the 2003 Gulf War.

Stormshadow is powered by a Microturbo TRI 30-30 turbofan and incorporates a great deal of low-observable characteristics. Guidance is by GPS and uses BAe's TERPROM (TERrain PROfile Matching) system. Approaching the target at low level, the missile then climbs to medium altitude to perform a target search. The nosecone is jettisoned to expose the Imaging Infra-Red seeker, which commences searching for a target that matches that in the pre-loaded targeting database. On finding a match, Stormshadow dives onto it and triggers the BROACH warhead on impact.

BROACH stands for Bomb, Royal Ordnance, Augmenting CHarge and is a munition for use against hardened targets such as bunkers. It incorporates an initial penetrating charge that punches into the bunker and a second charge that moves through the hole created by the first charge. This makes the Stormshadow superior to other cruise missiles such as the American Tomahawk for operations against hardened facilities.

Conclusion

Britain's development of stand-off weapons follows the trend of other guided weapons: over-ambitious requirements, over-runs (in time and money, figures quoted for Blue Steel show that its development cost had multiplied four-fold) and the usual moving of the goalposts as the threat changed. At first glance all these changes in threat, policy and requirement look like muddle. Indeed Sir Stanley Hooker summed up military aviation policy of the time by saying 'We were in, we were out, then we were in again and finally out. It was more like a boat race than a policy'.

Unlike other weapons the stand-off missile appears to have triggered a 'flap' when Skybolt was cancelled in 1962 leaving the UK without a credible deterrent. This might just be the reason that an updated assessment of the vulnerability of the V-bomber force remains a closed document. The assessment would have been grim, but reality could have been much worse. Ballistic weapons were to be the answer, but with these came a hidden agenda.

Stand-Off Weapons

Missile	Length ft (m)	Diameter in (cm)	Span ft (m)	Powerplant	Guidance
Blue Steel	34.9 (10.6)	68 (1.72)	12.9 (3.9)	Rocket engine	Inertial
Blue Steel Mk.2	34.9 (10.6)	68 (1.72)	12.9 (3.9)	4 x Ramjets	Inertial / Doppler
HP.106	40.5 (12.3)	65 (165)	31 (9.5)	8 x Turbojets	Inertial / Doppler
Bristol X12	31 (9.5)	28 (71)	5 (1.5)	1 x Ramjet	Inertial / Doppler
Avro W.140	38.2 (11.6)	30 (76)	6.7 (2)	Turbojet	Inertial / Doppler
Pandora / X.12 and Grand Slam II	50 (15.2)	38 (96.5)	6 (1.8)	1 x Ramjet	Inertial / Doppler
Stormshadow	16.75 (5.1)	–	9.8 (3)	Turbojet	Inertial GPS

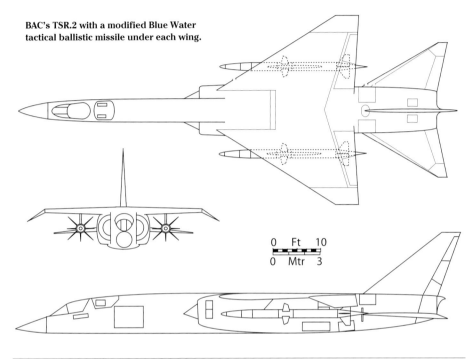

BAC's TSR.2 with a modified Blue Water tactical ballistic missile under each wing.

0 Ft 10
0 Mtr 3

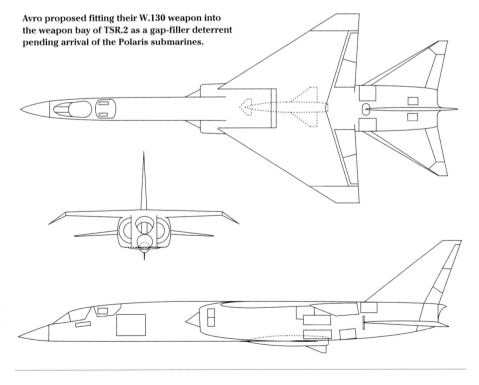

Avro proposed fitting their W.130 weapon into the weapon bay of TSR.2 as a gap-filler deterrent pending arrival of the Polaris submarines.

Chapter Nine

Ground-Launched Missiles

The heavy losses of the Bomber Command offensive from 1941 to 1945 had a major influence on post-war strategic planning. First of all was the Air Staff Requirement for a high-altitude, high-speed medium bomber to OR.229 / Specification B.35/46 to replace the Avro Lincoln, which produced the V-bombers. Second was the realisation that the OR.229 type could be a long time coming. The RAF needed to fill a capability gap between the Lincoln becoming obsolete (since it couldn't carry the first generation of atomic bombs, it effectively became obsolete on 6th August 1945, the day Hiroshima was attacked) and the arrival in service of the Vickers Valiant, first type for the V-Force,

which was due to reach squadrons in the mid-1950s.

To regain this bombing capability the RAF took delivery of eighty-eight American Boeing B-29s, which the RAF called the Washington B.1. Ever eager for a home-grown solution (that would require little dollar expenditure), the Air Staff determined that the answer lay with the two weapons that the Allies lacked at the end of the war: the flying bomb and the ballistic missile.

British forces had been offered flying bombs twenty years before the V-1 made its first flight, in the shape of the Larynx, which we first saw in Chapter One. Later, in 1940, Miles developed the Hoop-La, a Gypsy Major-

Soviet PVO Strany MiG-15s intercept a massed attack by RAF Red Rapier flying bombs.
Adrian Mann

powered monoplane to carry a 1,000 lb (454kg) bomb to Germany. Intended to be launched in waves, the cheap, mass-produced Hoop-La failed to grasp the imagination of the Air Staff, who, ever eager to have more men and aircraft under their command, dropped the idea.

By September 1945, with the lessons of the Nuremberg raid fresh in their minds, the situation had changed from the era of Hoop-La. The unmanned expendable bomber was initially seen as a means to gain longer range.

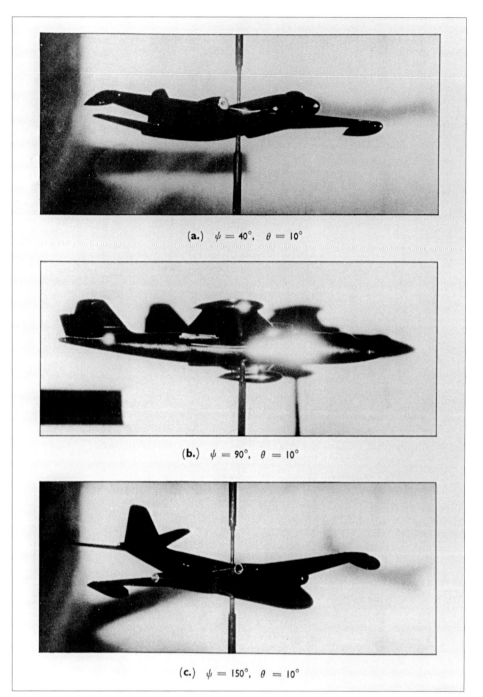

Radio and Radar Establishment used models of the Canberra to assess its radar cross-section. The models were highly polished and lights were shone on them to 'see' the reflection areas.
TNA WO 195/14767

(a.) $\psi = 40°$, $\theta = 10°$

(b.) $\psi = 90°$, $\theta = 10°$

(c.) $\psi = 150°$, $\theta = 10°$

The Soviet Union was vast and its industry had been moved lock, stock and barrel to the east of the Urals in 1941 to escape being over-run by the Germans. The Urals are a very long way from Bomber Command's bases in Lincolnshire, which presented a huge problem with the start of the Cold War in the late 1940s.

It is preferable to have your expensively trained aircrew and their costly aircraft return to fly another mission or two. They therefore require enough fuel for a return trip or onward flight to friendly territory, thus more or less halving the operational radius of the aircraft. Removing the crew and building the aircraft as cheaply as possible, thus making it expendable, allowed the entire fuel load to be used to carry the aircraft and its payload on a one-way mission. A state of affairs the Kamikaze had exploited to attack the US and Royal Navies at long range in the Pacific.

Blue Moon – Named Ever So Aptly

A study for a surface-to-surface atomic 'strategical rocket' was under way by 1945 for the General Staff. Called Menace, this was to be a ramjet-powered pilotless plane carrying an atomic warhead for 2,000nm (3,704km). A joint War Office and Air Ministry project, Menace's range meant that there was no suitable facility in the UK to test it when it was due for trials. This need for extensive range facilities prompted the setting up of the Long Range Weapons Establishment at Woomera in Australia. The main problem with Menace was its ramjet: with development problems occurring on a 6in (12.7cm) ramjet, there was no hope for one six times the diameter to power Menace which was therefore cancelled in 1947.

In 1950 the ramjet missile was re-examined, less ambitiously, to provide a 400nm (741km) range from a 14,000 lb (6,349kg) missile powered to Mach 2 by a pair of 30in (76.2cm) ramjets. Again, the state of the art could not provide the requisite ramjet performance nor the quantum leap in boost rocket motors required to lift the weapon off the ground.

So, it was back to turbojet types and even the possibility of crewing to solve the guidance and weapon aiming problem. In late 1951 the Minimum Conventional Bomber was drawn up which aimed to provide increased range, over-the-target altitude and speed while reducing production, training and maintenance costs. The use of the description 'conventional' by the RAE meant that it was crewed, gas turbine powered and re-usable; but it did not refer to its warload. By reducing the crew to a maximum of two and removing such luxuries as ejection seats and pressurisation, the bomber could provide better accuracy than the unmanned expendable aircraft, but still come in cheaper than conventional bombers such as the Valiant. Powered by a pair of Rolls-Royce Conway engines the Minimum Conventional Bomber, with a 10,000 lb (4,535kg) bomb load carried externally, could cruise at Mach 0.86 at 47,000ft (14,325m).

Of unconventional configuration, the fuselage was just large enough to house a cockpit similar in size to the de Havilland Mosquito, with H2S radar mounted behind and the engines, Rolls-Royce Conways, to the rear. The fuel was housed in the 45° swept wings, which had tailfins on the wingtips. A single large bomb (possibly the 'Special Store') was carried under the fuselage with an aerodynamic fairing to reduce drag. High explosive bombs could be carried in specially designed panniers. However, the idea of no pressurisation at such altitudes and the lack of ejection seats apparently failed to inspire the Air Staff,

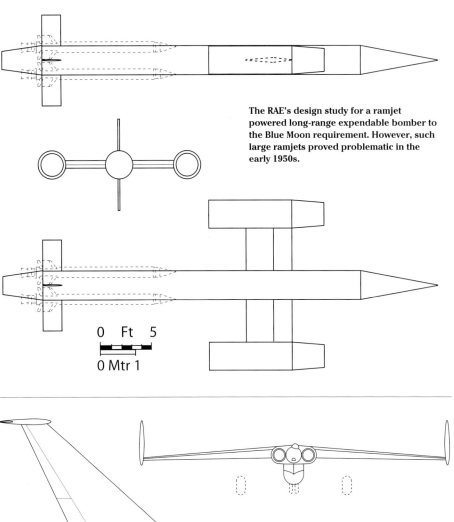

The RAE's design study for a ramjet powered long-range expendable bomber to the Blue Moon requirement. However, such large ramjets proved problematic in the early 1950s.

0 Ft 5
0 Mtr 1

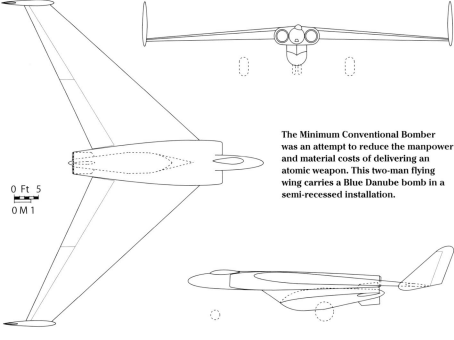

The Minimum Conventional Bomber was an attempt to reduce the manpower and material costs of delivering an atomic weapon. This two-man flying wing carries a Blue Danube bomb in a semi-recessed installation.

0 Ft 5
0 M 1

Moon requirement contains one of the earliest allusions to what we now call stealth technology: '7. Consideration should be given to the possibility of avoiding radar detection by use of an anti-echo coating or by any other means.'

Clearly research into such techniques was well advanced by 1945, such that they could be applied to aircraft in the early 1950s. Radar-absorbent materials (RAM) called DX1 and DS2 (carbon impregnated rubber sheet backed by brass 40-mesh), absorbing X- and S-band bands respectively, had been developed by Plessey and were apparently applied to a Boulton Paul Balliol during a series of trials by Boulton and Paul between 1951 and 1956. Later, models of the English Electric Canberra B.2 were used in 1959 radar echo measurement trials. The same year Canberra WX161 fitted with DX3 RAM flew from Boulton and Paul's Seighford airfield for trials against an AA No.3 Mk.7 radar that had been modified to use X-band. The service application of this work remains classified.

This all sounds very ambitious but, as on so many occasions, there was one major spanner in the works for Blue Moon: guidance. Bomber Command had expended a lot of effort in developing equipment and methods to enable its bombers to deliver their bombs on the target. By 1944, with the introduction of radio bombing aids such as Gee, Oboe and the H2S (which stood for Home Sweet Home), aircrews could navigate to the aiming point and deliver the payload, even through cloud. However, these methods, particularly Gee and Oboe, were limited in range due to the curvature of the earth, with their useful range being dependent on altitude. This 'useful range' was in the order of 400 miles (643km) for Oboe stations in eastern England. High-flying de Havilland Mosquitoes of the Pathfinder Force were used under Oboe control to mark targets for raids on eastern Germany, but both Oboe and Gee were useless over the ranges required for the Soviet Union.

Item 8 of the requirement stated that the guidance system: '...should confer the greatest possible immunity against all forms of enemy interference, both from the ground and from the air, that can be visualised.'

Item 9 covered tracking the missile and triggering the warhead over the target: '9. It should embody a means of signalling whereby its precise position immediately prior to detonation can be determined.'

Both of these were frankly impossible in 1945 and it would be a decade at least before Item 8 could become practicable with the advent of inertial systems. Developing such a

so the Minimum Conventional Bomber disappeared and it was back to the expendables.

OR.203 Issue 1, drawn up by the Air Ministry and distributed on 9th September 1945, called for an alternative to the manned bomber with a range in excess of 1,500nm (2,778km). This weapon was later assigned the MoS rainbow code 'Blue Moon'. The OR.203 type was to be flown at an altitude of 40,000ft (12,192m) and 1,300kts (2,408km/h) to deliver an atomic bomb within 4nm (7.4km) of the target. As a requirement, this was somewhat ambitious at a time when fighter jets were just pushing 500kts (926km/h).

Its guidance was to be immune from countermeasures and item Number 7 of the Blue

British Secret Projects: Hypersonics, Ramjets & Missiles

system in the late 1940s would be about as likely as the blue moon of popular myth, so perhaps the name was prophetic.

The only means available for such missions was a variant of the Rebecca and Eureka beacons developed during the war to allow accurate paratroop drops. Such a system was under development from 1953 to meet OR.3514 for a blind bombing aid for the V-bombers. Officially called Blue Sugar by the MoS it had a couple of other cover names; Eureka Mk.6 (a crash location beacon to disguise its true purpose for the RAF) and Robot Weatherman (to further confuse the workers at Ultra Electronics who built Blue Sugar).

Blue Sugar was to be deployed via a parachute by Pathfinder Canberras or Valiant B.2s (one prototype of the latter was built to meet Specification B.104D) to lay or clear a route across enemy territory. The system utilised some very smart packaging and deployment techniques that would not be out of place in modern space exploration vehicles. Prior to deployment, Blue Sugar was a 7ft 6in (2.28m)-long cylinder with a diameter of 16⅓in (42cm) but on landing the device levelled itself and erected a 40ft (12m) aerial and began transmitting its location. By doing this it of course became vulnerable to jamming or location, or even being kicked over and smashed up by the locals.

In fact Blue Sugar beacons would be useless as a bombing aid without another system called Blue Study. This was an automatic track control and bomb release computer for blind bombing. The Cat/Mouse computer method was used, with signals from secondary beacons such as Blue Sugar. Essentially an update of Gee-H and Oboe that used the SHORAN system, the Cat/Mouse technique required that the aircraft fly along a curved flight path at a range that brought its path over the target. A pair of stations in friendly territory transmitted signals to and received returns from the aircraft. As these stations were about 100miles (161km) apart they could triangulate the aircraft very accurately and transmit a bomb release signal.

It soon became apparent that a speed of 1,300kts (2,407km/h) would not be feasible for a long time and that the guidance system was fraught with problems.

In 1949 a series of studies was undertaken to find an expendable bomber capable of carrying a 10,000lb (4,535kg) 'Special Store' at altitudes up to 56,000ft (17,078m) at a speed of 600kts (691mph/1,111km/h). These could be launched from the ground by catapult or from a carrier aircraft, which would increase the available range. The RAE estimated that

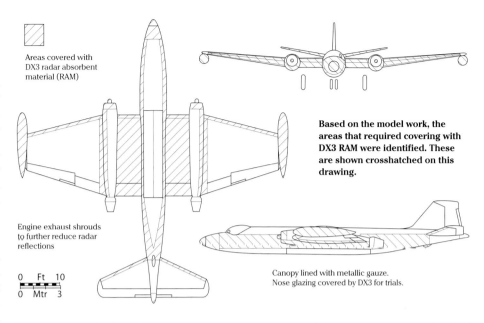

Areas covered with DX3 radar absorbent material (RAM)

Based on the model work, the areas that required covering with DX3 RAM were identified. These are shown crosshatched on this drawing.

Engine exhaust shrouds to further reduce radar reflections

Canopy lined with metallic gauze. Nose glazing covered by DX3 for trials.

such types would weigh in at 22,000lb (9,977kg) and be powered by expendable axial flow turbojets of the 'Griffith Type', an engine that ultimately became the Rolls-Royce AJ.65 Avon.

Two mid-wing designs, A and B, were drawn up for the Expendable Bomber, Type A having a jet on each wingtip while B had

engines buried in the wing roots. Both types had their Special Store integrated into the 62in (157cm)-diameter fuselage structure. However, the preferred designs were C and D, which basically were flying wings with a payload pod attached to a pylon on the wing undersurface, giving the impression of a parasol wing. This configuration permitted

Provisional drawing of Bristol Type 196 Medium Range Expendable Bomber variant of the same company's T188 research aircraft.

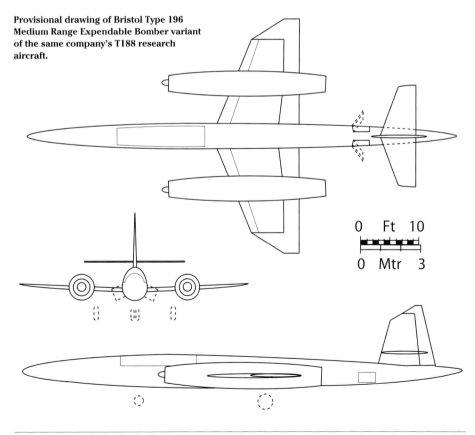

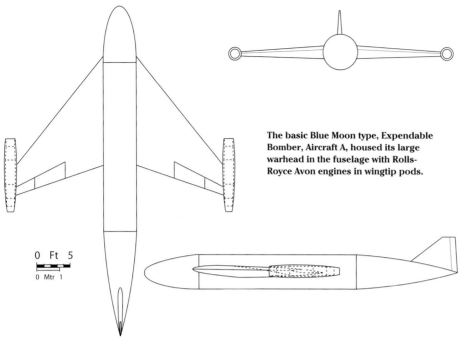

The basic Blue Moon type, Expendable Bomber, Aircraft A, housed its large warhead in the fuselage with Rolls-Royce Avon engines in wingtip pods.

0 Ft 5
0 Mtr 1

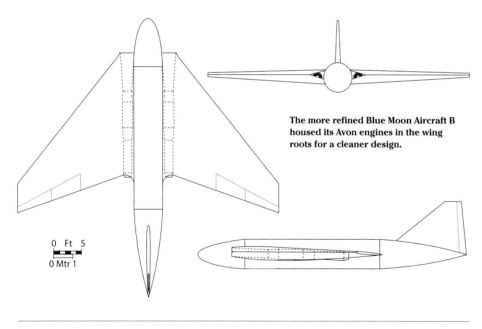

The more refined Blue Moon Aircraft B housed its Avon engines in the wing roots for a cleaner design.

0 Ft 5
0 Mtr 1

flexibility of warload by providing different payload pods to suit the mission, and the aircraft could continue as a flying wing after dropping the weapon pod. With the main engines fitted within the support strut, uprated or additional engines could be added without radical re-engineering of the wing structure. Conversion to manned use was possible by building a pod with a cockpit. As ever everything looked rosy in the RAE's studies.

This project was only expendable in the sense that it didn't return from the mission,

the Expendable Bomber had to deliver its payload. It depended primarily on height over target to provide immunity from interception, but was also to be fitted with countermeasures. A Window dispenser triggered by a sensor to detect anti-aircraft shell bursts and a 'Proximity Fuse Exploder' were considered, as was an automatic 'jinking' system which would trigger a corkscrew manoeuvre when an enemy fighter was detected.

Types C and D were considered the most feasible, due to their lighter and less complex

structure, flexibility and most importantly, better performance. However none of that would be of any use if the Blue Moon Expendable bomber failed to find its target. Ground based beacons were unreliable, so a return to the ancient art of navigation by the stars would be necessary.

OR.203 was downgraded from an Air Staff Requirement to an Air Staff Target on 29th January 1952 and soldiered on until August 1953 when OR.203 Issue 2 appeared.

So far Blue Moon had always been regarded as an unmanned aircraft, a factor that had hindered its development. Issue 2 changed that. In the eight years since Issue 1, much had changed in the guided weapons field. Fast aircraft were vulnerable to SAMs and high supersonic speeds, coupled with high altitude, were seen as the only way to defeat such defences. The benchmark SAM systems for Issue 2 were the projected air defence systems of the UK in the period 1963 to 1973.

The required range of 2,500nm (4,630km) was a start point, with increases to be achieved by adding fuel and engine stages to the basic Blue Moon. Nuclear warheads were to be carried; either a 30in (76.2cm) diameter/2,500lb (1,134kg) warhead (possibly a variant of Red Beard) or the 62in (157.5cm)/10,000lb (4,534kg) variety (no doubt a variant of Blue Danube).

Yet again guidance was the crux of the matter, with the new Staff Target stating: 'The form of guidance will depend to a large extent on the type of weapon selected as well as on the technical advances in possible systems to make feasible the accuracy required. However, the Air Staff wish to be free of any system which depends on aids placed inside enemy territory or on prior route reconnaissance.'

So, that ruled out a Blue Sugar-type system. The only other possibilities were the Blue Sapphire and Orange Tartan astro-navigation systems being developed by TRE. These were optical devices that could take automatic sightings of specific stars and calculate the aircraft's position. Blue Sapphire could only work at night, but its Orange Tartan derivative could operate in daylight.

Carriage of the larger-size warhead would need a big airframe with big engines. This was a non-starter. The ideas behind the OR.330/336 supersonic bomber, to meet RB.156 discussed earlier, were well into planning by 1954, so by 1955 the writing was on the wall for Blue Moon. Ballistic systems were the way ahead and OR.203 was cancelled on 22nd May 1955, superseded by OR.1139 – the Blue Streak ballistic missile.

Blue Streak – The Sandys Plan

Blue Streak is a name that, like TSR.2, provokes strong reactions in people. Hindsight is wonderful, but Blue Streak managed to fall between two stools. Had it been developed earlier, it would have entered service as the carrier for the UK's nuclear deterrent. Had it been cancelled later, it may have formed the basis of the UK space programme. Unfortunately it came to fruition at the wrong time: too late for use as a deterrent, too early for use as a launcher.

Its development is covered more than adequately elsewhere, in the depth the project deserves. Suffice to say Blue Streak, with its Rolls-Royce RZ.2 rocket engine (derived from the US Rocketdyne S-2 via the RZ.1), was from 1955 under development by de Havilland at Hatfield to meet OR.1139. This Medium Range Ballistic Missile (MRBM) was to form the core of the Sandys defence plan (Duncan Sandys was the then Minister of Defence) and would be housed in a series of underground silos strung across eastern England. Blue Streak was to carry an Orange Herald warhead.

Much of the research work for Blue Streak's re-entry system was undertaken using the Black Knight test vehicle at Woomera, while the RZ.2 rocket engine testing was carried out at Spadeadam Waste in Cumberland. After its cancellation as a weapon in 1960, in favour of the US Skybolt air-launched ballistic missile system (and later the Polaris submarine launched system), Blue Streak development was continued as a space launcher. In this role Blue Streak showed that it possessed unmatched reliability, no doubt due to the live firing of each complete system on the test stands at Spadeadam.

However Blue Streak was cancelled as a satellite launcher later in 1960, taking with it any hope of an indigenous UK launcher. It would eventually form the basis of the Europa booster, which ultimately led to Ariane.

Blue Streak was the last long-range ballistic launch system developed in the UK. With the signing of the Bermuda Accords in 1959 the UK bought the American Polaris system. As time progressed into the early 1960s, and with buying Skybolt, worries about losing the weapons design expertise prompted the UK government to upgrade Polaris to maintain 'a credible deterrent' rather than buy the next-generation US SLBM, Poseidon.

A rare photograph of the 'Stealth' Canberra WX161 at RAF Seighford while undergoing radar trials with Boulton and Paul. Dave Welch, via Phil Butler

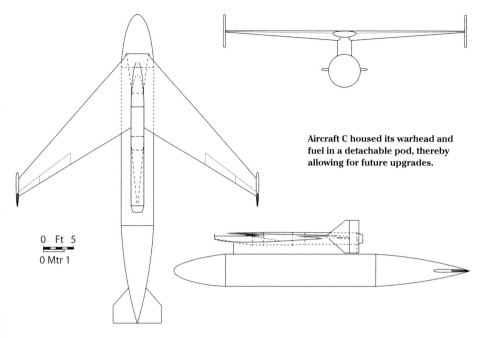

Aircraft C housed its warhead and fuel in a detachable pod, thereby allowing for future upgrades.

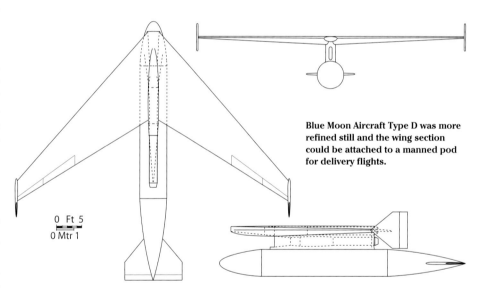

Blue Moon Aircraft Type D was more refined still and the wing section could be attached to a manned pod for delivery flights.

Army Tactical Support Weapons

Strictly speaking, although used strategically to terrorise populations, the German V-2 was a tactical weapon with a limited warhead size of 2,150 lb (975kg) and a limited range of 200 miles (322km): essentially a 1945 version of the Paris Gun of 1917.

The British Army had taken notice of the V-2's potential and wanted a rocket system to act as long-range artillery. This long-range rocket had been one of the GW projects on the GW Committee's list of seven at the end of the war. At a time when guided weapon ranges were quoted in yards, 'long range' meant more than 10 miles (16km)!

The early days of this work are very confusing. One of these projects was called Big Ben, which may be related to the Ben SAGW, but the name Big Ben had also been applied to the German V-2. Strange as it might seem, in its artillery missile guise Big Ben has been described as a ramjet-powered development of the Brakemine SAGW. As ever the early days of guided weapons prove baffling!

The first Army-specific artillery rocket was called Half-Pint. Intended to replace guns, Half-Pint may have been under development by Vickers.

By the end of 1954 the Army's requirements were firming up. The artillery was to have a suite of nuclear-tipped delivery systems at their disposal under direct authority of the field commanders. Three classes of weapon were proposed: a long-range 200 miles (322km) ballistic missile; a short-to-medium range 30 miles (48km) ballistic missile; and an atomic artillery shell for shorter ranges.

The long-range weapon became known as Black Rock, but progressed no further than a design study, probably because it overlapped with what the RAF saw as its territory of deep strike. The short-range nuclear artillery shell, known as Yellow Anvil, was also cancelled.

The short to medium range weapon prospered, leading ultimately to another of the body blows to British industry that punctuate this book: Blue Water.

The Staff wanted a surface-to-surface guided weapon (SSGW) that would be mobile, have a range of up to 30, preferably 35, miles (48 to 56km) and be able to carry a nuclear warhead. This weapon was to be used against troop and vehicle concentrations identified by aerial reconnaissance. A conventional warhead was also required for targets that did not warrant a nuclear weapon or for use in conventional warfare. Bear in mind that this was the era of the Tripwire response and as soon as Soviet forces crossed the Elbe, the war would become a nuclear affair.

Red Rose

In November 1954 the War Office approached English Electric concerning the development of a 30-mile (48km) range SSGW to meet a new Outline of Military Characteristics (OMC), the equivalent of an Air Ministry Staff Target. English Electric embarked on a design study with the blessing of the War Office, which was already committed to EE's Red Shoes SAGW (Chapter Four). The project was assigned the MoS rainbow code Red Rose in August 1956.

Meanwhile at Weybridge, completely unaware of the War Office interest and overtures to English Electric, Vickers was pursuing a private venture to fill such a requirement. Although the design team hadn't seen the OMC, Vickers were congratulated by the General Staff on the prescience of their design studies and their proposals were welcomed.

In 1956 Vickers proposed a couple of systems for what they called the '35 mile Artillery Weapon System'. The first involved a wingless missile transported in an articulated semi-trailer which was to be parked up with the front pointed in the desired launch direc-

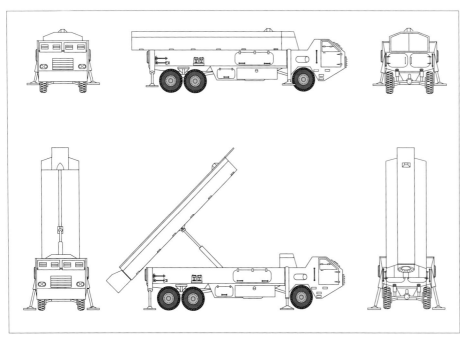

Vickers' design study for a 35nm missile to be carried on an articulated transporter to allow it to be concealed amongst the general service vehicles. via John Forbat

A later Vickers study for an all-terrain Transporter / Erector / Launcher for their 35nm missile. via John Forbat

British Secret Projects: Hypersonics, Ramjets & Missiles

tion, the trailer was then opened up and the launch rail raised to an inclination of 45° from horizontal. The rocket was fired and the launcher reloaded from a second trailer carrying a further three rockets.

The second proposal was an all-in-one cross-country vehicle, what is now called a TEL (Transporter-Erector-Launcher), but based on a 10-ton 6x6 truck chassis and armoured against both the rocket's blast and small arms. Again this would be aligned in the correct azimuth, the launcher raised and the rocket fired.

Vickers opted for the slant launch because they believed that an alternative vertical launch system required much time-consuming surveying of the launch site and setting up a launch pad. This was particularly relevant because the Army OMC had specified a maximum action time of sixty minutes, with a preference for thirty minutes. Another factor in Vickers' choice of slant launch was that, even with the launcher elevated, the system was easier to conceal in trees and villages.

Vertical launch required the rocket to turn over onto the correct azimuth after launch and Vickers believed that there was plenty of scope for a vertical launch missile to 'go rogue' at this stage and land on friendly forces. At least a slant-launched weapon was pointing in the general direction of the enemy!

The Army also advised Vickers that using existing vehicles would simplify the system, hence the use of an articulated launcher that could be moved by any tractor vehicle. One further reason for using existing vehicles was that the launcher could be easily disguised as a normal logistics vehicle. The launcher could then be 'hidden' amongst utility vehicles, a tactic adopted by Iraqi forces to conceal their Scuds in 1991.

Despite all this congratulatory 'back slapping', the Staff had one particular gripe with Vickers' design: vulnerability. The slant launch meant that the Vickers missile achieved an apogee of only 10,000ft (3,048m) and a maximum speed of Mach 1.3. This meant that the Vickers weapon could be intercepted by the latest SAMs.

The same conclusions were no doubt drawn about another proposal, this time from Bristol Aircraft's Guided Weapons Department. The Bristol bid was to be powered by ramjets, no doubt to provide adequate range. Ramjet propulsion suggested a maximum speed of Mach 2, again vulnerable to the next generation of SAMs. The work on the propul-

sion system was covered by the title RP.15 but, other than this, little is known about the weapon. Bristol may have modified its Red Duster SAM for this role, but the best example for such a change of role came from Stevenage.

Red Shoes Conversion

Against the Vickers and Bristol design studies, L H Bedford, Director of Engineering for English Electric Aviation (EEA) at Stevenage, proposed a variant of the company's Red Shoes SAM called the '30-mile RS Conversion'. The rainbow code Red Herring has been associated with this study. RS Conversion involved a larger 24in (61cm) diameter airframe to accommodate the 500lb (229kg) nuclear warhead and was to be launched from a standard Red Shoes launcher towed by the 4x4 Bedford RLHC 3-ton truck.

To achieve the thirty-mile range with the larger 1,000lb (454kg) nuclear warhead, the RS Conversion required additional boost power, and the standard four Goslings of Red Shoes became a sextet. All of this weighed in at 4,246lb (1,926kg) at launch. Guidance, that perennial problem for the guided weapon designer in the 1950s, was to be achieved by radar using the Army's old GW warhorse, Radar No.3, Mk.7.

The Staff gave this design a cool reception. They did not like the idea of strapping two more boosters to the weapon since field trials with Red Shoes had shown that these hindered ground handling. The bigger missile also required a 25% increase in the span of the boost fins, again making ground movement difficult. The idea of radar guidance, which could be jammed, did not impress either.

Essentially English Electric's RS Conversion was a quick fix that failed to convince the Staff, who wanted a compact, all-in-one solution. The RS conversion shared the Vickers design's vulnerability because it also used a slant launch. This prompted a major re-think at Stevenage. After all the next generation of SAMs were to be capable of intercepting tactical ballistic missiles and English Electric was developing such weapons.

So, back to the drawing board for English Electric but, as the reader will by now have come to expect, the firm had another project up its sleeve. In the absence of a home-built weapon, the American SSM-A17 Corporal missile had been purchased, with EEGW providing technical support in the UK. Britain had lagged behind the US in all the GW fields, especially ballistics, so purchasing the Corporal was no surprise to maintain capability. Corporal would soon be obsolete however, such was the pace of progress, and a replacement, preferably homegrown, was required.

Supporting the Army's Corporal missiles had shown EEA this weapon's shortcomings and it put this experience to good use in a new design. Described as Red Rose Ab Initio, this new project was a vertical-launch, inertially guided ballistic missile. The Ab Initio design dispensed with the strap-on boosts and was to be carried by a single 6x4 10 ton AEC Militant truck with the launch platform towed behind. EEA believed that vertical launch from a levelled platform simplified the entire system with the bonus of reducing the telltale blast area.

Red Rose Ab Initio was a completely new winged design, again 24in (61cm) in diameter, 25ft 3in (7.69m) long and weighing in at

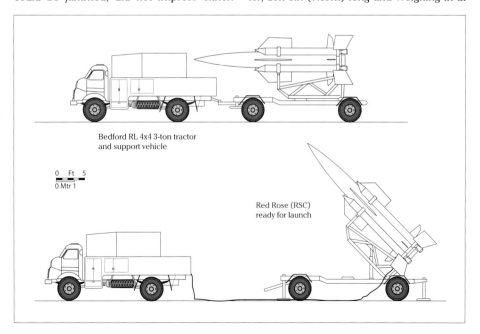

Bedford RL 4x4 3-ton tractor and support vehicle

0 Ft 5
0 Mtr 1

Red Rose (RSC) ready for launch

English Electric's Red Shoes SAM was converted into a tactical nuclear weapon. The General Staff were not impressed.

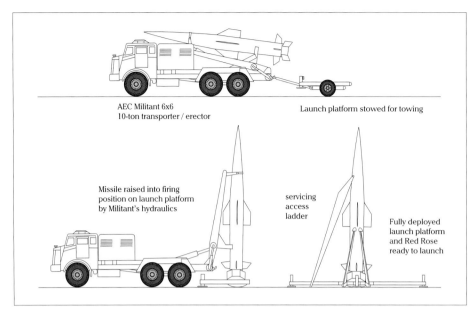

AEC Militant 6x6
10-ton transporter / erector

Launch platform stowed for towing

Missile raised into firing
position on launch platform
by Militant's hydraulics

servicing
access
ladder

Fully deployed
launch platform
and Red Rose
ready to launch

The Red Rose Ab Initio gained the General Staff's approval, despite being somewhat time consuming to set up.

5,700 lb (2,586kg) with a new 'combined boost-sustainer' rocket motor. This motor was designed to produce high thrust for the boost, but reduced its thrust by 90% for the sustain phase. Guidance was inertial, with errors of 125ft (38m) in line and length after a flight of 35 miles (56km), such accuracy being essential if the weapon was to be used to support friendly troops. Control was by tail fins initially, but was changed to the mid-body wings after the control surfaces with the tail fins became fixed. This later version was slightly longer at 26ft 8in (8.12m) long. Both designs required a small stage carrying boost fins to maintain stability in the early launch phase, but this detached once stable flight was established.

The Staff liked the Ab Initio Red Rose but, as time passed, the requirements and targets changed. The War Office drew up an outline requirement for what it now called the Corps Support Rocket (CSR). This would be carried and launched by a single vehicle, capable of off-road mobility and, importantly, air portable. Both English Electric's and Vickers' Red Rose had been designed to be air transportable, with the OMC stating: 'The system is to be transportable...desirable without breakdown of major items'.

The OMC had stated that the system was to be carried in a 'Britannic' aircraft: a Shorts project that became the Shorts SC.5 Belfast transport. Unfortunately the Belfast was a strategic freighter and so could not deliver Red Rose to tactical fields close to the fronts. The Armstrong Whitworth Argosy was to be the RAF's tactical transport for the late 1950s and 1960s, but it could not carry Red Rose in the configuration English Electric proposed.

Other than NATO operations in Western Europe, the intended *modus operandi* of the

UK forces in the 1960s was to act as a rapid deployment force. This imperial policing role entailed flying troops and equipment into what were called Mounting Bases situated at strategic points around the world. From these mounting bases troops and materiel would be carried to troublespots by tactical transports.

As well as strategic transports like the Belfast, the RAF needed new transport aircraft to fulfil this role. The design studies for new requirement OR.351, which led to the Armstrong Whitworth AW.681 STOL transport, would allow materiel to be delivered near the front; consequently the next generation of SSGW had to be air portable in that type of aircraft as well as the Argosy. English Electric complied with this requirement and produced Blue Water.

Blue Water

Not content with moving the goalposts on mobility, the War Office wanted range increased to 60 miles (96.6km) and a quicker launch time. To meet the new requirement A5077, EEA produced a stunning weapon that acquired the rainbow code Blue Water. Based on the Ab Initio Red Rose missile design, Blue Water retained the 24in (61cm) diameter body to house the nuclear warhead, but carried enlarged tail fins in lieu of the detachable boost fins.

However, the main difference between Red Rose and Blue Water was the launcher. Blue Water was carried by and launched from the same vehicle, a Bedford RLHC 3-ton truck with a launch rail mounted on the rear of the chassis. This was raised to an almost vertical attitude and levelled by sighting a theodolite through an aperture in the launcher and adjusting the stabiliser pads.

Targeting information and fuzing was carried out by the crew in an attendant Land Rover carrying the computer equipment, with technical support in a pair of mobile workshops that were again based on the Bedford 3-tonner.

Blue Water was powered by various rocket motors and this may have been its downfall. The motor was of a two-phase design, with a high-thrust initial phase to boost the missile followed by a second sustainer phase. Rather than being two separate stages, with the boost stage falling away when expended, the motor used petal valves that were opened by the pressure of 150psi (1,034kPa) exerted by the second phase burning. Two motors (Saluki and Aspin) were tested in a 17in (43.2cm)-diameter (0.7 scale) test vehicle fired in Australia and in a full-scale unguided test vehicle called Jinker. The trials got as far as Jinker flight tests at the Aberporth Range in 1960 and two full-scale development examples were fired using the Phoenix 24in (61cm) rocket motor. These trials showed problems with the motor and its valve, creating delays in the development of the whole system.

A variety of nuclear warheads were proposed for Blue Water, including the RO.106 warhead capsule with a Tony physics package and GM.462/Big Brother. English Electric also considered fitting Blue Water with a French nuclear warhead to allow sales to Switzerland. A further nod to Europe was that Blue Water became the first British weapon project to be developed using the metric system, odd given that it was based on a missile with a diameter of 24in (61cm). Whether this contributed to its delay is not mentioned.

In 1961 NATO doctrine changed from the Tripwire to Flexible Response, with the prospect of a war escalating in stages to the use of tactical nuclear weapons such as Blue Water. Then, out of the blue, in August 1962 Peter Thorneycroft, newly appointed Minister of Defence, issued the cancellation order. There was little or no consultation with any advisers, such as Sir Solly Zuckerman who was his Chief Scientific Adviser. Zuckerman believed that a tactical nuclear battle in Germany was the road to ruin, leading only to the escalation of any conflict and was glad to see the back of Blue Water from that point of view. He stated: 'My own view, which I made perfectly clear, was that Blue Water should go. While I recognized that PT.428 [Chapter Four] was highly ambitious from a technical point of view, it made more sense to spend such money as was available on a system that had some ostensible military purpose, rather than on one that I thought had none.'

Blue Water was cancelled in 1962 to cut costs and the British Army subsequently purchased the larger and less capable Honest John from the USA. This cancellation astounded English Electric at Stevenage, which was already reeling, having had the PT.428 SAM scrapped to save Blue Water, and now had to take this second blow.

Thorneycroft needed to save money and it was believed that the forthcoming TSR.2 could fill the tactical nuclear role under better command and control than a missile on the battlefield. From 1962 the British Army used American ballistic missiles, and in the late 1970s Honest John was replaced by the Vought Lance.

Blue Water lived on for a bit longer however, because it was suggested as a stand-off weapon for TSR.2 in the 'dash for deterrence', but by the time TSR.2 was cancelled in 1965 Blue Water had been killed off completely. To

English Electric began development of Blue Water but it was BAC (GW) who brought it to the stage seen here. The system was highly mobile on its Bedford RLHC truck. BAE Systems via Tony Buttler

BAC Blue Water system setting up. The theodolite operator is checking the vehicle alignment prior to elevating the missile. A photograph of the system ready to launch is included in the colour section. BAE Systems via Tony Buttler

Blue Water in travelling and launching positions.

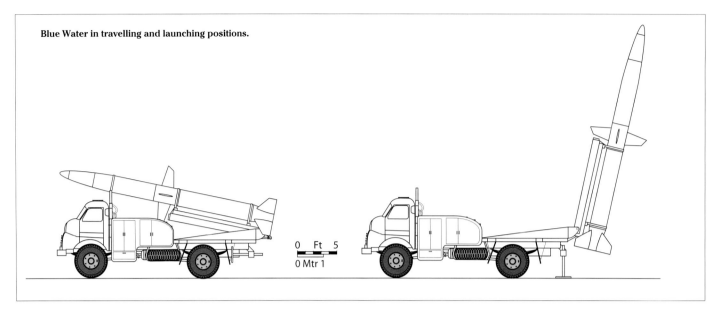

0 Ft 5
0 Mtr 1

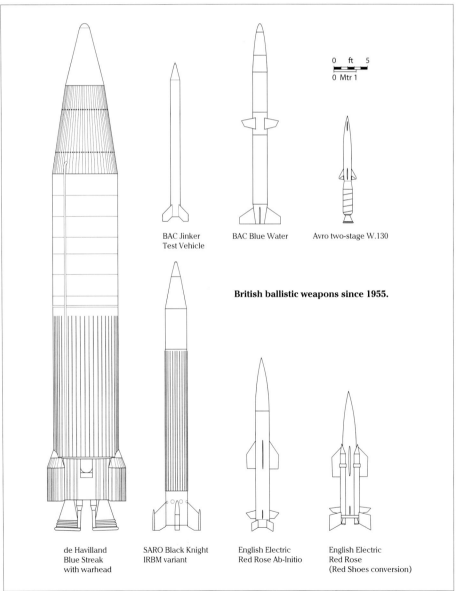

0 ft 5
0 Mtr 1

BAC Jinker
Test Vehicle

BAC Blue Water

Avro two-stage W.130

British ballistic weapons since 1955.

de Havilland
Blue Streak
with warhead

SARO Black Knight
IRBM variant

English Electric
Red Rose Ab-Initio

English Electric
Red Rose
(Red Shoes conversion)

Shown on the test stand at Spadeadam Rocket Research Establishment in 1962, the de Havilland Blue Streak was to have formed the basis of the UK's nuclear deterrent. HSD via T Panopalis

serve as an air-launched weapon the Blue Water airframe was modified by tapering the rear fuselage and adding an aerodynamic fairing over the rocket nozzle to reduce drag. This fairing was blown off when the motor ignited.

One other notable SSM proposed in the early 1960s, mentioned briefly in the chapter on stand-off weapons, was the Avro/Hawker Siddeley W.130. Originally proposed as an air-launched weapon for TSR.2, the 4,500 lb (2,041 kg) W.130 as an SSM came in two versions: two-stage with a booster weighing 7,500 lb (3,401 kg) giving a range of 400 nm (740 km) and a three-stage version weighing in at 20,000 lb (9,071 kg) with a range of 1,200 nm (2,222 km). Ground-launched W.130, like its air-launched counterpart, received short shrift from the Controller of Guided Weapons and Electronics.

Flying Bombs

The German wartime V-1 flying bomb or 'Buzz Bomb' had also influenced British thinking. In 1949, keen to have a cheap flying bomb weapon that could be launched in waves at the Soviet Union (a Hoop-La for the jet age), the Air Ministry asked for tenders for an expendable bomber. This weapon was to be launched from ramps, powered by an expendable gas turbine and would have a payload of 5,000 lb (2,268 kg). It would be called the High Speed Expendable Bomber (HSEB)

The requirement for this flying bomb was issued in December 1950 as OR.1097 with the official specification, UB.109, (UB = Unmanned Bomber) issued in February 1951. Vickers, Bristol and Boulton Paul all submitted designs for the specification.

The missile was to have a range of 400 miles (714 km) at 500 kts (926 kph) and an altitude of 45,000 ft (13,716 m). Powered by a cheap expendable turbojet and as noted to be capable of carrying 5,000 lb of bombs, the HSEB was to carry these to a target and drop them under command guidance. The guidance system would be capable of handling a great many HSEBs at the same time, which should ensure that the defences would be saturated. This guidance system was to be called Tramp and be based on the Gee H and Oboe systems developed during World War Two.

Vickers' bid would be known as the Expendable Bomber, and there were two versions, the EB.15 and EB.16. Bristol tendered their Type 182 and Boulton Paul the P.123. For development purposes the Ministry of Supply named the project Red Rapier.

The Vickers types were of comparatively simple construction in mild steel and, as the company had embarked on a private venture even before the development contracts were

issued, they were ahead of Bristol and Boulton Paul. A full-scale manned test vehicle was planned but this came to nought. Instead Vickers built and flew the 1/3-scale Type 719 which was to be dropped by a Washington B.1 bomber that had been seconded for trials at Woomera. Originally for use in Blue Boar trials, this aircraft was also fitted out for the Red Rapier trials, and in fact was the same Washington that later caused the delays to Green Cheese development.

The Vickers Type 725, the full-scale prototype powered by three Rolls-Royce RB.93 turbojets, was under construction when the entire project was cancelled in September 1954.

Boulton Paul produced a design study for UB.109 called P.123. This was different in that it used a swept wing, a butterfly tail carried the control surfaces and it was powered by a pair of Rolls-Royce RB.93 turbojets in underwing pods. As with the Vickers proposal, a manned version was planned to carry out much of the development work, with the option of producing a manned bomber version.

Bristol's Type 182 on the other hand was a more technically advanced machine. Its structure comprised a set of mouldings using an asbestos-reinforced plastic called Durestos. This had originally been used for drop tanks,

W E W Petter, the brilliant aircraft designer behind such types as the English Electric Canberra and the Folland Midge, whose wing was used for Blue Rapier. via Tony Buttler

but its use soon spread to airframe components. Bristol compared an all-steel structure with the Durestos and steel structure, and found that Durestos was much lighter.

For some reason, Bristol, despite having its own aircraft design company, selected a

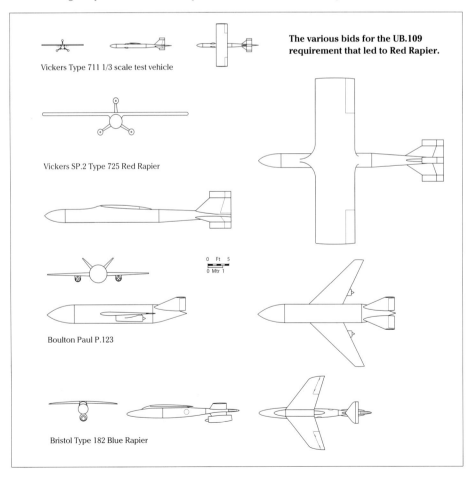

The various bids for the UB.109 requirement that led to Red Rapier.

Vickers Type 711 1/3 scale test vehicle

Vickers SP.2 Type 725 Red Rapier

Boulton Paul P.123

Bristol Type 182 Blue Rapier

Missile	Length ft (m)	Diameter in (cm)	Span ft (m)	Powerplant	Guidance
Blue Streak	61.5 (18.75)	120 (328)	–	Rocket engine	Inertial
Red Rose	23 (7)	24 (61)	4.4 (1.3)	Rocket motor	Inertial
Blue Water	25 (7.6)	24 (61)	7.2 (2.2)	Rocket motor	Inertial
Red Rapier	45.4 (13.8)		32 (9.7)	3 x turbojet	Radio beacon
Blue Rapier	33.8 (10.3)		20.8 (6.3)	1 x turbojet	Radio beacon

planform that had been developed by the famous designer W E W 'Teddy' Petter for his lightweight fighter, the Folland Midge, later to become the Gnat. As ever Petter proved enigmatic and the reason for adopting his design is not clear. Perhaps this planform fitted the Durestos construction methods.

However, rather than go straight for the Durestos structure from the beginning, Bristol built a retrievable test vehicle using light alloy, which sported a retractable undercarriage! In addition Bristol Engines developed an expendable engine for the Type 182 called the BE.17. It will come as no surprise to the reader that, with supreme irony, this expendable engine becomes a very successful powerplant for a variety of rather non-expendable aircraft. In this guise it was named Orpheus and, yet another link to Petter, powered the Folland Gnat trainer plus the Gnat and Hindustan Aeronautics Limited (HAL) Ajeet lightweight fighters (HAL built the Gnat under licence as the Ajeet).

The Bristol Type 182 had a new lease of life after Red Rapier was cancelled. In Chapter Eight mention was made of 'The Pattern of the Offensive' discussion paper written in 1954 which raised concerns about the survivability of the V-bombers on missions into the Soviet Union. The paper considered the Soviet Air Defences and foresaw a quantum leap in capability with the arrival of the first Soviet SAMs in 1960. How prescient the writers were, as Gary Powers found out on May Day 1960 when his American Lockheed U-2 reconnaissance aircraft was shot down by the PVO-Strany's SA-2 Guideline SAMs.

The paper considered several different scenarios:

- The new OR.336 / RB.156 supersonic bomber.
- The existing V-Force with stand-off weapons.
- The existing V-Force with a diversionary missile.
- A high-speed/high-altitude missile (Blue Streak).
- A low-level bomber aircraft (ultimately TSR.2).

Option 2 ultimately became the Blue Steel stand-off missile but Option 3, the diversionary missile, would have been fulfilled by a modified Bristol Type 182 fitted with extra fuel tanks, jammers and other ECM equipment in lieu of a warhead to act as a decoy. It became known as Blue Rapier.

Blue Rapier was to possess similar performance to the V-bombers and carry out similar feint attacks and jamming missions to those performed by various aircraft types during the 1941 to 1945 offensives against Germany. Obviously the RAF couldn't (or wouldn't) perform these missions with V-bombers that could be better employed carrying bombs, so Blue Rapier got the job.

By 1956 it was becoming clear that the medium- and intermediate-range ballistic missile was the way forward and that the low-level mission was the only option for the V-Force. Rapiers, Red and Blue, therefore dis-

appeared. However, Red Rapier isn't forgotten, but lives on in the cruise missiles that performed remarkable feats on our TV screens in January 1991 in Baghdad.

Having looked at the Red Rapier Short-Range Expendable Bomber and the Blue Moon Long-Range Expendable Bomber, what was to be used for intermediate ranges? As ever there was a British compromise, from a remarkable source, in the shape of the June 1955 proposal for the Bristol Type 196, an unmanned medium-range expendable bomber based on the Type 188 research aircraft powered by a pair of BE.36 turbojets. The basic 188 airframe was to be stretched to 76ft (23.2m), the cockpit and life support systems removed and a 4,000 lb (1,814kg) warhead installed. Performance estimates included a 2,000nm (3,704km) range at Mach 3 and an altitude over the target of 84,000ft (25,601m).

The objective was to produce a strategic weapon that would be in service before the OR.330 derived supersonic bomber, filling an expected gap in deterrent capability. Despite drawing up a draft requirement specifying the intended in-service date as 1962 and examining the proposal, the Air Staff did not issue a requirement. The reason given was that the guidance systems were not up to the job and the size of the nuclear warheads was still a great unknown. The attached drawing is based on descriptions given for the Type 196 in Ministry documents – to date no originals have been found.

Conclusion

In the end apart from Chevaline (a British-developed update of the Royal Navy's Polaris submarine-launched ballistic missiles), whose development was driven by the politics of nuclear weapons, none of the UK's ballistic systems entered service. The cancellation of missiles such as Blue Water had an immediate and devastating impact on British industry. Blue Streak, as indicated above, appeared on the scene at the worst possible time. The perceived wisdom is that, had Blue Streak development continued, its transformation into a viable and profitable satellite launcher would have followed. Access to space was on the minds of the British developers and policymakers but, apart from a self-confessed reliance on the Americans, space access for the British was to be winged, reusable and very high-tech. It is time to look at hypersonic vehicles.

The Folland Gnat, designed as a lightweight fighter by Petter: its wing found its way onto Bristol's Blue Rapier. via Tony Buttler

Ramjets in Britain

In 2007 it is possible to fly non-stop by sched- uled airliner from London to Australia in less than a day. Hailed as a major breakthrough when it first became possible in the first years of the 21st century with the introduction of Airbus A340 and Boeing 777 long-range air- craft, a 1957 aircraft developer would have been astounded if you had told him. Not because it could be done, but that it would take all of eighteen hours. He would have expected it to take two. In the fifteen years fol- lowing the Second World War aircraft speed increased by leaps and bounds. Had this pace been maintained, hypersonic strike aircraft, airliners and trans-atmospheric vehicles should have been in service by the mid-1970s. Such vehicles didn't appear and are still nowhere to be seen in the early 21st century. Why not?

Much effort has been expended on hyper- sonic research, but very little has reached the flying hardware stage. Interest in this field has waxed and waned over the last half-century with the advanced projects offices of the air- craft companies churning out design study after design study. Despite this effort there is still no overt evidence of a manned aircraft capable of cruising at Mach 5 plus.

In the United Kingdom, discussions on higher Mach numbers began in 1954. It was becoming obvious that a future jet-powered threat to the UK would require a high-speed response. It was concluded that only a vehi- cle with Mach 3+ performance would offer any prospect of intercepting an inbound high- speed threat. A long-range, high-speed SAM or interceptor aircraft would be required. Air- craft with such performance do not come out

May 1944 and with the German V1 offensive opening, the newly developed RAE propulsive duct for the Spitfire has been rushed into service to take on the robot weapons. Adrian Mann

of the blue, so it was recognised that a research aircraft to explore this regime would be required and discussions with that aim began in mid-1954.

By 1956 the Royal Aircraft Establishment (RAE), National Gas Turbine Establishment (NGTE) and Ministry of Supply (MoS) had set up a working party that drew up guidelines for the study of types capable of high supersonic and hypersonic cruise. Rather than being an ultimate goal, Mach 5 was identified as the threshold of a regime where the problems of high-speed flight would be encountered. These guidelines evolved into Experimental

Requirement ER.181, issued in 1957, that outlined the need for studies to identify the problems, develop the technologies and formulate the procedures involved in hypersonic flight.

The Ministry envisaged progressing up the Mach scale in a series of steps from the Mach 2 of ER.134, an experimental requirement of 1952 that was fulfilled by the Bristol 188. Any research aircraft arising from these ER.181-derived studies would be required to be self-accelerating, have an all-up weight of 30,000 lb (13,600kg) and be capable of fifteen minutes cruise at speeds in excess of Mach 4. The specifications were finalised and design studies invited from the aircraft manufacturers.

The Power for Mach 5

The received wisdom in the 1950s was that the only powerplant that could operate at such speeds was the ramjet. According to the propulsion people it was the 'Engine of the future!'.

The ramjet was the only air-breathing engine capable of operating at such speeds, so it was the obvious choice to power any aircraft to meet ER.181. Since in such flight regimes the engine is of supreme importance, it is only right that the history of the British ramjet should be covered before looking at the aircraft studies.

Jet Propulsion Basics

There now follows a basic introduction to gas turbines and their main features with a brief summary of the main types of high-speed powerplant. This introduction will help clarify many of the terms and descriptions in the following chapters.

A reciprocating engine uses a piston to draw in the fuel, compress it, absorb the power and expel the exhaust in a series of strokes. Rather than having one power stroke every four in its cycle, a jet engine has a continuous power cycle. Jet engines use either forward motion or turbomachinery to 'draw in' and compress the air prior to adding fuel and burning the mixture. The exhaust gases, expanding because of what thermodynamicists call heat addition, take the easiest escape route – out of the back of the engine. Because they have higher velocity than the surrounding air, these gases generate the thrust that propels the aircraft. Jet engines also have the advantage of being scaleable: to gain more power, build a bigger engine.

Jet engines can be split into two basic types: Those with turbomachinery (turbojet and turbofan) and those without (ramjets).

Ramjets – originally known as 'athodyds' (Aero THermODYnamic Duct) in the UK,

Lorin ducts in Germany and 'flying stovepipes' in the USA – rely on forward motion to force (ram) air into the engine intake. This ram compression works best at high speeds. Consequently ramjets cannot produce static thrust (power output with the engine stationary, as with an aircraft awaiting take-off) and work best at Mach numbers higher than 1. Ramjets are usually referred to as the simplest form of jet engine because they have no moving parts. This author has spoken to engineers, such as Roy Hawkins who was involved in ramjet development at Bristol Siddeley, who might dispute that view.

Turbomachinery – Gas Turbines

A basic gas turbine differs from a ramjet in using two sets of bladed rotating disks (the turbomachinery) arranged to perform specific tasks, separated by a combustion chamber.

Gas turbines can be axial flow, where the air travels linearly through the engine, or centrifugal flow, where the air moves outwards before travelling linearly.

In centrifugal flow engines the air is compressed by rotating a disk with vertical plates on the surface in a shaped chamber. These plates decrease in size towards the edge, compressing the air as it moves from the centre of the disk to the periphery, normal to the direction of flight, before turning again to enter the combustion chamber.

Axial flow engines use a series of bladed stages to compress the air, which moves axially along the engine in the opposite direction to flight. For high-speed flight the axial flow gas turbine is ideal and has been the engine of choice for Mach numbers above 1.5, and it is axial flow gas turbines that will be referred to from now on.

At the front of an axial jet there is the compressor section. This has a series of rotating bladed disks and, like a propeller, these move air to the rear. Between each compressor stage are stators, which are fixed blades attached to the compressor casing that direct the air onto next compressor stage at an optimum angle, producing even flow and thereby increasing the efficiency of the blades. These disk/stator pairs are called stages and, rather than producing thrust, each successive stage occupies a smaller volume than its predecessor and so compresses the incoming air in relation to the ambient pressure outside the engine. The ratio of the ambient pressure to that at the end of the compressor section is called the Pressure Ratio. As the air is compressed, the temperature of that air increases. This hot air then passes into the combustion chamber.

In the combustion chamber, fuel is mixed with the hot, compressed air and invariably ignites (some engines have ignition sources similar to spark plugs). The burning fuel/air mixture and the expanding gases take the easiest route to the lower pressure of the atmosphere.

As the expanding gases exit the combustion chamber they pass through the turbine section. This is also a series of bladed disk stages, but as the gas passes through each stage, its volume increases. As the gas impinges on the turbine blades, the turbine disks rotate. The turbine stages increase in size towards the rear of the engine, to match gas expansion rates, and are fixed to a shaft that connects the turbine stages to the compressor stages. Therefore, as the turbine rotates, the compressor draws air into the engine and the entire process is continuous. Suck, squeeze, bang, blow, with one moving part. In theory!

Sounds simple? Indeed 'simple' was how Frank Whittle described the process to Lord Hives, Chairman of Rolls-Royce, when Whittle demonstrated his first centrifugal jet engine, the Whittle Unit (WU). Lord Hives' response was: 'Don't worry. We'll soon design the simplicity out of it.'

Powerplant Components

The engine itself should be thought of as the middle section of a powerplant. At the front is an intake and diffuser. At the back is a jet pipe and occasionally a reheat section, known in the USA as an afterburner and particularly in the early days, augmentation.

The intake captures the air prior to passing it to the compressor. A basic intake is a circular duct but, as the aircraft speed increases, the intake has to control the volume of incoming air (known as the Mass Flow) and, if the aircraft is moving supersonically, slow the air down before it reaches the compressor, which is incapable of accepting supersonic airflow. The shape of the intake serves to induce shockwaves in the mass flow with air velocity falling dramatically across the zone of the shock wave. Aircraft with high supersonic performance have the intake shaped to induce such shockwaves, with variable geometry intakes being used to manage them once they have been induced.

An intake diffuser uses the venturi effect whereby fast moving air exhibits a reduction in pressure and vice versa. A diffuser is a duct whose cross-sectional area changes along its length. The duct narrows just behind the intake then opens out again just before the compressor face. This causes the air to slow down and its pressure to increase. This pre-compression means that the compressor has less work to do to achieve the same pressure ratio.

Aircraft flying in a variety of speed regimes may require variable intakes that alter their geometry to match the mass flow to the aircraft speed, such as moveable ramps in a two-dimensional intake such as Concorde.

A jetpipe's raison d'être at the back end is to expand the exhaust gases to match the ambient pressure. This expansion has the effect of accelerating them, producing more thrust than a simple exhaust would make. Like a diffuser, a jetpipe works by varying the cross-sectional area and it can also be variable.

Reheat can add as much as 50% to the thrust available from a gas turbine. Neat fuel is added to the exhaust and is burned in the excess oxygen not consumed in the combustion chamber. This adds heat to the reaction, causing more expansion and generating more thrust; it also uses a lot of fuel very quickly

Types of Gas Turbine

The case described above is a basic axial turbojet in which all the mass flow passes through the engine core. A turbofan is a turbojet with additional compressor stages passing some fraction of their mass flow into a concentric duct on the outside of the core engine. This bypass air can be mixed with the exhaust or form a concentric layer around the engine exhaust stream.

The proportion of the mass flow passing through the duct is shown by the Bypass Ratio (BPR). Military turbofans, such as the Rolls-Royce RB.199 in the Panavia Tornado, have small BPRs of around 0.5 to 1.0 whereas a large turbofan, such as a Rolls-Royce Trent for a civil airliner, may have a BPR greater than 8.

The Semantics of High-Speed Powerplants

One of the main constraints on gas turbine operation is the Turbine Entry Temperature, TET. As outlined above, the compressor causes the air temperature to increase. The combustion process also adds heat, raising the exhaust gas temperature accordingly. The turbine blades must be able to operate at such elevated temperatures, rather than deform and lose efficiency. This is a balancing act, as higher TET produces higher efficiencies in the engine and allows an aircraft to operate at higher Mach numbers as the ram effect coupled with the compressor means that the mass flow entering the combustion chamber is already at a high temperature.

TET can be controlled but, as noted above, this has a knock-on effect on efficiency. The turbine blades can be made of thermally resistant alloys such as Nimonic, or designed to have cooling passages within to carry cooling air tapped from the compressor. Cooling can be so effective that the blades can be white hot, but still retain their structural integrity. Despite these steps the TET is still the limiting factor in high-speed propulsion systems using turbomachinery, with the limit for turbojets being around Mach 2.5.

The obvious answer was to bypass the turbomachinery to produce a bypass turbojet, with the best example of this being the Pratt and Whitney J58 as used in the Lockheed SR-71 Blackbird Mach 3 reconnaissance aircraft.

The J58 has six large ducts running fore and aft along the exterior of the engine. At low speeds the engine functions as a reheated turbojet. At high speeds these ducts carry most of the mass flow, bypassing the last few compressor stages, combustion chamber and turbines to re-enter the engine at the reheat section. The engine effectively runs as a ramjet at high speeds. The J58 has been described as a turboramjet, but since some of the mass flow passes through the turbomachinery, bypass turbojet is more accurate. The limit for the J58 has been quoted at around Mach 3.2.

In a true turboramjet all of the mass flow bypasses the turbomachinery and all combustion occurs as reheat, with the powerplant using a single intake and jetpipe. These can either have a single bypass duct, the so-called 'up-and-over' turbojet as in the Wright XJ-67-W-1/XRJ-55-W-1 for the Republic XF-103, or the duct burning turboramjet, more like a turbofan in which combustion occurs in the bypass annulus. The XF-103 was to have been a Mach 3 fighter for the USAF but it was cancelled in 1957 before the first example had flown. Both isolate the turbomachinery by gates in the intake ducts or by variable stators that rotate to form shutters at the compressor face.

Robin Jamison and Roy Hawkins of Bristol Siddeley Engines Ltd Ramjet Department viewed the use of the term turboramjet as an exercise in semantics and preferred to use the term 'combination engine'. This is defined as a powerplant that uses a separate turbojet and ramjet, which share a common intake but have separate jet pipes. The turbojet and ramjet are used either together or separately depending on the Mach number. Typically, below Mach 1.0 the turbojet powers the aircraft, between Mach 1.0 and Mach 2.5 both powerplants operate, and then

above Mach 2.5 the turbojet is shut down and isolated leaving the ramjet to power the aircraft. These were the focus of much research by Bristol Siddeley Engines Ltd.

Turborockets

A favourite of Rolls-Royce, the turborocket is essentially a ramjet with a rocket-driven compressor that produces static thrust. A small rocket engine within the engine drives a turbine that is connected to a compressor. This provides enough compression for the ramjet burners to operate. Once the aircraft is airborne and travelling at sufficient speed to provide ram compression, the rocket is shut down and a clutch system allows the compressor to freewheel or, more accurately, windmill.

Flashjet

Like the turborocket, the flashjet was of interest to Rolls-Royce. Essentially it is a gas turbine that uses the expansion of liquid hydrogen to turn a turbine, with the expanded hydrogen then being burned in a reheat section.

Having now established a foundation on which to build the story, it is time to present an outline of the origins of ramjets in Britain. This story is closely linked with the development of guided weapons, and the story of one cannot be told without the other.

Early Ramjet Development Work in the UK: RAE and NGTE

In the dark days of May 1940 the Royal Aircraft Establishment (RAE) was looking for ways of improving the performance of the Supermarine Spitfire interceptor. RAE scientists (including Hayne Constant, an advocate of Whittle's jet propulsion work) began to look at a 'propulsive duct' for the Spitfire Mk.I. The duct they developed was 48in long, 30in wide and 15in deep (122 x 76 x 38cm) and would be fitted under the centreline of the Spitfire. The duct was to be slung below the fuselage and fed with gasolene from the aircraft's tanks.

Although the system was never flight tested, bench tests indicated that the speed increase was not sufficient enough to warrant continuation of the project. In the end the drag of the external mounting and internal pressure losses of this installation proved too high and the work was stopped to concentrate on more immediate problems. Ultimately more efficient piston engine supercharging (courtesy of Stanley Hooker and the two-stage supercharger) and more powerful Merlin engines achieved the improved performance.

However, in 1943 a new threat had appeared on the horizon – the V-1 flying bomb. Intelligence had indicated that only high-performance aircraft such as the new Hawker Tempest piston fighter and the Gloster Meteor jet fighter could intercept these high-speed weapons. The Tempest was not yet widely available and the Meteor was a long way from entering service, while the more numerous Spitfires could only attack the V-1 by diving on it. Again the RAE looked at a propulsive duct to boost the Spitfire. A D Baxter and C W R Smith at Farnborough looked at the 1940 RAE work by Constant and concluded that the duct could be made to work. Again the same problems with drag and pressure losses were encountered and the V-1 had been beaten before the propulsive duct was ready.

The GAP Committee

The difference at this later stage in the war however was that the gas turbine was under development and emerging as the way forward for interceptor aircraft. New ramjet work was to be carried out to power a guided weapon, possibly Ben as described elsewhere, for use against the German V-1. As the war progressed the more immediate need was for a weapon to destroy Japanese Kamikaze aircraft.

As related in Chapter One, the Guided Anti-aircraft Projectile (GAP) Committee had been set up in early 1944 to investigate the possibility of using guided projectiles to intercept high-speed aircraft and, in all probability, the V-1.

The GAP committee examined the liquid fuel rocket and the ramjet in depth, and the ramjet was seen as having most development potential, particularly in range. As this projectile would be supersonic, some means of testing a ramjet under supersonic conditions would be required. While no such facility existed in the UK, there was more than one way to skin a cat.

After Rolls-Royce had taken over wartime gas turbine production, Power Jets R&D Ltd (later to become the National Gas Turbine Establishment) had become involved in the development of reheat to boost the thrust of the early jets. As an adjunct to this work, two engineers at Power Jets, R Smelt and D J Smigton were developing a 6in (15cm) ramjet using a PD.1 burner. A North American Mustang I fighter was borrowed from the RAE to conduct a series of ramjet tests.

The theory behind this was that the design of the Mustang's cooling system, like F Meredith's system for the Spitfire, was such that it actually produced thrust as the incoming air was heated by the radiator; the heat expanded the air and thrust was generated as it exited the rear. The net result was that any drag from the radiator fairing was nullified by the thrust from the radiator exit. By fitting a total of twelve ramjets in a circular duct downstream of the radiator, the hot air from the radiator simulated the temperature rise achieved by the pitot intake system of a supersonic ramjet. As ever, ingenuity had provided the answer to a problem that at first sight looked insurmountable.

Rather than using a single ramjet in a housing under the fuselage, Power Jets had fitted the twelve PD.1 ramjets into a 28in (71cm)-diameter duct placed behind the circular radiator of the Mustang I. Twelve were employed because the measurement systems in use were unable to detect the rise in thrust for a single 6.1in (15.5cm) ramjet only. The systems could measure the thrust increase of this mul-

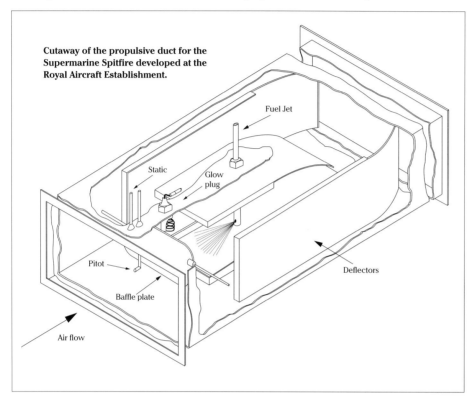

Cutaway of the propulsive duct for the Supermarine Spitfire developed at the Royal Aircraft Establishment.

Fuel Jet

Static

Glow plug

Pitot

Baffle plate

Deflectors

Air flow

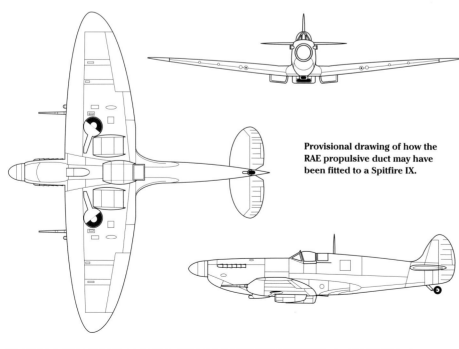

Provisional drawing of how the RAE propulsive duct may have been fitted to a Spitfire IX.

tiple installation and the results would then be adjusted accordingly. The system was flown in a Mustang I powered by an Allison V-1710 engine, which had been attached to the Royal Aircraft Establishment.

The reason for choosing the Allison-engined variant was more to do with ease of access to the radiator duct. Unlike the Rolls-Royce Merlin variants of the Mustang, the earlier models had large doors on the underside of the fairing that opened and closed depending on the flight conditions. These doors could be modified to accommodate the ramjet support structure and associated systems. The resulting increase in speed only amounted to 50mph (80km/h) at best, with a corresponding reduction in endurance; however the primary reason for this work was related to guided weapons.

Little Ben and the 7.2in Ramjet

Under the auspices of the GAP committee, work also began on a 7.2in (18.2cm) ramjet for a guided weapon. In 1946 the RAE set up the Controlled Weapons Department at Farnborough and the Guided Projectile Establishment (GPE) at Westcott to develop a Guided Anti-aircraft Projectile (GAP). The size was governed by the fact that this was the biggest ramjet that could be bench tested in the test rig at the RAE's Powerplant Division at Pyestock.

This ramjet was to be flight tested in a test vehicle being developed in conjunction with GPE at Westcott. The 14ft (4.27m)-long vehicle had a pitot intake and was boosted by solid rocket motors and a central body held the gas pressure system that fed fuel to the staged combustor system. Before the end of the war a total of eight cold firings had been carried out to investigate boost separation. It was intended that this ramjet would power a guided weapon called Little Ben and use the same guidance system as LOP/GAP.

While GPE was concerned with developing the weapon at Westcott, the RAE Powerplant Division had in 1946 merged with Power Jets R&D to become the National Gas Turbine

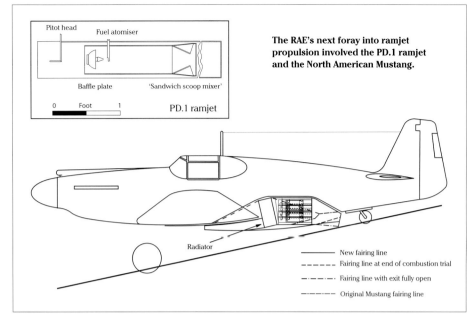

The RAE's next foray into ramjet propulsion involved the PD.1 ramjet and the North American Mustang.

Establishment (NGTE) at Pyestock under the directorship of Roxbee Cox. NGTE became concerned with the development of the ramjet and combustor, while the Projectile Development Establishment at Aberporth was involved in the flight tests.

Flight testing of the 7.2in (18.3cm) ramjet showed that its performance was marginal, especially at speeds greater than 600mph (965km/h) where the higher internal flow velocity caused problems with the staged combustor. When the secondary combustion zone ignited, it caused the primary combustion zone to be extinguished, with little or no thrust being developed.

Combustors: Keeping the Fires Burning

The RAE continued with its ramjet research and, due to fuelling and combustor limitations, believed that smaller multiple ramjets possessed more scope for successful development than larger ramjets. As a result the RAE, in the guise of the Gas Dynamics Department, pursued the development of 6in (15cm) and 10in (25cm) ramjets with simple

combustors. These ramjets were built and tested by the Bristol Aeroplane Company and Bristol Aero Engines at Filton, with the first contract for the Jet Test Vehicle (JTV) being placed in September 1949. RAE and Bristol flight tested their designs at every opportunity and could be accused of taking shortcuts to obtain the desired results. One of these shortcuts was the use of gasolene as fuel. (Bear in mind that the RAE was a scientific establishment and therefore more interested in the theoretical and technical aspects of ramjets, rather than producing a practical propulsion system.)

The National Gas Turbine Establishment at Pyestock on the other hand had different ideas, and so did a company called D Napier and Son. The NGTE had grown up from Whittle's Powerjets Ltd and did want to develop a practical powerplant. NGTE and its predecessor also had a background in using test rigs to develop engines. Oddly enough Napier, latecomers to the gas turbine field, had a close relationship with the National Gas Turbine Establishment. This may be because its main

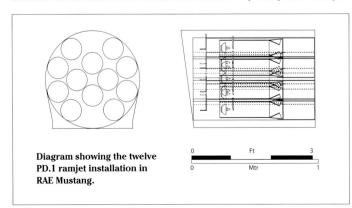

Diagram showing the twelve PD.1 ramjet installation in RAE Mustang.

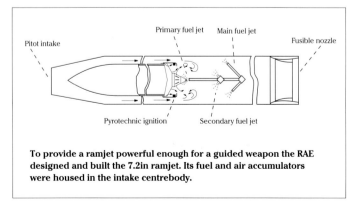

To provide a ramjet powerful enough for a guided weapon the RAE designed and built the 7.2in ramjet. Its fuel and air accumulators were housed in the intake centrebody.

Launch of a JTV.1 with tandem boosts.
Bristol Collection via Richard Vernon

JTV.1 awaiting fitting of boosts and transport to the test range. Note the XTV.2 in the background.
Bristol Collection via Richard Vernon

industry competitor, Rolls-Royce, had taken control of gas turbine development and production and Napier believed that they had to catch up. The NGTE produced a more complicated combustion system than that developed by the RAE, but the NGTE was willing to talk to other workers in the ramjet field.

The GAP studies in the UK were echoed in the USA, where in January 1945, the US Navy Bureau of Ordnance placed a research contract with Johns Hopkins University's Applied Physics Laboratory (APL) to develop a ramjet-powered guided weapon to defend ships.

The project was called Bumblebee and continued throughout the 1940s. By June 1945 APL had flown a 6in (15cm) 'Burner Test Vehicle' (based on the exhaust tubing from a Republic P-47 Thunderbolt fighter) over a distance of 6.25 miles (10km). This success led the APL team to begin development in September 1946 of an 18in (45.7cm) vehicle called Cobra. Close liaison between the US and UK led to the secondment of NGTE engineer Rhys Probert to the Bumblebee project in 1946.

The Bumblebee team had developed a two-stage combustor that appeared to work. Probert returned to the UK in mid-1947 and imparted his knowledge to his colleagues at NGTE. This included fitting fuel injectors upstream of the combustor in the intake diffuser and a separately fuelled pilot combustor.

NGTE concluded that the combustion system was the key to efficient ramjet performance and that a practical ramjet should run on kerosene, a safer fuel than gasolene. Keeping the engine lit in flight was a balancing act between fuel and air mixtures so without an efficient combustor the engine would not produce sufficient thrust to provide range for the planned guided weapons. NGTE, through rig testing, opted for a pilot combustor using one third of the fuel flow, with the remaining fuel flow being directed to a main combustor. If the main combustor was extinguished, the pilot combustor could relight it, but the main benefit was that the pilot/main combustor system allowed the engine to be 'throttled back'. Full power could be used for the acceleration phase of the flight. When the vehicle reached a specified Mach number, fuel flow to the main combustor could be reduced, with the pilot combustor providing enough thrust for cruise. Based on this work, NGTE and Napier developed a 16in (40.6cm)-diameter ramjet, the NRJ.1.

British Secret Projects: Hypersonics, Ramjets & Missiles

Right: **The intake of an early Thor ramjet on an XRD.1 showing the centre body and auxiliary intake. Notice that it is possible to see straight through the engine, as it has no flow-straightening grid.** Bristol Collection via Richard Vernon

Below: **Three images of a Thor ramjet intake in flight.** Bristol Collection via Richard Vernon

Bottom Left: **The other end of a later Thor showing the six fuel sprays, flame holders and annular duct for cooling air.**

Bottom right: **The flame holder of the BS.1003 Odin ramjet for the CF.299 SAM.**

Napiers were contracted to build a test vehicle to fly the NGTE ramjet design and the Napier Ramjet Test Vehicle (RJTV) was the result. Boosted by eight 7½in (19cm) Demon boost rocket motors, the RJTV flew successfully in a programme that increased the speed and altitude flight envelope in stages.

While the NGTE had been working closely with Napier, RAE had a similar relationship with Bristol Aero Engines. Bristol's newly established Guided Weapons Department had in 1949 embarked on Project 1220, the Surface-to-Air Guided Weapon (SAGW) that would become Red Duster.

Bristol began to develop a ramjet for this SAGW and, under the influence of the RAE, concentrated on small-diameter ramjets, typically the 6in (15cm) unit. This ramjet was flown on the JTV.1, but its performance was

poor. The RAE ideas on ramjet combustors were based on using a single-stage combustor system, with strontium pyrotechnic flares to maintain combustion in the duct. A simple solution that appeared to work, but the ramjets based on this design didn't produce the thrust levels that the calculations predicted, especially when they were scaled up to counter this lack of thrust. A further problem was that the operating duration of such an engine was limited by the flare's burn time with a corresponding effect on range.

In the meantime, Bristol Aero Engines had

signed a technical exchange agreement with the Boeing Aeroplane Company in Seattle. When a Bristol Ramjet team, including Robin Jamison, travelled to the USA in 1951 to consult with Boeing, they concluded that the small ramjet was a waste of time and began scaling up their engines from 10in (25.4cm) to 14in (35.6cm) and ultimately to 16in (40.6cm). Further visits to Marquardt and APL convinced the Bristol team that bigger ramjets were the way forward. The resulting BB.1 (Bristol Boeing type 1) and BRJ.1 to 3 (Bristol RamJet type 1 to 3) ramjets formed the basis of the Red

Robin Jamison, the driving force behind Bristol's ramjet work. Rolls-Royce Heritage Trust via Roy Hawkins

Duster flight test programme, but they still employed the RAE single-stage combustor and consequently lacked performance.

The development of Red Duster and the Thor ramjet has been covered in Chapter Four but, in summary, Bristols adopted the NGTE pilot combustor system for the Thor, Britain's first production ramjet. This was improved upon by the addition of features developed by Roy Hawkins (who joined Bristol Aero Engines from the RAE Aero Dept in 1956). Hawkins had improved the combustor of the BRJ.800 series of M3 ramjets for Blue Envoy and, on that weapon's cancellation, these improvements were transferred to the Thor to produce the ultimate Thor, the BS.1009. This was fitted to Bloodhound II and remained in RAF service until 1989.

Having developed the Thor, Bristol, or Bristol Siddeley Engines Ltd (BSEL) as they were by 1958, became involved in the development of a new ramjet for the SIGS SAM. As shown in Chapter Four SIGS became the CF.299 Sea Dart SAM and was fitted with a BS.1003 ramjet. The BS.1003 incorporated more innovations from Roy Hawkins, particularly in the flame holder and mixer, which produced a powerplant that could power the Sea Dart to Mach 3.5 and a range in excess of 50 miles (80.5km), all in an airframe 14ft (5.35m) long.

With two ramjet-powered SAMs under development, the focus turned to the long-range, high-speed cruise regime of the stand-off missile. Chapter Eight shows the difficulties of producing a missile to meet the 1,000 mile (1,609km) OR.1149 requirement, which was eventually 'de-spec'd' to OR.1159 with a range of 600 miles (965km). Bristol Aero Engines and BSEL expended considerable effort in producing a ramjet that could fulfil this tricky requirement.

The Advanced Propulsion Research Group
The work on a ramjet suitable for long-range cruise tweaked the curiosity of Robin Jamison. Jamison had worked at Rolls-Royce on their earliest gas turbines, the Griffith CR.1 and CR.2. When these were shelved in favour of Whittle designs in 1944, Jamison continued work on control systems and, more importantly, on reheat. Stanley Hooker had moved to Bristol Aero Engines in 1948 and was building a research and development team with an eye to future gas turbine work. Encouraged by Hooker, Jamison eventually took a position at Bristol Aero Engines and, through his gas dynamics expertise, became involved

with ramjet development. Jamison's right-hand man in the ramjet field was R J (John) Lane, who had joined Bristol in 1954.

From the start Jamison and Lane saw the potential in the ramjet within the 1950s climate of ever-increasing aircraft speed and Jamison produced a series of design studies for aircraft that would utilise the ramjet. As Whittle's turbojet was to shrink the world, Jamison saw the ramjet as the way to make the world even smaller. With Hooker in charge of overall propulsion development, Jamison and Lane got to work to conduct research that would produce the powerplant of the future. This ultimately led to the setting up of the Advanced Propulsion Research Group (APRG) at BSEL in 1962. APRG not only conducted ramjet research but also worked on a variety of applications such as the reheat system for Concorde, before eventually being wound up in 1969.

In 1958, as missile ramjet work was starting to come to fruition, Bristol's Ramjet Department published its Report 2093: 'The possibilities of air breathing propulsion for hypersonic vehicles'. In this Jamison and Lane outlined how hypersonic flight could be achieved with ramjets and turbojets rather than by the use of rockets. The key was to be the use of ramjets in conjunction with turbojets to produce a powerplant capable of operation from a standing start through to hypersonic speed, without the need for rockets. This was known as the 'Combination Engine' and this would form the basis of the various design studies undertaken into hypersonic flight in the UK. However before looking at these engine and aircraft studies, two items critical to hypersonic flight must be covered – fuel and structures.

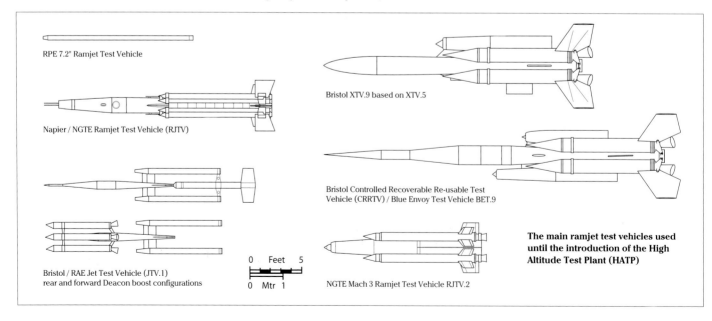

RPE 7.2" Ramjet Test Vehicle

Napier / NGTE Ramjet Test Vehicle (RJTV)

Bristol / RAE Jet Test Vehicle (JTV.1)
rear and forward Deacon boost configurations

Bristol XTV.9 based on XTV.5

Bristol Controlled Recoverable Re-usable Test Vehicle (CRRTV) / Blue Envoy Test Vehicle BET.9

NGTE Mach 3 Ramjet Test Vehicle RJTV.2

0 Feet 5
0 Mtr 1

The main ramjet test vehicles used until the introduction of the High Altitude Test Plant (HATP)

Chapter Eleven

Fuel and Materials
for Hypersonic Flight

Specification ER.181 had stated that any research aircraft to meet the requirement should be air breathing. While that ruled out a purely rocket-powered aircraft right from the start, it did allow a range of other propulsion systems and fuels to be considered. Jet fuel, which invariably means a type of kerosene, comes in a variety of grades and JP-4 was the standard military grade back in the 1960s. JP-4 was 'wide-cut' kerosene, which means that the fuel was blended from a wider range of hydrocarbon fractions than straight kerosene fuels. The boil-off range of a wide-cut fuel falls between 50 and 220°C, which means that they are highly volatile.

As flight speeds increased, the attendant thermal effects on the airframe would be conducted to the fuel in the tanks. Wing tanks were especially prone to this, being wide and flat. As the fuel was heated it became unsta-

ble and it soon became apparent that normal aviation fuels were not suited to high-speed flight. It was known that kerosene such as JP-4 was particularly susceptible to 'cracking' and forming gummy deposits when subjected to high temperatures for long periods. A further reason lay in the fact that the energy output of conventional jet fuels was low in comparison to their mass. For a high-speed aircraft this meant that more time would have to be spent in reheat, requiring more fuel, which in turn required a larger, heavier airframe. The vicious spiral that affects high-speed flight rears its head with the fuel as well as the airframe.

The received wisdom was that high-speed propulsion systems would require exotic fuels to maintain performance at elevated temperatures and perhaps even supersonic combustion, where airflow through the

The last Avro 730 in RAF service awaits its fate at RAF Boscombe Down in 1996. The 730 was the first large aircraft fabricated from stainless steel.
Adrian Mann

engine exceeds speeds of Mach 1. These exotic fuels eventually took two forms: 'zip' fuels based on boron compounds and the cryogenic fuels such as liquid hydrogen. Zip fuels were under development in the late 1950s to provide high performance in aircraft such as the North American F-108 long-range interceptor and the North American XB-70 Valkyrie Mach 3 bomber.

Initial attempts at producing more energy from conventional jet fuels and hence more power from the engines was achieved by adding powdered boron. Despite providing the required power increase the exhaust was poisonous, which thus created a hazard for ground crews. Secondly, the boron tended to

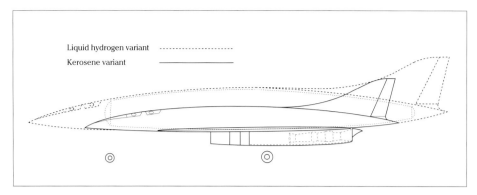

Liquid hydrogen variant ·····················

Kerosene variant ─────────────

BAC conducted a series of fuel comparisons for their P.42 Study. Here the difference in airframe size between liquid hydrogen and kerosene is obvious.

deposit on metal surfaces in the engine itself, particularly the turbine sections of the turbojets. Such coatings reduced the efficiency of the turbomachinery and represented a hazard to any technicians servicing the engines. However, using the boron-treated fuel solely for reheat to provide a speed boost over the target solved these problems. This meant a separate fuel system was required for the boron-treated fuel or the boron additive: more weight and complexity.

As an alternative to this boron additive, the USAF and US Navy were investigating other boron compounds for what became known as 'chemical' or more commonly 'zip' fuels. Zip fuel was actually ethyl borane. The increased performance of zip fuels (it was thought that a 10% increase in range and higher cruising speeds would be attained) would compensate for their higher cost of development and production (and new infrastructure) while providing a much improved capability for the weapons systems using them.

By the turn of the decade it was becoming obvious that the high-speed high-altitude bomber would be incapable of competing with the ballistic missile in the deterrent stakes. The XB-70 bomber programme was cancelled and the airframes then under construction transferred to a research programme investigating the possibility of a supersonic transport (SST).

Cryogenics

Cryogenic fuels were familiar to the aerospace industry as a rocket fuel, particularly in high-performance rockets. Liquid Hydrogen (LH_2) has the highest Specific Impulse (Isp) of any fuel. Specific Impulse is used to compare the performance of rocket motors and is defined as pounds of thrust produced per pound of fuel consumed per second, and expressed in seconds. This superior performance possessed an allure all of its own to the high-speed aircraft and powerplant developers, who saw LH_2 as a means to attain the necessary performance from their propulsion

systems. In the US LH_2 had been proposed for the Lockheed CL-400 Suntan Mach 3 reconnaissance aircraft, but had failed to achieve the range requirements.

Despite preferring to use kerosene as its rocket fuel of choice (with either High Test Peroxide or Liquid Oxygen as the oxidant), the UK rocket engine developers did turn to LH_2 for higher-powered engines such as the Rolls-Royce RZ20 for Blue Streak. Since it was becoming clear that to produce high performance from a rocket needed cryogenic fuels, it was realised that high performance from an aircraft would also need cryogenic fuels.

LH_2 had a couple of perceived advantages in the high-speed aircraft field: it possessed three times the thermal energy per unit of mass of kerosene and it was cold. Producing LH_2 involved lowering the temperature of hydrogen gas below its boiling point of -252.7°C. Once liquefied the LH_2 only required a slight pressurisation to remain in this phase, allowing the LH_2 to be stored and handled relatively easily.

Stagnation and friction effects can increase the skin temperature of an aircraft many times over. For example, research had shown that a 75° delta wing with a leading edge radius of 2mm would reach a maximum temperature of 525°C without any cooling when flying at Mach 5. By pumping the cold LH_2 around the critical parts of the airframe, the airframe was then not only cooled, but the LH_2 itself was warmed up prior to being injected into the engine. The airframe acts as a heat exchanger, a pre-heater for the engine fuel system, using the heat from the airframe to preheat the hydrogen before being fed to the combustors. This is called regenerative cooling.

From the airframe designer's point of view, however, the use of cryogenic fuels had many drawbacks. The trebling of the energy per unit mass is attained by a consequent fourfold increase in volume due to hydrogen's much lower density. This required a larger airframe to hold the tanks and carry the necessary insulation. Interestingly the insulation

was to prevent the build-up of condensation and ice on the outside of the airframe rather than keeping the LH_2 liquid. Of course the larger airframe meant greater weight, greater wetted area and therefore more drag. This required more powerful engines and more fuel. The vicious spiral went ever upwards.

One interesting outcome of the research work done at BAC Warton was that fuel comparison studies conducted on LH_2- and kerosene-powered variants of the company's P.42 EAG.3303 study showed that there was very little difference between the two fuels. LH_2 had a slight advantage in the range stakes, but this was outweighed by the complexity of cryogenic systems. An entirely new infrastructure would be required to handle cryogenically fuelled aircraft. Based on these findings BAC thus concluded that for a research aircraft in the speed range up to Mach 5, kerosene was the answer.

So in the 1960s the UK aircraft companies saw kerosene as the optimum fuel for high-speed flight, at least in the Mach 3 to 5 range. For higher speeds kerosene still had the edge over more exotic fuels. BSEL had been conducting research into improving kerosene-fuelled ramjet performance for stand-off weapons; particularly increasing the speed at which the ramjet-powered vehicles would fly.

This work was carried out in parallel with studies to produce a scramjet: a supersonic combustion ramjet that, rather than using an intake diffuser to slow the incoming air to below Mach 1, could run at mass flows in excess of Mach 1. The fuel would be injected and burned in this supersonic flow. Because the intake diffusers constituted a major component of the total drag, the idea was that the amount of drag would be reduced by dispensing with the diffuser. However supersonic combustion has been likened to keeping a candle lit in a hurricane and even in the early 21st century scramjets are still at the experimental stage.

It was anticipated that scramjets would work best with hydrogen fuel, but as the BSEL work progressed it became clear that scramjets were beyond the technology of the day and that subsonic combustion, meaning normal ramjets, could provide a solution.

Exotic Fuels

With this in mind the research engineers at BSEL set out to attempt to increase the performance of their ramjets, ultimately showing that it was possible to run kerosene-fuelled ramjets in the HATP test rig at Mach numbers up to 7. Of course these were experimental ramjets and no doubt only functioned for seconds, but they had proved that it was possible to run such ramjets at high Mach numbers.

BSEL's engineers also looked at another boron compound, pentaborane. This was considered as a fuel for the BS.1012 combination powerplant (see Chapter Thirteen). In this application parametric studies had concluded that by using pentaborane the endurance of a Mach 5 aircraft could be almost doubled. However pentaborane shared ethyl borane's drawbacks.

The next course of investigation was improving the fuel for conventionally fuelled ramjets, which made density the area of interest. JP-4 has a density of between 0.75 and 0.8g/cc so Handley Page's rational for using diesel for its HP.106M stand-off weapon had been that the denser fuel (0.83g/cc) gave longer range. There were also high hopes for Shelldyne, a synthetic fuel. These fuels are derived from coal or natural gas rather than petroleum and synthesised by a process developed by Franz Fischer and Hans Tropsch in the 1920s. The Fischer-Tropsch process provided the German armed forces with much of its fuel during the Second World War as Germany's access to sources of crude oil diminished. Amid concerns about energy security and rising oil prices, interest in synthetic fuel has increased in the first decade of the 21st century.

Developed by Shell in conjunction with BSEL, Shelldyne, while having a lower energy per unit of mass, was denser (1.08g/cc) than JP-4 and so had higher energy per unit volume. This meant that for the same volume of Shelldyne, the aircraft's range was still improved. Shelldyne was particularly associated with the BS.1012 combination powerplant for the Hawker Siddeley APD.1019 research aircraft (see Chapter Sixteen). The ultimate use for Shelldyne-type fuels (as JP-10, for the very same reasons outlined above) was as a fuel for the cruise missiles that spearheaded many of the conflicts the USAF has been involved in during the last two decades.

By 1965 BSEL had developed the engine, the BS.1012, and a fuel, Shelldyne, for a high-speed cruise aircraft and it had shown that these could power an aircraft through all phases of flight. With a propulsion system in place the aircraft companies now had some performance figures to work into their own studies.

This graph clearly illustrates the balancing act between aircraft speed and airframe material.

Materials and the Heat Barrier

Alongside fuels, materials also posed new challenges to the designers of high-speed aircraft. In less than fifty years aircraft structures had gone from bamboo and canvas to complex structural components chemically etched or machined from single billets of exotic alloys. Materials would govern what could and could not be built, but without new materials technology the high-speed aircraft would never be built.

With the performance figures for the putative propulsion systems now available the aircraft companies (by 1965 the British Aircraft Corporation, BAC and Hawker Siddeley Aviation, HSA) could draw up their design studies with an eye on a practicable engine system. The aerodynamics could be worked out on the new computers such as Deuce (Digital Electric Universal Computing Engine) that were replacing the traditional slide-rule. However a new 'barrier' was being encountered – heat.

Any body moving through the atmosphere at speed will generate heat in two ways. The first is the frictional effect of the air moving over the surface of that body and the second is by stagnation. Stagnation occurs where the air builds up in front of a surface, becomes compressed and consequently the temperature of that air increases. When applied to aircraft these phenomena are known collectively as kinetic heating. The heat generated by kinetic heating is transferred to the airframe, increasing its temperature, and this will affect the integrity of the airframe in the

short or long term depending on the severity of the heating and the airframe material.

Kinetic heating is a fact of life in high-speed flight, but the degree of heating can be minimised by careful manipulation of the flight regime. This may involve limiting the speed, limiting the time spent at high speed or by flying at higher altitudes where kinetic heating is minimised in a less dense atmosphere. This manipulation somewhat complicates matters because flying too high can reduce the efficiency of the engines and gives less lift, while flying too low increases the thermal effects on the airframe. As a result the vehicle has to fly in a fairly rigid speed/altitude 'corridor'. Sir Frank Whittle's original observation, that to fly fast the aircraft had to fly high, is particularly pertinent to hypersonic vehicles.

Stagnation temperature is typically a function of Mach number; for example, at Mach 4 the stagnation temperature can reach 400°C (752°F). The temperature increase is most severe in the intake ducts (where precompression occurs prior to entering the engine), with temperatures almost double those seen on the lower surface of the wing. For an aircraft flying at Mach 5 for example, its lower wing surface temperature would rise to approximately 550°C (1,022°F) whereas in the intake duct the temperature would be in the region of 1000°C (1,832°F). Prolonged exposure to such temperatures can wreak havoc with an aircraft's structure and systems. In time the structure materials lose their strength properties and in due course failure will occur.

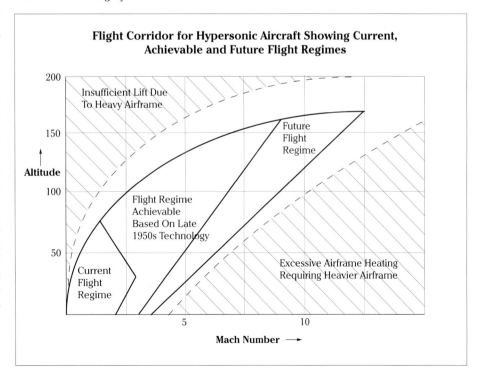

Flight Corridor for Hypersonic Aircraft Showing Current, Achievable and Future Flight Regimes

There are a number of ways to deal with this heat build-up. Using the fuel as a heat sink can cool the airframe, either by conduction or by active circulation of fuel around the airframe as has been described. Another less complicated method has the airframe constructed from materials that can sustain repeated heating and cooling to high temperatures, the so-called hot structures. A further technique involves coating the exposed area with heat-resistant refractory materials or by the materials themselves forming protective oxidised layers.

In the early 1960s three materials were considered as being the most suitable for the structure of a hypersonic cruise vehicle: titanium, stainless steel and a nickel alloy called Inconel. Titanium, as well as being light and strong, possessed good heat-resisting properties. However, Mach 4 would be titanium's thermal limit, so higher Mach numbers would require more resistant materials. Stainless steel, Inconel and tantalum are heavy and rather difficult materials to work and fabricate, but they possess superb heat resistance, which makes them ideal for Mach 4. This resistance is helped by the formation, when heated, of oxide layers that act as insulation to the airframe.

However, even if the airframe could be made of heat-resistant material, the chances are that the structure would be immensely heavy compared with an aircraft designed for Mach 2. Over the years the vicious spiral of Mach number and structural weight has severely restricted the development of hypersonic vehicles. Studies have shown that to produce a viable hypersonic vehicle the structural weight fraction would need to be in the region of 15% of the all-up-weight. This, however, was half that of the supersonic aircraft of the 1960s, which had a structural weight fraction in the region of 30% of all-up weight. Any construction techniques that worked toward reducing this would be a major step toward the ultimate goal. How could this be achieved? The answer lay in the method of fabrication.

Fabricating the Airframe
During the Great War Hugo Junkers, the German aircraft pioneer, began producing all-metal aircraft. The Junkers J 1, the first purpose-built all-metal monoplane, first flew in 1915 and later all-metal Junkers types such as the J 4 biplane (also designated J.I) were used in battle. Junkers' designs initially used mild steel in their construction but later moved on to a lightweight high-strength alloy of aluminium called Duralumin that has a density of around 3.0g/cc. Originally a trade

name, Duralumin (or Dural as it was often called) has dominated aircraft construction since the 1930s.

In the 1920s a French engineer called Marcel Wibault patented an improved method of all-metal construction that dominated the aircraft industry until the end of World War Two. Both Junkers and Wibault's construction techniques relied on the use of rivets to join the components. These were later referred to as mechanical fasteners in the aviation industry because rivets conjured up images of Victorian heavy engineering and sweaty chaps with big hammers. The technique relied on the two components being overlapped, producing a double thickness along the joint. Holes were drilled through the overlap and a fastener inserted and secured. The application of fasteners to these types of joints increased the aircraft's structural weight by as much as 30% of the structural weight, which could represent around 5% of the all-up weight of an aircraft.

When it came to high-performance aircraft any weight shaved off the total take-off weight, however small, represented an improvement in performance not to mention material cost. As noted above, high-speed aircraft were by necessity constructed from materials that were either costly (in the case of titanium), heavy (in the case of stainless steel) or both (in the case of nickel-based Inconel and Nimonic).

Titanium is one of the most abundant elements in the Earth's crust, but until recently it has remained in the realm of very high-technology specialist applications principally because it was so difficult to separate from its ore. Today we see titanium everywhere, in bicycles, sports cars and even spectacle frames, and in some applications it has usurped aluminium and steel as the material of choice. Back in the 1950s however, titanium was used solely in the aerospace industry. Titanium, when alloyed with aluminium and/or other elements, possesses high tensile strength (on a par with some steels) and is light, its density being in the region of 4.5g/cc. It was first used for aircraft structures in early jets such as the North American F-86D and F-100 for areas around the jet pipe. These were non-structural skin areas where temperatures would be too high for aluminium alloys. Titanium alloy for large-scale structural use was first used on the Lockheed A-11/SR-71 series, but it was an expensive and difficult material to work with and new manufacturing techniques had to be devised. The Lockheed A-11 was the first aircraft to have its main structure fabricated in titanium, with almost 93% of

the airframe constructed using this material. Titanium had been earmarked for the earlier Republic XF-103 Mach 3 interceptor, but this was cancelled before any metal was cut.

As noted titanium was very expensive to produce, typically twenty times more expensive than aluminium alloy. Many aircraft parts required different techniques to aluminium, and chemical and machine milling of components became the norm. Welding was employed to put together titanium components much more than fasteners, with a consequent saving in weight.

Hard and heavy, Inconel (a US-developed nickel alloy) and Nimonic (a UK-developed nickel alloy) had been developed for turbine blades in jet engines. These alloys were particularly durable in high temperature applications but possessed a high density, typically more than 8.2g/cc. While they were fine for smaller structures, such as the exteriors of the Mercury and Gemini space capsules, larger structures for cruise vehicles were a different matter. In time these difficulties were overcome.

Having seen the trials and tribulations of stainless steel fabrication at Avro during the construction of the Avro 730 reconnaissance bomber and the Blue Steel stand-off weapon (see Chapter Eight) plus the ongoing saga of the Bristol Type 188 research aircraft, BAC Warton investigated in detail the pros and cons of stainless steel and titanium during its P.42 design study (described later). The choice appeared to be governed by mission profile and cruising altitude; (design studies rarely get involved with fabrication problems). The paper on the structure of the aircraft by C Christianson, Senior Engineer: Project Research, concludes with: 'It is interesting to note that the stainless steel aircraft of 1,336ft² (124.2m²) starting to cruise at 75,000ft (22,860m) will have only 100nm (185.2km) more range than the 1,700ft² (157.9m²) / 85,000ft (25,908m) titanium variant.'

As with the fuel question it appeared that a more conventional solution would be the best compromise, but this comparison ignored any fabrication and operational problems.

A later Hawker Siddeley design study, APD 1019 E2, was to be fabricated from tantalum alloys. Tantalum would be an easier material to work with, especially in sheet form, but tantalum alloys possessed very high density (typically 16.6g/cc) and had poor resistance to oxidation at high temperatures. Adding 5 to 20% chromium to the alloy improved its resistance to oxidation a thousand fold, but coating the components with compounds such as molybdenum disilicide also improved resistance to oxidation. A further reason for pursuing a welded airframe was the need to maintain a uniform coating over the airframe components. The drilling involved in riveting or bolting would damage these coatings and the fasteners would require a coating before fabrication. The entire assembly would then require re-coating to maintain the required degree of resistance. Welding would be much simpler from this aspect.

If used in an aircraft's primary structure, a tantalum airframe would be good for Mach 7. For the Mach 5 application of the APD 1019 E2, coated tantalum alloys were intended for the areas where heat build-up would be greatest, the nose, leading edge and intake, while the remainder of the structure was to be constructed in nickel alloy.

Hot Systems

While an airframe could be made thermally resistant, fuel, avionics and payload presented further challenges. At a cruising speed of Mach 3, the temperature within the airframe would reach 220°C, rising to 470°C at Mach 6. This necessitated some form of cooling for crew and critical systems pending development of temperature resistant systems. The degradation of fuel (kerosene fuel degrades to a gummy sludge when subjected to temperatures above 200°C for prolonged periods), electronics and weapons systems would be a big problem. Reconnaissance cameras and explosives were particularly sensitive to thermal effects. Overall this would have been a major obstacle in the development of a usable hypersonic vehicle (that is, a vehicle for a particular role such as a strike aircraft) as opposed to a research aircraft.

Given these thermal effects, the crew, avionics and any payload would require active cooling systems. Such cooling systems would then add to the weight of the aircraft, with the inevitable knock-on effect on performance. The Bristol 188 research aircraft carried a cooling plant to protect its pilot and systems but such equipment would represent a significant weight penalty to an already heavy hypersonic aircraft. The vicious spiral of speed against weight was present all of the time.

Another point to consider is the visibility of the pilot. To fly an aircraft the pilot needs to see the outside world. While a hypersonic vehicle in cruise mode could probably only go in a straight line or perform very slow turns where vision is not important, some means of seeing the aircraft surroundings is required

for take-off and landing. British RB.156 studies of the mid-1950s for a Mach 3 reconnaissance aircraft had looked at indirect vision systems using TV cameras and periscopes but, whatever the means of looking outside, some transparency would still be required. Transparencies could be constructed from borosilicate glass, or even faired over with heat shields. Even if the transparencies could be heat resistant, those in the airframe, given the different thermal expansion rates and ranges of glass and metal, still pose a problem. Of course an operational type would require radar and sensors, whose antennae would require heat-resistant, radio frequency transparent fairings. These materials also needed to be developed.

Fuelling the propulsion system at such high temperatures, especially if the fuel is being used for cooling, presented a major problem. Kerosene jet fuel will break down if subjected to high temperatures, but only if allowed to settle in the pipe work. If the fuel doesn't gum up, how easy is it to start the ramjets? These matters made cryogenic fuels attractive due to their cooling properties, but there were also drawbacks.

Repeated heating and cooling of the airframe, the Bauschingle effect, would play havoc with the aircraft structure, and so would the high frequency vibration generated by the ramjet powerplant. This vibration produces an effect called 'brinelling' where the vibration of two components against each other produces a hardening around the point of contact. This may lead to the area becoming brittle and prone to failure. The new construction techniques noted above would also have to be developed to cope with such harsh conditions.

Yet another point to consider, aircraft are by necessity constructed with removable panels to gain access to the internal systems. Seals to prevent ingress of hot air to the various equipment bays would themselves need to be temperature resistant. The landing gear would require special tyres and possibly a cooled bay to protect them. With air at Mach 4 reaching 600°C at stagnation, the slightest gap between any panels or doors would create a high temperature jet capable of severe internal damage.

Provision of electrical power would pose a considerable problem. The turbomachinery in a combination engine could drive a generator in the early phases of a flight, but how would the aircraft, operating on ramjet power alone, generate electricity? One suggestion was a ram air turbine (RAT). Many jet aircraft possess RATs for use when engine power is lost because they can provide electrical

power for critical systems and the power-assisted controls such aircraft require. Most are retractable and can be deployed as required. However their means of operation (effectively a wind generator) means that they produce a lot of drag on a hypersonic aircraft. Such turbines would no doubt be fitted in the air intakes where the air velocity would be lower than on the exterior but, as noted previously, the intake experiences the highest temperature. Producing a RAT resistant to high temperatures would be a challenge. A limited-endurance research aircraft could probably function on battery power, but large batteries add further weight to an already heavy system. However an operational type would require far more power for its sensors and systems, so a generator would be needed.

Assuming new materials could overcome all of these problems, how could they be tested under realistic high-speed conditions? How could such temperatures be simulated without the high costs of repeated test flights? The Bristol Type 188 proved to be of little or no use in its intended role of investigating thermal effects of airframes, and that was at speeds of Mach 2 only. To examine the effects of cruise and heat soak at Mach 3 meant that another means of testing airframe materials was required. The RAE did have test vehicles such as the CTV-5 (whose design evolved into the Skylark sounding rocket). There were also the Leopard and the Jabiru, three-stage Mach 9 test vehicles that were flown at Woomera to provide materials testing in the high-speed environment. Nevertheless a cheaper method of testing materials on the ground under controlled conditions was required. The solution was novel to say the least. Bristol Aero Engines constructed a ramjet test facility at Filton that was used in the development of the Thor and BRJ-800 series ramjets for the Bloodhound and Blue Envoy SAMs. By placing samples in the efflux of a ramjet, new materials could be subjected to conditions not dissimilar to that of high-speed flight.

The sound barrier may have been breached in the late 1940s, but in the late 1950s it was the heat barrier, or rather the 'thermal thicket', a term originally coined by none other than the great American broadcaster Walter Cronkite, that posed the problems. There were so many unknowns, any one of them preventing the design from reaching the goal and all of them representing additional weight and complexity. The complexity was becoming more apparent as the study progressed. More and more questions arose at every turn.

Chapter Twelve

Standing Start to Mach 5 – The Combination Engine

Aircraft with two different engines, usually a mix of piston (for efficient cruising) and jet (to boost speed or take-off performance), were common in the late 1940s, mainly due to the poor performance of the early jets. The example of the Spitfire from 1940 shows ramjets could, in theory, provide a much-needed boost to piston-engined aircraft.

The first British proposal to use ramjets to boost jet performance involved Fairey and the National Gas Turbine Establishment (NGTE) in March 1956. The Avon-powered Fairey Delta Two research aircraft, also known as the Type V or Project 34, smashed the absolute world speed record with an average over two runs of 1,132mph (,1,822km/h). However, even before this achievement, Fairey at Hayes had investigated a means of increasing the FD.2's maximum speed in a form that would also allow it

to act as a re-usable testbed for ramjets. One of these studies, from July 1955, involved fitting the FD.2 with a pair of 16in (40cm) ramjets to provide an increase in maximum speed of Mach 0.4. The ramjets, variants of the Napier NRJ.1, were to be provided by the NGTE at Pyestock and would have been fitted on underwing pylons. NGTE was more than happy with this proposal since it would also provide it with a test vehicle for the Establishment's Ramjet Test Vehicle (RJTV), which had been designed to investigate the principles of flying ramjets for missiles and aircraft.

The RJTV, with its onboard fuel and control systems, would have been modified for an alternative pylon mounting with the fuel and control systems installed within the aircraft. This would have significantly reduced the length and weight of the ramjet. An aircraft weight increase of 600lb (272kg) was antici-

Hawker's P.1134 on a test flight under the power of its combination engine. Adrian Mann

pated for the ramjets with their ancillary electrical systems including a separate fuel and ignition system plus a throttle lever.

While the ramjet-equipped FD.2 was capable of Mach 1.8 plus, its Rolls-Royce Avon R.14 was limited to Mach 1.75 above 36,000ft (10,973m). Although a difference of 0.05 sounds insignificant, it has considerable effect on the performance of a turbojet, leading to high Turbine Entry Temperatures. Increasing an aircraft's performance by adding a pair of ramjets may have sounded ideal in the mid-1950s, but flying an aircraft with ramjets was fraught with very basic problems.

Ramjets only start to become effective from around Mach 0.8. While the RJTV was filled with fuel and flown from a ground launcher at the ambient temperature, the FD.2 would be flying at 36,000ft (10,973m) or more. The ambient temperature at this altitude would be in the region of -40°C (-40°F), which would present considerable problems in lighting the ramjet. As the ramjet intakes would not be faired over there would also be considerable 'cold' drag caused by the ramjet intakes.

A further complication lay in the design of the FD.2 itself. Its intakes would not perform efficiently at higher speeds, having been optimised for supersonic flight in the region of Mach 1.5. To get the benefits of the additional power from ramjets, the FD.2 would need considerable modification to its intakes with possibly variable geometry ramps.

All things considered it was an admirable idea, indeed it may have helped keep the World Air Speed Record in the Fairey 'trophy room'. In the end the ramjets were never fitted. Perhaps they were mismatched from the start. The FD.2 was designed and built for Mach 1.5, which at the time was at the limit of turbojet capability, and so a British air speed record in excess of Mach 1.8 was not to be.

While not a true combination powerplant (the ramjets and turbojets shared neither intake nor jet pipe) the Fairey FD.2 study did show that the UK industry saw the ramjet as a means to increase the performance of jet aircraft. The next development would involve Napier in the powerplant for the English Electric Aviation P.10, which would see performance more than doubled.

OR.330 and the P.10

The RAF had conducted reconnaissance operations over the Soviet Union with impunity throughout the early 1950s using the English Electric Canberra. By 1954 it was

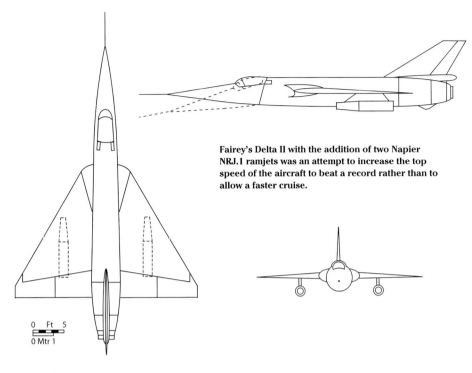

Fairey's Delta II with the addition of two Napier NRJ.1 ramjets was an attempt to increase the top speed of the aircraft to beat a record rather than to allow a faster cruise.

anticipated that a strategic reconnaissance force to support the V-bomber force was required. To cover this specification R.156 was drawn up with Operational Requirement OR.330 and issued in 1954. A dedicated reconnaissance platform, the R.156 would require very high performance to ensure immunity from the Soviet supersonic jet fighters that the RAF and the Ministry of Supply believed were in the pipeline.

As time progressed the specification was modified as RB.156 to include a bombing role, which in turn evolved into OR.336, a supersonic bomber requirement that would ultimately replace the RAF's V-bombers in the late 1960s. The contractors went to their

drawing boards and submitted their designs. Invitations to tender for R.156T (which was worked up around Operational Requirement OR.330) were issued to the UK aircraft manufacturers in 1954. A V Roe, English Electric, Handley Page, Shorts and Vickers received a positive response to their proposals and were requested to continue their design studies for further analysis by the Ministry. The full story of R.156 can be found in 'British Secret Projects: Bombers since 1949'.

Rear view of the English Electric P.10 with its integrated ramjet and RB.123 turbojets. A true combination engine sharing an intake, but having separate jetpipes. Model by John Hall

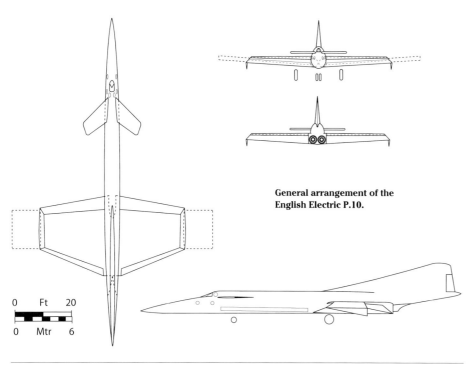

General arrangement of the English Electric P.10.

0   Ft   20

0   Mtr   6

P.10 and RP.1

From a ramjet standpoint the OR.330 story is most important, since it is probably from his involvement in one of the tenders that Robin Jamison formed his opinions on the combination engine. All of the companies except one tendered turbojet aircraft capable of Mach 2.5. The sole exception was English Electric Aviation at Warton who produced a very advanced aircraft capable of Mach 3 cruise using a ramjet integrated into the wing, with an RB.123 turbojet in the wing root.

From 1954 Napier and the NGTE were heavily involved in the P.10 propulsion system, with a two-chamber test rig being built at Pyestock in June 1956, but by September that year NGTE had taken overall charge of the engine test rig. The P.10's integrated ramjet comprised a series of twelve ramjet combustors buried within its low-aspect-ratio wings. Also known as the 'Split Wing Ramjet' the entire leading and trailing edges of each wing were open and acted as a wide two-dimensional intake and exhaust. The intake diffuser inside the wing structure acted as a large fuel tank, with a variable area exhaust within the trailing edge provided by a hydraulic actuator-driven ramp. Between the diffuser and the exhaust lay the ramjet burners in square section bays.

The RB.123 turbojet in each wing root provided power for take-off and acceleration to ramjet light-up speed (ramjets cannot operate when the aircraft is stationary). They also provided electrical power plus an added boost through the transonic region, particularly around Mach 1.2 where the thrust/drag margin would be at a minimum and intake pressure not high enough to light the combustors. Acceleration at lower altitude was suggested but the stress on the airframe would be untenable compared to operation at height. It was from this work that EEA (and others) developed its ideas for a 'flight corridor', where an aircraft flies a narrowly defined flight path to balance heat build-up, altitude and acceleration. Maintaining this flight path was usually a function of the intake pressure whereby, if the aircraft climbed at a

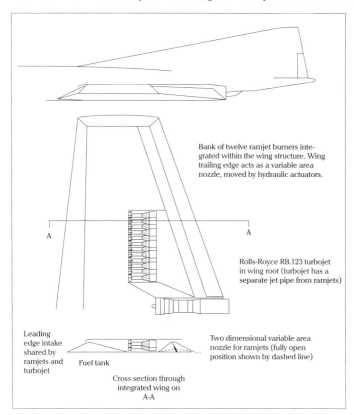

Bank of twelve ramjet burners integrated within the wing structure. Wing trailing edge acts as a variable area nozzle, moved by hydraulic actuators.

Rolls-Royce RB.123 turbojet in wing root (turbojet has a separate jet pipe from ramjets)

Leading edge intake shared by ramjets and turbojet

Fuel tank

Two dimensional variable area nozzle for ramjets (fully open position shown by dashed line)

Cross section through integrated wing on A-A

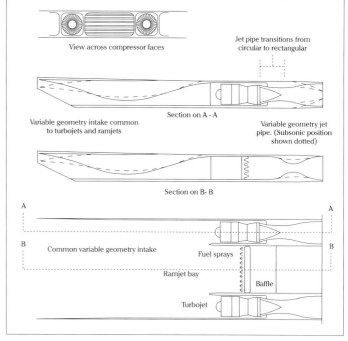

View across compressor faces

Jet pipe transitions from circular to rectangular

Section on A - A

Variable geometry intake common to turbojets and ramjets

Variable geometry jet pipe. (Subsonic position shown dotted)

Section on B- B

Common variable geometry intake

Fuel sprays

Ramjet bay

Baffle

Turbojet

Above: **Jamison's initial combination engine for a Mach 3 airliner was soon superseded by a more compact design.**

Left: **Simplified diagram of the integrated ramjet wing.**

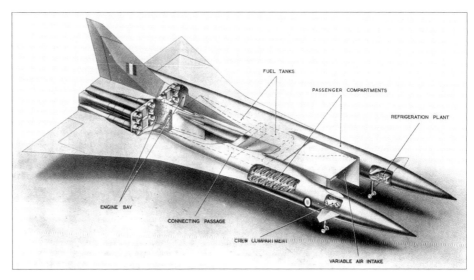

The Mach 3 airliner that Jamison intended to power with his combination engine. The port nose is occupied by a refrigeration unit to cool the passenger accommodation. Rolls-Royce Heritage Trust via Roy Hawkins

constant speed, the pressure at the inlet decreased. To maintain a constant pressure the aircraft accelerated and, by careful selection of intake pressure, the aircraft could stay within the flight corridor.

Barnes Wallis believed that flight corridor could be used to produce a viable hypersonic aircraft. Wallis' theory was that by flying at extreme altitude, typically 150,000ft (45,720m), the thin atmosphere would mean less kinetic heating. This would allow a Mach 5 aircraft to be built using conventional materials apart from the leading edges of the flying surfaces and nose. Bristol Aero Engines' John Lane on the other hand showed that this was not possible, because of excessive engine temperatures and structural weight. Lane's reports impressed the MoD by their regularity and particularly their concise and incisive analysis. These proved to be a model for future MoD reporting.

At some point in this work Bristol Aero Engines was approached by the MoS to help in the P.10's ramjet development and the company quite possibly took over the work from Napier. Evidence for this lies in an English Electric briefing paper on the P.10 and also in a November 1956 letter from Stanley Hooker, chief engineer at Bristol Aero Engines. Hooker had been invited by the Director of Engine R&D at the MoS to submit a tender for a turborocket to TE.10/56 but he replied that Bristol was busy working on developments of the Olympus and the BE.47 engine projects and therefore: 'Under the circumstances we do not feel entitled to tender for the above specification (TE.10/56) Nonetheless, we are extremely interested in it and Jamison is studying the performance of this unit in relation to the possible performance that can be achieved in the P.10.'

This appears to show that, despite having lost out to the Avro 730, (selected to meet OR.330 in May 1955), work on the P.10 integrated ramjet aircraft continued under an MoS contract. In fact the P.10 was revived at a later date and proposed as first a long-range fighter and later as a: '...clandestine reconnaissance aircraft'. The Avro 730 was itself cancelled in 1957.

Shades of the Lockheed YF-12 and SR-71, but the P.10 possessed performance on a par with these types and pre-dated them by more than five years. The integrated ramjet wing was also the basis of English Electric's P.10D

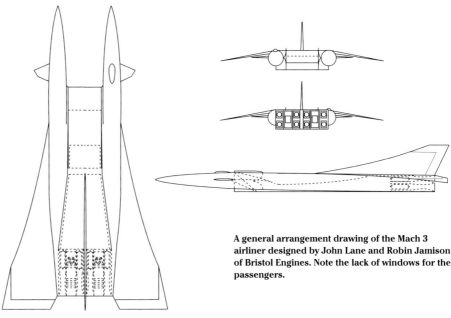

A general arrangement drawing of the Mach 3 airliner designed by John Lane and Robin Jamison of Bristol Engines. Note the lack of windows for the passengers.

stand-off weapon to meet OR.1159, with Bristol giving this later work the title RP.10. Robin Jamison looked at the P.10 aircraft and saw its potential, but considered the integrated wing far too complicated.

Supersonic Airliner

By 1957 the axe had fallen on many of the advanced projects that British companies were involved in. Bristol had lost the Blue Envoy Mach 3 SAM, but its BRJ.800 cruise ramjet was adopted for the OR.1159 stand-off missile (selected for development as the BRJ.824 on the Avro W.114, Blue Steel Mk.2, see Chapter Eight). While work continued on the development of the BRJ.800 series of ramjets, the Ramjet Research Department began looking for more applications for this type of power unit.

Jamison rightly saw that any high-speed aircraft, with a turning radius proportional to airspeed, would only be useful in applications that involved point-to-point flights; that is, reconnaissance or transport. Having seen the dedicated OR.330 reconnaissance aircraft cancelled in 1957, Jamison turned his attention to a transport. The turbojet/ramjet mix provided power throughout all phases of the flight and Jamison intended applying the combination engine to a transport.

In a June 1959 paper entitled 'Power for the long-range supersonic airliner', Robin Jamison outlined his views on how a Mach 3 airliner could be developed. He proposed a twin-fuselage aircraft with a propulsion system, designated RP.18, fitted in a connecting bay. The bay would house two large turbojets, such as the Bristol Olympus or de Havil-

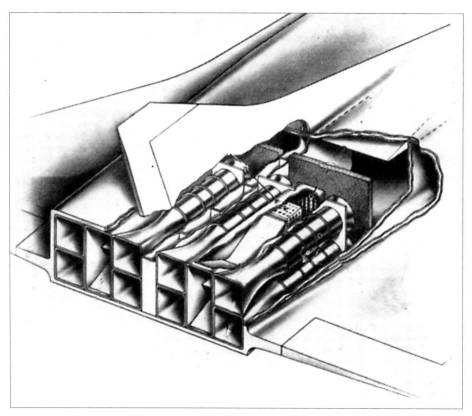

Jamison's final engine design for the Mach 3 airliner. Rolls-Royce Heritage Trust via Roy Hawkins

High Mach from Kingston

Sydney Camm at Hawker and his assistants John Fozard and Ralph Hooper had been looking at high-speed aircraft for some time. Hooper had drawn up a couple of studies for a turborocket-powered Mach 3 research aircraft and interceptor as far back as 1956. Camm and his design team visited the RAE in November 1958 and according to Camm's diaries were advised that the RAE were: 'Concerned about the general running down of the research programme on manned flight and it was suggested that a Mach 3-4 sustained flight research vehicle would receive their support.'

However, Fozard intended to use Jamison and Lane's combination engine concepts to power a research aircraft that could meet ER.181.

ER.181 was intended to form the basis for a staged progression up the Mach scale from 3 to 5 and to prompt the aircraft companies into action. Power for the new studies was to be a combination engine from Bristol Engines, called the RP.20. One of these project studies involved a Hawker research aircraft in the 30,000 lb (13,608kg) all-up-weight class. RP20 was in fact a follow-on to some earlier propulsion studies called RP.11 and 12 that had been intended for a Vickers Barnes Wallis 'Swallow' type design study for a Mach 3+ aircraft. This project had itself replaced Wallis' Mach 5 studies.

The airframe for RP.20 was designated P.1134 in the Hawker design series. Fozard produced four designs over a five-month period from November 1958. Three of these addressed the first stage of the project, Mach 3+, while the fourth addressed the Mach 4+ regime. Few details of this work survive, only a few general arrangement drawings and some notes from the Chief Designer Sydney Camm's diaries, with very little to differentiate variants as the study progressed. This paucity of information may indicate how serious the companies were about the prospect of such developments leading to hardware. There was always someone in the Ministry willing to fund such paper studies but, when it came to major funding for hardware, the cupboard was bare. As stated, P.1134 was the project designation covering all this Mach 3 to Mach 5 work; so, to aid clarification, numbers have been used to identify the variants.

The Mach 3+ Designs

In mid November 1958 Stanley Hooker and Robin Jamison of Bristol Engines visited

land Gyron (Bristol would take over DH's engine interests in November 1961), separated by a bay containing a series of ramjet combustors. The ramjets and turbojets shared a variable geometry two-dimensional intake, but had separate jet-pipes; in other words, a combination engine.

Both fuselages held passenger accommodation, with the flightdeck in the starboard

John Fozard of Hawker. Designer of the P.1134, but would gain fame with the Hawker Siddeley Harrier and Sea Harrier. Brooklands Museum

nose. The port nose carried the large refrigeration plant necessary to keep the passengers, crew and systems at a bearable temperature.

Intended to possess Mach 3 performance, Jamison's airliner was fitted with a delta wing very similar to that of Bristol's Blue Envoy SAM (see Chapter Four), the first serious attempt at a vehicle to cruise at Mach 3+. Parametric studies soon showed that this twin-turbojet/single-ramjet combination engine would not deliver the required performance, so Jamison and Lane sought to increase performance and reduce the engine size.

The new installation was indeed more compact and allowed the installation of a pair of combination engines. Each engine comprised two turbojets stacked one on top of the other on either side of a ramjet duct. A common intake fed the ramjet and both pairs of turbojets, but each had its own jet pipe. Two of these combination engines were installed in a compact engine bay between the twin fuselages.

Like most design studies, no real consideration was given to the problems of Mach 3 flight apart from commenting on the need for thermal-resistant structures and systems. In any case such an airliner was very much a leap in the dark at a time when Mach 2 was pushing the envelope for military aircraft. A research aircraft would make a worthwhile contribution to the field and as ER.181 had been issued in 1957 it was time for some action.

Graph showing the flight regime of the Hawker P.1134. Note the points where the turbojets and ramjets stop and start.

Diagram showing the main elements of the Bristol RP.20 for the Hawker P.1134.

Camm and Fozard at Kingston. A month later a team from Rolls-Royce visited to discuss the choice of turbojet and the decision was taken to use the RB.146, a reheated version of the Avon. In January 1959 the possibility of using the de Havilland Gyron Junior was discussed, but the Avon was considered superior and a known quantity. It may sound strange that the core of this Bristol combination engine was to be a Rolls-Royce turbojet. However, during the 1950s Bristol had carried out licence production of the Avon to increase manufacturing capacity at a time when the Avon was much in demand for the Lightning and Sea Vixen fighters and Canberra bomber.

By March 1959, John Fozard had draughted the initial P.1134 study, with the Avon placed between a pair of ramjet ducts. In true combination engine fashion the different engines shared intakes but had separate jet pipes. This study was submitted to the RAE Aero Department for analysis, while Dr Walter Cawood, Deputy Controller of Aircraft (Research and Development) at the Ministry of Supply, also requested information on P.1134.

P.1134/1 had a very sleek wing with 10° of anhedral mounted on a broad, boxy fuselage containing the propulsion system. The very thin wing, with a leading edge sweep of 70° and trailing edge sweep of 34°, had an arrowhead planform. The entire rear portion of each wing formed an elevon with a hinge line normal to the fuselage centreline. Twin uncanted, all-flying, vertical stabilisers provided lateral stability. Since these fins lacked sufficient area to maintain lateral stability at high speed, additional vertical surface area was required. The P.1134/1 used a pair of ventral fins mounted on the lower rear fuselage that folded upwards through 120° to provide adequate ground clearance for take-off and landing. Construction was to be in stainless steel, despite its attendant fabrication woes, and Fozard entered discussions with the RAE Structures Department to discuss the effects of kinetic heating.

The P.1134/2 design showed much variation on the P.1134/1, mainly in the forward fuselage with the intakes being moved forward to just behind the cockpit. A further modification was the addition of unswept, tapered canards or foreplanes, just behind the intake lips, flush with the bottom of the intake ducts. The ventral fins were deleted

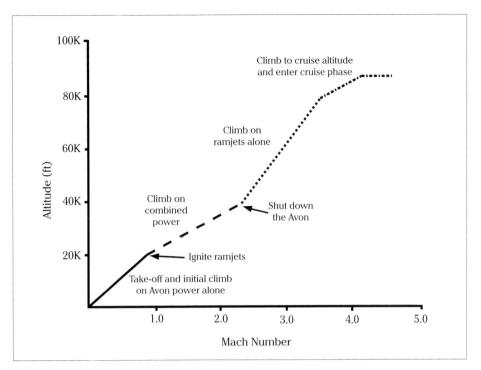

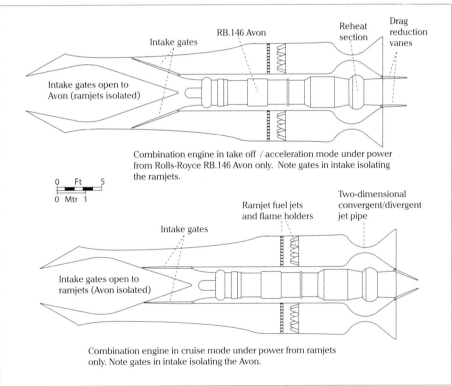

Combination engine in take off / acceleration mode under power from Rolls-Royce RB.146 Avon only. Note gates in intake isolating the ramjets.

Combination engine in cruise mode under power from ramjets only. Note gates in intake isolating the Avon.

Hawker P.1134

Type	Length ft (m)	Span ft (m)	Weight lb (kg)	Powerplant
P.1134/1	60 (18.3)	25 (7.6)	30,000 (13,605)	2 x Ramjet / RB.146
P.1134/2	60 (18.3)	25 (7.6)	30,000 (13,605)	2 x Ramjet / RB.146
P.1134/3	64.5 (19.7)	30 (9.1)	30,000 (13,605)	2 x Ramjet / RB.146
P.1134/4	63.5 (19.6)	25 (7.6)	30,000 (13,605)	2 x Ramjet / RB.146

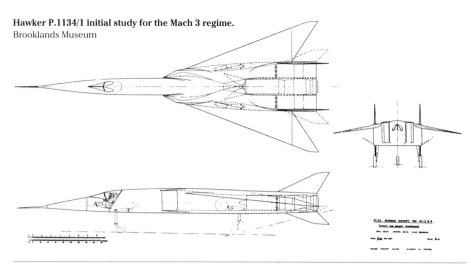

Hawker P.1134/1 initial study for the Mach 3 regime.
Brooklands Museum

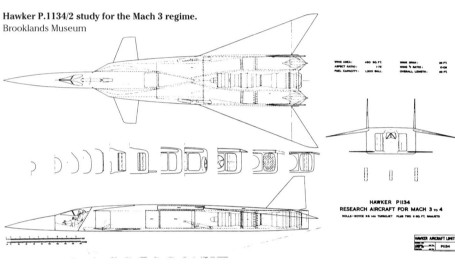

Hawker P.1134/2 study for the Mach 3 regime.
Brooklands Museum

HAWKER P1134
RESEARCH AIRCRAFT FOR MACH 3 TO 4

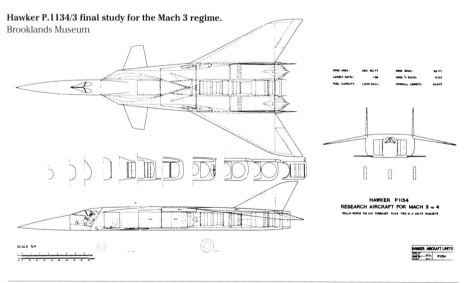

Hawker P.1134/3 final study for the Mach 3 regime.
Brooklands Museum

HAWKER P1134
RESEARCH AIRCRAFT FOR MACH 3 TO 4

and the vertical stabiliser area increased accordingly by making the fins taller and broader. The wings remained unchanged from the original /1 variant but were moved

further aft, with no change in aspect ratio and retaining the large elevons.

John Fozard further modified the /2 variant, in particular the wings and tail fins, to pro-

duce the P.1134/3. The aspect ratio of the wings was decreased, with more curvature added at the tips. The large elevons were replaced by narrow chord elevons, whose hinge line lay parallel to the trailing edge. The tail fins were altered to have small fixed sections and large rudders. The /3 variant would form the basis of Hawker's bid to investigate the Mach 3 to 4 flight regime.

Towards Mach 5

The bid for the Mach 4+ aspect of the specification was to be the P.1134/4, drawn up at the request of the RAE Aero Department in April 1959. This variant used the 'traditional' hypersonic planform, a 75° anhedral delta, mounted on a broad fuselage with a single highly swept fin. The cockpit glazing was changed, with the higher temperatures generated at Mach 4+ necessitating the use of multiple panes rather than the four-section 'V' windscreen of the predecessors.

By June 1959 the project was dead. Prior to April 1959 Camm had received a letter from Cawood at the MoS stating that Hawker was duplicating the Bristol 188 Mach 2 research aircraft. Camm states in his diaries: 'This, of course, was quite incorrect and Dr Cawood was politely told so.' Cawood replied thanking Camm for the reports on P.1134 and continued: '…but at the same time advising us to discontinue with the project. Although they are enthusiastic about the need for such a research vehicle, we could not hope for any official financial support.'

There would be no more funds for the P.1134 project and Fozard went on to work on the Harrier. Ralph Hooper on the other hand continued with Mach 3 studies and penned the P.1138 series in late 1959. This included a VTO naval interceptor with eight Rolls-Royce RB.153 turbojets. Another study for P.1138 was a very sleek 75° delta with four dorsal RB.153s. Described as a Mach 3 Military Aircraft it appeared to carry an AI radar in the AI.23 mould.

The Pros and Cons of the Combination Powerplant

The combination powerplant posed a number of problems to Fozard, the sheer size of the propulsion system being one. Another would have been isolating the turbojet during the cruise phase. In the cruise, the intake gates would close off the inlet to the turbojet, leaving the ramjets to use the maximum airflow. In the low-speed flight regime, the gates would have opened, allowing airflow to the Avon turbojet that would provide the power.

A further consideration, shown by the breadth of the P.1134 fuselage, is the need to

Rear view of the Hawker P.1134/3 showing the jet pipes and the planform. Model by John Hall

Looking very sleek and suited to its intended Mach 4+, the P.1134/4 was a departure from its predecessors. Model by John Hall

The P.1134/4 used the same RP.20 combination engine as the other studies, as can be seen from this rear view. Model by John Hall

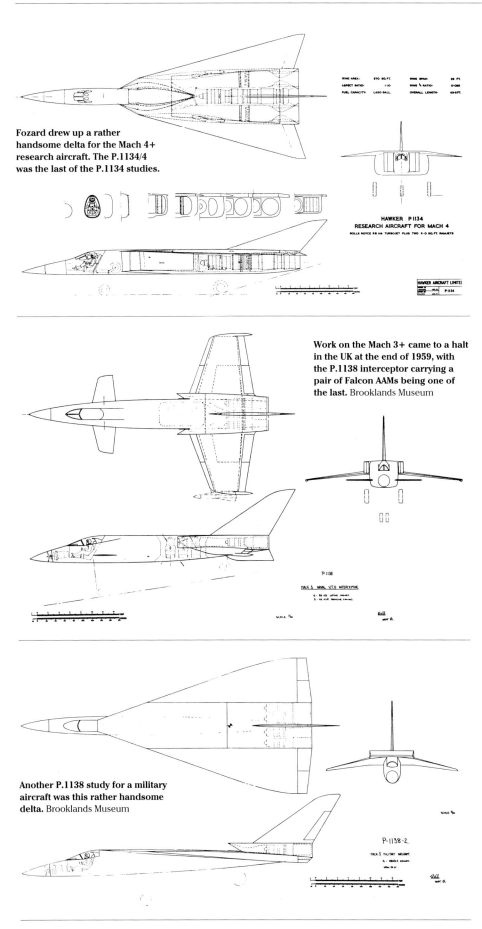

Fozard drew up a rather handsome delta for the Mach 4+ research aircraft. The P.1134/4 was the last of the P.1134 studies.

HAWKER P 1134
RESEARCH AIRCRAFT FOR MACH 4
ROLLS ROYCE RB 146 TURBOJET PLUS TWO 9·0 SQ.FT. RAMJETS

Work on the Mach 3+ came to a halt in the UK at the end of 1959, with the P.1138 interceptor carrying a pair of Falcon AAMs being one of the last. Brooklands Museum

Another P.1138 study for a military aircraft was this rather handsome delta. Brooklands Museum

have airflow around the engines to cool the engine bay, further increasing the size of an already large engine installation. As had been found with the NGTE test rig for the split wing ramjet, fitting a cylindrical ramjet in a box-shaped duct reduced the problems of cooling the outside of the ramjet. Circular cross-section ramjets were also easier to cool internally than a rectangular type.

The main drawback to the combination powerplant was its size and weight. From take-off until about Mach 0.9 the ramjets played no part in the flight. At speeds greater than Mach 2 the turbojet was throttled back in stages until it was shut down just above Mach 2.2. Therefore the ramjets represented a considerable weight penalty for much of the flight. The sheer size of the installation with its large jetpipes would have contributed significant base drag, but this could have been reduced by shaping the rear fuselage and by fitting moveable plates on the rear fuselage. One drawing of the P.1134/3 shows such plates on either side of the Avon's jetpipe.

The RP.20 and the P.1134 fell by the wayside, possibly in the turbulent times that preceded the amalgamation of the aircraft and aero-engine companies in the first years of the 1960s. The project provided the fundamental information on how the combination engine could be implemented, but RP.20 used fairly old ramjet technology with basic colander flame holders and large combustors. The years from 1958 had seen ramjet technology improve significantly. A new series of ramjets with BS prefixes began to appear and these heralded a new era in ramjet development.

The P.1134 might have been dead and buried by June 1959, but in March 1960 Camm visited Dr Cawood at the MoS and was informed that: 'Official interest was rising in the high-speed research vehicle in view of the changes in defence policy etc. Mach 5 is now being talked about.'

A week later Camm visited the Royal Aircraft Establishment to meet Sir George Gardner, Director RAE, and L F Nicholson, Director General Scientific Research (Air) at the Ministry of Aviation. Camm noted that: 'The Mach 5 research vehicle was mentioned and it seemed that our efforts were recognised as having triggered off an interest in such aircraft.'

Thus the door was opened for a new series of design studies for aircraft and engines, with the engine designers full of new ideas and keen to put the new computers and test facilities to work. This was especially true at Bristol Siddeley Engines, who now had this new generation of power units to work on.

Standing Start to Mach 5 – The Combination Engine

Chapter Thirteen

High-Speed Powerplants – A New Generation

By 1959 ramjet research and development at Bristol Siddeley Engines Ltd (BSEL) was in full swing with the High Altitude Test Plant (HATP) in operation. Work on the 18in (45.7cm) BRJ.800 series of Mach 3 ramjets for Blue Steel Mk.2 had taken over where the Blue Envoy powerplant had left off and this engine brought a radical change in combustor and fuel systems compared with its 16in (40.6cm) predecessors.

Using the BRJ.800 combustor and ancillaries, the ramjet research department began to look at a ramjet specifically for aircraft propulsion. Up until this point the focus for aircraft ramjets had concentrated on fitting the engine within the aircraft in a non-optimum installation; as with the RP.20/P.1134.

The options were to develop a ramjet capable of pod mounting (which would ease cool-

ing, maintenance and allow easier engine change) or carrying out a complete re-examination of ramjet propulsion for aircraft and integrating the ramjet and airframe to optimise the performance of both.

With the merger of Bristol Aero Engines and Armstrong Siddeley Motors in 1958 to form BSEL, the ramjet projects were relabelled in a BS series (for Bristol Siddeley) followed by a sequential number starting at 1001, although the studies ran more or less concurrently. These included design studies aimed at hypersonic aircraft powerplants.

Work undertaken by Roy Hawkins on the combustors for BS.1001 and BS.1002, and particularly the BS.1003 for the SIGS surface-to-air missile (Small ship Integrated Guided weapon System, see Chapter Four), contributed significantly to improved ramjet per-

An RAF Transport Command Hawker Siddeley 1019A5 Mach 5 transport aircraft receives its final checks before taking off for a trooping flight from RAF Brize Norton to RAF Changi in Singapore.
Adrian Mann

formance. Hawkins' analysis of the flow regimes within the flame holders and combustors of ramjets provided a better understanding of how the ramjets operated, improving their efficiency and consequently their range and thrust levels.

The first of the BS series was called BS.1001, a 13in (33cm)-diameter controllable thrust ramjet for the NIGS surface-to-air missile (New Naval Guided Weapons System, see Chapter Four). NIGS was then superseded by SIGS, a Bristol Guided Weapons design based on the RP.25 that used a BS.1003 integrated ramjet. BS.1003 ultimately

British Secret Projects: Hypersonics, Ramjets & Missiles   155

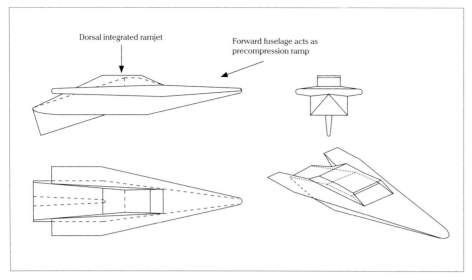

Dorsal integrated ramjet

Forward fuselage acts as
precompression ramp

The initial application for the BS.1010 ramjet was a
Mach 7 cruise missile. This early study shows the
engine in a dorsal position, which was not ideal.

A much simplified diagram showing the effect on
thrust of increasing speed and temperature due to
real gas effects.

became the Odin ramjet in the Sea Dart SAM.

The BS.1002 was intended to be an integrated ramjet for long-range high-speed missiles and manned aircraft flying at Mach 4.5 at 90,000ft (27,432m). BS.1002 had a nominal cross section of 500in² (3,226cm²) and used a fixed geometry arrangement. It soon fell by the wayside, to be replaced by the later BS.1010 studies.

The next two projects were based on the older Bristol 18in (45.7cm) BRJ.824. First came the 20in (50.2cm) BS.1004, that was aimed at a SAM, designated RP.21. Then the 21½in (53.4cm) diameter BS.1005 was intended for the Bristol X-12 stand-off weapon to arm the Avro Vulcan (see Chapter Eight).

The BS.1005 is of interest because it represents the earliest attempt to develop a fully variable geometry ramjet for aircraft that was reusable, rather than a one-shot missile engine. As has been noted above, ramjets are optimised to operate in a particular Mach number range, outside of which the efficiency falls, thereby affecting thrust and range. A second factor was that optimising the ramjet to the flight regime would allow the vehicle to cruise. To address this, the intake and jet pipe configuration needed to be changed. Early ramjet test vehicles such as the post-war 7.2in (18.3cm) ramjet carried fusible nozzles. These eroded away as the speed and thrust levels rose to provide the correct shape for higher speeds, but this was

not practical for re-useable ramjets. The BS.1005 led to a pair of research engines, the R.1 and R.2, designed to investigate the possibilities for aircraft propulsion.

R.1 was a fixed geometry ramjet intended for acceleration applications and to provide data on the fuel system, combustor and flame holder for the next step, the R.2. The R.1 combustor and intake were also used in the BS.1001.

The R.2 was to utilise a fully variable intake and jetpipe, provided by a translating spike and plug nozzle respectively. The mechanisms for these were housed in the engine centrebody that carried the diffuser and flame holder. In the event, only the plug nozzle was variable and the work on R.2 was carried over to the BS.1006, a design study for a podded variable geometry ramjet suitable for aircraft use.

The next pair of Bristol Siddeley project studies were the BS.1007, an engine for a Mach 2.2 air-launched decoy in the Blue Rapier mould, and BS.1008, a Mach 1.2 low-altitude drone. Neither of these progressed beyond the study phase.

BS.1009 saw a return to the Ramjet Department's roots, the Thor used in the Bloodhound SAM. Thor was upgraded with modifications to the intake, diffuser and nozzle to improve the performance of the Bloodhound III, thereby increasing its range to over 75 miles (120km). When the nuclear-armed, command guidance Mk.III was cancelled, the BS.1009 was fitted to Bloodhound II, further extending that weapon's capability.

Hypersonic Ramjets
Robin Jamison still had an interest in high-speed aircraft propulsion and embarked on a design study for a Mach 7 cruise vehicle, which he called a long-range cruise missile. This description may have been a ruse to raise funds for the project, which acquired the designation BS.1010 when work began in 1961.

Mach 7 was chosen as the upper limit for the engine as it had been shown that this speed was the limit for subsonic combustion with conventional fuels such as kerosene. Beyond Mach 7 the propulsion system would require supersonic combustion and the supersonic combustion ramjet was far too complex and exotic to contemplate develop-

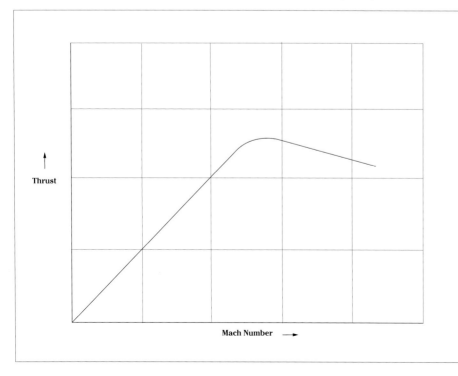

Thrust

Mach Number ⟶

British Secret Projects: Hypersonics, Ramjets & Missiles

An artist's impression of the definitive BS.1010 vehicle from a Bristol Siddeley publicity brochure.
Rolls-Royce Heritage Trust via Roy Hawkins

ment in the early 1960s. BS.1010 was to be integrated into the airframe of a vehicle using the undersurface to provide precompression for the intake. Rocket-boosted to Mach 4, a BS.1010-powered missile would then accelerate to Mach 7 and 90,000ft (27,432m). This Mach range meant that the engine would be required to operate under a wide variety of conditions and so a variable geometry engine configuration was selected.

The BS.1010 engine comprised a fixed section carrying the fuel jets and cooling system that was built into the lower structure of the vehicle. This would form the fixed surface of a ramjet duct whose variable geometry capability would be provided by a moving cowl that rotated around a hinge point on the forward fuselage. In its fully extended position the cowl would be optimised to operate at Mach 4, the start of the acceleration phase. As the vehicle gained speed, the cowl moved upwards to gradually match the intake and exhaust areas to the Mach number until the target speed of Mach 7 had been attained.

Mach 7 presented a considerable challenge to the combustion system designers in the Ramjet Development Department. Despite the Mach 4 to 7 performance envelope, the BS.1010 was still operating under subsonic combustion. This meant that prior to entering the combustion chamber the air entering the intake had to be slowed to subsonic speed in the diffuser. As described earlier, slowing air not only increases its pressure but also, in accordance with the laws of physics, increases its temperature.

However, the laws of chemistry also conspired to challenge the ramjet designer. Mach 5 is the delineation point that separates supersonic from hypersonic. It's a nice round number and while it might sound like an arbitrary selection in the Mach range, it isn't. From around Mach 4.5 a phenomenon called gas dissociation begins to occur, whereby the kinetic heat starts to break chemical bonds in the air. The energy from burning fuel in the engine is also consumed by breaking and making chemical bonds in the combustion process rather than producing thrust. This affects the levels of available thrust, causing thrust levels to decrease as the Mach number, and hence the combustion temperature, rises. This is particularly true for hydrocarbon fuels but hydrogen is not affected, one reason that made it the high-speed fuel of choice.

Temperatures in the region of 2,175°K (1,900°C) could be encountered in the intake

and diffuser, with even higher temperatures around 2,500°K (2,227°C) on the combustion chamber and exhaust duct walls. Consequently some means of preventing damage to the structure was required. Two methods were employed in the BS.1010: the first used refractory materials such as ceramics, Nimonic or tantalum while the second incorporated ceramics with an active cooling system. The latter was used in the areas where thermal effects were greatest, such as the lining of the combustion chamber and the exhaust.

An integrated installation was the way forward, using the forward fuselage as a precompression ramp, while the rear fuselage provided a large area for exhaust expansion. Having worked out these aspects, a planform best suited for Mach 7 was the next objective.

American Influence

By 1960 Bristol Siddeley's ramjet development department had a good idea of the performance of the BS.1010 engine and began studying a possible vehicle for the engine. Jamison despatched Roy Hawkins to the USA where much of the work on high-speed aerodynamics had been performed in the 1950s.

Hawkins was an aerodynamicist who had come to Bristol Engines from the RAE Aero Dept where, amongst others, he had worked with German aerodynamics specialist Dietrich Kuchemann on the Blue Envoy SAM. Hawkins looked around for a suitable configuration and came up with a shape similar to that of the Boeing X-20 Dynasoar (DYNamic SOARing), an American re-useable spacecraft that the US Air Force had been developing to allow routine access to space. The North American X-15 research aircraft was doing the groundwork for the Dynasoar with a view to gaining experience of the high-alti-

tude/high-speed regime. However, both projects suffered cancellation and curtailment after the US government changed its policy from that of gradual engineering development to an out-and-out space race with the Soviet Union.

The initial BS.1010 missile study bore a distinct resemblance to a Dynasoar without fins, because Hawkins considered it to be the best configuration. Bristol had a very amicable relationship with the US aerospace companies, especially Boeing with whom BSEL had shared a partnership in the early ramjet development for SAMs. Boeing's designers shared Hawkins' view and were no doubt happy to see their work on Dynasoar continued, even in the UK. Hawkins returned to Britain with his findings and development work on the vehicle's shape continued. Hawkins claimed that in developing the BS.1010 he was merely following a directive from Robin Jamison, as Jamison had become rather blinkered in his views on hypersonic flight. Hawkins was adamant that while Jamison saw the BS.1010 as a configuration for a future cruise vehicle, Hawkins approached it as a paper study to indulge his boss! He saw no future in it.

An early design study showed the propulsion system mounted in a dorsal position with a very narrow delta wing. Further work saw this configuration modified and, like Dynasoar, the BS.1010 vehicle sprouted fins at the tips of the highly swept wings. While Dynasoar was intended to fly into space and re-enter the atmosphere, the BS.1010 was to cruise for long periods in the upper atmosphere. The nose and leading edges became less bluff and, since the BS.1010 was unmanned, the shape became much sleeker.

The next major change was the location of the ramjet. One of the reasons hypersonic aircraft are only good for 'straight and level'

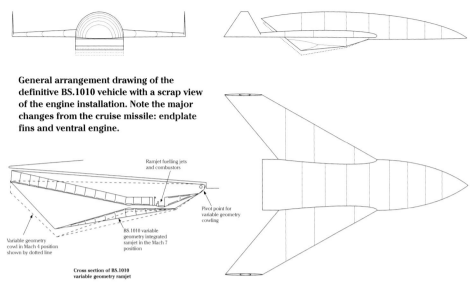

General arrangement drawing of the definitive BS.1010 vehicle with a scrap view of the engine installation. Note the major changes from the cruise missile: endplate fins and ventral engine.

Ramjet fuelling jets and combustors

Pivot point for variable geometry cowling

BS.1010 variable geometry integrated ramjet in the Mach 7 position

Variable geometry cowl in Mach 4 position shown by dotted line

Cross section of BS.1010 variable geometry ramjet

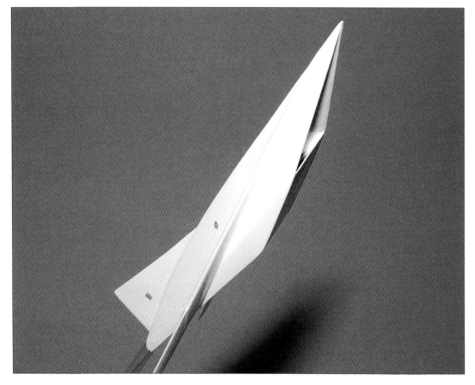

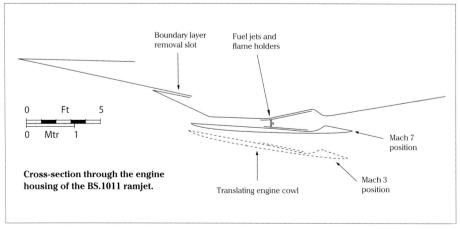

Boundary layer removal slot

Fuel jets and flame holders

0   Ft   5

0   Mtr   1

Mach 7 position

Cross-section through the engine housing of the BS.1011 ramjet.

Translating engine cowl

Mach 3 position

applications is that the turn radius of an aircraft is proportional to the square of the speed. This leads to a hypersonic aircraft being restricted to 'point-to-point' sorties of global range. A further complication is that their propulsion systems react badly to off-axis flow into the intakes. Moving the ramjet to a ventral location allowed the flow into the intake to be undisturbed by changes in angle of attack during manoeuvres. This change also allowed the application of deflected thrust to reduce drag. The outcome was a particularly handsome aircraft that certainly looked the part, but it remained a design study.

The Very Rapid Reaction Force
In 1960, two roles were envisaged for a manned hypersonic aircraft: reconnaissance and transport, both point-to-point applications. English Electric approached BSEL for a powerplant for a reconnaissance aircraft capable of speeds in excess of Mach 4. The BS.1011 was suggested, being essentially a BS.1010 with five reheated turbojets installed in a bay above the ramjet. This logical evolution can be seen on a drawing of the BS.1010 with the turbojets scribbled in. Never considered seriously for further development, BSEL produced a design study based around the BS.1011, which they called 'The Mach 7 Transport'.

This was intended to carry up to seventy troops at Mach 7 to reinforce the forces still based 'East of Suez'. The idea was that materiel was pre-positioned at what were called 'Mounting Bases', such as Butterworth in Malaya, but the man-power was kept in Europe. In the event of a perceived threat, troops would be flown in at very high speed from the UK in these Mach 7 transports and then carried to forward airfields in the proposed new generation of airlifter, the Hawker Siddeley HS.681.

The Mach 7 transport had a rather fishlike appearance with a large intake to the engine bay under the forward fuselage. The variable geometry wings helped low-speed flight under turbojet power, being swept back for high-speed cruise. Two rocket packs were fitted on the rear fuselage to boost the aircraft through the transonic zone, in a method similar to the RB.123s on the English Electric P.10. These rockets were to be jettisoned after use. The crew and passengers were accommodated in a dorsal compartment where they

It may sound unlikely, but the vehicle in the photo above is a Bristol Siddeley Engines Ltd passenger aircraft capable of carrying 70 people at a speed of Mach 7. Model by John Hall

were considered to be subject to a more benign heating regime.

What the BS.1010 vehicle and the Mach 7 Transport demonstrate is the coming together of engine and airframe. The airframe is an integral part of the engine and vice versa. However, looking at the Mach 7 Transport, when it came to designing aircraft the aircraft builders probably had the aesthetic edge over the engine team!

Towards a Practical Powerplant

While no specific requirements were issued for hypersonic types, the aircraft companies still had their project study groups looking at the various possibilities. As will be related in the next chapters, the project offices of English Electric (to become BAC Warton) and Hawker Siddeley Aviation (HSA) at Kingston were looking at hypersonic aircraft. These design studies needed accurate figures for engines, their installation weight and performance, so they approached the engine companies, who in turn needed similar data for airframes.

What the aircraft companies wanted was an engine that could propel an aircraft from a standing start to Mach 5 without using disposable rockets as required by ER.181. Such an aircraft had by necessity to be large and required a powerplant to match. Further impetus came from classified symposiums, one on very high-speed flight held in July 1963 that covered aircraft studies, but also an earlier symposion on high-speed air-breathing engines from December 1962. These symposia alerted the engine and airframe companies to the fact that the RAE was once more blowing hot on hypersonic flight. Therefore at the end of 1962 BSEL commenced the BS.1012 engine project study to power a large Mach 5 cruise vehicle.

Such studies were funded by the MoD and MoA, who wished to maintain an interest in these developments. The MoD (while not issuing an official specification or requirement) called for a range of 4,000nm (7,408km), cruise at 80,000ft (24,384m) at Mach 5 in an aircraft with an all-up weight (AUW) of 400,000lb (181,437kg). The engine specification was for a dry thrust of 14,000lb (622.7kN) at take off and 50,000lb (222.4kN) in the cruise. Kerosene was the preferred fuel, with the turbomachinery based on the Olympus 593 turbojet for Concorde or the BS.100 turbofan for the Hawker P.1154 supersonic V/STOL fighter.

As an initial proposal BSEL drew up the BS.1012/1, a combination engine with up to eight engine units installed under the aircraft wing. The basic unit comprised a reheated

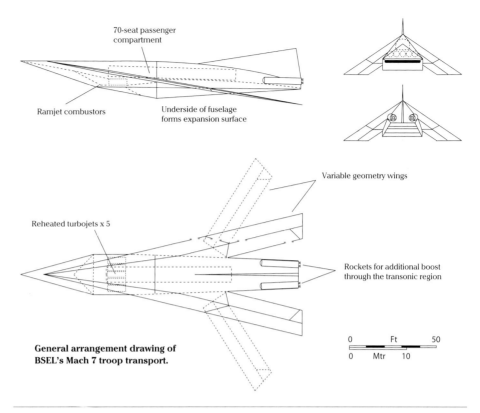

General arrangement drawing of BSEL's Mach 7 troop transport.

70-seat passenger compartment

Ramjet combustors

Underside of fuselage forms expansion surface

Variable geometry wings

Reheated turbojets x 5

Rockets for additional boost through the transonic region

Olympus or BS.100, a combination ramjet for acceleration and a high-speed ramjet for the cruise. The turbojet was isolated from the mass flow by a series of shutters forward of the compressor, while the variable geometry intake ramp could be fully extended to seal off the combination ramjet in the cruise. Intakes for high-speed aircraft pose particular problems at Mach numbers greater than 2. Intake shock management by variable geometry intakes became a major factor in the aircraft flying at all.

What John Lane and Robin Jamison became particularly concerned with was taking engine integration to its full extent by using the undersurface of the aircraft and shaping it to produce compression ahead of the intake. This would allow a much shortened, and therefore lighter, intake system for the aircraft.

As can be seen from the drawings, the BS.1012/1 was large, with a lot of complex machinery in the intake. In hypersonic aircraft, given the materials involved, 'big and complex' invariably means heavy: in this case 60,000lb (27,211kg). The size of the installation also produced a lot of drag in the underwing installation.

Concerns about the size of the /1 prompted a radical change in the BS.1012/2. This used a duct-burning turbofan, with the BS.100's fan feeding a ramjet duct surrounding the turbomachinery, rather than separate combination

and high-speed ramjets. The two-dimensional intake was fully variable, with the turbomachinery isolated by inlet guide vanes that acted like shutters. The problem with the intake/diffuser weight was to be addressed by fitting a cascade intake, which would shorten the length by directing the airflow through a series of vanes. Weighing in at 50,000lb (22,675kg), the BS.1012/2 had a better power/weight ratio than the BS.1012/1 but, with six units installed, still had a large powerplant.

Rather than make the jump to a 40,000lb (18,144kg) aircraft using six or eight engine units, BAC and HSA proposed small research aircraft. HSA's APD.1019E2 was to use a single BS.1012/3, a compact combination engine based on the BS.1012/2. Olympus turbomachinery formed the core, with an annular bypass combustion chamber rather than a combination ramjet. The annular chamber was fed at low speed by a 48in (1.22m) zero-stage fan ahead of the compressor. High-speed power was provided by a trio of ramjets on either side of the core engine. The turbomachinery and annular duct were totally isolated by hemispherical clamshells in the intake, leaving the mass flow to enter the high-speed ramjets. The /4 studies involved applying future turbomachinery projections to the /3.

Using the experiences of the previous studies, BSEL developed the BS.1012/5, /6 and /7

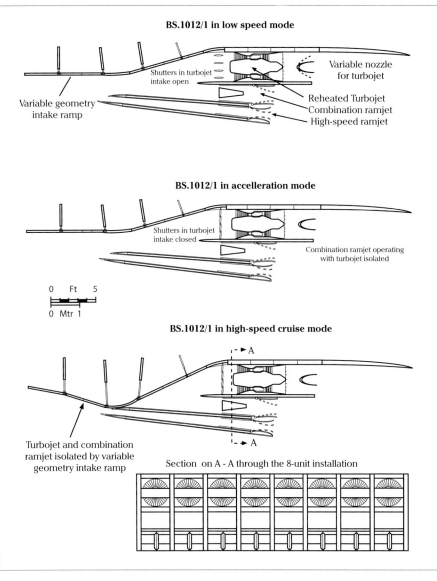

BS.1012/1 in low speed mode

Variable geometry
intake ramp

Shutters in turbojet
intake open

Variable nozzle
for turbojet

Reheated Turbojet
Combination ramjet
High-speed ramjet

BS.1012/1 in accelleration mode

Shutters in turbojet
intake closed

Combination ramjet operating
with turbojet isolated

0   Ft   5

0 Mtr 1

BS.1012/1 in high-speed cruise mode

Turbojet and combination
ramjet isolated by variable
geometry intake ramp

Section on A - A through the 8-unit installation

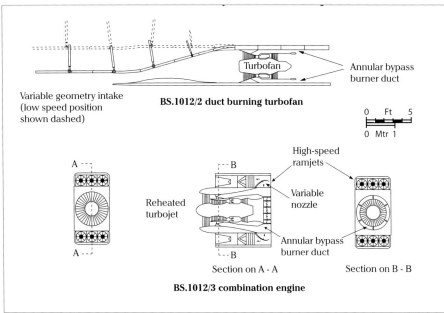

Variable geometry intake
(low speed position
shown dashed)

Turbofan

Annular bypass
burner duct

BS.1012/2 duct burning turbofan

0   Ft   5

0 Mtr 1

High-speed
ramjets

Reheated
turbojet

Variable
nozzle

Annular bypass
burner duct

Section on A - A

Section on B - B

BS.1012/3 combination engine

To power a more conventional airliner (that is, one designed by an airframe builder rather than by an engine builder) required a new approach. The BS.1012/1 integrated turbomachinery with ramjets. However it was a very large engine.

The BS.1012/2 integrated the engine with the airframe to reduce size, but the compact BS.1012/3 would make an ideal powerplant for a research aircraft.

concepts. These were based on the /2, but with isolation of the turbomachinery and the addition of a high-speed ramjet based on the BS.1010 configuration. They had the potential to achieve Mach 7.

The BS.1012/7 was re-fanned with a 56in (1.42m) zero stage fan and possessed a simpler installation. As such it would allow an aircraft to take off, accelerate, cruise at Mach 7, decelerate, land and taxi with one air-breathing propulsion system, but it also had another trick up its sleeve – thrust deflection.

Weight and Drag Reduction by Jet Deflection

Recent developments in fighter propulsion have included thrust deflection to enhance manoeuvrability. Prior to that becoming all the rage, deflected or rather vectored thrust was generally perceived as a method of achieving vertical and short take-off for short-range close support aircraft such as the Harrier. Back in the early 1960s when Hawker and BSEL were developing the Harrier's P.1127 predecessor and its Pegasus engine, these companies were also looking at deflected thrust for another role. Jet deflection could not only improve take-off and landing performance, but it could also act as an aid to drag reduction in hypersonic vehicles. Such vehicles were proving difficult to develop as the studies showed their structures and powerplant would be so heavy that their performance might be, at best, borderline. Deflected thrust might provide just enough improvement in performance for the vehicle to be viable.

Westland's Jet Deflection Meteor

Such work dated back to the early 1950s. In 1953 the Westland Aircraft company proposed, designed and built a research aircraft to investigate the reduction in take-off and landing distances of jet aircraft, with particular relevance to naval aircraft. Under a NGTE contract, Westland took a Gloster Meteor Mk.4 fighter and re-engined it with more powerful Rolls-Royce Nene turbojets. These engines were modified by fitting a Westland-developed jet deflection system in the jet pipe. This system deflected the turbojet exhaust downward at an angle of 60° from the engine axis by the use of a flapper valve and guide vane/cascade mechanism in the jet-pipe. This required considerable modification to the aircraft: this included the fitting of Meteor PR Mk.10 outer wing panels, a Mk.8 tail unit, nose undercarriage from an NF.11 and main gear from an F.4. This mongrel resulted in a Meteor with the longest wingspan of any variant.

The most obvious external change was to the engine nacelles, which were extended much farther forward than on other variants. This was due to the requirement to keep the line of the deflected thrust as close to the aircraft centre of gravity as possible. As a consequence of these extended nacelles, small endplate fins were added to the tail to maintain lateral stability.

As a testbed the aircraft worked very well and proved capable of flying at speeds as low as 65kts (120km/h). The first application for jet deflection on a UK aircraft was the Saunders Roe P.177. The P.177 was a mixed-powerplant interceptor (using a DH Spectre rocket engine and a DH Gyron Junior turbojet) and was intended to provide air defence for the RAF and Royal Navy. The Naval version, as ever with a more demanding flight envelope, required some means of reducing the approach speed for landing. The solution was deflected thrust. Thrust deflection cascades were installed between the turbomachinery and the reheat section, exhausting a portion of the thrust through a ventral port between the undercarriage bays. The Saunders Roe P.177 was cancelled in the 1957 White Paper, the aim being to cut defence costs, but also because the P.177 was superseded by the advances made in SAMs in the preceding five years. The P.177 was advertised as a manned missile, so the cost could now be cut by deleting the man.

Capitalising on its work for the Meteor, Westland's bid for a new carrier strike aircraft, the 1954 M.148 and NR/A.39 requirement, used jet deflection for take-off and landing. A rather handsome twin-finned tailless type, the Westland M.148 type used two DH Gyron Juniors with jet deflection. However its lacklustre performance saw it being rejected early on in the competition. No such problem for the Short Bros bid for M.148, the PD.13. This was a very advanced aircraft that, on paper, far exceeded the performance requirement,

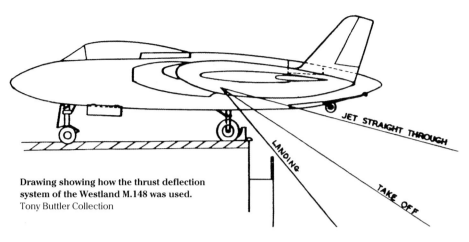

Drawing showing how the thrust deflection system of the Westland M.148 was used. Tony Buttler Collection

Model of the Westland M.148 showing the jet pipes deflected downwards. Tony Buttler Collection

Model of the Westland M.148 showing the jet pipes in straight-through position. Tony Buttler Collection

High-Speed Powerplants – A New Generation 161

but it came third in the tender contest behind what ultimately became the Blackburn Buccaneer. The advanced nature of the PD.13 brought the potential for delay with it.

While the Nene Meteor proved the concept to be sound, as far as the application to naval aircraft was concerned, jet deflection was overtaken by the angled deck, steam catapults and improved arrester gear. High-performance jets could operate from carriers without jet deflection so the deflected Nene Meteor was forgotten about. However, this was not the end for jet deflection.

Research work done at the RAE and at the aircraft companies had shown that an appreciable gain in range could be attained for a high-speed aircraft by using jet deflection. The effect is most pronounced at high values of Gross thrust/Net thrust (Fg/Fn) and low Lift/Drag (L/D) ratios. On paper this also provided advantages at Mach 5 to 7 where deflecting the thrust provided lift. Jet deflection allowed a reduction in wing incidence,

which in turn led to a reduction in induced drag therefore producing longer range. As a method of reducing drag, this turned out to be better than reducing the wing area.

Wing incidence can be varied to increase or decrease lift. Increasing the incidence will increase lift, at the cost of a consequent increase in drag. By reducing the incidence and generating the difference in lift by deflecting the jet thrust, the same amount of lift can be generated at a lower angle of incidence. This in turn would allow an aircraft to fly with its wings at a shallower angle of attack, which in turn reduced drag and ultimately allowed a smaller wing. This meant that the aircraft had less drag and therefore more range. A further spin-off was that the smaller wing was lighter and conferred a considerable weight saving. It was also hoped that jet deflection could be used to reduce the landing speed when deflected at 64°. All-in-all deflecting the thrust looked like a winner to the aircraft designers.

Larger values of Fg/Fn obtained with the BS.1012 proposed by BSEL seemed to offer the promise of range improvement at Mach 2.5 and beyond. For the BS.1012 to be capable of powering an aircraft to Mach 7, it would produce a lot of thrust, especially when taking off with duct burning. This would be more than enough for a conventional take-off, so BSEL engineers proposed using this excess thrust to improve take-off (and landing) performance, provide additional lift in the cruise and consequently reduce drag. For take-off, the efflux was to be deflected through a cascade in the exhaust duct at an angle of 50°. Studies showed that optimum take-off performance was reached if the thrust was deflected two seconds before unstick.

As noted above, the effect of thrust deflection is most pronounced at high values of Fg/Fn ratio and low Lift/Drag ratios. In short, jet deflection would allow a hypersonic aircraft to be smaller, lighter and/or possess increased range. Another benefit of thrust deflection is that it could provide a greater nozzle area for exhaust expansion at high speed, while reducing the base drag at lower speeds, again helping to reduce the overall drag.

In practice the deflection of the high-temperature efflux from a turbojet in reheat or a ramjet at full chat would present a considerable challenge to the engineers. The materials for the deflection vanes/ducts, high-temperature alloys such as Nimonic and exotic metals like tantalum, were difficult to fabricate and would need much pilot engineering, while the actuation mechanisms would require further development. Ceramic coatings or tiles in the rear fuselage and jet pipe areas seemed to provide the optimum solution to the high temperatures, especially if the rear fuselage was to be used as an expansion zone. Actuators would also be critical for the operation of the intake ramps and the shields for the turbojet.

Deflected thrust provided a possible solution to the vicious spiral of weight and power. By reducing drag in a variety of ways deflected thrust allowed a smaller wing. In turn the airframe could be lighter, which was very important in a field where the materials used in the airframe's fabrication are much heavier than in conventional aircraft. Very important in a field where every pound shaved off the weight could mean the difference between success and failure.

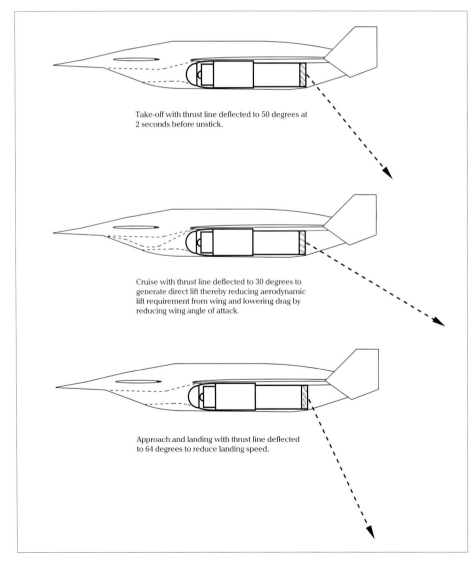

Take-off with thrust line deflected to 50 degrees at 2 seconds before unstick.

Cruise with thrust line deflected to 30 degrees to generate direct lift thereby reducing aerodynamic lift requirement from wing and lowering drag by reducing wing angle of attack.

Approach and landing with thrust line deflected to 64 degrees to reduce landing speed.

Diagram showing the deflection system on the APD.1019E2 and E5 research aircraft. This system allowed the E2 and E5 to have smaller wings thereby reducing drag and airframe weight.

Chapter Fourteen

Derby's Alternatives to the Combination Engine

The reader might have gained the impression that BSEL and their ramjets were the only game in town for hypersonic propulsion systems. As ever there was more than one way to skin a cat when it came to aircraft powerplants.

Rolls-Royce in Derby didn't show much interest in the ramjet, their preference being turbomachinery, concentrating on the development of the turbofan and rocket engines. While BSEL's Advanced Propulsion Research Group had worked on combination engines, Rolls-Royce at Derby followed a different tack.

Like BSEL, Rolls-Royce did see the ramjet's potential as a high-speed propulsion system for the future, but the lack of static thrust prompted R-R's designers to look at some means of operating a ramjet from standstill. Rolls-Royce had considerable experience in liquid-fuelled rockets, particularly Liquid Oxygen (LOX) and kerosene, for the RZ2 motors in the Blue Streak ballistic missile programme. Drawing the experience of turbomachinery and rocket engines together they produced what is called a turborocket.

One of the earliest mentions of the turborocket as a propulsion system for a British design study dates from 1953 with a Hawker Mach 3 research aircraft drawn by Ralph Hooper. This sleek design was powered by a

pair of Armstrong Siddeley Motors (ASM) 30in (76.2cm) turborockets fitted at the tips of rectangular wings in a configuration not dissimilar to the French Nord Aviation Trident rocket-powered interceptor flown in 1953. As such powerplants do not appear out of the blue, a brief introduction to the turborocket and its flashjet sibling will help.

A variety of names have been applied to the turborocket including Air Turbo Rocket, Rocket Compressor Engine and Ducted Fan Rocket. The NGTE preferred Turborocket, so

A Hawker Mach 3 research aircraft powered by a pair of Armstrong Siddeley turborocket engines begins a turn to return to base after a successful flight. Adrian Mann

that is the name used throughout this work.

To overcome the lack of static thrust in ramjets, an alternative to the weight and complexity of mounting a turbojet and a ramjet in the same installation was sought. The solution was a compressor stage added ahead of the main ramjet combustion chamber. A turbine

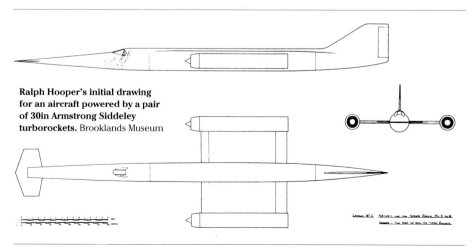

Ralph Hooper's initial drawing for an aircraft powered by a pair of 30in Armstrong Siddeley turborockets. Brooklands Museum

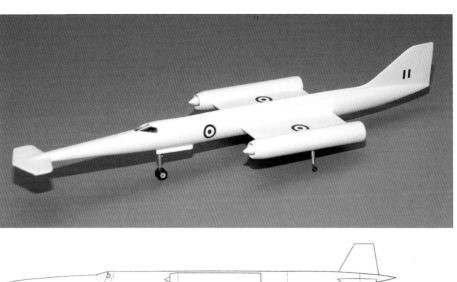

John Hall's model shows the layout of the first Hawker turborocket aircraft. Model by John Hall

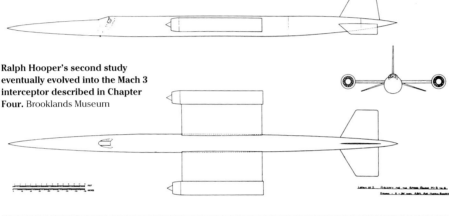

Ralph Hooper's second study eventually evolved into the Mach 3 interceptor described in Chapter Four. Brooklands Museum

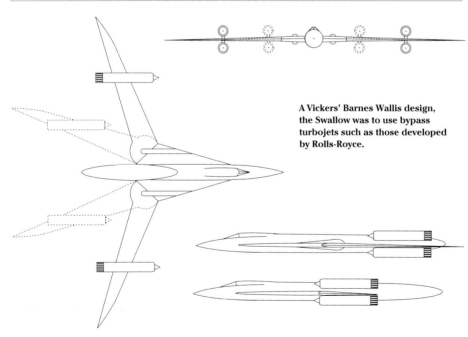

A Vickers' Barnes Wallis design, the Swallow was to use bypass turbojets such as those developed by Rolls-Royce.

was reduced gradually and the compressor windmilled. The engine then ran in pure ramjet mode for the remainder of the flight until airspeed fell below that required to provide ram compression. The rocket would then be re-ignited for the approach and landing.

The origins of the turborocket are hazy and perhaps, like many aeronautical innovations, they lie in wartime Germany. German expertise in the application of liquid-fuelled rocket engines and the propensity of Germany's engineers to fiddle with new technology may have led to the turborocket. One of the earliest mentions of the concept is in a 1950 paper by the Aerojet Engineering Corporation in the USA. The first appearance in the UK is a de Havilland Engines paper from 1951, a period when de Havilland was heavily involved in developing supersonic propulsion systems such as the Gyron jet engine.

The NGTE looked at the turborocket as a means to power aircraft in the Mach 2.5 to 4 regime, beyond the performance range of conventional turbomachinery. NGTE proposed a variety of engine types categorised by engine geometry. These were:

- Type A – An impulse type turbine with the turbine blades arranged on the periphery of the compressor driven by gas in a separate duct.
- Type B – Miscellaneous schemes that do not fit into the other categories.
- Type C – The compressor is driven by a gearbox fitted with a clutch to allow windmilling.
- Type D – The compressor is driven by turbine blades within the compressor flow path.

The seemingly odd placing of the miscellaneous schemes in the Type B category *may* allude to de Havilland's original turborocket work. The later Rolls-Royce and Armstrong Siddeley Motors designs *might* then have been added later as Types C and D.

The above categories were further subdivided depending on the type of fuel involved:

- Category I – Rocket runs on liquid methane (CH_4) and an oxidant (liquid oxygen), while the reheat section runs on kerosene.
- Category II – Rocket runs on high test peroxide (HTP, a solution of 85/15 ratio hydrogen peroxide in water.), while the reheat section runs on kerosene.
- Category III – Rocket runs on methanol and an oxidant (liquid oxygen), while the reheat section runs on kerosene.

In essence the options came down to geared or non-geared compressors, with Rolls-Royce

placed downstream of a small rocket combustion chamber drove this compressor either directly or via a gearbox. The exhaust from this rocket fed into the main mass flow of the engine ahead of the fuel injectors, where more fuel was added, and the 'back end' acted as a ramjet combustion chamber. The turborocket could function as a compressor-augmented ramjet for take-off. As speed built up, the flow of liquid oxygen to the rocket

British Secret Projects: Hypersonics, Ramjets & Missiles

developing specialist clutches for its geared turborockets. By 1956 NGTE had drawn up a specification, TE.10/56, for a turborocket and invited tenders from the engine manufacturers. Armstrong Siddeley, Rolls-Royce and D Napier and Son tendered design studies, while Bristol Engines declined to tender because, according to their chief engineer Stanley Hooker, they had their hands full with the Olympus and the BE.47, a turbojet for short-haul transport aircraft.

ASM tendered the P.170 turborocket, Napier a design called the E.237 and Rolls-Royce the PP.27, although this designation may refer to the brochure title.

On paper, turborockets looked great. They were lighter and cheaper than a high temperature turbojet, with the bonus of operating up to Mach 4. However, when proposed for guided weapons they were heavier and produced lower acceleration rates than Boost Rocket Motors (BRM) and ramjets. Turborockets were suggested for the Blue Envoy SAM, as a back-up in the event of the failure of the BRJ.800 ramjet. Studies showed that the acceleration was too low, so BRMs were still required. In the light of these findings the turborocket was dropped in favour of the BRJ.800 ramjets. However, the acceleration rate was not so much of an issue for aircraft and the turborocket could have an applica-

tion in that field. Turborockets were most suitable for pod mounting and as such made thrust deflection easier. Thus a potentially better solution than fitting cascades in the jetpipe was having the entire turborocket engine mounting turning and deflecting the thrust to the required degree.

Another interesting engine concept studied by Rolls-Royce was the Flashjet. The Flashjet's basic principle was the same as a standard gas turbine except that it did not burn fuel in a combustion chamber to expand the working fluid. Instead liquefied gas, such as hydrogen, was vaporised 'in a flash' that increased its volume and, as it escaped to atmosphere, drove a turbine that in turn drove the compressor. The flashjet utilised a heat exchanger in the jetpipe to add heat to the cryogenic fluid, which was then injected into the mass flow, went through the turbine stages and then into a reheat section where it would be burned to produce thrust. This had two advantages: first the heat exchanger cooled the incoming air, thereby reducing the temperature of the air as it entered the engine, and secondly the potential was there to use the cryogenic fuel as the medium in regenerative cooling system.

The downside of the flashjet was the added complication of using cryogenic fuels such as liquid methane or hydrogen, plus the addi-

tional weight of a heat exchanger. There was also the thermo-mechanical effect of taking liquid hydrogen at -253°C and raising its temperature to 597°C. The flashjet was only really suitable for large aircraft, such as an air-breathing satellite launcher.

Rolls-Royce also looked at ducted turbojets or turbofans (true turbo-ramjets) where the turbomachinery was bypassed and closed off, with the mass flow being diverted around the core to a reheat section acting as a ramjet burner. The engine would operate as a normal reheated turbojet or turbofan up to a point where turbine entry temperatures began to reach the engine's limit. Incoming air was then diverted into annular ducts around the engine core's turbomachinery and into the reheat section. The core engine would be isolated by closing the inlet guide vanes to act as shutters, blanking off the compressor face. The engine operated as a ramjet until the Mach number dropped and the incoming air temperature came within acceptable levels again.

So, having had a very brief look at the development of high-speed propulsion systems and the factors involved in building and fuelling high-speed aircraft, it is time to look at some of the hypersonic design studies that were undertaken to make use of these systems.

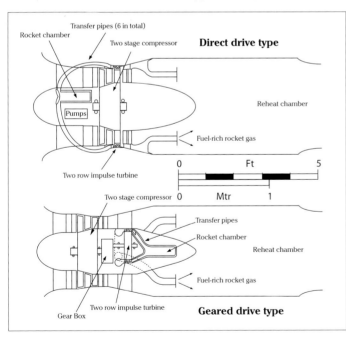

Above: **The NGTE examined the turborocket in detail and eventually two main types evolved, geared turbine and direct drive.**

Top right: **Rolls-Royce favoured the geared turbine with a clutch system. This drawing shows the main components of the engine.**

Right: **Rolls-Royce researched the Bypass Turbojet such as Types B, C and O, that could isolate the turbomachinery and run as a ramjet.**

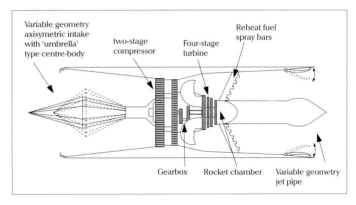

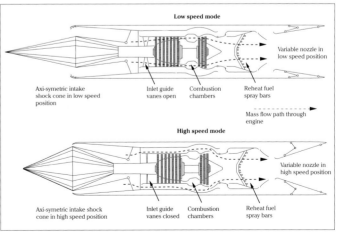

Chapter Fifteen

Warton's P.42 Studies

BAC's P.42 research aircraft accelerates away from the camera on a test flight over the North Sea.
Adrian Mann

The English Electric Company entered the aircraft business as English Electric Aviation (EEA) to build aircraft for other companies as part of the wartime shadow factory programme to boost aircraft production. Construction of Handley Page Hampden and de Havilland Mosquito aircraft at the factories around Preston had allowed EEA to get a good idea of what it took to build high-performance aircraft.

After the war was won, with the only item missing from the show being a design team, EEA decided to get into the aircraft design and

manufacturing business and gathered a team under the leadership of W E 'Teddy' Petter. During the war Petter had been Chief Designer at Westland Aircraft and had designed types such as the Whirlwind and Welkin. When the Air Staff issued the B.3/46 requirement for a jet-powered bomber to replace the Mosquito, Petter and his design team produced what would become the Canberra. This was an outstanding design that, in its PR.9 guise, was still in frontline RAF service over Afghanistan more than fifty years after its first flight. Petter's next major project was the P.1 supersonic research aircraft, which was later turned into the P.1B Lightning – the only wholly British supersonic fighter. Although first designed by Petter, who left EEA to join

Folland Aircraft in 1950, much of the development of the Lightning was carried out under a new Chief Designer, Frederick Page. Page remained Chief Designer throughout the turbulent late 1950s and early 1960s.

By the mid 1950s EEA had diversified into guided weapons, developing the Thunderbird SAM and what would become the Blue Water SSM. This broad range of interests allowed the company to gain experience in the high-technology/high-performance end of the business, with supersonic aircraft as well as the technology and systems that such machines require. By 1960 aircraft were making the transition from being an airframe on which weapons were hung, to being a weapons system whose performance is

English Electric's P.10 Mach 3 reconnaissance aircraft study provided a baseline on which to start the Mach 5 P.42 study. Model by John Hall

dependent on the integration of airframe, powerplant, avionics and weapons. The aircraft companies' advanced projects offices continued with design studies for future requirements. In the late 1950s hypersonics looked like the way forward: allowing immunity from interception, high-speed transportation and, most tantalisingly, access to space. English Electric believed that speeds above Mach 5 held the promise of more efficient aerodynamics, such as reduced drag, with the attendant improvement in aircraft payload/range performance.

In the years after the issue of Specification ER.181 in 1958, the aircraft companies attempted find their feet in the unstable political and military climate that had affected the military aircraft construction business since late 1957. By 1960 the company amalgamations demanded by Duncan Sandys (who was Minister for Aviation by this time) were more or less complete – the dust was settling.

As ever the military aircraft designers were looking on the bright side for the future, and ER.181 had prompted paper studies. As noted above the MoS and RAE had blown hot and cold on high-speed vehicles, but by 1960 they were blowing hot again. Warton dusted off the design from their last high-speed project, the P.10 reconnaissance aircraft. This was the third time (fourth if the P.10D stand-off weapon is included) that this project had been resurrected, having been suggested as the basis for a long-range fighter and later as being suitable for a 'covert reconnaissance aircraft'. The designers considered the P.10 from a 'lessons learned' point of view and a paper by an anonymous author (possibly F G Willox, Chief Project Research Engineer) titled 'Some Lessons From Earlier Work' stated that: '...an appreciable amount of project assessment is required, especially on fuel requirements for the whole flight, before a finalised aircraft and propulsive system will emerge.'

As well as indicating the scale of the challenge, the paper also pointed out that the companies were pretty much on their own on the subject of hypersonic aircraft: 'We are not surprised at the reluctance of the RAE to show what they believe to be a feasible layout or quote precise operational performance and cost, or even the usual overall details of propulsion, structure weight ... L/D, etc.'

Which suggests that the RAE, normally keen to pass on its views on how a problem should be approached, was maintaining a

hands-off approach for some reason. In that vein the paper continued with: 'There is a clear need for practical project and other research in which industry must play a full part.'

The report's author then recalled 1956 when he had lectured to the likes of Dr Walter Cawood, Deputy Controller of Aircraft (Research and Development) at the Ministry of Supply, on the subject of high-speed flight and its problems: 'Amongst the slides I showed was the next one, which illustrates the now familiar concept of the flight corridor. I laid great stress on the importance of high temperature material and propulsion research if this corridor was not to close into a heat barrier.'

The concept of the flight corridor had been demonstrated in Bristol Aero Engines Ltd Report 2093 written by John Lane in 1958 and is best shown on a graph of velocity vs altitude. Lane's graph shows the corridor narrowing as the speed and altitude increase, before opening up at orbital velocities. More or less a function of air density the corridor is defined by regions where flight produces excessive heat in the denser, lower atmosphere and poor lift in the upper less dense atmosphere.

Interestingly the author of the English Electric report makes an admission that seems to be at odds with EEA's previously stated beliefs: 'I also showed Slide 20 which illustrates the advantages to be gained in range up to Mach numbers approaching 5. Even after three years of intensive work, I remember that this curve was a sheer guess.'

This might explain the RAE's hands-off approach. Perhaps it already knew that the companies were on a hiding to nothing by

pursuing hypersonic flight. The report's author concluded that there were still many unknowns, with the most important one being: 'What sort of operations do we want to carry out at Mach numbers above 2½ to justify the large expenditure involved?'

...and: 'We would very much like to hear more from the Air Staff about the flight plans and other operational possibilities that would interest them.'

English Electric/BAC would wait a long time to hear from the Air Staff, but embarked on a series of design studies to investigate the various aspects of high-speed flight, particularly materials and aerodynamics. These grew into project studies for aircraft. One of these BAC studies, designated P.42, produced a range of fifty designs that would cover everything from basic research to satellite launching. However, the early studies concentrated on matching the airframe to the propulsion system and formed the basis of more advanced studies under government contract.

Warton's P.42 research received a good reception at the Ministry, so the company was awarded a contract for further studies in July 1963. This Ministry of Aviation Research Contract No.KD/2X/2/CB7(c) was to carry out studies of the feasibility of hypersonic flight as applied to:
- Long-range high-speed-cruise aircraft
- Recoverable launch vehicles
- Boost Glide vehicles
- Space planes

Particular aspects of hypersonic flight were to be covered in these studies, with the long-term view being to identify fields that would require further, more detailed, research.

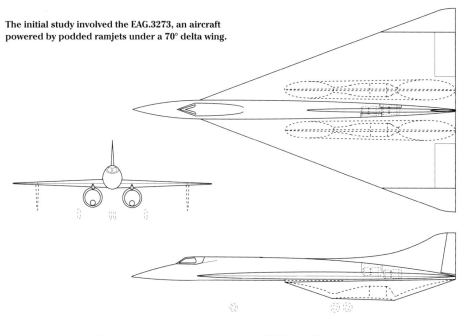

The English Electric / BAC Studies

The MoA contract was awarded as a result of the in-house studies that EEA/BAC Warton had carried out in response to ER.181. This earlier work was carried out in conjunction with Bristol Siddeley Engines Ltd and Rolls-Royce, with both companies offering their engine projects. As would be expected, the engines and airframes evolved hand-in-hand.

Given the close relationship of airframe to engine, the evolution of the P.42 studies is best described in terms of the engine system. The first of them used podded ramjets but, as BSEL and Rolls-Royce developed their engine projects, the aircraft changed to take advantage of improvements in the state of the art. The other significant change was the flight regime. Initially the aim was for Mach 5 and beyond, but as time went on the speed came down to Mach 4. This was no doubt due to the realisation that the technology to deal with Mach 5, particularly materials plus the

approach of real gas effects in the engines, made Mach 4 a more attractive if not attainable goal.

As for the design studies themselves, they are identified by their EAG number. The EAG (possibly standing for English Electric Aircraft Group, no-one really knows) nomenclature describes drawings English Electric produced as part of design studies, conforming to a system initiated by the Society Of British Aircraft Constructors in 1948. The number can refer to a specific drawing or block of drawings rather than a particular project. They are sequential and their use continues at BAE Systems to date.

The earliest design study for P.42 was the EAG.3273; a fairly simple-looking ramjet-powered delta. However, the features that typify hypersonic flight were apparent already: 70° delta, large fin and fold-down wingtips. The ramjets were mounted under the wings, no doubt to aid cooling, but also because this installation permitted trials of different engines. The ramjet intakes and jetpipes were also profiled to maximise efficiency.

In addition to the ramjets, the EAG.3273 was to be powered by a pair of retractable Rolls-Royce RB.162 turbofans to provide thrust for take-off, acceleration to ramjet light-up speed and also a 'go around' capability in the event of a baulked landing. Although no specific engine was identified, the ramjets

EAG.3273's large delta wing is shown to advantage in this photograph. Model by John Hall

The layout of the EAG.3277 is shown off well in this photograph. Model by John Hall

may have been the BS.1002, BSEL's first foray into aircraft propulsion.

EAG.3277 – Shaping the Future

While the EAG.3273 had ramjets fitted in underwing pods, the smaller EAG.3277 used one of these pods in a fully integrated fuselage installation with the same wing planform. Also, like the pods of the EAG.3273, the nose was profiled to provide a precompression ramp and the rear fuselage was shaped to provide an expansion surface for the exhaust. This configuration is interesting in that it has occurred time and again in hypersonic aircraft studies, most notably from the USA in the late 1980s. Auxiliary power was again provided by Rolls-Royce RB.162 turbofans.

EAG.3280 – High-Speed Spey

Reminiscent of a Soviet MiG Design Bureau aircraft, the EAG.3280 took the P.42 research study back into conventional territory. Powered by a pair of developed Rolls-Royce RB.168 Spey turbofans, this aircraft was intended to have a maximum speed of Mach 4.5. How the RB.168 was to be 'developed' is not alluded to, but a bypass system was a possibility. The EAG.3280 also formed the basis of one of the earliest air-breathing satellite launch systems; with modifications including a large payload bay between the engines, a lengthened fuselage and new engines.

As a launch vehicle the EAG.3280 was to be re-engined with a pair of Rolls-Royce Turborockets, possibly a variation of the FPS.146 series of studies.

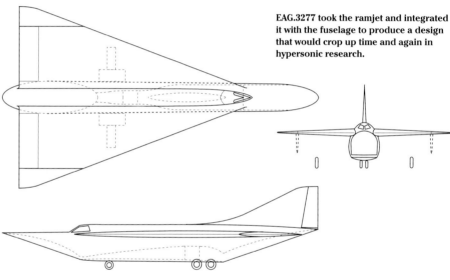

EAG.3277 took the ramjet and integrated it with the fuselage to produce a design that would crop up time and again in hypersonic research.

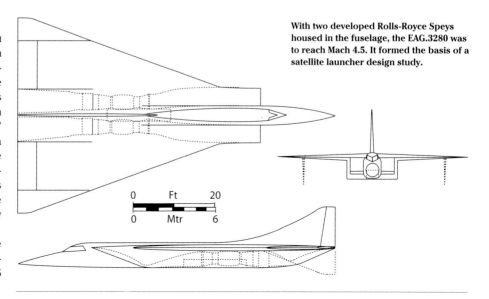

With two developed Rolls-Royce Speys housed in the fuselage, the EAG.3280 was to reach Mach 4.5. It formed the basis of a satellite launcher design study.

0   Ft   20
0   Mtr   6

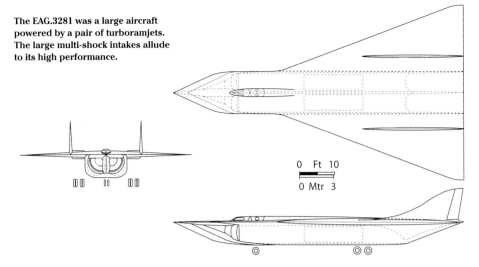

The EAG.3281 was a large aircraft powered by a pair of turboramjets. The large multi-shock intakes allude to its high performance.

0 Ft 10
0 Mtr 3

EAG.3281

This study was driven by the availability of what the drawing calls 'Turboramjets'. It is unclear what particular flavour of turboramjet this refers to, but the installation and the size of the airframe suggests that a bypass turbojet was to be applied to the study. Such bypass turbojets, designated Type 'C', were under development by Rolls-Royce for use in high-speed aircraft studies.

The two-seat EAG.3281 was a much bigger aircraft than its predecessors, 100ft (30.48m) long, perhaps alluding to the need to develop a practical use for such a vehicle by allowing for a payload. This study continued with the integrated intake and jet pipe of the EAG.3277, but on a grander scale. The intakes were of the two-shock quarter-cone type arranged under the nose. Twin fins were mounted on the upper surfaces of the wings.

EAG.3282/2 and EAG.3282/3

These studies shared a similar fuselage, but the wing type differed substantially. The /2 was fitted with an anhedral delta while the /3 sported a low-mounted delta with no anhedral or dihedral. Both types were to use a pair of BSEL BS.1012/3 combination engines in the rear fuselage and Mach 4 performance was expected from them both.

John Hall's model shows the complicated intake of the EAG.3281 to advantage. Model by John Hall

This variant, the EAG.3282/1 housed its four RB.153 turbojets in underwing fairings. This variant formed the basis of the later EAG.3303.
Model by John Hall

British Secret Projects: Hypersonics, Ramjets & Missiles

The two BS.1012/3 combination engines of the EAG.3282/3 were housed in a wide ventral housing reminiscent of the North American XB-70 Valkyrie. The /2 also carried three guide vanes on the rear fuselage to reduce drag and maximise the expansion area for the engines.

EAG.3299 – Return of the Ramjet

This study saw the return to the podded ramjet, with the Bristol Siddeley BS.1005 or R.2 variable geometry ramjets fitted under the wings. It is notable for two reasons:

1. The very large boost rocket motor to accelerate the aircraft to ramjet light-up speed, which for the R.2 would be about Mach 2.5. This booster was 4ft 10in (1.47m) in diameter, 75ft (22.8m) long and weighed in at 100,000 lb (45,359kg) – it generated a thrust at take-off in the region of 175,000 lb (778.4kN). No solid rocket motor of this size had been attempted in the UK but it may have been related to the 3ft (0.91m)-diameter Bristol Aerojet Stonechat used in the RAE Falstaff test vehicle referred to in Chapter Two.

2. The launch trolley to ensure the aircraft reached the correct angle of incidence at the right moments during take-off. This was no doubt because the pilot would be under high acceleration during the roll and may not have been able to control the aircraft, given that the ensemble would reach the 200mph (322km/h) unstick speed in just ten seconds.

The launch system operation involved the trolley being rolled under the aircraft and the trolley jacks raised and engaged on the spools on the aircraft wing undersurfaces. The jacks were raised to lift the aircraft and booster off the ground so that the trolley could carry the aircraft and booster forward. The complete ensemble was to be towed to the end of the runway and prepared for take-off. The rocket motor was ignited and the ensemble set off down the runway. After two seconds the jacks began to lift the aircraft into flying attitude at around 5° of incidence. After ten seconds the ensemble should have accelerated to 200mph (322km/h) and the angle of incidence been raised to 15°. At this point the trolley was to be released and the aircraft would climb away on rocket power, the trolley being brought to a halt by parachutes. While all this was happening the ramjets were prepared for lighting. By the time the aircraft had reached Mach 2.5 these would be started and begin to generate thrust. As the thrust increased the aircraft would accelerate further and as the rocket motor lost power it would be jettisoned. The aircraft would then continue to climb to cruise altitude.

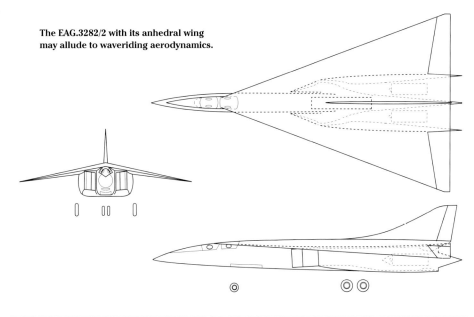

The EAG.3282/2 with its anhedral wing may allude to waveriding aerodynamics.

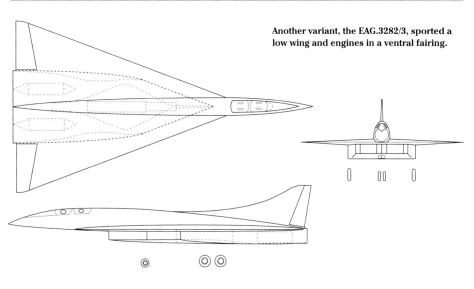

Another variant, the EAG.3282/3, sported a low wing and engines in a ventral fairing.

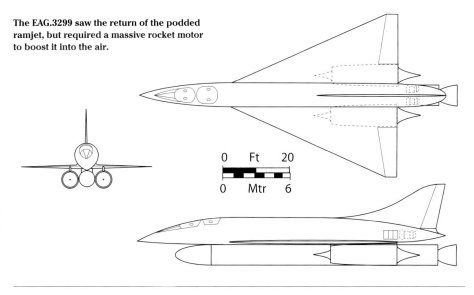

The EAG.3299 saw the return of the podded ramjet, but required a massive rocket motor to boost it into the air.

0   Ft   20
0   Mtr   6

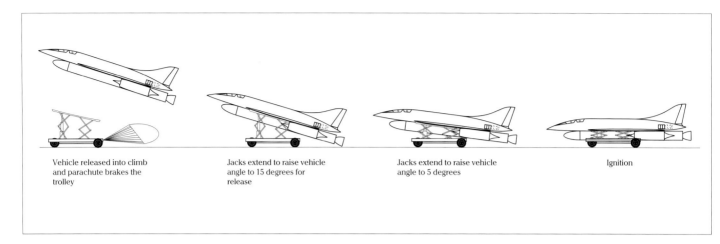

Vehicle released into climb and parachute brakes the trolley

Jacks extend to raise vehicle angle to 15 degrees for release

Jacks extend to raise vehicle angle to 5 degrees

Ignition

The EAG.3303 was powered by a quartet of Rolls-Royce RB.153 turbojets, in this case fuelled with kerosene.

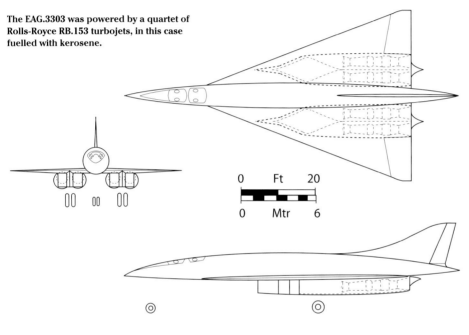

The EAG.3299 was to be launched from a trolley. The above diagram shows the launch sequence (minus the smoke and noise).

EAG.3303/2 – Liquid Hydrogen

This study, a variation on the previous ramjet-powered design, clearly illustrates the difference in size between a kerosene-fuelled aircraft and an LH$_2$-fuelled aircraft. As shown in the chapter covering fuels, the size of an LH$_2$ tank would be considerably larger than the fuel tank for an equivalent kerosene-fuelled type. Power for this aircraft was to be provided by a quartet of Rolls-Royce RB-153 bypass turbofans, modified to burn hydrogen. This study may also have been aimed at satellite launching because it is illustrated with an 'air-launched rocket' payload. Whether this is a stand-off missile or a space payload booster is not clear, but it may mark the change toward developing a space launcher.

Air-Breathing Boosters

By 1963 the focus of the Warton P.42 studies had shifted from a research aircraft to a more practical use: satellite launching. Having had the shock of their lives in 1957, when the Soviets launched their Sputnik satellite, the Americans, acting in what could be described as something of a flap, all but abandoned development of air-breathing re-usable launchers and focused on the straight-up rocket solution. According to an unpublished memoir by John Lane, the Americans had actually 'lost' all the data they had amassed on air-breathing high-speed propulsion systems.

Expendable boosters were seen by the British as an expensive and inefficient method of lofting a payload into space. The materials and equipment used in the construction of an expendable rocket booster are always lost, usually either burning up or crashing into the ocean where they are beyond recovery. In the late 1950s such equipment was based on recently developed

The change to liquid hydrogen fuel increased the fuselage size considerably.

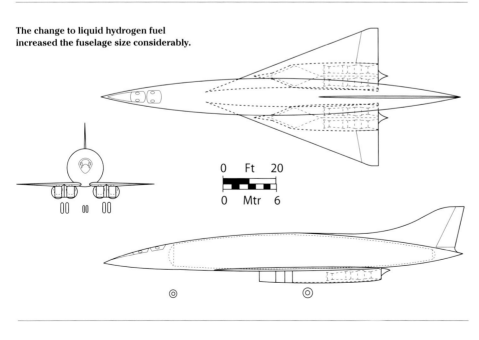

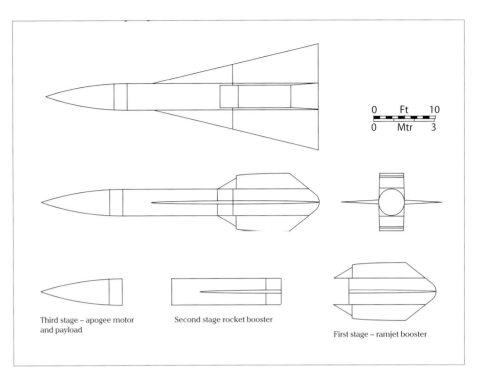

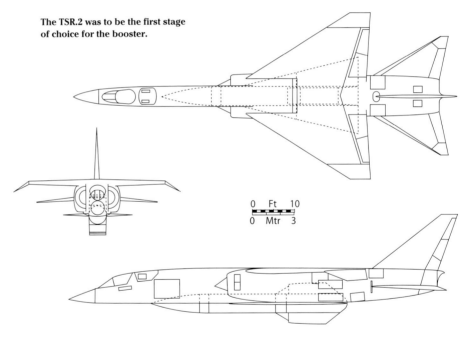

Bristol Siddeley proposed this ramjet-powered booster for launching small satellites.

Third stage – apogee motor and payload

Second stage rocket booster

First stage – ramjet booster

The TSR.2 was to be the first stage of choice for the booster.

ballistic missiles. This technology was very expensive and the launch preparations required a lot of highly skilled manpower, not to mention the need for specialist facilities, usually in a remote area and preferably near the equator. The reason for the equatorial launch site is that the rocket can gain extra velocity from the rotation of the Earth so a launcher lifting off from an equatorial site can carry a greater payload than one launched from higher latitudes.

John Lane and Robin Jamison at Bristol Siddeley Engines had already pondered the possibilities of using the ramjet's high Mach number performance to power an expendable rocket booster. Initially their studies envisaged a ramjet-powered aircraft carrying a rocket booster. Lane and Jamison studied the possibilities, concentrating on the propulsion system for such a vehicle and leaving the airframe studies to the aircraft companies. This may explain a discrepancy in 'the paperwork'. Many of BAC's P.42 studies list the engine as being the 'BSEL BS.1011/2'. This is odd for two reasons. The first is that the BS.1011 was, according to BSEL's paperwork, an integrated translating cowl ramjet with five turbojets and was not studied in great detail. The second is that the former BSEL engineers this author has interviewed claim that there was no such design study! Suffice to say, the drawings appear to show a BS.1012/3-style engine, so perhaps the BS.1011/2 was merely a set of weight and performance data dished out to the airframers, rather than a proper submission as the BS.1012/3 was. Like the intriguing gaps in paper trails, such nebulous studies remain the bane of the aviation historian!

Early proposals to use a TSR.2 as a first stage were drawn up by Bristol Siddeley who ran a study to produce a small delta-winged booster, powered by a pair of ramjets, with the final stages being rocket powered. Semi-recessed in the TSR.2 bomb bay, this would deliver a 400 lb (181.4kg) payload to Low Earth Orbit (LEO). As can be seen from the accompanying drawing, shoe-horning this booster into a TSR.2 would have been an interesting exercise!

Meanwhile at Warton, the P.42 team began to look at air-breathing boosters more seriously. They intended to modify the EAG.3280 study to carry a rocket powered two-stage booster in a bay behind the cockpit. This was to be capable of delivering a 500 lb (226.7kg) payload in to a 100-mile (160km) LEO. Modifications included lengthening and widening

the fuselage, extending the length of the undercarriage leg, adding TSR.2-style twin wheels and fitting a large bay between the intakes/engine bays.

However, in the early 1960s a 500 lb satellite was not much use (the wonder of miniature solid-state circuitry was in its infancy) and these studies only really served to illustrate the potential in the concept. A bigger payload was needed, so a bigger air-breathing booster would be required, especially if a manned spaceplane was the payload.

Manned spaceflight has had no place in the UK space effort since the mid-1960s. The UK has specialised in constructing satellites and space hardware without the need to develop its own launcher. Expendable launchers based on the Blue Streak MRBM evolved into the Europa programme and later Ariane, but the UK has eschewed heavy involvement with the boosting business. This may be a result of the UK's location in higher latitudes (and resulting payload restrictions) and the lack of a 'safety zone' into which an aborted

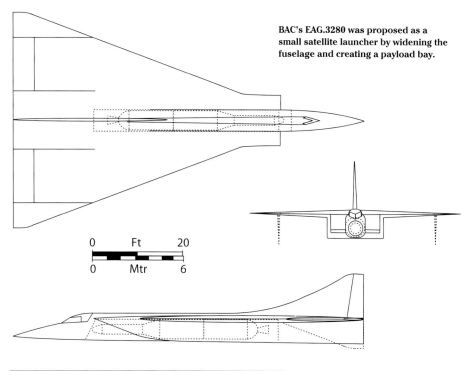

BAC's EAG.3280 was proposed as a small satellite launcher by widening the fuselage and creating a payload bay.

0   Ft   20

0   Mtr   6

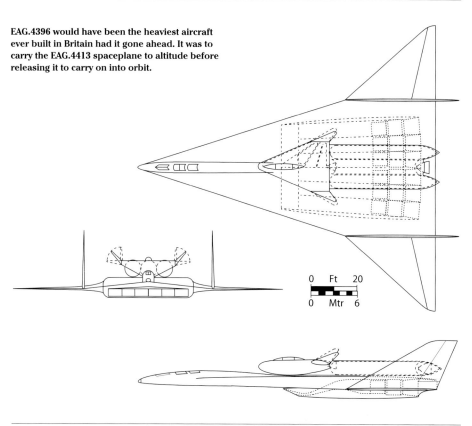

EAG.4396 would have been the heaviest aircraft ever built in Britain had it gone ahead. It was to carry the EAG.4413 spaceplane to altitude before releasing it to carry on into orbit.

0   Ft   20

0   Mtr   6

future space requirements of the Royal Air Force. Drawn up in 1962, the AST laid out the following: 'The vehicle should be capable of using existing airfields, be a single-stage vehicle carrying crew, navigation, communications and life support systems plus a payload of 2,000 lb (746,5kg) to an apogee of 600 nautical miles (1,111km). It should have the capability of tracking, identifying and intercepting satellites.'

Ambitious stuff, even today! The Defence Research Policy Committee thought that the development of an air-breathing first stage could only be done as a by-product of a hypersonic aircraft. In the end offensive space systems were deemed to be extravagant and inflexible: 'An independent British space programme would cost more than we could reasonably afford.'

As ever in military programmes, the participants were hoping someone else would foot the bill for the research and development, in this case the booster would be developed on the back of the hypersonic airliner. BAC, on the other hand, took the opposite view.

EAG.4396

This design, an air-breathing Mach 4 launch aircraft, formed the basis of a rather more in-depth study of structure, propulsion and aerodynamics than its predecessors. The double-delta planform, chosen because it would be self-trimming at Mach 4, also had an aft aerodynamic centre making a dorsal payload more feasible. The wing formed the airframe with the six Rolls-Royce Type C turboramjets housed in the thickened inboard section, which also held much of the kerosene fuel.

The booster was to be 150ft (45.7m) long, with a span of 130ft (39.6m) and the all-up weight was to be almost 500,000 lb (226,757kg). The EAG.4396 would have been the heaviest aircraft designed and built in the United Kingdom. The payload, BAC's manned spaceplane based on the EAG.4413 study and weighing in at 198,000 lb (89,795kg) with its rocket booster, was to be launched from the back of the EAG.4396 at Mach 4.0.

The size of the engine installation was governed by the need for a long intake trunking. Despite using the aircraft undersurface for external precompression (whereby the surface ahead of the intake lip is shaped to compress air before entering the inlet) and so reducing the powerplant's sensitivity to incidence changes, the intakes were longer than optimum. This was due to the large undercarriage being housed within the engine housing, under the diffuser throat. The undercarriage itself was a *tour de force*, allowing

launch vehicle could fall. Plans to launch satellites into polar orbits from Norfolk were scuppered by the developing oil and gas industry in the North Sea.

In the light of this it was looking as if air-breathing boosters, launched from a conventional airfield, would allow large satellites to be launched from the UK. This set the scene for the issuing of some rather ambitious Operational Requirements by the Air Staff. OR 9001, later changed to Air Staff Target AST.1450, was a document outlining the

British Secret Projects: Hypersonics, Ramjets & Missiles

the EAG.4396 to operate from runways with a Load Classification Number (LCN, a standard measurement for the load-bearing capacity of paved surfaces) of 60, a figure that included 30% of the military airfields in the UK. No mean feat when the requirement to halt a 500,000 lb (226,757kg) aircraft in an aborted take-off would entail some heavy-duty braking systems, but BAC considered it worthwhile. The EAG.4396's undercarriage showed that, as well as the aerodynamic and materials challenges posed by hypersonic flight, seemingly mundane components such as the brakes can also impact an aircraft's development.

BAC built wind tunnel models of the EAG.4396 and tested them in the 9ft x 7ft (2.7m x 2.1m) low-speed tunnel at Warton. This revealed a tendency to pitch up, especially at low speeds, something that could: '...be an embarrassment in take-off and landing conditions'. However, this wind tunnel work showed that the pitch-up tendency could be cured by modifying the leading edge with, for example, a dog-tooth.

One outcome of such 'an embarrassment' could be crew ejection. Ejection by conventional means would be possible in the conditions quoted above, but was a non-starter at Mach 4 and so BAC decided that an ejection capsule would be required. This, of course, is another of those relatively mundane but important items that in fact bring added complication to high-speed aircraft development.

EAG.4397 – Hypersonic Transport

As has been already related in the chapter on the BS.1010 powerplant, the main drive in hypersonic research had been a military transport aircraft. EAG.4397 shared the wing and engine components of the EAG.4396 booster, but with a cabin to accommodate one hundred passengers and 3,000 lb (1,360kg) of freight above the centre section. The main difference was the large single fin, made possible because there was no need to carry a dorsal payload.

Two questions not addressed (and possibly skirted around if asked) were how was the passenger cabin to be cooled and how would the passengers react to the G-forces involved? By the 1960s the travelling public (and the deploying squaddie) had become used to being transported in what could only be termed as a shirtsleeve environment in Bristol Britannia and de Havilland Comet airliners. The troops would probably be fit enough to cope with the 3 to 4G they would be subjected to during accelerations to Mach 5, but then what about the travelling public? A comfortable 68°F (20°C) is fairly easy to

maintain in a subsonic airliner when the outside temperature is below zero, hot air tapped from the engine compressors being used to heat the cabin. However, in a hypersonic aircraft the skin temperature could be in the region of 400°F (200°C), which is a different matter altogether. Some form of cooling system is required and, while a crew cockpit can be cooled effectively with a fairly compact system, a large passenger cabin is another matter. Such was the size of these

cooling plants that Robin Jamison addressed this problem by using a twin-fuselage airframe with the cooling system in the forward portion of the port fuselage of his Mach 3 airliner of the late 1950s. As for the G-forces, no reference was ever made to them!

BAC calculated that the EAG.4397 would have a rather unimpressive range of 2,000nm (3,704km), but BSEL was positive that engine developments could produce a more useful 3,000nm (5,556km).

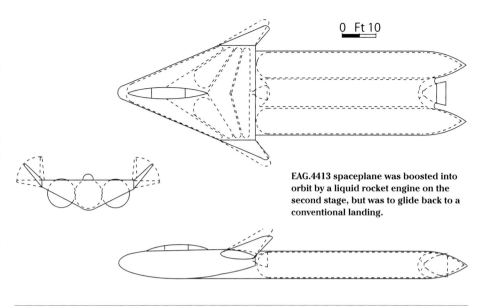

0 Ft 10

EAG.4413 spaceplane was boosted into orbit by a liquid rocket engine on the second stage, but was to glide back to a conventional landing.

BAC based their EAG.4397 Mach 4 transport aircraft on the EAG.4396 booster.

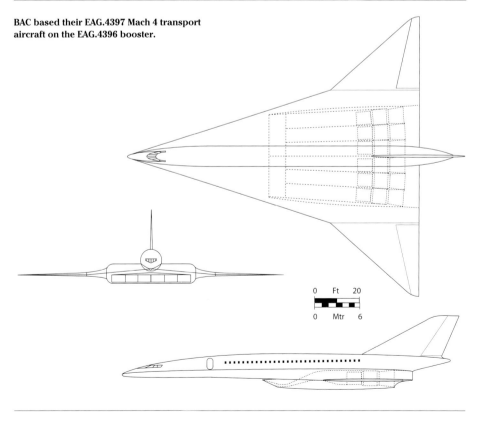

0   Ft   20
0   Mtr   6

BAC also looked at slower, less complicated
supersonic boosters such as the EAG.4409,
seen here carrying the EAG.4413 spaceplane
in a ventral installation.

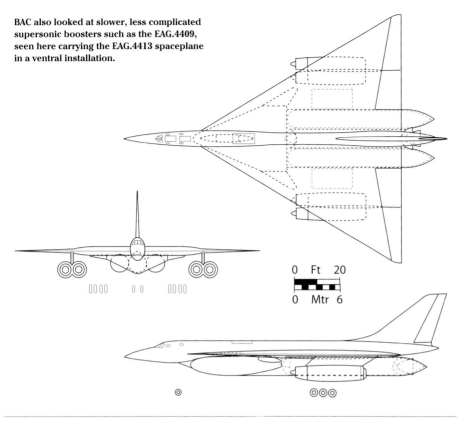

nology from bomber and fighter development had allowed the aircraft companies to
embark on supersonic passenger transports,
ultimately leading to Concorde. Using a Mach
2.2 aircraft to lift a satellite booster seemed
like a logical step.

One of BAC's studies to produce a satellite
booster was the EAG.4409, with a configuration not unlike the American Convair B-58
Hustler bomber. The EAG.4409 had a somewhat small diameter fuselage, but its 60° delta
wing had a thickened inboard section holding the fuel for the mission. The four engines
were to be reheated turbojets rated at
50,000 lb (222.4kN) such as a developed
Olympus or RB.167 (the latter was a supersonic turbojet for a Concorde predecessor).
These were mounted under the wings in
paired pods on pylons with each engine having a circular intake with a conical centre-
body, simplifying their installation.

The payload, BAC's EAG.4413 orbital
spaceplane and rocket booster, was suspended under the fuselage/inboard wing sections. The EAG.4413's outer wings were to be
folded to the horizontal position while the
spaceplane was attached to the carrier. One
feature of the EAG.4409 was the ejection system. Being mounted ventrally the crew of the
spaceplane would not be able to use their
ejection seats. Given the furore caused by the
lack of ejection seats for the Avro Vulcan
bomber's 'back-seaters' BAC must have pondered an escape system for the spaceplane's
crew.

The solution was a conduit passing through
the fuselage of the carrier aircraft. On ejection
from the 4413 spaceplane, hatches on the
carrier would blow off and the ejecting crew
would pass though the conduit. Well, that
was the idea but perfect timing would be
required.

EAG.4409

As work on a hypersonic booster aircraft continued, it was becoming apparent that such
high speeds would pose considerable engineering challenges. Meeting these challenges

was going to take a long time, with a first flight
for a Mach 4 aircraft being delayed until the
late 1970s. In the early 1960s the technology
to produce a supersonic aircraft to achieve
Mach 2 cruise was maturing. Indeed the tech-

EAG.4412 – Practical Possibility

It may strike the reader as odd that this chapter contains a reference to a subsonic aircraft.
However in the air-breathing booster studies,
BAC looked at as many possibilities as they
could, including the Vickers VC-10 airliner
and Avro Vulcan. Looking not dissimilar to a
Vulcan, the EAG.4412 carried the same
EAG.4413 spaceplane and booster as the
other launcher studies, but being subsonic
with a launch speed of Mach 0.9 it would pose
fewer difficulties and would probably represent an achievable goal.

The EAG.4413 space plane was the
intended payload for many of BAC's air-
breathing boosters. Based on the P.55 lifting
body studies, the manned spaceplane would
have weighed 17,600 lb (7,983kg), with the

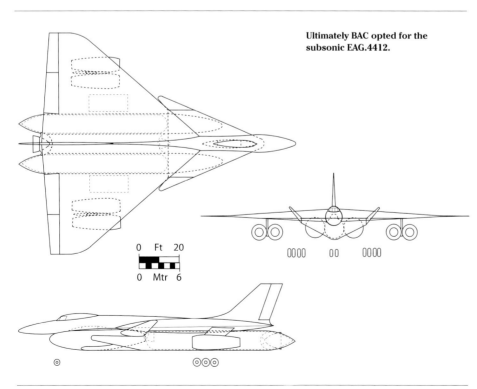

booster and fuel tanks weighing 178,400 lb (80,920kg). However the weight could vary depending on the booster because slower boosters were capable of carrying a heavier payload.

EAG.4416 – Flashjet

This study is particularly interesting because it is one of the few aircraft projects to use the Rolls-Royce flashjet. As related in the propulsion chapters, high-speed powerplants invariably produce no static thrust. As can be seen in the general arrangement drawing, the engine installations were large at 50ft (15.2m) in length. Pylon mounting would ease the engine fitting in that each could be identical, but that would also mean there would be no propulsion system components within the wings. This in turn would make the entire wing volume available for the liquid hydrogen tanks. Also notable in this study is the size of the moving wingtips (5% of the wing area) that could be deployed to increase stability and generate compression lift.

EAG.4424

This study is essentially the same aircraft as EAG.4416 but with internally mounted Rolls-Royce Type C ducted turbojets. The difference in size between hydrogen and hydrocarbon fuels becomes obvious in these studies.

EAG.4435

This project was described as a boost aircraft intended for use as a satellite launcher and a long-range cruise vehicle. As ever the fin area is large to maintain stability at high speeds, with folding wingtips being dispensed with, possibly due to the weight of the actuators. This large two-seat aircraft is powered by what are described as 'scaled' BS.1011/2 engines in a triple installation at the tail. By identifying the engines as being scaled, the project study designers could use the performance figures quoted in engine manufacturer's brochure as a baseline from which to work from. In the case of the EAG.4435, the rating of the 'Scaled' BS.1011/2 is specified as being 1.47 times that of the baseline BS.1011/2. If the BS.1011/2 possessed a take-off thrust of 60,000 lb (266.9kN) the Scaled BS.1011 for EAG.4435 would have been 88,200 lb (392.3kN).

EAG.4446

EAG.4446 was one of the last P.42 air-breathing boosters and departed from its predecessors in both planform and payload carriage. The planform was very much like that of the 4435 study, but with a forward fuselage and

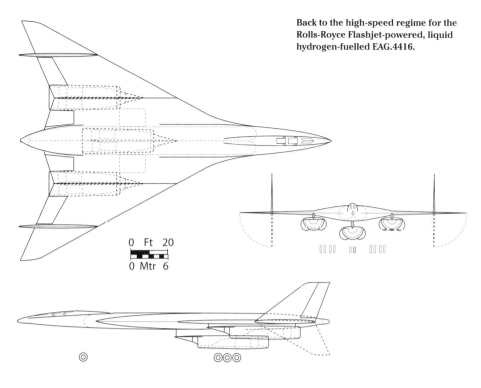

Back to the high-speed regime for the Rolls-Royce Flashjet-powered, liquid hydrogen-fuelled EAG.4416.

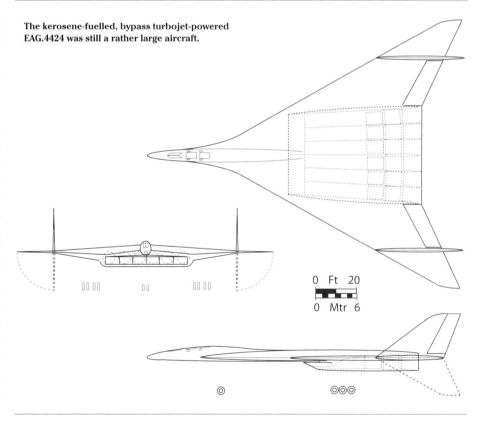

The kerosene-fuelled, bypass turbojet-powered EAG.4424 was still a rather large aircraft.

ventral BS.1012/2 combination powerplant rather than the BS.1011. The size of the engine installation shows how much the aircraft design was driven by the powerplant. This allowed the EAG.4446 to reach Mach 5.5 with a payload faired into the rear of a booster stage. The undercarriage retracted into large fairings in the wings, while the engines were arranged across a ventral bay, sharing a common intake and diffuser that allowed an optimum intake length. The final stage was based on the EAG.4413 spaceplane.

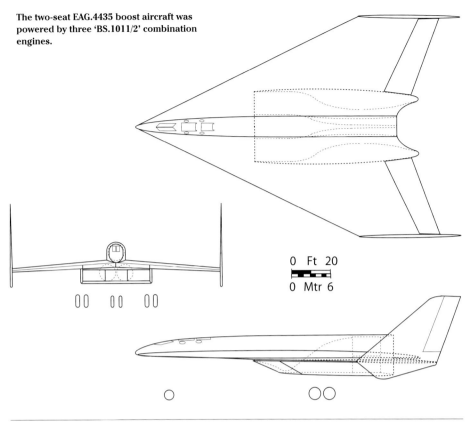

The two-seat EAG.4435 boost aircraft was powered by three 'BS.1011/2' combination engines.

0 Ft 20
0 Mtr 6

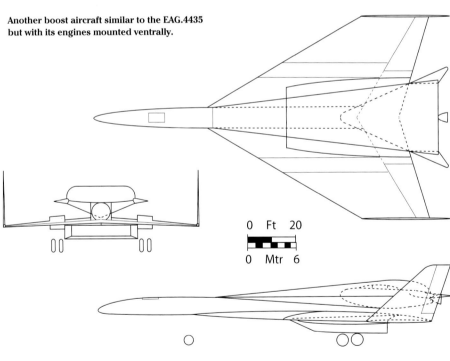

Another boost aircraft similar to the EAG.4435 but with its engines mounted ventrally.

0 Ft 20
0 Mtr 6

P.42 as a warplane produced two studies, both of similar configurations and including a planform that could almost have come straight from the Blue Envoy missile of 1956. They were intended to present a high-altitude/high-speed threat that would be very difficult to counter, with a speed of Mach 4.0 at 90,000ft (27,432m). There was also a requirement to zoom-climb to 120,000ft (36,576m) if necessary. The first was EAG.4426, a 90,000lb (40,823kg) two-seat strike aircraft in the same class as BAC's TSR.2. Intended for Mach 4.5, this 85ft (26m)-long machine was to be powered by a pair of Rolls-Royce type C 'turboramjets', with an SLS (Sea Level Static) rating of 27.000lb (120.1kN), installed in the thick inboard sections of the double-delta wing. These were to be fed by a single two-dimensional intake mounted under the wing centre section and the aircraft's undersurface would be used as a precompression ramp.

This study featured a translating nose that would improve the pilot's vision on landing but also form a heat shield in the high-speed flight regime. Weapons were to be carried internally in bays within the thickened inboard section of the wing. They could also be carried externally under the wings or on a centreline station under the engine bay. The practicality of releasing weapons from the internal bays was not addressed, but some form of ejection mechanism would be required. Further weapons, possibly stand-off weapons, were to be semi-recessed in the upper surfaces of the inner wing, being launched outwards and upwards. BAC had a penchant for such overwing weapons installations; particular examples include the Lightning F Mk.3 and Jaguar strike aircraft. Of course, external stores would restrict performance; Mach 4 was only possible with internal weapons.

This type may have been drawn up in response to the Air Staff requirement OR.346 or 355, a Buccaneer/TSR.2 replacement. Interestingly the draft of requirement OR.355 was dismissed by the Air Staff as being 'too conservative'. This is even more interesting when the eventual TSR.2 replacement, the Tornado, is considered.

Opposite page:

The EAG.4426 was a TSR.2 replacement powered by a pair of Type 'C' turbojets. Model by John Hall

Rear view showing the size of the jet pipes and the drooping outer wing panels, which are about one third through their range of movement.

The 'Blue Envoy'-style planform of the EAG.4426 is clear in this view. All three models by John Hall

The Strike Aircraft

As ever, BAC wanted to apply the techniques learned in developing a hypersonic aircraft to perform the more usual role of high-performance aircraft, warfare. Oddly enough the driving force behind these studies was not a requirement to produce a warplane, but rather a request from BAC's Guided Weapons Dept at Luton. The GW division was developing a high-altitude defence system as a follow on to Thunderbird and looked to Warton for information on future threats.

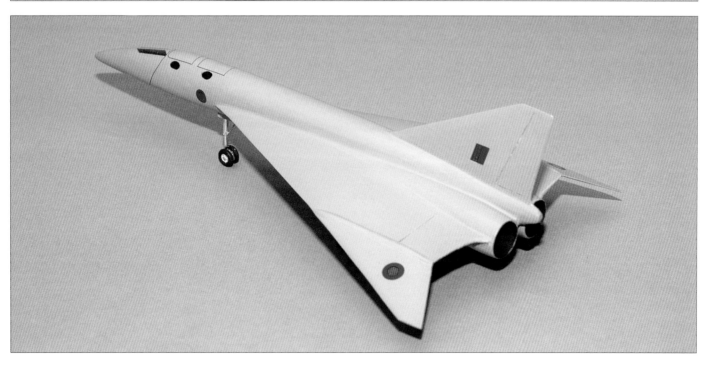

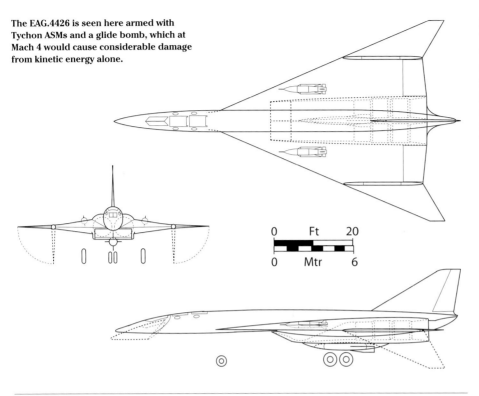

The EAG.4426 is seen here armed with Tychon ASMs and a glide bomb, which at Mach 4 would cause considerable damage from kinetic energy alone.

0 Ft 20
0 Mtr 6

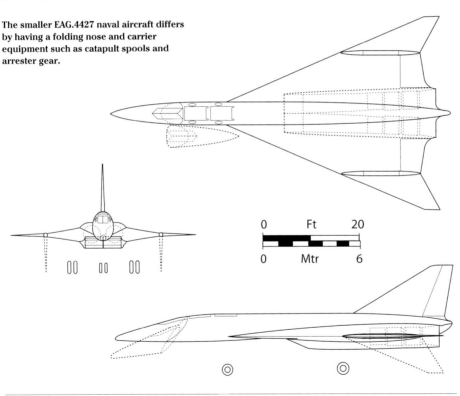

The smaller EAG.4427 naval aircraft differs by having a folding nose and carrier equipment such as catapult spools and arrester gear.

0 Ft 20
0 Mtr 6

EAG.4426

The drawing on this page shows the 4426 armed with two BAC Tychon stand-off missiles semi-recessed on the upper wings and a ventral 'glide-bomb'. The glide-bomb is interesting as, when released at high Mach numbers, even a weapon with a small explosive charge can cause considerable damage to a target solely by kinetic energy. Recent studies into weapons for high-speed aircraft have highlighted this and have proposed guided tungsten or depleted uranium darts, the so-called 'rods from the gods'.

EAG.4427 – Naval Strike Aircraft

The next type was half the size of EAG.4426, weighing 45,000 lb (20,411 kg), and it was again a two-seater but was intended to fill a naval strike role, probably as a Buccaneer replacement to OR.346. Whether carrier operations would be the forte of this type is not specified, but the scaled Rolls-Royce Type C ducted turbojets with an SLS rating of 13,500 lb (60KN) would have possessed more than enough thrust for service aboard carriers. Concerns were raised about the low-speed handling of the aircraft for carrier operations, but there were applicable features such as a folding nose, reducing length by 10ft (3.28m) and outer wing panels that reduced span from 34ft (10.36m) to 22ft (6.7m). Of course the folding wing panels were originally intended for use at high speed where they supplied additional side area for improved lateral stability.

This type would also be fitted with external stand-off weapons, but its main role was to be 'radar busting', now given the acronym SEAD or Suppression of Enemy Air Defences. Like the larger 4426, missiles would be mounted on overwing stations, with an additional single centreline hardpoint under the engine housing. No internal weapons bay was planned for the 4427.

EAG.4441 – Reconnaissance Aircraft

Clearly identified as a reconnaissance aircraft in the BAC paperwork this study shared the double-delta planform of the EAG.4396 and EAG.4397 studies. This was aimed at a Mach 5 regime and was to be powered by a pair of BS.1012/2 combination engines. Again these are 'scaled' to produce more thrust than the brochure engines, in this case 57,600 lb (256.2kN) at take-off. The fin area is extensive and the rear fuselage was shaped to allow the maximum expansion of the gases. The underwing zone ahead of the intakes serves, as usual, as a precompression ramp.

P.42 in Summary

BAC Warton's P.42 study covered many aspects of the hypersonic flight regime, from research aircraft to satellite booster via reconnaissance and strike aircraft. The study lasted almost five years but, as ever, very little reached the hardware stage apart from a few low-speed wind tunnel models. As an exercise in identifying potential problems in the field, the P.42 work was a success. Areas for further research included structures, materials, systems and propulsion and a full-scale research aircraft would not have been possible until these areas had been investigated. Much of that work would have been carried out on a small scale at the aircraft companies, the Royal Aircraft Establishment and, for subjects that were not security-sensitive, the universities.

Pressure of work on BAC's TSR.2 meant that the P.42 design team was transferred to that project and by 1964 work on P.42 came to an end. Work on space launch systems continued with an analysis of re-usable recoverable rockets such as the MUSTARD (Multi-Unit Space Transportation and Recovery Device) project. Ultimately in the 1980s what came to be called space access led to the development of HOTOL. Designed as an unmanned, re-usable, single-stage-to-orblt vehicle, HOTOL (HOrizontal Take-Off and Landing) was to carry satellites into low Earth orbit and use conventional runways for launch and recovery. HOTOL's power came from a Roll-Royce RB.545 Liquid Air Combustion Engine (LACE) that liquefied air to separate oxygen, which in turn was passed to a rocket engine. This allowed HOTOL to carry less oxidant at take-off, reducing weight and maximising payload. HOTOL lives on in the Reaction Engines Ltd Skylon and LAPCAT projects, which use the LACE principle in their engines.

By the early 1970s Britain had abandoned all work on launch systems, even the expendable launchers that would prove to be a

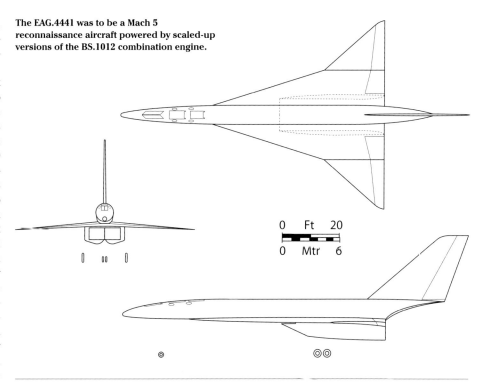

The EAG.4441 was to be a Mach 5 reconnaissance aircraft powered by scaled-up versions of the BS.1012 combination engine.

0 Ft 20
0 Mtr 6

money-spinner in the satellite-launching boom of the late 1970s and 1980s. Yet again, timing had proved less than impeccable, too early to be useful and cancelled before it would show its potential. How a launcher such as the EAG.4396 would have fared will never be known, but P.42 served its purpose in identifying what research was required. It also showed how difficult this would be.

P.42 Studies

Type	Span ft (m)	Length in (cm)	L/E Sweep	Weight lb (kg)	Powerplant
EAG.3273	45 (13.7)	75 (22.6)	70	50,000 (22,676)	2 x RB.162 2 x BSEL ramjets
EAG.3277	36 (10.9)	65 (19.8)	70	50,000 (22,676)	2 x RB.162 1 x BSEL ramjet
EAG.3280	45 (13.7)	75	70	50,000 (22,676)	2 x RB.168-31R
EAG.3281	56 (17.1)	106 (32.3)	70	20,0000 (90,703)	2 x 'Turboramjets'
EAG.3282	42.5 (12.9)	79 (24)	70	10,0000 (45,351)	2 x 'Turboramjets'
EAG.3299	36 (10.9)	85 (25.9)	70	10,0000 (45,351)	2 x RB.162 2 x BSEL ramjets
EAG.3301	42.5 (12.9)	62 (18.9)	70	10,0000 (45,351)	4 x RB.153
EAG.3303 (kerosene)	42.5 (12.9)	88 (26.8)	70	10,0000 (45,351)	4 x RB.153
EAG.3303 (Hydrogen)	42.5 (12.9)	116 (35.3)	70	10,0000 (45,351)	4 x RB.153
EAG.4396	130 (39.6)	155 (47.2)	73/50	500,000 (226,757)	6 x Rolls-Royce Type C
EAG.4397	130 (39.6)	155 47.2)	73/50	500,000 (226,757)	6 x Rolls-Royce Type C
EAG.4409	105 (32)	140 (42.7)	60	500,000 (226,757)	4 x reheated turbojets
EAG.4412	105 (32)	130 (39.6)	50	500,000 (226,757)	4 x Rolls-Royce Type B
EAG.4413	40 (12.2)	45 (13.7)	70	17,600 (7,982)	1 x Rolls-Royce rocket
EAG.4416	123 (37.5)	165 (50.3)	70	500,000 (22,6757)	6 x Rolls-Royce Flashjets
EAG.4424	123 (37.5)	150 (45.7)	70	500,000 (22,6757)	6 x Rolls-Royce Type C
EAG.4426	46 (14)	87 (26.5)	70	-	2 x Rolls-Royce Type C
EAG.4427	34 (10.4)	62.5 (19)	70	45,000 (20,408)	2 x Rolls-Royce Type C
EAG.4435	78 (26.8)	97 (29.6)	70	500,000 (226,757)	3 x BS.1011/2
EAG.4441	62.5 (19)	148.5 (45.3)	70	-	2 x BS.1011/2
EAG.4446	75 (22.8)	80.5 (24.5)	70	500,000 (226,757)	6 x BS.1012/2

Chapter Sixteen

Advanced Projects
from Kingston

While BAC was working on the P.42 at Warton, Hawker Siddeley Aviation (HSA) at Kingston was also examining hypersonics closely. Rather than the 'broad brush' studies at Warton, HSA's research was more focused, specifically on a research aircraft, and grew out of the July 1963 RAE Symposium on Very High-Speed Flight. Under MoA contract KD/2X/1/CB7(C) awarded in 1963, the Advanced Projects Department examined high-speed flight, particularly the detailed structural and systems analysis for a Mach 5 to 7 aircraft that would pave the way for practical applications.

This project study, designated APD.1019, initially covered a single-seat research aircraft with an AUW of 70,000lb (31,751kg) and capable of a fifty minute sortie with around twenty minutes of flight at Mach 5. Further research was to look at advanced fuels such as Shelldyne as a means to increase

endurance. HSA considered a research aircraft a necessary tool in the advancement of the science, to prove the materials and propulsion systems, and there was the prospect of HSA applying this experience to an advanced military or civil aircraft.

HSA considered the materials, systems and techniques to be so unusual that only by building and flying a research aircraft could the designers even begin to attack the thorny problem of hypersonic aircraft for service. The research aircraft would show the real problems of hypersonic flight. While BAC Warton were 'throttling back' to Mach 4 for its studies, HSA was determined to stay above Mach 5, in fact the company saw higher speeds as the key to satellite launching. HSA's view was that a second stage powered by a supersonic combustion ramjet to beyond Mach 7 was the best bet for satellite launching.

A pair of Hawker Siddeley APD.1019E2 research aircraft climb away from their base on the first hypersonic formation flight. Adrian Mann

As for the uses of a Mach 5+ aircraft, HSA also saw the transport as the logical employment, which it estimated could have a range of 5,800nm (10,741km) when using exotic fuels such as Shelldyne or pentaborane. The other possibility was an anti-satellite missile launcher based around OR.9002, the Air Staff's requirement for a counter-satellite system. HSA suggested that the use of a hypersonic aircraft as a launch platform for an anti-satellite missile would reduce the size of the missile and provide a performance improvement by lifting the missile above the denser, and therefore draggy, lower atmosphere.

Eventually the focus of Kingston's research centred on an aircraft to be constructed from nickel alloy and powered initially by the Bris-

182   *British Secret Projects: Hypersonics, Ramjets & Missiles*

tol Siddeley BS.1012/3 combination engine Later the BS.1012/7, based on the Olympus 593 high-pressure core engine with a 56in (142cm) diameter zero stage fan, was to be installed. The BS.1012/7, although larger than the /3, possessed a smaller 'D'-shaped cross-section with simpler intake ducting that could be installed within the airframe more efficiently. All in all, the /7 produced more power, less drag and a simpler, lighter installation. At the back-end the /7 was to be fitted with a cascade jet deflection system comprising mechanically rotated deflectors built into the rear fuselage. Thrust deflection was to take advantage of the excess thrust available to reduce drag and improve take-off and landing performance.

The aim was to have this aircraft flying by around 1970 but in reality, given the now familiar delays due to fabrication problems plus the attendant political wrangling, the first flight for what would be called the APD.1019/E2 would most likely have been in the late 1970s. By July 1964 Hawker Siddeley Aviation's Advanced Projects Department had prepared an interim report on their activities and, most importantly, their findings to date. This report, 'Hypersonic Vehicle Research Studies', made very interesting reading.

A Small Research Aircraft

According to the report, the Advanced Projects Department saw no massive stumbling blocks in developing the 1019/E2, apart from the usual design problem, but it did identify two areas of concern. The first was finding actuators that would work in the high temperatures of the intake and exhaust. Bristol Siddeley had a system called Beaver that used recirculating ball bearings and screw jacks, but one of HSA's suggestions was a new hydraulic system using liquid metal as the working fluid. This was no doubt borrowed from the nuclear power side of Hawker Siddeley's business where liquid metal coolant was used in reactors.

The second concern was electrical power generation under ramjet propulsion. Generally aircraft carry generators that run off the accessory drives of their gas turbines. In the BS.1012 the turbomachinery would be isolated; turning only slowly to stop the bearings from seizing up. No drive would be available for the generator, and therefore no electrical power. The solution on conventional aircraft is a RAT, the Ram Air Turbine, which pops out into the air stream in the event of engine failure. At first glance the RAT is an easy answer, but how long would it survive in a Mach 7 airflow? Not long is the answer and, while a small research aircraft could use battery

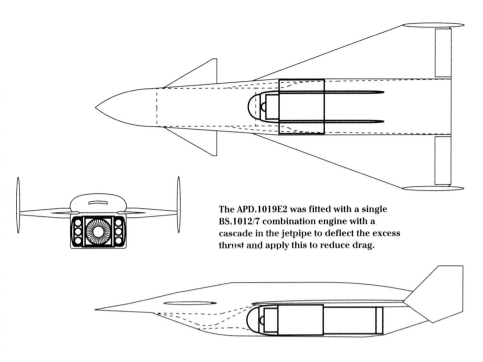

The APD.1019E2 was fitted with a single BS.1012/7 combination engine with a cascade in the jetpipe to deflect the excess thrust and apply this to reduce drag.

General arrangement of Hawker Siddeley's 'Small Research Aircraft', the APD.1019E2.

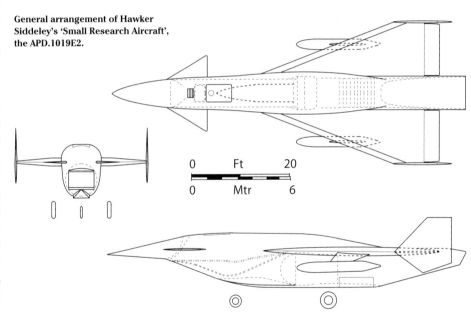

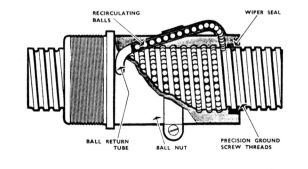

Bristol Siddeley's ingenious 'Beaver' recirculating ball actuator system. Such dry systems would have been required on hypersonic aircraft because of the thermal effects on hydraulic fluids.
Rolls-Royce Heritage Trust via Roy Hawkins

The APD.1019E5 larger twin-engine Mach 7 aircraft was considered as the launch platform for an anti-satellite system. Model by John Hall

Two sets of components that would experience the maximum temperatures would be the intake diffuser and the jetpipe. Both would need the problematic actuators as well as insulation to protect the rest of the airframe. Insulation would have been ceramics, light and more than adequate for non-structural areas, but only a refractory metal such as Nimonic or tantalum could be used where the component was subject to structural loading. The ceramic was to be a replaceable item because, in areas such as the jet pipe, it would be subjected to high acoustic loading that would cause damage over a period of time. This point would be particularly applicable to the next study in the APD.1019 series, the /E5.

power for a short flight, an operational type with radars and systems to operate could not rely on a battery. This was a problem that had to be solved before practical applications could be found.

The APD.1019/E2 was to be a 70ft (21.3m) canard delta with endplate fins on the 26ft 3in (8m)-span mainplanes. It sported a two-dimensional chin intake with the nose undersurface ahead of the intake shaped for external precompression. In standard fit, the aircraft was to have an AUW of 65,000lb (29,483kg), 22,000lb (9,979kg) of which was kerosene fuel. With two underwing drop tanks, each containing another 225 gallons (1,023 litres), the all-up weight would rise to 69,000lb (31,298kg). The fuel in the tanks

would be used up in the early phase of the flight, with the tanks being jettisoned before Mach number exceeded the safe carriage speed. Maximum speed with tanks aboard was considered to be around Mach 0.96.

As stated, the structure would be nickel alloy, probably Nimonic, in corrugated sandwich form, with the insulated wing fuel tanks fabricated from titanium. The nickel structure would be adequate for Mach numbers around 5 but, as HSA's goal was Mach 7, exposed areas such as the leading edges would need a more thermally resistant material. One material suggested was tantalum, a heavy but heat-resistant metal used for turbine blades and currently a major component in electronics.

APD.1019/E5 – Up the Mach Scale

To provide the speed increase to Mach 7 this variant of the 1019 would be provided with a second BS.1012/7 engine in a larger airframe and a wider fuselage. APD.1019/E5 was to be 82ft 6in (25.1m) long with a span of 34ft (10.3m), which dimensionally was approximately 18% larger than the /E2. The all-up-weight was 109,400lb (49,623kg) of which 41,600lb (18,869kg) was fuel. This twin-engined study, which HSA considered most suitable for use as a bomber, would benefit from the use of advanced fuels. Estimates for endurance included almost fifty minutes at Mach 5 with a still air range of 2,780nm (5,749km).

Apart from the additional engine, the principal changes in the APD.1019/E5 were the materials. For flight in excess of Mach 5, HSA believed that the Nimonic leading edges should be replaced by niobium alloy, and for the Mach 7 application tantalum alloys. Both would require coating with anti-oxidation material before they could be used. As already noted in the materials chapter, such coatings had great influence the fabrication techniques. Other methods to reduce the thermal effects of stagnation on the leading edges were to increase their radii or replace the leading edges with silicon nitride. With a melting point of 3452°F (1900°C) silicon nitride would handle the temperature, but its lack of fracture resistance would make fabrication difficult, particularly for complex shapes. Another aspect of the Mach 7 design was that, while the wing undersurface was not subject to stagnation temperatures to the same extent as the leading edges, it would still need some additional insulation. This insulation was to be applied as tiles attached

General arrangement drawing of the APD.1019E5.

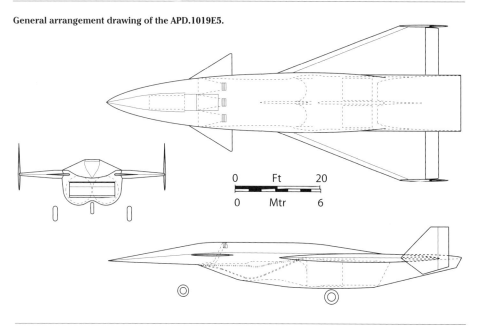

to the structure at overlapping angles like the shingles on a roof.

Mach 5 Transports

Like BAC, HSA saw the first practical use of hypersonic aircraft to be a transport. The Advanced Projects Department surmised that the military would be the first customer for such a transport but that once established in service the airlines would beat a path to HSA's door. The APD.1019/A1 was to be the civil version, burning kerosene, while the military /A5 variant would operate on exotic fuels such as pentaborane and Shelldyne. In fact the /A5 would carry both fuels; Shelldyne for the turbomachinery and pentaborane for the ramjets.

Comparative studies had shown that Shelldyne and pentaborane would confer improved range, typically 6,800nm (12,594km) against 4,650nm (8,612km) for kerosene. These exotic fuels would be very expensive, but HSA surmised that the military would be happy to pay up for the improved performance. This was the era of the Mounting Base (with pre-positioned military equipment awaiting troops to be flown in if trouble flared up) and the A5, carrying 100 troops, would allow such rapid deployment.

Power for both versions would be provided by a six-unit BS.1012/2 installation in an underwing nacelle. As ever, the area forward of the intakes formed precompression ramps, reducing intake length and therefore structural weight. The wing could almost

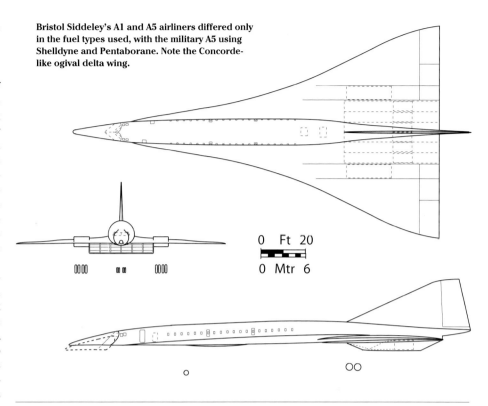

Bristol Siddeley's A1 and A5 airliners differed only in the fuel types used, with the military A5 using Shelldyne and Pentaborane. Note the Concorde-like ogival delta wing.

have come from Jamison's 1958 twin-fuse-lage transport described in Chapter Twelve, it being an ogival delta similar to what would become Concorde.

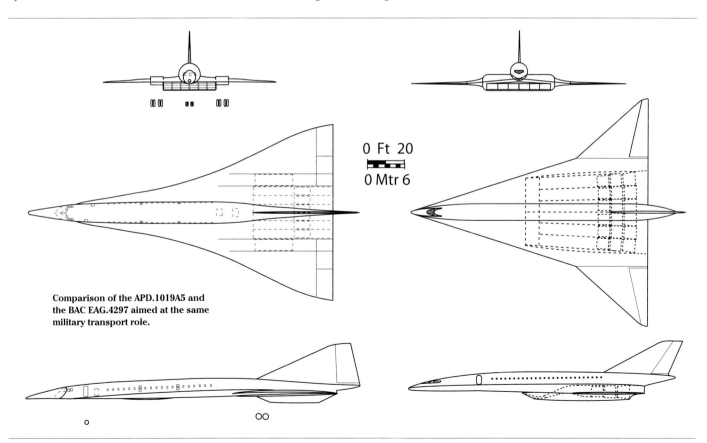

Comparison of the APD.1019A5 and the BAC EAG.4297 aimed at the same military transport role.

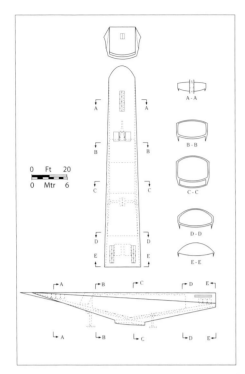

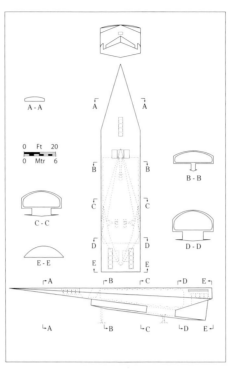

Far left: **The ultimate air-breathing aircraft could have been this APD.1019H1 liquid hydrogen-fuelled, scramjet-powered, vertical landing wedge.**

Left: **The H2 actually surpassed its sibling, the H1, in performance, so the accolade of ultimate aircraft has to go to the APD.1019H2 second stage aircraft.**

Lower left: **This photograph of the Rolls-Royce FPS.16 turborocket-powered Hawker Siddeley APD.1019E6 shows the planform and engine installation.** Model by John Hall

Bottom left: **This view of the turborocket-powered APD.1019E6 illustrates how the engine pods tilt to provide drag reducing deflected thrust.**
Model by John Hall

The A1 was to have an AUW of 465,000 lb (210,920kg) with a 20,000 lb (9,072kg) payload while the A5 was slightly heavier at 472,790 lb (214,454kg) a small penalty for the significant increase in range.

Flying Wedges

As discussed already BAC had pursued a fairly conventional route in its quest for a satellite launcher, finally opting for Mach 4 or less. However Hawker Siddeley, as we have noted, preferred higher Mach numbers and designed accordingly. HSA proposed a series of aircraft capable of speeds in excess of Mach 7, which were to be launched from a booster aircraft. These second-stage aircraft were wingless lifting bodies that would be powered by that 'Holy Grail' of propulsion, the Supersonic Combustion Ramjet or Scramjet.

Scramjets are still seen as the key to high-speed flight, but their development has been fraught with problems over the years. John Lane and Roy Hawkins at Bristol Siddeley conducted a series of design studies and practical trials that showed that the scramjet had to be of sufficient length to allow the injection, mixing and combustion to all take place within the supersonic mass flow. This really requires a long engine for that to occur properly and it all happens more or less instantaneously, but Lane and Hawkins discovered that the engine was prone to choking at low Mach numbers. There is also the small matter of the heat build-up caused by the need to slow the air from the Mach 12 of the airflow to a reasonable Mach number within the engine, typically Mach 3.

Hydrogen was the fuel of choice for the scramjet as it does not suffer the thrust loss caused by the dissociation of molecules under real gas effects. Mixing of fuel and air is also simplified by using hydrogen but in its liquid form it can also be used for regenerative cooling.

British Secret Projects: Hypersonics, Ramjets & Missiles

The second-stage aircraft design studies really did prove that for hypersonic flight the integration of the propulsion system with the airframe was total. The airframe was basically an engine and a fuel tank, with a bit of space reserved for crew and payload. HSA proposed the three-seat APD.1019/H1 aircraft (their term!), which was intended to be capable of Mach 10 at 100,000ft (30,480m) and to carry a 2,000 lb (907kg) payload with an AUW of 117,000 lb (53,070kg), 37,000 lb (16,783kg) of which was to be liquid hydrogen fuel. Powered by a single scramjet, this wingless wedge was to land vertically under the power of ten Rolls-Royce RB.189 lift engines. The H1 had the appearance of two back-to-back wedges and was 112ft (34.1m) long with a 'span' of 21ft 6in (6.5m). The vertical landing was to be on three legs with the cockpits and lift engines buried in the fuselage and isolated behind sealed doors.

Another design, the H2, was twin-engined and slightly larger at 125ft (38.1m) long with a width of 24ft 6in (7.5m) and weighing in at 128,500 lb (58,286kg); to land the heavier H2 required twelve RB.189 lift jets. The H2 was a true flying wedge, this difference between the H1 and H2 being due to the intakes. H1 was to be fitted with the eponymous Ferri intake designed by Antonio Ferri at the General Electric Applied Sciences laboratory, with such intakes becoming the choice for hypersonic applications. Ferri's intake for the H1 could slow the air flow from Mach 10 to Mach 4 by the triggering of shockwaves. The H1 on the other hand used a double plane intake within the diamond-shaped engine installation.

Performance-wise, despite being smaller, the H1 with its Ferri intake performed better than the H2, being capable of acceleration to 21,400ft/sec (6,523m/sec) while the H2 could only reach 16,900ft/sec (5,151m/sec) before its fuel ran out, according to the parametric studies. The main factor in this would have been the higher fuel fraction of the H1.

The Rival from Derby
Ramjets and scramjets were not the only potential means of propelling a Mach 5 aircraft. As shown in the chapter on the development of high-speed propulsion systems, there was also the turborocket. In late 1963 Rolls-Royce supplied HSA with details of its FPS (Future Propulsion Study) 146 turborocket and the Advanced Projects Department then drew up a design study to put it to use. Appendix 5 of HSA's July 1964 'Hypersonic Vehicles Research Studies – Hypersonic Aircraft with Other Engine Systems' details an aircraft with alternative powerplant, the turborocket.

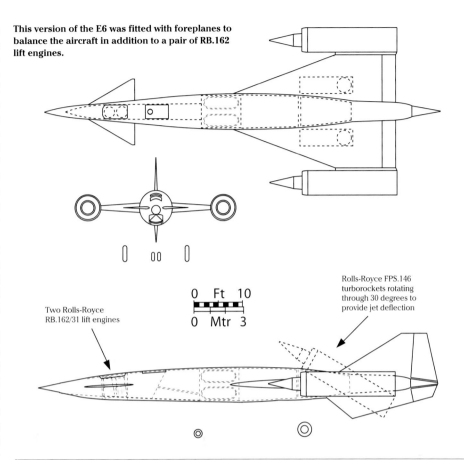

This version of the E6 was fitted with foreplanes to balance the aircraft in addition to a pair of RB.162 lift engines.

Two Rolls-Royce RB.162/31 lift engines

0 Ft 10
0 Mtr 3

Rolls-Royce FPS.146 turborockets rotating through 30 degrees to provide jet deflection

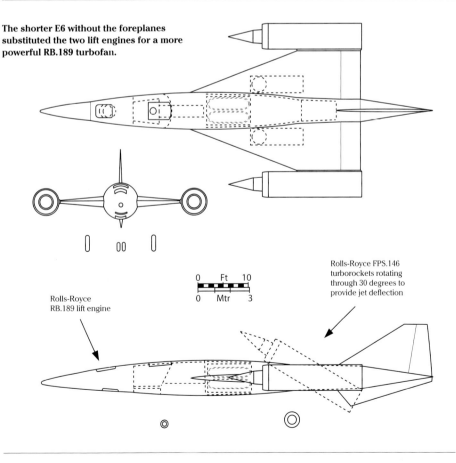

The shorter E6 without the foreplanes substituted the two lift engines for a more powerful RB.189 turbofan.

Rolls-Royce RB.189 lift engine

0 Ft 10
0 Mtr 3

Rolls-Royce FPS.146 turborockets rotating through 30 degrees to provide jet deflection

Hawker Siddeley APD.1019 Design Studies

Type	Length ft (m)	Span ft (m)	Weight lb (kg)	Powerplant
APD.1019E2	70 (21.3)	26.25 (8)	65,000 (29,478)	BS1012/7
APD.1019E5	82 (25)	34 (7.6)	109,400 (49,614)	2 x BS1012/7
APD.1019A1	187 (57)	97 (29.6)	465,000 (21,088)	BS.1012/2
APD.1019A5	187 (57)	97 (29.6)	472,790 (214,417)	BS.1012/2
APD.1019H1	112 (34.1)	21.5 (6.55)	117,000 (53,061)	Scramjet
APD.1019H2	125 (38)	24.5 (7.5)	128,500 (58,276)	Scramjet
APD.1034S	62 (18.9)	43.7 (22.9)	35,700 (16,190)	RR Type 'O' turboramjet

General arrangement drawing of the Hawker Siddeley 1034S fighter.

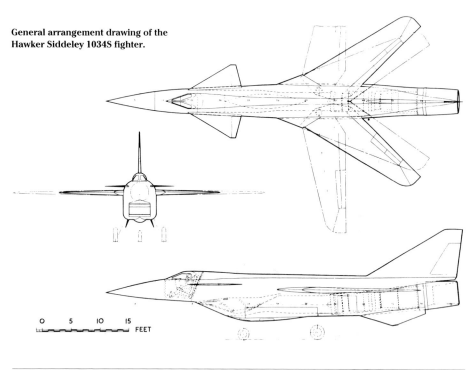

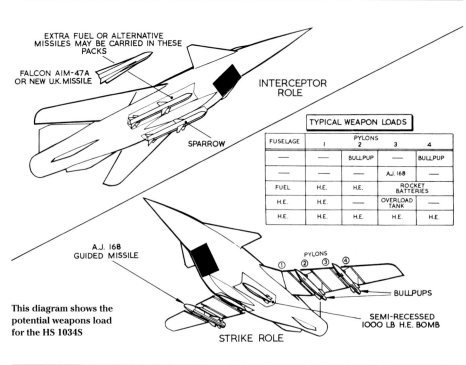

This diagram shows the potential weapons load for the HS 1034S

FUSELAGE	PYLONS			
	1	2	3	4
—	—	BULLPUP	—	BULLPUP
—	—	—	AJ.168	—
FUEL	H.E.	H.E.	ROCKET BATTERIES	—
H.E.	H.E.	—	OVERLOAD TANK	—
H.E.	H.E.	H.E.	H.E.	H.E.

TYPICAL WEAPON LOADS

The resulting APD.1019/E6 was an elegant canard delta with the FPS.146 engines mounted in wingtip nacelles, fed by axi-symmetric intakes with the Rolls-Royce 'umbrella' intake centre body. This lack of integration made the application of thrust deflection look much easier on paper, because the pods could be mounted on rotating bushes. However, practice was a different matter. Some heavier support structure was required in the wings and, while allowing the thrust to be directed as required to a limit of 30° from horizontal, the engine lacked the reverse thrust capability of a cascade design. The FPS.146 also used the more complex 'umbrella' intake centrebody, but on the whole the turborocket weighed only 60% of the BS.1012/7 powerplant on the APD.1019/E2 above. Another benefit of the rotating pod was that, given the sensitivity of high-speed powerplants to air entering the intake at an angle, rotation of the entire pod allowed better fine-tuning of intake incidence to optimise airflow to engine in the cruise.

The E6 had a higher structural weight of 20,350 lb (9,230kg), which was more than the E2's 16,980 lb (7,702kg) because of its longer fuselage and the need for a heavier wing structure to support its engine mounting. Nevertheless, the powerplant weights of the two types were almost identical. This was because the E6 carried a pair of RB.162/31 lift jets in a nose bay to balance the aircraft during take-off and landing under deflected thrust. Another factor in the weight question was the need to carry an additional 6,500 lb (2,948kg) of liquid oxygen (LOX) and its associated equipment. In the end the AUW of the E6 was 78,150 lb (35,448kg) as opposed to the E2's figure of 65,140 lb (29,547kg), a 20% difference.

The FPS.146 ran in rocket mode (that is, the combustion chamber burnt kerosene and liquid oxygen to drive the compressor) up to a speed of Mach 3.5 at which point the LOX supply was to be cut and the turbomachinery windmilled. The engine would then run in ramjet mode up to the design Mach number of 5.

Two variants of the E6 were designed, with the basic difference being the canard or, in the then current parlance, foreplane. Both spanned 34ft 2in (10.42m) but the variant with the foreplane was 85ft (25.9m) long and had the pair of RB.162/31 lift jets forward of the cockpit. The shorter canard-less variant was 80ft (24.4m) long and substituted the RB.162s for a single RB.189.

In the performance stakes the E6 would beat the E2 hands down in the climb, taking seven minutes to reach the Mach 5 cruise speed and altitude, whereas the E2 needed sixteen minutes. However the E6 used 30% more fuel to do this. HSA suggested correctly that this might have been due to the turborocket operating at a lower temperature than the BS.1012/7's ramjets … but this was the point of the turborocket.

As with any matter where two different approaches are taken to meet the same goal, there are pros and cons to each type. The E2 study may have had the edge, because its propulsion hardware would be based on a fairly mature core engine, the Olympus 593, whereas the FPS.146 was still a paper study. The E2, with its simpler intake and diffuser system, may have had an easier development than the E6, the E2's smaller airframe would make for a lighter and possibly more efficient vehicle. However, the decision was never made because the entire APD.1019 research expired in the late 1960s. What the APD.1019 studies showed clearly was that there was more than one way to approach a problem, even in the same design office.

High Mach Military
Like BAC at Warton, HSA ran design studies for military applications of its earlier hypersonic studies. With Hawker's history of providing single-engined fighters for the RAF, one feels that nothing less would have been expected. One example was the Advanced Project Group's 1034S/0102, which dated from 1965 and covered a reconnaissance and strike fighter. It was based on an earlier study called the /0101, which had looked at a fighter aircraft that was also capable of strike and reconnaissance. The /0102 design placed more emphasis on strike, hence the S.

The 1034S was to be a Mach 4 variable geometry canard design powered by a Rolls-Royce Type 'O' engine, described as a 'reheated turbofan'. The two-dimensional chin intake was fully variable and the nose undersurface acted as a precompression ramp. The powerplant would be expected to function as a bypass engine at speeds above Mach 2.5.

Construction was to be mainly titanium for heat resistance, with the sensitive equipment house in insulated bays. The wings and canards were to be fitted with a blowing system using air tapped off the engine compressors. A total of ten weapons points were

provided, with a pair of ventral weapons bays and four pylons per wing, all of which rotated with the wing sweep between 14° and 70°. A pulsed Doppler radar would be fitted with 'Ferret' electronic warfare equipment and sideways-looking airborne radar (SLAR) or reconnaissance cameras in the ventral bays, which could also carry fuel. Weaponry included the American AIM-7 Sparrow AAMs (no doubt to be replaced by the Hawker Siddeley XJ.521 Sky Flash at a later date), Bullpup and AJ.168 (Martel) Air to Surface Missiles up to a maximum weight of 10,000 lb (4,536kg). In the air-to-air role the 1034S would weigh 35,700 lb (16,193kg) at take-off

with full fuel, Sparrows or a pair of high performance AAMs designed for Mach 4 launch, possibly a member of the Family clan (see Chapter Three). In this role the operating radius would have been in the region of 575nm (925km). The 1034S met the usual fate of 1960s design studies – stuck forever on the drawing board.

The APD.1019 and 1034 research taught HSA a great deal about hypersonic flight but for now, like the BAC work on P.42, that work languishes in the archives of Britain's long-gone aircraft developers and builders. However, as we shall see presently, perhaps all this work was not in vain

Hawker Siddeley APG.1034S was a Mach 4 variable geometry strike aircraft. Model by John Hall

Another view of the APG.1034S, but with its wings in the unswept position.

'Bright Promise'

*Thus the following review must be set against the bright
promise of today may not see tomorrow's fulfilment.*

[Aeronautical Research Council, Report on Hypersonics, 1965.]

The premise of the British Secret Projects
series is to show how the UK aircraft industry
rose to the challenges of ever-advancing
technology in an ever-changing world. That
very few of the projects shown in this book
went as far as the mock-up stage, never mind
having metal bashed on them, will come as
no surprise to anyone with the least interest in
aviation. More than anything it is the innovation and creativity of the people involved that
should be celebrated.

As noted in the introduction, these were
the designers and engineers who built the
modern world and allow you, the reader, to
carry on with your comfortable life in the
knowledge that the airliner you travel in won't
ditch with engine trouble, and that your new
car can go for 18,000 miles (28,968km)
between services. If you bought this book
thinking that it was full of flights of fancy,
you'd be correct. But these flights of fancy
pushed the technology to produce what
Michael White has described as 'The Fruits Of
War', which today have become necessities.
Without the work described in this book,

much of the 'push' would have been missing.

But what became of the hypersonic aircraft? In his unpublished memoir on ramjet
development at Bristol Aero Engines and
BSEL, John Lane describes a series of papers
he wrote with Robin Jamison on air-breathing
high-speed propulsion systems. Lane makes
a very interesting statement: 'The papers
caused quite a stir when they came out and
were ahead of the field. The work was trotted
around the US by the author for Rolls-Royce
in the 1980s. The author found that the US had
not recorded their own work and had forgotten most of it.'

By 1985 the US had embarked on the Cop-
per Canyon hypersonic studies and the
National Aerospace Plane (NASP) and by
1989 rumours were rife of a hypersonic aircraft operating from the western United
States. Perhaps like the cavity magnetron, the
atomic bomb and that unsung hero of the
Second World War, the strain gauge, Britain's
high-speed propulsion research went across
the Atlantic, to live on and even reach the
hardware stage.

The ultimate aim, Britain's
ultimate What-If?: A Mach 4
air-breathing booster for a
two-stage spaceplane. The
British Aircraft Corporation's
Warton Division studied such
types in the mid-1960s.

Colour Photo Album

Eurofighter Typhoon of the Royal Air Force banks away from the camera to reveal a pair of MBDA Meteor ramjet-powered beyond visual range AAMs on the fuselage and MBDA ASRAAM imaging Infra-Red guided AAMs on the wing pylons. Courtesy of Eurofighter Gmbh www.eurofighter.com/medialibrary

Close up of MBDA ASRAAM air-to-air missile on a Royal Air Force Typhoon.
Courtesy of Eurofighter Gmbh www.eurofighter.com/medialibrary

A trials round for the Hawker Siddeley / Matra Martel beside a Sea Vixen during test launches. This example is the AS.27 anti-radiation missile. BAE Systems

Left: **The crew of a Spartan armoured personnel carrier on alert, ready to use the Shorts Starburst man-portable SAM against attacking aircraft.**
Copyright Thales Air Defence

Below: **A Royal Air Force Phantom launches a Hawker Siddeley Dynamics Sky Flash semi-active AAM. The motor has just fired as the weapon is ejected from its semi-recessed mounting.**
BAE Systems

Bottom left: **Most surface-to-air missiles have been proposed for defending ships. Here a Shorts Javelin is launched from the stern of a warship. Note that the tail fins are fully deployed and the sustainer motor has just ignited.**
Copyright Thales Air Defence

Bottom right: **This rare photograph shows a development version of the de Havilland Red Top AAM beside an English Electric Lightning. The 'pencil' seeker head and swept tail fins allude to its Blue Jay / Firestreak lineage. Production Red Tops had triangular tail fins and a hemispherical 'IR-dome'.** BAE Systems

An Officer and NCO of the Royal Artillery prepare to launch a Blue Water surface-to-surface Corps Support Weapon. Despite being compact and capable of rapid deployment, Blue Water was cancelled in 1962. Tony Buttler Collection

Compare this production Red Top with the development round. This Lightning sports a large fin fillet as increased fin area was necessary when carrying Red Top. Production Lightning F.3 and F.6 were fitted with a larger, squarer fin to address this. BAE Systems

A Gloster Javelin launches a de Havilland Firestreak air-to-air missile during armament practice camp.

Above left: **A close up of a Hawker Siddeley Dynamics Sky Flash semi-active air-to-air missile showing the black rectangles of the Thorn-EMI fuse system and the black spots on the wings used to differentiate between Sky Flash and the AIM-7 Sparrow.** via Author

Above right: **A spectacular sight as HMS *Edinburgh* launches a Hawker Siddeley CF.299 Sea Dart area defence SAM from its forward launcher.** Crown Copyright/MOD

Left: **John Fozard's Hawker P.1134 design study utilised the Bristol Engines combination powerplant employing two ramjets and a Rolls-Royce Avon. This variant, the third in the series was to explore the Mach 3.5 regime.** Model by John Hall

Below left: **Hawker's P.1100 swept wing Hunter combined the Rolls-Royce Avon with a pair of rocket engines such as the de Havilland Spectre. This was to produce a supersonic interceptor armed with a pair of DH Blue Jay Mk.3 AAMs.** Model by John Hall

Opposite page:

A formation of Handley Page Victors inbound to their targets, release Handley Page's HP.106M stand-off weapons, developed to OR.1149. Adrian Mann

British Aircraft Corporation TSR.2 aircraft as they may have been operated by the RAF in the 1960s. These aircraft carry the air-launched variant of the Blue Water tactical ballistic missile. This combination was considered as a stop-gap deterrent pending the deployment of Polaris. Adrian Mann

British Secret Projects: Hypersonics, Ramjets & Missiles

Opposite page:

A scenario from the 1960s showing Bristol Blue Envoy Stage 1¾ SAMs intercepting a flight of Myasishchev M.52 (NATO Reporting Name *Bounder*) supersonic bombers over the North Sea.
Adrian Mann

This Hawker Mach 3 research aircraft dates from the late 1950s and shows the highly swept delta wing considered to be ideal for this speed range.
Model by John Hall

This page:

Above right: **English Electric's P.42 studies included the massive two-seat EAG.3281, powered by a pair of unspecified turboramjets.** Model by John Hall

Right: **A Royal Air Force Panavia EF.3 fitted with MBDA ALARM anti-radiation missiles on its ventral pylons. The EF.3 is a variant of the F.3 fighter, modified to carry out the Suppression of Enemy Air Defences (SEAD) role. This aircraft is also carrying an ASRAAM air-to-air weapon.**
Crown Copyright/MOD

Below left: **A Panavia Tornado GR.4 carrying a pair of MBDA Stormshadow stand-off weapons. The underwing stores include 'Hindenburger' 1,500-litre (330-Imp Gal) drop tanks inboard and Sky Shadow Electronic counter measures pods outboard.** Crown Copyright/MOD

Below right: **Displaying its Hawker Siddeley Dynamics XJ.521 Sky Flash AAMs, a Royal Air Force Phantom FGR.2 peels away from the camera.**
Crown Copyright/MOD

Glossary of Terms

AAM   Air-to-Air Missile

AAGW   Air-to-Air Guided Weapon. Superseded by AAM

ABM   Anti-Ballistic Missile

ADE   Armaments Design Establishment

ADM   Atomic Demolition Munition

ADRDE   Air Defence Research and Development Establishment

AEI   Associated Electrical Industries – Radar manufacturer

AEW   Airborne Early Warning

Afterburner   see reheat

AFV   Armoured Fighting Vehicle

AGE   Admiralty Gunnery Establishment

AI   Air Interception when applied to radar.

Aircraft Mach number   The speed of an aircraft measured relative to the undisturbed air at the aircraft's altitude divided by the speed of sound at that height.

AMES   Air Ministry Experimental Station

APDS   Armour Piercing Discarding Sabot

Apogee   Highest point reached by a rocket in flight

ARI   Airborne Radar Installation

ASE   Admiralty Signals Establishment

ASM   Armstrong Siddeley Motors

ASR   Air Staff Requirement – outline of what the subject has to do. The basis of the development programme.

AST   Air Staff Target – formed the basis of a feasibility study for the Requirement.

ASW   Anti-Submarine Warfare

ATGW   Anti-Tank Guided Weapon

Avro   A V Roe aircraft company

AWA   Armstrong Whitworth Aviation

AWE   Atomic Weapons Establishment

AWRE   Atomic Weapons Research Establishment

BAe   British Aerospace, became BAE Systems

BAC   British Aircraft Corporation

BAJ   Bristol Aerojet. Rocket motor casing manufacturer.

BMEWS   Ballistic Missile Early Warning System

Booster   High-thrust rocket motor or engine used to launch a vehicle. Usually short-lived, sometimes disposable.

BSEL   Bristol Siddeley Engines Ltd

BTH   British Thomson Houston – radar manufacturer

BVR   Beyond Visual Range

Cascade   A series of vanes or aerofoils arranged in a duct used to direct mass flow, for example in an air intake or thrust reverser.

CIWS   Close-In Weapon System. Short-range ship defence system.

Combination engine   A high-speed propulsion system where the low-speed regime (<Mach 2) is powered by a turbojet, with the high-speed regime (>Mach 2) powered by a ramjet. Speeds higher than Mach 5 could use a scramjet.

Command Guidance   Ground-based guidance system tracks target and missile and transmits guidance cues to the missile, via a command link, to bring the target and missile together.

Continuous Wave (CW) radar   Signal is repeated and transmitted continuously at constant frequency and wavelength.

DACR   Direct Acting Close Range. Gun-based naval anti-aircraft / missile system. Now called a CIWS.

DGW (Proj)   Director, Guided Weapons (Projects)

DGW (R&D)   Director, Guided Weapons (Research and Development)

DGW (R)   Director, Guided Weapons (Research)

DH   De Havilland – aircraft company

DHP   De Havilland Propellers – Guided weapons branch of de Havilland. Became Hawker Siddeley Dynamics.

DCIGS   Deputy Chief of the Imperial General Staff.

DRPC   Defence Research Policy Committee

ECM   Electronic CounterMeasures

EEA   English Electric Aviation

EECo   English Electric Company, parent group of EEA and D Napier and Son.

Ekco   E K Coles – radar manufacturer

Elint   Electronic Intelligence

EMIED   Electrical and Music Industries, Engineering Division

ESM   Electronic Support Measures

EUREKA   Navigation system comprising a ground beacon responding to signals from REBECCA.

EW   Electronic Warfare

GEC   General Electric Co (The British one)

GW	Guided Weapon
GWS	Guided Weapon System – as fitted to Royal Navy vessels. Refers to complete installation (launcher, magazine, fire control) rather than just the missile.
HP	High-Pressure, as applied to gas turbine compressors and turbines.
HSA	Hawker Siddeley Aviation – aircraft division of Hawker Siddeley
HSD	Hawker Siddeley Dynamics – Guided Weapons division of Hawker Siddeley. Formerly de Havilland Propellers.
HTP	High Test Peroxide. Solution of 85/15 ratio Hydrogen Peroxide in water.
ICBM	Inter-Continental Ballistic Missile
ICI	Imperial Chemical Industries
IMI	Imperial Metal Industries
INS	Inertial Navigation System
IR	Infra-Red
IRBM	Intermediate Range Ballistic Missile
JATO	Jet Assisted Take Off – original acronym, now RATO.
LABS	Low Altitude Bombing System – nuclear weapon delivery method. Known as loft bombing in the United Kingdom.
LP	Low Pressure, as applied to gas turbine compressors and turbines.
Mach Number	A speed divided by local speed of sound.
MBT	Main Battle Tank
MBDA	Matra BAe Dynamics Alenia – European consortium
Mid-course guidance	Keeps the missile on a trajectory that will place it in a position for the terminal homing system to acquire the target. Also allows the seeker to be aligned on the target.
MIRV	Multiple, Independently-targeted, Re-entry Vehicle
MoD	Ministry of Defence
MoS	Ministry of Supply. The Ministry in charge of everything from 'boot laces to atoms'. Responsible for aerospace contracts and management thereof. Dissolved with the creation of the MoD in 1958.
MRBM	Medium Range Ballistic Missile
NGTE	National Gas Turbine Establishment
OR	Operational Requirement

PCB	Plenum Chamber Burning
PDE	Projectile Development Establishment
PDGW (R&D)	Principal Director, Guided Weapons (Research & Development)
PDSR	Principal Director Scientific Research
PERME	Propellant and Explosives Research and Manufacturing Establishment
Predictor	Fire control equipment for AA guns. Tracks the target and feeds directional information to gun-laying system predicting where the target will be when the shells arrive. An early fire control computer.
Pulse radar	Radar where the signal is in the form of short bursts. Commonest form of radar.
PVO-Strany	Protivo-Vozdushnoi Oborony Strany (Soviet air defences)
RAE	Royal Aircraft Establishment
RARDE	Royal Armament Research and Development Establishment
RATO	Rocket Assisted Take-Off
RED OWL	Not a Rainbow Code, but an acronym: Remote Eyes in the Dark Operating Without Light. Developed by the RAE as a low-light TV system for helicopter pilots.
Reheat	Thrust augmentation by injecting neat fuel into the exhaust flow between the turbine and the propelling nozzle. This fuel burns thereby increasing the temperature and the velocity of the gas as it leaves the nozzle.
REME	Royal Electrical and Mechanical Engineers
RPV	Remotely Piloted Vehicle. Now called UAV.
RRE	Radar Research Establishment / Royal Radar Establishment
RSRE	Radar and Signals Research Establishment
RV	Re-entry Vehicle
SACLOS	Semi-Automatic Command to Line Of Sight. Method of gathering a missile onto the correct heading after launch.
SAGW	Surface-to-Air Guided Weapon, since superseded by SAM
SAM	Surface-to-Air Missile
Saro	Saunders Roe.
SEAD	Suppression of Enemy Air Defences

Semi-Active Radar Homing (SARH)	Method of missile guidance whereby the seeker homes in on the radar energy reflected off the target. The illuminating radar is separate from the seeker.
SLAR	Sideways Looking Airborne Radar
SLBM	Submarine Launched Ballistic Missile
Snap up / down	Ability of an aircraft / missile to intercept targets above or below its current flight level.
SNEB	Société Nouvelle des Etablissements Brandt – 68mm rocket.
Specific Impulse (Isp)	Used to compare rocket engine performance. Pounds of thrust produced per pound of fuel consumed per second. Units are Seconds.
SRDE	Signals Research and Development Establishment
SRS	Summerfield Research Station
SSM	Surface-to-Surface Missile
SST	Supersonic Transport
STOL	Short Take Off and Landing
STOVL	Short Take Off Vertical Landing
Sustainer	Rocket motor or engine used to keep vehicle in flight after boosting.
TACAN	Tactical Navigation system. UHF navigational aid giving bearing and distance of aircraft from a ground station.
Target Illumination Radar (TIR)	Radar transmitting a signal whose reflection is used by semi-active radar homing seekers.
TRE	Telecommunications Research Establishment, became Radar Research Establishment in 1953, but renamed Royal Radar Establishment. Became Royal Signals and Radar Establishment in 1980 when Signals Research and Development Establishment was merged.
UKADGE	UK Air Defence Ground Environment
UAV	Unmanned (or Uninhabited) Air Vehicle
V/STOL	Vertical / Short Take Off and Landing
VTOL	Vertical Take Off and Landing
WRE	Weapons Research Establishment at Woomera, South Australia.

The Ministry of Supply Colour Codes

Codenames have long been a feature of military activity and equipment has always had an official designation, a service name or a company sales title. Occasionally such equipment also acquires a name from its users, usually derogatory.

In the immediate postwar era the Ministry of Supply, tasked with co-ordinating the development of British weaponry, instigated a system of nomenclature. Although no official name for the system has been unearthed, it has become known as the series of colour (or rainbow) codes. These names were a colour followed by a noun and were intended to give no clue of the system's purpose, unless it was a matter of deception, as was the case with the Yellow Sun nuclear bomb.

Everyday terms were used initially, such as Orange Cocktail or Red Duster, but as these became used up somewhat surreal names were applied instead, such as Orange Poodle or Green Stymie. Please note that in official British documents the equipment names were always capitalised. However, to aid readability, this practice has not been perpetuated in the main body of the text of this book. The following list is complete as far as is known and is certainly the fullest list published. It includes aviation and non-aviation equipment.

BLACK ARROW
Three-stage Saro satellite launcher that launched Britain's first satellite, Prospero.

BLACK KNIGHT
Saro research rocket used to test re-entry vehicles for BLUE STREAK.

BLACK MARIA
Fighter Identification System interrogator for Identification Friend or Foe (IFF) system to meet OR.3538 and used in conjunction with Mk.X IFF system.

BLACK PRINCE
Proposed satellite launcher comprising BLUE STREAK + BLACK KNIGHT + a third stage. Unofficial name for BSSLV (BLUE STREAK Satellite Launch Vehicle). Also known as BLUE STAR.

BLACK ROCK
Long-range ballistic Surface-to-Surface Missile (SSM) for the British Army.

BLUE ANCHOR
Type 87 X-band CW tracking and Target Illumination Radar for fixed-base BLOODHOUND.

BLUE BADGER
Atomic Demolition Munition (ADM) and landmine transported on a truck.

BLUE BISHOP
Previously called GREEN JANET. Portable 2.5Mw & 5Mw nuclear powerplant.

BLUE BOAR
Mk.1 TV guided glide-bomb to OR.1059. Mk.2 was the H2S guided version.

BLUE BOY
Twelve-channel speech encryption system for VHF radio.

BLUE BUNNY
Truck-mounted nuclear landmine and ADM. Official name for BROWN BUNNY / BIG BERTHA, later became BLUE PEACOCK. The first UK Atomic Demolition Munition (ADM) and Landmine.

BLUE CAT
Boosted fission warhead and thermonuclear primary.

BLUE CEDAR
X-band version of AA No.3 Mk.7 radar built by British Thompson Houston for heavy anti-aircraft gun fire control system.

BLUE CIRCLE
Spoof codename for concrete ballast in nose of Panavia Tornado F.2 fighter in lieu of type's Marconi AI-24 Foxhunter radar. First installed in the Buccaneer while awaiting BLUE PARROT radar. (Blue Circle is a trade name for cement).

BLUE DANUBE
UK's first operational plutonium fission weapon. Mk.1 atom bomb to meet OR.1001. RAF designation: Bomb, Aircraft, HE 10,000 lb MC.

BLUE DEVIL
T.4 bombsight taking drift and ground speed from GREEN SATIN.

BLUE DIAMOND
EMI Engineering Division built AA No.7 Radar. Used to control Bofors guns and became the radar element of YELLOW FEVER.

BLUE DIVER
ARI 18075 UHF barrage noise jammer for V-bombers.

BLUE DOLPHIN
BLUE JAY Mk.5 CW radar-guided version of BLUE VESTA.

BLUE DUCK
ASW missile that became IKARA.

BLUE ENVOY
Stage 1¾ SAGW Mach 3.2 200-miles range heavy SAM to OR.1146. Cancelled 1957.

BLUE ERIC
Crash programme to produce a Harrier ECM pod for Falklands War in 1982.

BLUE FALCON
Demonstration radar developed by Ferranti that became BLUE VIXEN.

BLUE FOX
Air Interception radar for Sea Harrier FRS.1

BLUE FOX (1955)
Small-diameter, low-weight, unboosted fission warhead. Renamed INDIGO HAMMER.

BLUE GRANITE
Fusion weapon test. Original (and possibly correct) name for PURPLE GRANITE.

BLUE GUM
Search procedure for lost submarine contact.

BLUE HARE
BLUE PEACOCK nuclear landmine mounted on truck for the British Army, but with a smaller warhead.

BLUE HAWK
GEC-Marconi Multimode radar.

BLUE JACKET
MRG-G5FT Air data navigation system for Buccaneer.

BLUE JAY
Development name for FIRESTREAK AAM to meet OR.1117.

BLUE JOKER
AMES Type 87 balloon-borne S-band radar system for low-level threats from early 1950s.

BLUE KESTREL
Radar of Merlin ASW Helicopter.

BLUE LABEL
Marconi development radar for the Stage 2 air defence system.

BLUE LAGOON
IR equipment for detecting aircraft in flight.

BLUE MERCURY
Centurion Crocodile flamethrower tank.

BLUE MOON
Long-range expendable bomber to meet OR.203.

BLUE OAK
Super-computer at AWRE Aldermaston used to simulate nuclear explosions

BLUE ORCHID
Doppler navigation equipment used by anti-submarine Westland Wessex.

BLUE PARROT
AIRPASS III / ARI.5390 radar fitted to the Buccaneer.

BLUE PEACOCK
Truck-mounted nuclear landmine and ADM. Official codename for BROWN BUNNY/ BIG BERTHA, formerly BLUE BUNNY. The first UK Atomic Demolition Munition (ADM) and landmine.

BLUE PERSEUS
Centurion flamethrower kit.

BLUE RANGER
BLUE STEEL flight trials / carriage by V-bomber to Australia.

BLUE RAPIER
Bristol Aircraft plastic unmanned decoy and flying bomb, to supplement the short-range RED RAPIER.

BLUE RIBAND
Biggest, highest power, air defence radar in the UK. Intended to acquire targets for Stage 2 SAGW, but cancelled in 1957.

BLUE ROSETTE.
Short-case, high-yield, strategic gravity bomb casing to meet OR.1144 for a supersonic reconnaissance bomber R.156D to OR.336, the Avro 730.

BLUE SAGA
ART 18105 RWR for Vulcan.

BLUE SAPPHIRE
Star-sighting astro-navigation system.

BLUE SHADOW
ARI 5856 SLAR for Canberra B.6 on ELINT duties.

BLUE SILK
ARI.5885 / GPI Mk.4A Doppler Navigation radar for nuclear strike aircraft. Improved GREEN SATIN.

BLUE SKY
Fairey FIREFLASH beam riding AAM to meet OR.1088.

BLUE SLUG
Anti-ship missile based on SEASLUG airframe.

BLUE STAR
Unofficial name for BSSLV (BLUE STREAK Satellite Launch Vehicle). Also known as BLACK PRINCE.

BLUE STEEL Mk.1
OR.1132 rocket-powered strategic stand-off missile equipping V-bombers to Spec UB.198, with inertial guidance and invulnerable to countermeasures.

BLUE STEEL Mk.2
Long-range powered guided bomb to OR.1159, met by Avro W.112 with four BRJ.824 ramjets and two rocket boosts.

BLUE STONE
Unit.710 External Neutron Initiator for GREEN GRASS warhead in VIOLET CLUB and YELLOW SUN Mk.1.

BLUE STREAK
Ballistic missile to meet OR.1139.

BLUE STUDY
Automatic track control and bomb release computer for blind bombing. Essentially an update of Gee-H and Oboe.

BLUE SUGAR
Air-droppable radio beacon and long-distance blind bombing aid for the V-Force.

BLUE TIT
Probably an early in-house Ferranti name for SEA SPRAY radar.

BLUE VESTA
BLUE JAY Mk.4, a collision-course development of BLUE JAY to OR.1131, became RED TOP.

BLUE VIXEN
Air Interception radar for Sea Harrier FA.2.

BLUE WARRIOR
Jammer for use against VT-fused artillery shells.

BLUE WATER
Air-portable nuclear-armed ballistic surface-to-surface missile (SSM) originally to replace 30-mile-range Honest John SSMs.

BLUE WHALE
AWRE study into the effects of atmospheric nuclear explosions on high frequency radio paths.

BLUE YEOMAN
AMES Type 85 3D tactical control and early warning radar.

GREEN APPLE
Window for drift measurement over sea.

GREEN ARCHER
Radar FA No.8 X-band mortar location radar based on **BLUE DIAMOND**.

GREEN BACON
Light anti-aircraft picket radar for Bofors units.

GREEN BAMBOO
High-yield warhead for a strategic gravity bomb and a stand-off powered guided bomb for the V-Force.

GREEN BOTTLE
Device for homing on U-boat signals.

GREEN CHARM 3
Tungsten anti-tank round for the Challenger 2 main battle tank gun, replacing depleted Uranium rounds following environmental concerns.

GREEN CHEESE
Fairey anti-ship missile based on BLUE BOAR airframe with an EMI-developed RED DEAN X-band radar seeker.

GREEN FLASH
Green Cheese replacement.

GREEN FLAX
RED SHOES Surface-to-Air Guided Weapon (to Stage 1½) with CW radar. Renamed YELLOW TEMPLE in 1957.

GREEN GARLAND
IR fuse for BLUE JAY.

GREEN GARLIC
Prototype radar leading to AMES Type 80 Long Range Early Warning radar.

GREEN GINGER
AMES Type 88 Tactical Control and surveillance Radar and AMES Type 89 height-finder radar for THUNDERBIRD II / VR.725.

GREEN GODDESS
Military fire engine based on a Bedford RLHC 4x4 or RLHZ 4x2 chassis. May be a colloquial name.

GREEN GRANITE
First UK thermonuclear warhead design concept, it was used as a basis for subsequent designs.

GREEN GRASS
An interim megaton weapon deployed to get a high-yield warhead into service quickly. The last purely British nuclear warhead to be deployed.

GREEN HAMMOCK
Doppler navigation for low-altitude bombing.

GREEN JANET
Portable nuclear powerplant. Became BLUE BISHOP.

GREEN LIGHT
Test vehicle for visually guided maritime SAM that became Short SEACAT.

GREEN LIZARD
Barnes Wallis variable geometry gun-fired SAM.

GREEN MACE
RARDE-developed rapid-firing 5in (12.7cm) heavy AA gun that used a fin-stabilised dart and discarding sabot.

GREEN MINNOW
Radiometer.

GREEN PALM
ARI 18074 VHF jammer for V-Force.

GREEN PARROT
Royal Navy Westland Whirlwind VIP transport. Colloquial name.

GREEN SALAD
UHF homer for Hunter and Buccaneer.

GREEN SATIN
Self-contained Doppler Navigation aid for V-bombers.

GREEN SPARKLER
Stage 2 Command Guidance with active terminal homing SAGW.

GREEN STYMIE
Communications via radar system fitted to a Hastings for trials by RRE.

GREEN THISTLE
IR lock/follow seeker system incorporating BLUE SAPPHIRE and BLUE LAGOON.

GREEN WALNUT
Blind-bombing equipment for Eureka and BLUE STUDY.

GREEN WATER
A Ministry air defence study that worked up OR.202 for a 150-mile ramjet-powered pilotless interceptor / SAGW.

GREEN WILLOW
AI.20 X-band AI radar for single seat fighters that became RED STEER.

GREEN WIZARD
W H Sanders AA gun calibration instrument.

INDIGO BRACKET
ARI.3518 centimetric jamming system fitted to V-bombers that used carcinotron valves.

INDIGO CORKSCREW
AMES Type 86 Continuous Wave target illumination radar for the Bristol BLOODHOUND II and the English Electric THUNDERBIRD II

INDIGO HAMMER
Formerly named BLUE FOX. Small lightweight unboosted plutonium-based fission warhead and thermonuclear primary.

INDIGO HERALD
Small lightweight unboosted plutonium based thermonuclear primary.

ORANGE BLOSSOM
ESM on C-130 Hercules.

ORANGE COCKTAIL
Experimental mid-course update guidance system for RED DUSTER.

ORANGE CROP
Racal MIR-2 high and low band ESM for Lynx and Sea King naval helicopters.

ORANGE HARVEST
ARI.18144 Passive maritime ESM on Shackleton and, latterly, Westland Lynx.

ORANGE HERALD
A large core-boosted large fission weapon for BLUE STREAK missile to OR.1142.

ORANGE NELL
Design study for missile to defend against sea-skimming guided weapons.

ORANGE PIPPIN
Ferranti Light Anti-Aircraft fire-control radar.

ORANGE POODLE
Low-altitude radar system.

ORANGE PUTTER
Tail warning radar on English Electric Canberras, V-Force and electronic intelligence Canberras of 51 Squadron.

ORANGE REAPER
Thales KESTREL ESM on Royal Navy Merlin helicopters.

ORANGE TARTAN
Automatic day and night astro-navigation aid.

ORANGE TOFFEE
British Thompson Houston (BTH) SAGW guidance / Target Illumination Radar for BLUE ENVOY.

ORANGE WILLIAM
Fairey Project 6 anti-tank / anti-aircraft missile system for Royal Armoured Corps.

ORANGE YEOMAN
AMES Type 82 3D tactical control radar for BLOODHOUND Mk.1 system built by Metrovick.

PINK HAWK
Stern-attack AAM based on a reduced specification RED HAWK that eventually became BLUE SKY / FIREFLASH.

PURPLE GRANITE
Two-stage thermonuclear warhead. BLUE GRANITE may be the correct designation, but records are confused.

PURPLE PASSION
Cover name used for a UK sub-kiloton nuclear warhead for British Army Davy Crockett spigot mortar. Not adopted.

RED ANGEL
Unguided anti-ship rocket for use against Soviet cruisers in the Sverdlovsk class.

RED BEARD
Tactical nuclear weapon to OR.1127, in service 1962-1971 as Bomb, Aircraft, HE 2,000 lb MC.

RED BIDDY
Infantry Platoon Anti-Tank Rocket cancelled in 1953 in favour of RED PLANET.

RED BRICK
CW TIR development system for Stage 1½ SAM by British Thompson Houston that resulted in INDIGO CORKSCREW.

RED CABBAGE
Experimental coherent phase integration radar to detect small targets in sea clutter.

RED CARPET
X-band jammer designed by RRE circa 1958.

RED CAT(S)
UK version of Radio Corporation of America (RCA) Black Cat ground-mapping radar that contributed to development of RED CHEEKS.

RED CAT
Low-level, propelled, controlled air-to-surface guided weapon to OR.1125.

RED CHEEKS
Bomb guidance system using BLUE SHADOW.

RED DEAN
Vickers active AAM with GEC X-band active seeker. To meet OR.1105 / Joint Naval Requirement AW.281. Led to Red Hebe.

RED DEVIL
Proposed bombing system that used RED SETTER and GREEN SATIN.

RED DRAGON
Aircraft repair and upgrade project.

British Secret Projects: Hypersonics, Ramjets & Missiles

RED DROVER
SLAR to be fitted to the R.156T/OR.330 aircraft.

RED DUSTER
BLOODHOUND I SAM.

RED ELSIE
Ground-bursting anti-personnel mine developed in conjunction with Canada.

RED FLANNEL
Q-band H2S that used long fixed aerials with narrow azimuth.

RED FOX
Re-packaged export version of BLUE FOX for non-Sea Harrier applications.

RED FOX
1955 proposal for an atomic successor to TALLBOY and GRAND SLAM heavy bombs for delivery by fighter-bomber types.

RED GARTER
Tail warning device for V-bombers that provided audio warning from tail warning radar. Replaced by ORANGE PUTTER.

RED GODDESS
Colloquial name for modern (that is, post-1970) fire engines used by the UK Military during the 2002 fire fighters' strike.

RED HAND
Joint Naval/Army ship/ground-to-air missile. Cancelled in 1950 because it was duplicating the beam-riding work for SEASLUG.

RED HAWK
Radar-guided, collision-course AAM with four wrap-around boosts to meet OR.1056.

RED HEATHEN
Early study for SAGW leading to RED DUSTER and RED SHOES and regarded as a land-based, longer ranged SEASLUG.

RED HEBE
Vickers proposal for a continuous wave semi-active AAM developed from RED DEAN to meet OR.1131

RED HERRING
English Electric proposal for a ground-to-ground missile, possibly a development of RED SHOES.

RED INDIAN
EMIED Light Anti-Aircraft Artillery fire control computer for Bofors guns.

RED KING
Larger calibre (45mm) version of RED QUEEN twin-barrelled anti-aircraft gun.

RED LIGHT
ARI 18146 ECM system for V-bombers. Search /

lock / jam X-band jammer on Victor Mk.2 for use against AI radars.

RED MAID
Medium AAA development.

RED NECK
OR.3593 High-resolution radar reconnaissance system fitted in underwing pods on Handley Page Victor.

RED PLANET
Infantry Platoon Anti-Tank Rocket developed with RED BIDDY but cancelled in 1953.

RED QUEEN
AMES Type 12 Mk.2 GCI radar which was a modified Type 15 Mk.2.

RED QUEEN
Twin-barrelled 42mm anti-aircraft gun built by Oerlikon. Cancelled in favour of Mauler and PT.428 missile systems.

RED RAPIER
Specification UB.109T for an unmanned bomb or expendable bomber. Vickers SP.2, Bristol 182 and Boulton Paul P.123 proposed.

RED ROBIN
RED BRICK CW radar in a static installation for RAF THUNDERBIRD II. RAF bought the Bloodhound II.

RED ROSE
Surface-to-surface tactical nuclear missile for the British Army to replace Honest John and, later, the Corporal surface-to-surface missile. English Electric and Vickers tendered bids for RED ROSE.

RED SEA
Predictor for Gun X1 heavy anti-aircraft gun.

RED SETTER
Experimental SLAR for V-bombers to be used with RED CHEEKS producing high-definition pictures but limited in range.

RED SHOES
English Electric THUNDERBIRD I mobile Stage 1 SAGW. Replaced by YELLOW TEMPLE / GREEN FLAX with CW radar.

RED SHRIMP
ARI 18076 and ARI 18025 barrage noise jammer equipment for Avro Vulcan for use against long-range detection radars.

RED SLUG
Revised name for SEASLUG suggested by Guided Weapons Advisory Committee on 23/9/48.

RED SNOW
An anglicised US W-28 thermonuclear warhead for YELLOW SUN Mk.2, BLUE STEEL Mk.1 and

Mk.2, BLUE STREAK MRBM SKYBOLT ALBM and others.

RED STEER
ARI 5919 rearward-looking active tail warning radar for V-bombers. Development of AI.20 GREEN WILLOW.

RED TOP
De Havilland IR AAM based on FIRESTREAK Mk.4.

RED TULIP
Moving Target Indicator for phase coherent radar.

VIOLET BANNER
IR seeker for RED TOP.

VIOLET CLUB
Emergency capability high-yield strategic weapon for V-bombers. Large unboosted pure-fission bomb. RAF designation: Bomb, Aircraft, HE 9,000 lb HC.

VIOLET FRIEND
A proposal for a UK-based ABM system using BLUE YEOMAN and FPS-16 radars. Used BLOODHOUND SAGW.

VIOLET MIST
Successor to BLUE PEACOCK ADM/landmine for the Army.

VIOLET PICTURE
Plessey ARI 18120 UHF homing system fitted to Buccaneer, Whirlwind, Hunter and Sea Vixen.

VIOLET RAY
X-band TIR for Stage 1 SAGW possibly to meet OR.2065.

VIOLET VISION
Modified RED BEARD nuclear warhead for the Corporal SRBM in UK service.

YELLOW ANVIL
Warhead for a British Army artillery-fired atomic projectile (AFAP).

YELLOW ASTER
H2S Mk.9 reconnaissance radar for Victor and Valiant, interim to RED NECK. Essentially BLUE SHADOW with improved CRT/Photographic recorder.

YELLOW BARLEY
Wide-band passive radar warning receiver that indicated when an offensive radar had locked on to an aircraft.

YELLOW BUNTING
Details unknown

YELLOW DONKEY
Possible precursor to BLUE ANCHOR CW. Target Illumination Radar for GREEN FLAX SAM.

YELLOW DUCKLING
IR submarine detection system using lead tellerium sensors to detect the wake of submerged submarines. Ultimately led to Infra-Red Linescan systems.

YELLOW DUSTER
Bristol SAGW for Stage 1½ . Possibly refers to a RED DUSTER fitted with the Continuous Wave seeker from YELLOW TEMPLE.

YELLOW FEATHER
Homing system for Radar and IR missiles including CW radar seeker test programme.

YELLOW FEVER
Fire Control Equipment No.7 Mk.4 Light AA gun fire control system for the Bofors L/70 comprising BLUE DIAMOND radar and an analogue computer.

YELLOW GATE
Loral 1101 ESM for Boeing E-3D Sentry, Hawker Siddeley Nimrod MR.2 and R.1. Possibly only refers to the pod.

YELLOW GODDESS
Green Goddess military fire engine modified for use in Northern Ireland. Modifications included fitting wire-mesh riot screens on windows and tamper-proof lockers.
A colloquial name prompted by its yellow paintwork.

YELLOW JACK
On-mount, tachymetric sighting system for Light Anti-Aircraft artillery whose radar element was called ORANGE PIPPIN

YELLOW LEMON
Decca Al Mk.17 Doppler navigation equipment for Naval fighters to meet AW.301.

YELLOW RIVER
AMES Type 83 Fire Control radar, AA No.3 Mk.9 Tracking and illumination radar for Stage 1 SAGW.

YELLOW SAND
EMI anti-ship homing bomb with its guidance system developed by Smiths.

YELLOW SUN
High-yield strategic bomb for the V-Force.

YELLOW TEMPLE
English Electric THUNDERBIRD II Stage 1½ guided weapon. Originally called GREEN FLAX then YELLOW TEMPLE then VR.725.

YELLOW TIGER
Developed BLUE CEDAR Fire control radar for RED SHOES.

YELLOW VEIL
Whittaker ALQ-167 jamming pod for Lynx.

A Royal Air Force Strike Command Avro Vulcan B.2 carries an Avro W.105 Blue Steel stand-off missile. Despite many attempts to replace it, Blue Steel remained the mainstay of Britain's nuclear deterrent until relinquishing that role to the Royal Navy's Polaris system in 1968.

The Ministry of Supply Colour Codes

Appendix Two

Operational Requirements

GSOR.1000 Swingfire on Chieftain MBT. Chieftain was too far into development to adopt Swingfire.

GSOR.1010 Infantry-portable Swingfire that eventually became Golfswing.

GSOR.1013 Swingfire wire-guided heavy anti-tank missile.

OR.202 Green Water 50-mile range pilotless interceptor / SAGW, possibly superseded by Blue Envoy.

OR.329 F155T high-altitude fighter. Cancelled 1957.

OR.330 Specification R.156 leading to Avro 730 M3 supersonic bomber. Vickers SP4; English Electric Aviation P.10; HP100 and Shorts all bid. Also referred to as RB.156T. Cancelled 1957.

OR.336 Specification RB.156T for a Mach 3 medium-range reconnaissance bomber. Reconnaissance bomber variant of OR.330 led to the Avro 730.

OR.337 Mixed-powerplant fighter. Saro SR.177 selected.

OR.346 Mach 2+ multi-role Buccaneer/TSR.2 replacement for RN & RAF.

OR.355 TSR.2 replacement. Doubts about high / fast prompted a change to low level at Mach 1.2. Criticised as too conservative.

OR.356 Supersonic V/STOL. Hawker P.1154 for RAF. Specification SR.250. Joint requirement with AW406. Cancelled.

OR.357 Maritime reconnaissance requirement leading to Hawker Siddeley Nimrod.

OR.1009 Uncle Tom 1,000 lb Anti-ship rocket

OR.1015 Sight for Bootleg tossed torpedo. Requirement withdrawn July 1947.

OR.1056 Air-to-air homing or beam-riding missile. Red Hawk.

OR.1057 Air-to-surface controlled or homing missile. Nozzle.

OR.1058 Anti-submarine homing weapon. Zeta (later called Pentane). Joint Naval requirement AW.59 Too big / heavy for small-ship helicopters.

OR.1059 Control of bombs (initially for 10,000 lb weapon but should be applicable to 5,000 lb or 1,000 lb Superseded earlier and narrower requirement for homing anti-capital-ship bomb Journey's End. Became Blue Boar.

OR.1060 High-speed airborne tossed torpedo. Bootleg BA.290.

OR.1088 Blue Sky. Fairey Fireflash AAM.

OR.1089 Control of bombs. TV guidance. Superseded OR.1059.

OR.1097 Short Range Expendable Bomber. Red Rapier and possibly Blue Rapier.

Expendable bomber is an archaic term for a cruise-type flying bomb.

OR.1105 Heavy AAM with GEC X-band active seeker. Cancelled.

OR.1117 Covered AAMs. Firestreak and Red Top.

OR.1118 Red Cheeks inertia-controlled 5,000-lb bomb. Follow-on from AST 1101.

OR.1123 Green Cheese anti-ship missile based on Blue Boar airframe with an EMI seeker.
Intended for use by Blackburn Buccaneer. Cancelled 1956.

OR.1124 Stage 1 air defence system. Leading to Red Duster.

OR.1125 Red Cat Stand-off bomb for OR.324. Intended to arm the Avro 721.

OR.1127 Red Beard tactical nuclear weapon in service 1962-1971 as Bomb; Aircraft; High explosive 2,000 lb MC. Known as the 30in bomb and the Javelin Bomb before Red Beard name adopted for a fission gravity bomb.

OR.1131 Armament for high-altitude fighter to F.155T. Covered Red Hebe and Blue Vesta.

OR.1132 Blue Steel stand-off missile for V-Force. Strategic air-launched stand-off missile for the V-Force.

OR.1132(II) A cheaper optical SAGW for the Army that led to Rapier.

OR.1135 Simple ABM system to be incorporated into Stage 2 air defence system Violet Friend based around Marconi / English Electric studies to defend against ballistic missiles at 5,000 miles.

OR.1137 Stage 2 air defence system. Cancelled 1957.

OR.1139 Medium Range Ballistic Missile. Blue Streak. Cancelled 1960.

OR.1140 Nuclear warhead for defensive SAGW. 1956-1957 then superseded by OR.1154

OR.1141 Megaton warhead for OR.1132 Blue Steel, drawn up in January 1956.

OR.1142 Megaton warhead for OR.1139 MRBM Blue Streak.

OR.1144 Blue Rosette bomb casing for the supersonic bomber to R.156D

OR.1145 Stage 1½ SAGW, leading to Thunderbird II.

OR.1146 Stage 1¾ air defence system, leading to Blue Envoy.

OR.1149 Air-launched missile with a range of 1,000nm (1,852km). Superseded by OR.1159.

OR.1154 Nuclear warhead for Stage 1½ SAGW

1957-1958; then superseded by OR.1167

OR.1155 Defence system against ballistic missiles. Superseded OR.1135; but never issued. Follow-on to Violet Friend requirement. 1958

OR.1157 Warhead for ABM system. 1957

OR.1159 Long-range guided bomb; to be met by Blue Steel Mk.2. Superseded the too ambitious OR.1149. Cancelled 12/59 due to the problems with Blue Steel Mk.1. Superseded by OR.1187 written for Skybolt.

OR.1160 Megaton warhead for OR.1159 missile. Red Snow 1.1 MT; transferred from Blue Steel Mk.1 and Yellow Sun Mk.2. Cancelled 1959 with Blue Steel Mk.2. 11/6/58.

OR.1161 Small (500 lb) megaton warhead for future defensive and offensive missiles. Cancelled.

OR.1166 Nuclear headed SAGW. Command-guidance Bloodhound III.

OR.1167 Nuclear warhead for medium-range SAGW to OR.1166. TONY (R.106). Yield approximately 10 kilotons.

OR.1168 Advanced tactical ASM for TSR.2. Martel.

OR.1169 Bloodhound II. Entered service with RAF.

OR.1173 Joint Navy/RAF requirement for tactical ASM. AS.30 on Canberra.

OR.1177 Improved kiloton bomb casing for the OR.1176 warhead. WE.177 Red Beard replacement.

OR.1179 Nuclear warhead for UK Skybolt. RE.179 chosen after several other proposals.

OR.1182 Long-range stand-off bomb. Avro W.140 turbojet-powered stand-off missile and Bristol X-12 ramjet-powered missile.

OR.1187 Air-launched ballistic missile. Skybolt: issued 26/4/61; re-issued 29/8/62. Cancelled 22/2/63.

OR.1193 Air-to-air Missile. Dates from early 1960s.

OR.1194 Retarded 1,000 lb HE bomb for TSR.2. Hunting Engineering and Portsmouth Aviation Ltd bid for this.

OR.3576 40in-diameter radar for fighters. Pulsed J-band radar with a J-band CW illuminator. For use with the Fairey SARW. Led to GEC AI.18 (Sea Vixen; OR.329) 1954.

OR.3578 Airborne radar reconnaissance equipment. To be fitted to the V-bombers.

Radar Nomenclature

Radars and electronic warfare equipments are classified by the frequency band that they occupy in the electromagnetic spectrum: usually a letter, for example X-band. Not as simple as it looks as the categorisation of the radio frequency bands has changed in the period covered. The bands listed in this work are contemporary and are listed as they were in the original sources, with no correction to recent revisions being made.

Perhaps the best summary of these band categories has been written by Stuart Slade and is reproduced, in its entirety, with Stuart's permission.

Radar Frequency Band Designations
There are two quite separate systems for designating radar frequencies. The older one is based on wavelength and was originated during World War Two. It goes as follows:

The original wavelength used for search radars was 23cm. This became known as L-band (for Long).

When shorter wavelengths (10cm) were introduced, these became known, quite logically, as the S-band, S standing for Short.

When fire control radars (3cm wavelength) entered service they were designated the X-band radars – because X marks the spot.

It was then hoped that an intermediate wavelength would combine the advantages of both. This was C-band (C = Compromise). When the Germans decided to introduce short-wavelength radars, they selected a frequency of 1.5cm. This became known as K-band (K = Kurz, the German word for short).

Unfortunately, the Germans, with unparalleled Teutonic precision, had selected the one radar frequency that is absorbed by water vapour so the K-band radars don't work in rain or fog. Postwar this was countered by selecting frequencies either just over K band (Ka or K-above) or just under it (Ku or K-under).

Finally, the first radars operated with metre-long wavelengths. These were designated P-band (P standing for Previous).

This system was complex, clumsy and difficult to use. Consequently it was replaced by a rationalised system based on frequency with the designations running from the A band to the P band.

Old P-band = Modern A/B band (100 - 500MHz)
Old L-band = Modern C/D band (500MHz - 2GHz)
Old S-band = Modern E/F band (2GHz - 4GHz)
Old C-band = Modern G/H band (4GHz - 8GHz)
Old X-band = Modern I/J band (8GHz - 20GHz)
Old K-band = Modern K band   (20GHz - 40GHz)

Select Bibliography

A great deal of primary material has been consulted for this book. Much of this is held by The National Archives at Kew (AIR 20, AVIA 6, AVIA 28, AVIA 54, AVIA 65, DSIR 23). Further original material is held at the Brooklands Museum, REME Museum, North West Heritage Group at Warton. Private individuals also allowed access to their material, including unpublished memoirs.

A Vertical Empire: C N Hill; Imperial College Press, 2000.
Air Defence at Sea: Rear Admiral J R Hill; Motorbooks, 1988.
Aeromilitaria: Air-Britain; various issues.
Anti-Aircraft Artillery: Ian V Hogg; Crowood Press, 2002.
Anti-Ballistic Missiles: Dr Jeremy Stocker; Charterhouse Lecture, April 2005.
BAe Active Skyflash and AIM-120 AMRAAM: Dr Carlo Kopp; Australian Aviation, June 1994.
Blue Envoy's Peaceful Legacy: Chris Gibson; Prospero, British Rocketry Oral History Project, 2005.

Britain and Ballistic Missile Defence, 1942-2002: Dr Jeremy Stocker; Frank Cass, 2004.
British Research and Development Aircraft: Ray Sturtivant; Haynes.
British Secret Projects – Jet Fighters since 1950: Tony Buttler; Midland Publishing, 2000.
British Secret Projects – Jet Bombers since 1949: Tony Buttler; Midland Publishing, 2003.
Cambridge Aerospace Dictionary: Bill Gunston; Cambridge University Press, 2004.
Cold War: Wayne D Cocroft and Roger J C Thomas; English Heritage, 2003.
Cold War Hot Science – Applied Research in Britain's Defence Laboratories 1945-1990: ed Robert Bud and Philip Gummett; Science Museum, 1999.
Flight and Aircraft Engineer; various editions.
Flight International; various editions.
Good Company: A R Adams; British Aircraft Corporation, 1976.
Illustrated Encyclopaedia of Rockets and Missiles: Bill Gunston; Salamander, 1979.
Hawker's Hypersonic Secrets: Air Pictorial; Nov 2000.
Jane's All the World's Aircraft: Jane's Publishing; various editions.

Jane's Weapon Systems: Jane's Publishing; various editions.
Journal of the Royal Aeronautical Society: various editions.
Missile Systems: Philip Birtles and Paul Beaver; Ian Allan, 1985.
Project Cancelled: Derek Wood; Jane's, 1976.
Rolls-Royce Aero Engines: Bill Gunston; PSL, 1989.
Sleeve Notes: Rolls-Royce Heritage Trust Bristol Branch; Issues 33 to 38.
Spacelists 14 and 19: John Pitfield; Rocket Services, 2001.
The Early Development of Guided Weapons in the UK 1940-1960: S R Twigge; Harwood, 1993.
The Fruits of War: Michael White; Simon and Schuster, 2005.
The Secret World of Vickers Guided Weapons: John Forbat; Tempus, 2006.
Violet Friend: Chris Gibson; Air Pictorial, Nov 2001.
World Encyclopaedia of Aero Engines: Bill Gunston; PSL, 1998.
World's Missile Systems: General Dynamics Pomona, 1975.

Index

AIRCRAFT & AIRCRAFT PROJECTS

ENGINES & MOTORS

MANUFACTURERS

MISSILES

We hope that you have enjoyed this book . .

Midland Publishing book titles are carefully edited and designed by an experienced and enthusiastic team of specialists. A catalogue detailing our aviation publishing programme is available upon request from the address on page two.

Our associate company, Midland Counties Publications, offers an exceptionally wide range of aviation, military, naval, railway and transport books and videos, for purchase by mail-order and delivery around the world.

To request a mail-order catalogue or order further copies of this book, contact:
Midland Counties Publications
4 Watling Drive, Hinckley, Leics, LE10 3EY
Tel: 01455 254 450   Fax: 01455 233 737
www.midlandcountiessuperstore.com